B C L

The sociology of the Third World

Disparity and involvement

The sociology of the Third World

Disparity and involvement

J. E. GOLDTHORPE

Senior Lecturer in Sociology, University of Leeds

CAMBRIDGE UNIVERSITY PRESS

CAMBRIDGE

LONDON · NEW YORK · MELBOURNE

Published by the Syndics of the Cambridge University Press
The Pitt Building, Trumpington Street, Cambridge CB2 1RP
Bentley House, 200 Euston Road, London NW1 2DB
32 East 57th Street, New York, NY 10022, USA
296 Beaconsfield Parade, Middle Park, Melbourne 3206, Australia

Library of Congress Catalogue Card Number: 74-12979

ISBNs
0521 20521 2   hard covers
0521 09924 2   paperback

First published 1975

Photoset and printed in Malta by St Paul's Press Ltd

ACKNOWLEDGEMENTS

Acknowledgement is made to Princeton University Press for permission to reproduce on page 34 the figure from Kingsley Davis, *The Population of India and Pakistan*.

Thanks are due to President Nyerere for permission to quote from his 'Socialism and Rural Development', in *Essays on Socialism*, published by Oxford University Press, for which he holds the copyright.

CONTENTS

FOREWORD

BY THE RT HON. LORD BOYLE OF HANDSWORTH

When in 1968 I was invited to join the Pearson Commission on International Development, a senior civil servant advised me never to lose sight of the total relationship — not just the aid relationship — between richer countries and the Third World, and to regard this as 'an integral part of the attempt to make rational sense of Man's life on this planet'. Dr J. E. Goldthorpe, in the opening chapter of his book *The Sociology of the Third World* is surely making the same point when he says that '[Ours] is not a divided world. On the contrary, the world is one. The disparity in the living standards and ways of life of different societies and countries has arisen in a world in which all are increasingly involved with one another.'

The Report of the Pearson Commission, *Partners in Development*, encountered fairly severe criticism from the outset. In retrospect I think much of this criticism was justified, even though members of the Commission (as I still hope) performed a useful function in demonstrating that it was an illusion to suppose that, for the foreseeable future, private investment either could or should replace official aid flows. Some of the most important adverse comments on the Report were made at a follow-up conference held at Columbia University, New York, early in 1970. We were reminded that economic growth rates of five or six per cent would not necessarily deal with the most urgent problems of the world's population, and that the poorest twenty-five per cent of the world remained trapped in a situation of poor diet, bad health, illiteracy, and unemployment. In the words of Dudley Seers, then Director of the Institute of Development Studies at the University of Sussex, 'one could hardly talk of development having taken place in any true sense, if average incomes had risen, but at the same time inequalities had grown more severe, unemployment increased, and the lowest quarter of the population became absolutely poorer'.

During the years since 1970, the problem of 'Development in a Divided World' (I take the title from a collection of studies published by the Institute) has become even more urgent. The recent World Food Conference has shown that there is imminent danger of unparalled famine, and climatic changes have meant that arid zones are seriously encroaching on productive land. Furthermore what Dr Paul Streeten has called the 'world setting' is changing all the time: 'It is true not only that what you don't know doesn't hurt you ... but also that *what you do know does hurt.* This clearly reduces the patience with which the development process is viewed by the ruling elites in the underdeveloped world.'

In addition there is a growing and dangerous gulf of opinion within relatively wealthy countries like our own. R. H. Hutton, writing on Bagehot nearly a hundred years ago, could reflect that 'sympathy [with 'the toiling millions of men'], even when men really desire to feel it, is very much oftener coveted than actually felt by men as a living motive'. Not many of us, I guess, would care to advance, or feel confident of defending this view in a present-day university. I think Robert Kennedy was a good deal closer to the truth when he said, in one of his last speeches, that 'Today's young people appear to have chosen for their concern the dignity of the individual human being.' And they don't think the better of their elders when, in two consecutive general elections, Third World issues are almost totally ignored.

However, it remains essential to approach these issues from the standpoint of reason as well as commitment, and here, as it seems to me, academics, working in university departments or in institutes, have an essential part to play. In particular there are two approaches which seem to me not opposed but complementary. The first starts from the need to look more rigorously at certain very generalized concepts like 'development', and to enquire what precisely the providers of aid were trying to achieve, and what have been the objectives of the recipients. This is the approach of John White's valuable recent book *The Politics of Foreign Aid.*

The second approach starts from the need to comprehend the changing patterns of society within the Third World; and here sociologists, no less than economists or political scientists, have surely a major contribution to make. As Dr Goldthorpe says: 'The societies of the Third World are awkward to study, for ... while there is certainly material in them for the consideration of the more specialized social sciences such as economics and political science, these can lead to partial and misleading conclusions unless they are informed by a constant awareness of the whole whose parts they are studying. And this precisely is the contribution which the synoptic vision of the sociologist should enable him to make.'

When I read these words, I was reminded of the group discussions at the 1970 Columbia conference on 'structural change' in developing countries, and the difficulties we found (for there were very few sociologists among us) in tackling this part of the agenda. Whilst I would not for a moment pretend to be competent to evaluate Dr Goldthorpe's work, I hope it will be of interest to all those who feel a continuing concern with 'the dilemmas of a world of disparity and involvement'. It is also a reminder that sociology is, I am glad to say, a thriving discipline within the University of Leeds.

26 November 1974   Edward Boyle

PREFACE
AND ACKNOWLEDGEMENTS

It was with a somewhat narrowly East African focus that I came to Leeds in 1962. This has been a good place to seek a wider vision, with a strong and continuing interest in the Third World at all levels and in many departments throughout the University, and most especially a lively development seminar.

The idea of writing this book originated about the end of 1967, and I owe much to the encouragement of Professor A. H. Hanson at that time. Alas, he died before it was finished, and I pay warmly affectionate tribute to his memory. The first draft was written during a 'semi-sabbatical' session in 1971—2, and I am grateful to the University of Leeds, and my departmental colleagues in particular, for substantial relief from teaching and administrative duties during that period. It was revised during the summer of 1973 after a number of friendly colleagues had read it in whole or part, and I am grateful to them for saving me from many errors and indicating sources I had overlooked. It then had to be cut fairly drastically for publication, which was done in the spring of 1974. I regret that it has not always been possible to take account of the most recent contributions, even including some whose publication antedates that of this book.

I am grateful to Professor Gunnar Myrdal for permission to quote so extensively from his works, especially *Asian Drama*. I acknowledge with thanks the help of Mrs Catherine Chew in carrying out the laborious research and computations which went into the compilation of table 4.1. Mr Roger Appleyard also helped with some of the other statistical tables. For secretarial assistance I am grateful to Mrs Elizabeth McHale, Mrs Ruth Sweeney, Mrs Gena Lodge, Miss Alex Lutrzykowska, and Miss Helen Mitchell. Finally, I acknowledge with thanks the kindly help and guidance of the staff of Cambridge University Press at all stages from first discussions of the idea of the book to its publication.

December 1974

J.E.G.

1   Introduction and argument

Disparity and involvement

The transformation of human life through the application of science did not begin everywhere and at the same time; and the uneven onset of that transformation has created a situation without precedent in history. Rich and poor there have been since the dawn of civilization, but until recently the great majority of people in every country lived at or near subsistence level, and it was only a small minority in any country who were able to command enough resources to live an ampler life. What is completely new about the present world situation is that the real incomes of almost the whole populations of some countries have been raised far above subsistence, while those of other countries remain at or near that level. If the affluent industrial countries of the modern world are grouped into those of the 'West' and 'East', capitalist and communist, then the poor countries constitute a 'Third World' whose small command over resources distinguishes them from both. A central theme of this book accordingly is the wide disparity between rich and poor countries, together with the related disparity between rich and poor people within many Third World countries, whose wealthy families have as their standard of emulation the affluence of affluent societies elsewhere in the world. Such disparities are, indeed, a commonplace of contemporary discussion, expressed in phrases such as 'a divided world' and 'the ever-widening gap'.

But it is not a divided world. On the contrary, the world is one. The disparity in the living standards and ways of life of different societies and countries has arisen in a world in which all are increasingly involved with one another. A second major theme, then, is that of involvement or inter-relation — a theme which in some of the older literature, especially of social anthropology, was characterized as 'culture contact'.

'Until our day, human society has never existed.'[1] A generation ago it was still possible for anthropologists to write monographs about societies which, if not strictly 'untouched', had been affected by outside influences only to a limited extent. That was the golden age, the age of the Nuer, the Bemba, Tikopia, and Samoa, in which a social anthropologist could analyse a society as a single, unique form of human association with its own distinctive structure and culture to be explained mainly in its own terms. Now this is clearly no longer possible. The world has broken in, and the institutions of

1

the modern world — mines, political parties, armies, schools — have to be included as integral parts of the whole. Yet the pre-existing diversity of cultures, and the significance of those cultures for modern men, has certainly not vanished overnight, as we are reminded every day when we open the newspaper and read of language riots in an Asian state or deadly tribal rivalries in an African army. The societies of the Third World are awkward to study, for while the heritage and perspectives of social anthropology are necessary they are not sufficient, and while there is certainly material in them for the consideration of the more specialized social sciences such as economics and political science these can lead to partial and misleading conclusions unless they are informed by a constant awareness of the whole whose parts they are studying. And this precisely is the contribution which the synoptic vision of the sociologist should enable him to make.

'Industrialization' and 'development'

An industrial society may be briefly defined as one which makes lavish use of energy. Of all the discoveries and inventions which the rise of science brought in train, it is not without reason that the popular imagination has seized on one as signifying the start of the industrial revolution in history, and that one is the steam engine. Mainly by the use of heat engines burning fossil fuels, industrial development in what are now the affluent countries has literally put more power at the elbow of their inhabitants than was previously available to them from their own muscles, those of other animals, and a limited use of wind and water power. By the same token, the most striking and fundamental difference between rich and poor countries today lies in the vastly greater resources of energy commanded by the former.

If energy represents the critical difference in terms of physics, then in terms of economics the concomitant difference is capital. Heat engines and the machines they drive represent capital investment on a vastly greater scale than the simple tools of a non-industrial economy. Their use increases the productivity of labour; indeed, the very nature of work is transformed as it comes to be done by machines directed and controlled by men rather than directly performed by their own muscles. So wages are potentially high, and only a modicum of trade-union organization is needed to ensure that actual wages correspond closely to the productivity of labour. Industrialization accordingly involves a change from labour-intensive to capital-intensive methods, and this in turn entails a process of capital formation, initially by forced saving and a good deal of 'going short', later by using power-driven machines to make more machines. In this process there is a shift of the labour force out of 'primary' production (agriculture and other 'extractive' occupations like fishing and mining), into 'secondary' or manufacturing industry.

2

This is followed in the later stages by a further shift, as manufacturing becomes more capital-intensive, back into inescapably labour-intensive services, 'tertiary' and 'quaternary', as diverse as retailing, education, social welfare services, and entertainment. In this process the material standard of living, as represented by 'real' incomes (discounting changes in the value of money), rises greatly.

And in terms of social organization, industrial societies are large in scale. The application of heat engines to transport and communications increases the extent of the market and makes for a finer division of labour, more specialization, and greater interdependence between larger numbers of people. Moreover, much of the capital equipment of an industrial economy is itself large in scale and indivisible (oil refineries, electricity generating complexes, railways, air lines), so that the corporate organizations which control and operate it, whether publicly or privately owned, are inevitably large, complex, impersonal, and bureaucratic. Other organizations – political, administrative, educational – tend towards a similar pattern in relation to the advantages and economies of scale.

Such has been the experience of those countries and societies which have undergone the process of change we have come to know as industrial development. Such accordingly is the process which it is presumed will be undergone by others. Yet to make such a presumption is surely to beg a central question.

Non-industrial countries were first called 'underdeveloped' in a famous report to the United Nations in 1951;[2] then, when the word came to be thought of as derogatory, they were called 'developing' – an instance, surely, of what Myrdal calls 'diplomacy by terminology',[3] for it is by no means clear whether they all are, or can be. The very term 'development' and its derivatives needs to be handled with caution, for as Gellner has said, 'This language [i.e. that of economic growth] is misleading in as far as it suggests that what is at stake is something quantitative, a rate or speed or quantity of accumulation of goods. Ultimately, what is at stake is something qualitative – a transition between two fundamentally different forms of life.'[4] Furthermore, economists themselves find development an elusive concept, and they tend to refer it to conditions or processes which lie in the realms of psychology or sociology rather than economics. It is 'in the mind',[5] they say; it involves 'the upward movement of the whole social system';[6] it consists of 'the transformation of a tradition- or authority-bound society into a modern, innovating, experimenting, progressing one'.[7] To use such a term in defining our subject accordingly is to risk taking for granted what is actually problematic, a danger which is enhanced by the imprecision of the concept itself. It is for reasons of this kind that it seems best to avoid terms like 'the sociology of development' or 'of developing countries', and preferable to write of the sociology of non-industrial societies or of the Third World.

The units of analysis: 'countries' and 'societies'

For some purposes of analysis, the unit which we have to consider is the 'country'. 'Nation' and 'state' are not always appropriate; some of the countries in which we are interested are still colonies, and many more were until recently. We may think of a country as a defined geographical area with a government, whether independent or colonial, and the first reason for taking this as our unit of analysis is that it is the governments of countries which collect and issue statistics. Thus for example when we are making comparisons of G.N.P. per head, primary school enrolments, or infant mortality rates, the statistics which we find in the appropriate sources are for units like India, Nigeria, Peru, or British Honduras.

But we have to recognize that most such units are in a sense highly artificial, arbitrary creations whose boundaries might as well have been drawn along any other lines on the map, and which embrace a diversity of languages and cultures. Most countries in the modern world, that is, embrace within their boundaries diverse societies, for example, the many different tribes within a modern African state. At the same time, some societies transcend the boundaries of several countries, for example, a tribe like the Samia, parted by an arbitrary boundary between Uganda and Kenya; or the society of the overseas Chinese, which transcends the boundaries of Hong Kong, Malaysia, Thailand, Indonesia, etc.

Yet, though there is a sense in which it is an irrelevant, adventitious matter where boundaries happen to fall between countries, what begins as an arbitrary unit may end up by acquiring its own distinctive social characteristics – its own society, indeed. This process occurs as a result of the exercise of power. Governments do, after all, many other things besides collect and publish statistics; indeed, their statistical activities are merely one small by-product and manifestation of the fact that they exercise coercive power. Moreover, in general power is used in different ways and for different purposes in different countries. Thus for example the original demarcation on the map of Africa between the areas which later became Uganda, Kenya, and Tanzania could hardly have been more arbitrary. Yet since they became separately independent, the different policies of the three governments, the different political personalities and events which have influenced them, have created differences between them of an order which did not previously exist, so that it is not now by any means nonsensical to think of (say) Tanzania society being in certain respects different from that of Kenya.

Some perspectives in sociological theory

(A) THE CLASSICS

The division between the rich industrial nations, at that time confined to western Europe, and the rest of humanity was already a fact about the world

4

in which sociology emerged as a recognized discipline early in the nineteenth century. In the work of the classical sociologists we find accordingly a dawning awareness that modern industrial society was a phenomenon *sui generis* and constituted a distinctive type of society. Two related sets of large questions thus formed the major themes of early sociology. First, if what we now call modern industrial society is one type of society, what other broad types of society are there, what are their characteristics, and how may we distinguish between them? Secondly, by what processes does a society of one type transform itself, or become transformed, into a society of another? The answer to the first question depended largely on what term was chosen to characterize what we now call modern industrial society. If 'civilized', then obvious antonyms were 'primitive', 'rude', 'barbarous', or 'savage'. If 'capitalist', then other types of society might include 'feudal' and 'Oriental'. Answers to the second question constituted the theory of social change as it was then understood, and it was in such a context that the term 'social development' was then used, along with the equally grand concepts of evolution and progress.

Thus Comte counted it as one of the aims of sociology 'to discover through what fixed series of successive transformations the human race, starting from a state not superior to that of the societies of the great apes, gradually led to the point at which civilized Europe finds itself today' — that was in 1822. Social development was a product of intellectual development, which albeit somewhat unevenly had proceeded in three stages. Theological or fictive thought was associated with a military form of social organization, metaphysical thought with 'defensive militarism', and positive (or as we would nowadays say scientific) thought with industrial, peaceful social organization.[8] Somewhat similarly, Herbert Spencer classified societies in two ways — by the complexity of their organization, and into 'industrial' and 'militant' types. He did not mean by 'industrial' quite what we understand by the term today, and classed some simple and technologically primitive societies as industrial because they concentrated on peaceful production rather than war. Nevertheless he made it clear, by implication if not explicitly, that he regarded industrial societies as superior and more advanced from the evolutionary point of view, for he wrote of 'reversions' and 'partial reversions to the militant type of structure' in advanced contemporary societies including his own. The fundamental basis of his distinction was that anything involving coercion or compulsion is 'militant', while 'industrial' societies are based on the voluntary co-operation of free individuals.[9]

Spencer's lead was followed by Maine, who concluded from his study of ancient law that 'the movement of the progressive societies has hitherto been a movement from Status to Contract'.[10] Spencer and Maine together with the British economists from Adam Smith onwards laid the foundations for Durkheim's analysis of the social consequences of the division of labour,

5

with its distinction between mechanical and organic solidarity. Mechanical solidarity characterized a society in which there was little division of labour and people were like-minded because they performed similar tasks, and the structure of such a society consisted of homologous segments like clans. Durkheim probably erred in underestimating the extent of individual differences in such societies, and in overestimating the predominance of penal customary law in them. Organic solidarity was that of the complex society with a high degree of division of labour. Here the social structure consisted of interdependent associations, like industrial enterprises exchanging goods and services with one another. In such a society occupational and other groups would tend to develop their own different sub-cultures and become unlike-minded through performing unlike tasks. The solidarity of common values was less likely to be available to such a society accordingly. Durkheim differed from the British school in recognizing that self-interest mediated through free contract was not enough to secure the solidarity of such a society, since interest makes me today your friend, tomorrow your enemy. He accordingly rejected Spencer's extreme individualism, and looked rather to the rise of new sources of solidarity like professional ethics to maintain long-term non-contractual relations between individuals and groups and hence the solidarity of a highly differentiated society.[11]

Marx and Engels, it need hardly be said, differed sharply from the liberal tradition of Comte and Spencer. Their approach was based on historical materialism and stressed the importance of class conflict as a main explanation for social change. Like other nineteenth-century thinkers, however, they tried to put their ideas into a grand perspective of the stages in the development of man and society. In the earliest stage, property took its original form of tribal ownership, and the social order was an extension of the family. In a second stage, the slavery which had always been latent in the family became manifest as the dominant institution of society, and the social order was basically divided into two classes — citizens and slaves. This stage corresponded to the ancient city-states of Greece and Rome. The third stage of development was feudal, as in the Middle Ages, with peasant serfs instead of slaves as 'the subject class of producers'. And it was obvious enough that the bourgeois capitalist society of Marx' and Engels' own time had emerged from feudal society. When Marx became the correspondent of the *New York Daily Tribune* on Indian affairs, and became accordingly more aware of the civilizations of India and China, he characterized Oriental society, based on the Asiatic mode of production, as a kind of alternative to the Occidental stages of the city-states and feudalism. It was characterized by centrally controlled canalization and other public works, and in its social order the unifying function of the tribe was usurped by the despot and his ideological reflex the deity. Marx accordingly wrote in a summary way of the 'Asiatic, ancient, feudal, and modern bourgeois modes of production' as 'progressive epochs in the economic formation of society'.[12]

6

Tönnies contrasted the 'natural, organic' relations of the family, village and small town (*Gemeinschaft*) with the 'artificial' and 'isolated' condition of the city and modern industrial society (*Gesellschaft*) in which the original and natural relations of human beings to each other are excluded and every person strives for his own advantage in a spirit of competition. Western Europe had passed from a union of *Gemeinschaft* whose prototype was the family, through an association of *Gemeinschaft* with corporations or fellow-ships of the arts and crafts and 'relations between master and servant, or better between master and disciple', to an association of *Gesellschaft* with the rise of the joint stock company and limited liability. A fourth stage was possibly represented by movements like consumers' cooperation and British guild socialism, a revival of *Gemeinschaft* in forms adapted to conditions of *Gesellschaft* which might become the focus for 'the resuscitation of family life and other forms of *Gemeinschaft*'. No doubt his nostalgic analysis idealizes the harmony and integration of small-scale rural communities, but the notion of *Gesellschaft* like Durkheim's organic solidarity expresses an insight into the complex interdependence of modern industrial society while deploring the consequent impersonality.[13]

Hobhouse identified the four criteria of social development as scale, efficiency (which he linked with differentiation and specialization of the social structure), freedom, and mutuality. Though there might not be a rigid one-to-one relation (for example, Greek city-states were smaller than 'some of the great Empires of the middle culture'), yet on the whole there was a correspondence between the four criteria in the grand process of social development.[14] The concepts of freedom and mutuality express Hobhouse' position as a liberal social philosopher rather than belonging to the mainstream of sociology. His criteria of scale and 'efficiency', however, are clearly in line with the earlier work of Durkheim, and link it with the later contributions to which I refer below.

In this short introductory chapter I have done no more than allude to the work of some of the classical sociologists. In particular, Max Weber's seminal contribution has been omitted from this summary and finds its place in a later chapter. Enough has been said, however, to establish that the broad theme with which this book is concerned has been a major preoccupation of sociology since its first beginnings. Here, indeed, is yet another argument against a term like 'the sociology of development'. A better case could be made for the assertion that all sociology has been about 'development', or whatever term is preferred, than for the implication that its study is that of one limited area of social life like the sociology of the family or of industry.

(B) THREE RECENT CONTRIBUTIONS

The Wilsons and the growth of scale

Godfrey and Monica Wilson (née Hunter) were social anthropologists whose field experience in the 1930s, both in rural tribal societies in southern

7

Africa and in the rapidly growing urban industrial areas there, led them to try to construct a satisfactory theoretical framework for those observations from among the concepts and theories then available in sociology and social anthropology.[15] The key concept in their analysis of social change is the growth of scale of human relations, and in this they follow Hobhouse. In respect of political organization, language, economy, and religion alike, the change from primitive to civilized was a change from smallness of scale to largeness of scale. Further, not only has modern society a larger scale in space, but also in time.[16] Among the technologically most primitive peoples, like the Bushmen, the effective time-span was only that of the minimal kinship, three generations. Among the agricultural Bantu the time-span was longer, ten generations or so, as claims to land depended on genealogy. By contrast, the effective time-span of historical European societies embraced the thousands of years of western civilization, while modern science has enlarged that much further by making men aware of the millions of years encompassing the evolution of the universe and of life on earth.

The enlargement of scale entails a wider dependence of each individual on more people, both living and dead; and here the Wilsons follow Durkheim in an analysis of 'social density'. Further, 'complexity, control of the material environment and non-magicality, impersonality and mobility' characterize large-scale civilized society in contrast to primitive tribal societies, and these characteristics are 'necessarily connected with one another and with largeness of scale'.

A high degree of specialization is required for control of the environment; control of the environment makes for largeness of scale, which makes specialization profitable. Specialization and the accumulation of knowledge turn on the autonomy of the narrower relations (e.g. academic freedom) though there is increasing subordination in the wider relations (e.g. the autonomy of the businessman is limited by the law). Mobility is facilitated by the control of the environment and largeness of scale, and it also makes for efficiency: 'a career open to talents is a condition of maximum control of the environment'.

For the Wilsons, the stresses and conflicts which characterize southern African society are maladjustments or disequilibria arising from an unevenness of scale. 'The same people seek to be wider in scale in some ways than others.' For example, the world scale of production for a market of commodities like coffee is inconsistent with the attempts of Europeans to reduce the scale of the society involved in such production by limiting it to Europeans. Competition for land, related to competition for markets for agricultural produce, became accordingly a matter of maladjustment as a result of European farmers' attempts to monopolize the land near railways. Racial tension over the land issue (and related issues of soil erosion, overgrazing, and attitudes to cattle) were paralleled by racial tension in the copper-mining

8

industry. Here again the world scale of the market for copper, and the principle that mobility and a career open to talents are necessary conditions of economic efficiency, were inconsistent with wide differences in wages between white and black workers and opposition by European workers to the training and employment of Africans in skilled work. Racial exclusiveness was regarded as an instance of a disparity between the scale of economic and of religious ideas — the word religious being here used in a very wide sense. The underlying opposition is over scale, but it is muddled at every point: 'The same people complain that African agriculture is inefficient, but at the same time fear African competition in agricultural produce, and therefore oppose the development of tribal areas . . . Africans seek education and recognition as civilized men, but they cling to belief in witchcraft.'

Talcott Parsons, the pattern variables, and differentiation

From among the voluminous work of Talcott Parsons, the leading theoretician of recent American sociology, two contributions may be selected as having a bearing on the general theme of this book.

In his early work, Parsons clarified and elaborated Tönnies' distinction between *Gemeinschaft* and *Gesellschaft* into five 'major dilemmas of orientation' that confront an actor in a situation, 'choices that the actor must make before the situation has a determinate meaning for him' and before the appropriate action can be decided on accordingly. 'The five dichotomies which formulate these choice alternatives are called the *pattern variables*', and Parsons listed them as follows:

1. Affectivity versus affective neutrality.
2. Self-orientation versus collectivity orientation.
3. Universalism versus particularism.
4. Ascription versus achievement.
5. Specificity versus diffuseness.[17]

Though Parsons himself stated that 'a pattern variable is a dichotomy, one side of which must be chosen by an actor', it would appear more useful to think of the pattern variables as scales.

Within the Parsonian scheme of thought the processes of social change accompanying industrialization can be characterized in terms of shifts in the prevailing choices which are made of at least four of the five pattern variables. According to this view, industrialization involves a shift from affectivity to affective neutrality; from particularism to universalism; from ascription to achievement; and from diffuseness to specificity.

Affective neutrality is shown when an actor postpones or renounces immediate gratifications, and so is related to capital formation in industrializing societies which involves decisions to save and invest rather than expend resources in current consumption. Clearly there are overtones here of the Weberian Protestant ethic. Affective neutrality also character-izes social relations in industrial societies, which are contractual, im-personal, and calculating; the continuing need for affective gratification in such societies is largely met by more traditional institutions, especially the family.

Industrialization tends to erode particularistic exclusiveness like that in the Wilsons' example of the racial particularism of Europeans in southern Africa. Such particularisms are inefficient and lead to an under-utilization of resources. Indeed, the most highly industrialized societies, whether capitalist or communist, are those in which universalistic patterns prevail and careers are open to talents.

In the same way, achievement rather than ascription tends to be the basis for recruitment in a fully industrialized society. When people in less industri-alized societies recruit workers or admit pupils on the basis of kinship we call it nepotism and regard it as incompatible with the ways of a modern society.

And the finer division of labour and the greater complexity of organiza-tions in an industrial society are clearly related to the shift from diffuseness to specificity, from social relations which are wide in scope and all-embracing to relations in which, as Parsons puts it, the actor confines his concern with another to a specific sphere and does not permit other concerns to enter.

In a later work, Parsons combined evolutionary and comparative per-spectives in analysing changes in the social structures of societies 'ranging all the way from extremely small-scale primitive societies to the new super-national societies of the United States and the Soviet Union'.[18] From the evolutionary point of view, he says, the most important type of change is the 'enhancement of adaptive capacity'. This is seen in terms of a common paradigm, the leading feature of which is differentiation. Taking a familiar example, in predominantly peasant societies the household is both the unit of residence and the primary unit of agricultural production. The adaptive upgrading of such a society involves a separation of units or sub-systems in which specialized units such as workshops, factories, and offices are man-ned by people who are also members of family households. This does not mean that 'the older "residual" unit will have "lost function" . . . The house-hold is no longer an important economic producer, but it may well perform its other functions better.' Differentiation poses new problems of integration, for example that of creating new roles in which authority is not derived from kinship. 'Adaptive upgrading thus requires that specialized functional capacities be freed from ascription', says Parsons here in the terms of his earlier work. And there is the problem which as he puts it is opposite to that of differentiation and specification; it is that of establishing a new pattern of values appropriate to the new type of society. Here the thought echoes Durkheim's preoccupation with the problem of solidarity in a society in

10

which all men do not think alike. The establishment of new values may encounter severe resistance from groups adhering to older values which are no longer appropriate, a resistance which may be called 'fundamentalism'.

It may be helpful at this point to tabulate the terms in which different sociologists have characterized the basic processes of change.

Spencer	from simple	to complex
	from military	to industrial
Maine	from status	to contract
Durkheim	from homologous	to interdependent
	segments	associations
	from mechanical	to organic solidarity
Tönnies	from *Gemeinschaft*	to *Gesellschaft*
	(community)	(association)
Hobhouse	growth in: scale, efficiency (complexity), mutuality, freedom	
Wilsons	growth in: scale; complexity, control of the material environment and non-magicality; impersonality, social mobility; autonomy in the narrower relations, subordination in the wider	
Parsons (1951)	from affectivity	to affective neutrality
	from particularism	to universalism
	from ascription	to achievement
	from diffuseness	to specificity
Parsons (1966)	differentiation of sub-systems	

Fred Riggs and 'prismatic society'

Professor F. W. Riggs' contribution is based on his experience in the field of public administration especially in Thailand and the Philippines.[19] He takes as his starting-point the pattern variables of Talcott Parsons especially the fifth which distinguishes between diffuseness and specificity.

In a bold metaphor derived from the physics of light, Riggs first contrasts the 'fused' and 'diffracted' types or states of society. The 'fused' society is like white light, a blend of all colours, while the 'diffracted' society is one in which there is a complete separation of functions along, as it were, the whole spectrum.

In a 'fused' society a single structure tends to perform a wide range of functions, and to be functionally *dif*fuse in Parsons' sense accordingly. This applies especially to the family and kinship, an institutional cluster which in such societies performs a wide range of functions. In a 'diffracted' society, structures are functionally specific. Such a society can be thought of as having an economy, a polity or political system, an education system, etc., within which again are organizations performing specialized functions, such as for instance a bureau of labour statistics. Riggs accords with the Wilsons here in pointing to the autonomy of these specialized structures or sub-systems as well as their interdependence.

11

The contrast between 'fused' and 'diffracted' societies has important implications for the social sciences. 'Fused' societies are social anthropologists' societies. Their undifferentiated nature makes it both possible and preferable for them to be studied and analysed by one person (or sometimes a husband-and-wife team) — possible, because there is not so much to analyse as to be beyond the capacity of a single mind; and preferable, because social anthropologists are alerted by their training to look for and bring out the interconnections between things, for example the relations between the agricultural technology, the land tenure system, the kinship system, and the traditions of political authority. The social anthropologist's practice of giving primary attention to kinship is well adapted to the study of such societies, in which it may be found in practice that a full analytical description of the kinship system leaves little else in the social structure to be accounted for.

In 'diffracted' societies, by contrast, the specialization and relative autonomy of the major structures both demand specialized study by separate academic disciplines and are not essentially falsified by it. For example, in highly differentiated societies political leaders are reluctant to interfere with judges' legal decisions, and do so very seldom. Quite explicitly, indeed, political doctrines have been established in many of these societies asserting the separation of church and state, the distinction between the privy purse and public revenues, the independence of the judiciary, private property rights, academic freedom and the independence of the universities, freedom of the press, and so forth. It is accordingly quite possible and realistic to think, for example, of the law and politics as separate domains, and for political science and law to become two separate academic disciplines. Finer specializations within the major structures of society are mirrored in finer subdivisions in the social sciences; thus as Riggs writes, '"public administration" becomes partitioned off from government to permit the specialized examination of institutions for the execution of public policy; and correspondingly, "business administration" is demarcated from the more general subject of economics'.

Riggs now introduces the notion of the 'prismatic' society as one in which the diffraction process has started but remains incomplete, and 'the separate colours, though differentiated, are captive, "imprismed"'. The functional autonomy of institutions is incomplete, and the prismatic society pays no more than lip-service to doctrines of the separation of powers. This type of society is amenable neither to the methods of social anthropology nor to those of the specialized social sciences. Economic behaviour in a prismatic society, for instance, is unintelligible without noting its interaction with politics and administration, while agricultural and medical practices are linked with supernatural beliefs and rituals, and the family impinges alike

12

on politics, administration, market behaviour, religion, and education. At the same time, however, 'the emphasis on diffuse structures that characterizes anthropology has its own limitations in the study of an intermediate, prismatic society ... All the subsystems, in all their complexity, are already emergent, especially in the most industrialized parts of the society, the urban centres.' Social anthropologists tend accordingly to restrict themselves to the village; but in doing so they are taking as partial a view of the whole as their colleagues from the other social sciences, and the result is 'a curiously dissociated or schizoid image of the transitional society'.

Translating Riggs' metaphorical term 'prismatic' back into the more prosaic language of sociological analysis, such societies can be termed 'partially differentiated', though Riggs prefers to avoid the term 'differentiated' because, he says, it has also been used for what is more generally known as the 'plural society'. In a series of brilliant chapters in part two of his book, he has exemplified the possible scope and content of a 'pan-disciplinary' approach (as he prefers to call it) to these societies, combining the insights of economics, political science, and sociology.

Riggs is careful to avoid suggesting that the 'prismatic' state of society is necessarily a temporary stage. He makes little use of the word 'development' with its association with the idea of stages, and he explicitly dissociates 'prismatic' from 'transitional', with its connotation of moving toward the '"modern", that is, of "modernization"'. True, 'there are forces in the world which tend to increase the degree of diffraction'. Chief among these are the new techniques of death control, adopted widely because of their low cost and, as he puts it, 'a widespread desire to avoid death'. Administering these techniques demands a degree of diffraction, 'institutionalizing hospitals, clinics, medical and nursing services, immunization programmes'. Furthermore, population growth raises demands for economic production, which 'can only be raised by utilizing scientific knowledge and industrial techniques, creating capital, training technicians, professionals, specialists. Hence an overwhelming pressure is being exercised on every contemporary society in the direction of further diffraction.' Nevertheless, 'a prismatic social order might remain prismatic indefinitely. Indeed, ... it has its own equilibrating mechanisms.' Moreover, even though many of the present-day prismatic societies may become more diffracted eventually, the process may take decades or centuries. Meanwhile, they demand to be analysed and understood, and the need accordingly for social science is to take this state of society seriously and on its own terms. We need to elaborate and refine a conceptual apparatus or 'model' for understanding these societies which is neither that of social anthropology nor that of the specialized social sciences, and one which does not dismiss them as being merely in transition from one state to the other.

13

SUGGESTIONS FOR FURTHER READING

Peter Worsley, *The Third World*, London: Weidenfeld and Nicolson, 1964
Szymon Chodak, *Societal Development*, Oxford: Oxford University Press, 1973
Fred W. Riggs, *Administration in Developing Countries: The Theory of Prismatic Society*, Boston: Houghton Mifflin, 1964

2   Technology, society and population

The natural history of the human population of the earth from the emergence of *Homo sapiens* **to the present day**

There have been two great technological revolutions in the history of man — the neolithic revolution and the industrial revolution.* Each of these two great revolutions was accompanied by a population explosion.[1]

Ten thousand years ago man was a relatively rare species, living in small bands with (it may be surmised) some kind of kinship or familial bond, and making a living by hunting and food-gathering. Some such human groups exist to this day, or did until very recent years — most notably perhaps the Australian aborigines; a few small groups in Africa, such as those popularly named 'Bushmen', and including the Hadza of central Tanzania; the Andaman Islanders; and a few others. These are the genuine contemporary primitives — or rather, theirs are the genuinely contemporary primitive cultures. From studies which have been done of the population density of people living in this way, it may be surmised that the maximum possible human population of the earth in the paleolithic period was about 10 million, and the actual population possibly rose from about 1 to 5 million during the period.†

Between about 7000 and 5000 B.C. — seven to nine thousand years ago — occurred the first great technological revolution in the history of modern man. It involved a complex of inventions rather than one single crucial discovery; the domestication of a number of plant species, especially the grain

---

* By 'man' here is meant modern man, *Homo sapiens*. If we count the species ancestral to *Homo sapiens* and extend our time scale to the last million years, we could distinguish a first technological revolution corresponding to the making of the first tools, accompanied by population growth from perhaps around 100,000 or 150,000 individuals to perhaps 1 million — the paleolithic revolution.

† The land surface of the earth, excluding Antarctica, is 135.8 million square kilometres. In recent times the densities of hunting and food-gathering peoples ranged from 95 per 100 square kilometres on the west coast of North America — an exceptionally favourable habitat — through 10 per 100 square kilometres in the rest of North America and 8 per 100 square kilometres in Australia, presumably down to zero in other regions. If we allow an average of 8 per 100 square kilometres for the earth's land surface as a whole we arrive at a maximum of 11 million. The actual population was presumably a good deal less than this. (United Nations, *The Determinants and Consequences of Population Trends*, 1953.)

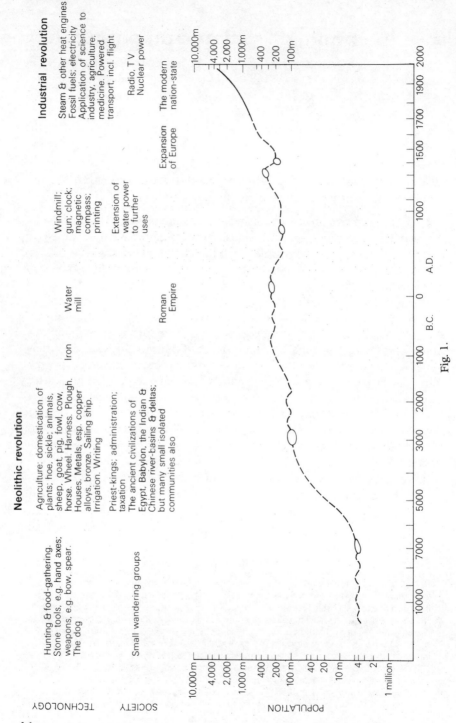

Fig. 1.

16

seeds, greatly increased the carrying capacity of the land, or at least of land in some parts of the earth, and also made possible the storage of food, and both necessitated and permitted the growth of a settled population. This in turn stimulated the building of houses, an advance on the temporary shelters of food-gathering wanderers. The domestication of a number of animal species had equally complex, and fundamental, effects on human social organization; these included sheep, goats, pigs, poultry, cattle, and horses. By adding the muscle power of other animals to that of men, they made possible the rise of techniques such as ploughing; they added a dependable food supply of meat and milk, together with other animal products such as leather; and they afforded the means of transport and trade between the new fixed settlements of human beings. Along with agriculture, therefore, went the rise of

Notes to Fig. 1. (Both time and population are plotted on logarithmic scales.)

Time is plotted on a logarithmic scale of years before A.D. 3000. This enables the long slow trends of the remote past to be somewhat 'foreshortened' while the rapid increase of the last 300 years can be seen without undue distortion.

In the same way, plotting population on a logarithmic scale enables the diagram to show changes in the relative increase rate. The neolithic population explosion from 5 million to 100 million is thus kept in the same perspective as the industrial population explosion from 500 million to (so far) 3,700 million.

The population estimates are derived from the United Nations, *The Determinants and Consequences of Population Trends*, 1953, and the article 'Population Growth' by J. V. Grauman in the *International Encyclopaedia of the Social Sciences*, vol. 12, 1968. The early estimates are, of course, extremely tentative and subject to wide errors.

An attempt has also been made to relate population trends to significant events in history, and especially to the history of technology. A valuable source here has been C. M. Cipolla, *The Economic History of World Population*, fifth edition, 1970; also the same author's essay 'Guns and Sails' in his *European Culture and Overseas Expansion*, 1970. A valuable earlier source is S. Lilley, *Men, Machines, and History*, 1948. Lilley's interpretation cannot be accepted entirely uncritically, since as an engineer he is more interested in devices than in the fundamental processes by which man utilizes his environment; hence the relative triviality of some of the inventions he lists, and the inevitable arbitrariness of his system of scoring, which underrates some really fundamental inventions. Further, he omits some inventions which first occurred in China or the Middle East and includes some only when they entered what he calls the 'mainstream' of Mediterranean—European culture. Most surprisingly, he nowhere includes the gun as a fundamental invention. Finally, the datings he adopts for some of the earliest inventions seem now to be too recent; thus he puts the neolithic revolution between 5000 and 3000 B.C., compared with Cipolla's date of 7000—5000 B.C. I have taken the liberty of re-dating Lilley's findings accordingly for the purpose of fig. 1.

The general correlation between technological innovation and population growth seems clear.

the first towns — and correspondingly that of specialized crafts and manu-
factures, by men who could exchange their products for the food that was
now available in a storable form. Other technological achievements of this
period included the rise and elaboration of metallurgy and the making of
tools and weapons of bronze and iron; the wheel, with its vast potential for
both trade and war; and the wooden sailing ship, which added a limited use
of another source of energy to human and animal muscle. And these technological developments were accompanied by remarkable economic, political,
and intellectual developments, including the rise of money and systems of
accounting; the rise of political authorities — mostly, it would seem, of the
'oriental despotism' type — wider than the kinship or neighbourhood principle; the invention of writing; mathematics, and its application to astro-
nomical observation, surveying and accounting; and the reckoning of time.

Although the neolithic revolution seems from our standpoint like a leisure-
ly affair compared with the industrial revolution of the present time and
recent history, it was nevertheless a dramatically rapid change compared
with the slow processes of evolution by natural selection, which had prevailed before the rise of culture. And like our own technological revolution it
was accompanied by a population explosion. By the time of which we have
worthwhile estimates, the largest human communities of people subject to a
common political authority numbered scores of millions. The Han empire of
China, Asoka's empire in India, and Roman rule around the Mediterranean
basin comprised populations of around 50–100 million each, and the world's
population at the beginning of the Christian era has been estimated at between 200 and 300 million.

Not that there was at any time a single neolithic culture or society. On the
contrary, although the technologies of transport and war made possible the
sort of empires we have just mentioned, they did not sustain a system of
communications and social interaction which ever approached the scale of
the whole earth. Even the empires remained comparatively isolated from one
another, while in areas which they did not conquer there continued to be
smaller human groups, developing in relative isolation both distinctive
cultures — different languages, technologies, kinship systems, systems of
political authority, etc. — and also distinctive physical characteristics through
the process known as genetic drift. During the neolithic period, therefore,
mankind came to be divided in two ways — by culture and by race.

After the great burst of innovative energy which is now generally regarded
as having occurred around 7000–5000 B.C., there followed some six thousand
years of relative technological stagnation. This stagnation was not quite
unrelieved, and we can distinguish two periods within it when significant
advances occurred. One accompanied the development of iron smelting,
apparently in about 1400 B.C., and its spread, together with some inventions
of minor importance such as the crane and the pulley at an early stage of

Graeco-Roman civilization. The other occurred during a period around A.D. 1000–1300, with the invention of the windmill (possibly independently in Persia in the seventh century and in Europe about 1100), the gun, the mechanical clock, the magnetic compass and other aids to navigation, printing, and the further development of some older inventions including improved harness, making possible a wider use of animal power, and the application of water power to wider uses. The first great expansion of European influence across the world, indeed, began centuries before the industrial revolution and was based on the technology of guns and sails.[2] Though the evidence is fragmentary, it seems not impossible that these periods of minor technological advance were also periods of population growth. In between such periods, and even to some extent during them, however, population grew very slowly, if at all, and from time to time experienced sharp setbacks. From the 200–300 million which modern authorities regard as a reasonable estimate for the world's population at the time of Christ, it possibly fell to not much more than half that number around the seventh century A.D., rose again to about the thirteenth century, and was then severely reduced by the pandemic of bubonic plague later named the Black Death.[3]

For long periods of history, therefore, most human communities seem to have experienced an irregular succession of 'good' and 'bad' periods. Good periods occurred when the climate was kindly, crops were good, there was an absence of killing outbreaks of disease, and political conditions were stable and not over-oppressive. Bad periods were those when natural calamities occurred, such as unfavourable weather conditions leading to crop failure, outbreaks of disease among crop plants, domestic animals, or the human population itself; or man-made disasters like war with its consequent ravages of looting and pillage, the destruction of stocks of food, the spreading of diseases by armies on the move, or the movement of people fleeing from oppression. In periods of general disorder and a lack of strong political authority, the prevalence of banditry and piracy would operate to make trade insecure and heighten the isolation of local communities and their dependence on their own resources. Isolated communities were at the mercy of local calamities such as a drought or a flood, or a purely local outbreak of disease. Offsetting these hazards, they did, it is true, also tend to develop immunity to local diseases and so experience a precarious balance, which might be upset by an incursion of outside influences involving large-scale movements of people, bringing in new diseases to which the population was not immune, or unfamiliar strains of existing diseases, and facilitating the spread of vectors such as the rat and the flea.

In larger political communities there was trade, and stocks of food would tend to be moved into stricken local communities from a wider area; deficits in one place would be made up by surpluses in another, and the security of trade would encourage people to keep stocks of food for sale and so provide

19

a reserve that could be drawn on in case of need. On the other hand, as has been suggested, large-scale movements of men and vectors of disease might also be associated with disastrous outbreaks of infectious disease and lead to population calamities. It is against such a background that we may see the decline in population that is thought to have accompanied the collapse of the Roman empire; on the other hand, the wars of the fourteenth century and the movement of armed forces may well have facilitated the spread of bubonic plague and played a part in the ghastly calamity the Black Death.

Whether locally or on a wider scale, there may well have been a cyclical tendency in population trends in pre-industrial conditions. Starvation or an epidemic would result disproportionately in the deaths of those always most at risk of death – the old and the very young. The survivors, now including a higher proportion of breadwinners than before, would in consequence have fewer dependants to support. They might experience a rise in their standard of living, and inherit rights to land and other assets sooner than they would otherwise have expected. Marriages postponed during the bad years would now take place, while existing marriages might be expected to be more fertile; the birth-rate would rise accordingly and a recovery or increase in numbers would take place until the next calamity.

Thus the birth-rate and the death-rate, the patterns of fertility and of mortality, were not independent of one another in pre-industrial conditions any more than they are today. In some cases, an awareness of the relation between population and resources may have led to the adoption of social practices and customs which had the effect of limiting births and keeping down the rate of population increase, and even in some cases to population decline. A number of examples of 'primitive' family limitation of this sort may be cited. One is the Pacific island of Tikopia, where the anthropologist Raymond Firth found an express awareness among people generally, but especially among the respected elders and chiefs, that on such a tiny island there could easily be too many people for the resources available. Population checks had in the past, Firth reported, included war and the driving out of some less-favoured people; more recently, in hard times and after family quarrels, 'sea voyaging' – virtually a form of suicide – was resorted to, when young men would set out in dug-out canoes determined never to return, and with only a small chance of fetching up on some other island, the nearest of which was some sixty miles away. But these were extreme measures, existing in memories but not commonly resorted to. Probably the most effective population check was a combination of celibacy and coitus interruptus. Younger sons married late, or never; and though they were not denied extra-marital satisfactions, they took care by means of coitus interruptus to ensure that pregnancy did not result. Abortion was sometimes practised, especially when an unmarried girl became pregnant, but that was rarely. More commonly, however, babies for whose future prosperity their elders saw little

20

prospect would be left face downwards, never to draw their first breath.[4] Other examples of pre-industrial family limitation are afforded by Tokugawa Japan, and rural England from the mid-seventeenth to the late eighteenth centuries, and these are dealt with more fully in the case-studies at the end of this chapter. And a more recent example is that of Ireland, where after the calamity of the potato famine of 1845—7 a spontaneous change occurred in the inheritance customs and other social arrangements of the peasant population. The importance of the undivided inheritance of land being now dramatically recognized, the Irish adopted patterns of life which involved many in perpetual spinsterhood and bachelorhood, while those who married tended to do so late in life and in many cases after a period of work abroad, especially in England, while younger sons with no prospect of inheriting the land made their way, with family help, out of the countryside altogether — to the towns, to England, or to America. Thus although, in deference perhaps to Catholic precept, married fertility-rates remained high, the general birth-rate was kept down to a level at which out-migration could cope with the natural increase of population, and the population declined continuously from 1848 till recent times.[5]

At other times and in other places, however, different attitudes and practices prevailed. Thus in England before 1640, and again after 1780, or in Ireland before 1848 there was something more closely approximating to the 'unchecked fertility' of the Malthusian model. Much may have depended upon the way in which people perceived their situation, and in particular which factor they thought of as limiting their opportunity and their prosperity. In some cases this was land, as in the island societies of Japan and Tikopia, and from time to time in some western rural communities. Elsewhere and at different periods, however, it may have been people. Thus in many traditional African societies, a successful and prosperous man was one who had plenty of children; the daughters could do household tasks as long as they stayed at home, and when they left to get married they became a source of bride-wealth in compensation; while sons could equally make themselves useful as small boys tending the goats, as bigger boys tending the cattle, and as young men lending their support and strength to defend their father in disputes. In such societies, accordingly, a high value was placed on fertility, and also on polygyny, since from the man's point of view the more wives the more children. Many African societies, at the same time, had plenty of land at their disposal and could practice 'slash-and-burn' shifting agriculture, in which a further premium was put on the services of young men for the hard and even dangerous work of cutting trees and clearing the bush, keeping wild animals at bay, etc. And 'Africa' was a concept unknown to many such peoples; there was no awareness of a continent as a limited land mass surrounded by sea, and in the state of knowledge which prevailed before modern times the situation was probably perceived as one in which there was no

21

limit to the land which was available, provided only that manpower was available to clear it of bush, wild animals, and (possibly) people of other tribes.

Over most of the world in pre-industrial conditions, the expectation of life was short; typically a new-born child might be expected to live less than thirty years, though the expectation of life would increase sharply once the extreme hazards of the early weeks and months were past. The working life was also short, so that men and women had scarcely finished bringing up a young family when the husband died and the wife (or wives, in those societies which permitted polygyny) became dependants on their own older children, or on other kinsfolk. The anthropological literature on kinship in pre-industrial societies, indeed, testifies to the extent to which provision for widows was necessary, and resulted in arrangements like the levirate, for example, among many African peoples. A short working life, high fertility, and large numbers of children born to each woman accordingly implied a high rate of dependency, which in turn tended to keep living standards low.

So in the first 1,650 years of the Christian era the population of the world scarcely doubled, and when the first modern estimates became available, it was about 545 million; but then the pace of increase began to quicken. From 1650 onwards the increasingly reliable estimates which we have of the world's human population show a sharp and ever-steepening increase. From an estimated 545 million in 1650, it topped 1,000 million in about the decade 1810—20. It then doubled in about a century, reaching 2,000 million somewhere about 1920 — a rate of increase which may be contrasted with the doubling in about the first sixteen or seventeen centuries of the Christian era. And by 1970 it had reached nearly 3,700 million, nearly a doubling in fifty years.[6]

Population in transition from pre-industrial to industrial conditions

A useful schematic analysis of stages in the transition from pre-industrial to industrial conditions was that of the demographer and eugenist C. P. Blacker.[7] According to this analysis, pre-industrial populations were characterized by a fluctuating and precarious balance between high fertility and high mortality, which he called the 'high stationary' stage. With the rise in the standard of living and the spread of modern scientific medicine, especially in the field of public health, populations pass into the 'early expanding' stage. In this second stage, the death-rate falls, but fertility remains high, and population increases at an accelerating rate. After a longer or shorter time, however, many countries have experienced a fall in the birth rate consequent upon the adoption of a small-family system. There has accordingly been a turning point, marking the beginning of the third stage which Blacker called the 'late

22

expanding' stage, when although population continues to increase the rate of increase slows up. When births and deaths are again in balance, but now at low levels, we have the fourth or 'low stationary' stage; while the possibility exists that the birth-rate may go below the death-rate, so that we have a theoretical fifth or 'declining' stage.

At the end of this chapter I give case-studies of three individual countries, namely India, England and Wales, and Japan, with the object of showing the different ways in which population trends have occurred and may be related to economic and other changes. Roughly speaking, using these three societies as examples, England and Wales may be said to have entered stage 2 in 1750; stage 3 began in 1877, a date which can be 'pin-pointed' by the Bradlaugh—Besant trial; while by about 1935 or 1940 stage 3 had come to an end, though whether the trends after 1940 deserve the term 'low stationary' is more doubtful. Japan entered stage 2 some time after 1868, and stage 3 came in with the dramatic drop in the birth-rate of 1947—57. India fairly clearly entered stage 2 after the great influenza catastrophe of 1919; whether stage 3 has been reached yet is doubtful.

However, useful as Blacker's analysis is, it will become clear that it does not exactly fit the population history of any of the three countries; still less, it must be emphasized, is it an inevitable sequence to be followed by all. When we come to translate 'high' and 'low' into actual figures, things become more difficult again. As has been pointed out by Drake, the present-day poor countries of the world had in the recent past birth- and death-rates which fluctuated between about 40 and 50 per thousand (like India before 1920), though death-rates in these countries have undergone dramatic falls in recent decades. It has been commonly assumed that pre-industrial western societies had similarly high birth- and death-rates until the late eighteenth

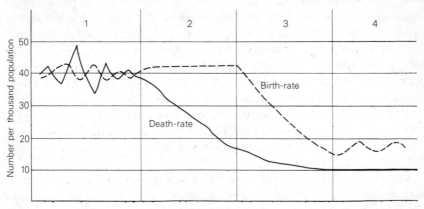

Fig. 2.
The population stages
(After C. P. Blacker, *Eugenics, Galton and After.*)

23

century; but Drake cites studies in England and Ireland, and adds his own of Norway, to suggest that in fact really high rates (that is, over 40) were not a universal characteristic of western countries before the industrial revolution. For example, the death-rate in England and Wales appears to have reached only 36 at its peak about 1740, and it never approached 40 at any time; while the birth-rate too was only around 36 to 37, though it stayed at that level for long periods during the industrial revolution between 1750 and 1870. In pre-industrial western societies, Drake suggests, 'preventive' rather than 'positive' checks (to use the Malthusian concepts) limited population growth; fertility was limited either through late marriage of women, or by birth control, in order to raise living standards; and this control may well have contributed in turn to higher per capita incomes there than in other non-industrial societies, and lower death-rates. These demographic characteristics of the West 'probably led to higher standards of living — associated with lighter burdens of dependency, higher lifetime return from investment in children (since fewer died before they reached working age), and attitudes of mind more conducive to the creation of an industrial society — than do the population mechanisms of many countries now at the pre-industrial stage of development. The higher birth- and death-rates of the latter might be said to have hindered industrialization, whereas the western demographic traits of two hundred years ago may well have favoured it.'[8]

Moreover, in the countries which first experienced the rise of modern science, especially medical science, and of industry and agricultural improvement, the fall in mortality was slow and gradual as new discoveries were made and new developments spread through the population. A Swedish poet attributed the rise in population in the early nineteenth century there to 'peace, vaccine, and potatoes',[9] which succinctly sums up the three major factors commonly involved in stage 2. Peace, security, and trade mitigated the effects of local disaster; medical improvements, of which vaccination against smallpox was a notable early example, lowered mortality; and the improvement of agriculture, including the introduction of new crops, enabled more food to be produced. In countries which experienced the impact of modern conditions at a later date, when the relevant knowledge and techniques were already fully developed in Europe, the changes which took place over a century or more in Europe were telescoped into a small number of decades, and the fall in mortality has been swifter accordingly. This has important consequences for world population trends at the present time, and I return to this point in a later section.

However, although the fall in mortality in some European countries (notably England) was slow and marked by painful setbacks, the first impact of the modern world on many previously isolated pre-industrial societies elsewhere was often disastrous. Military operations, the large-scale movements of people over wider areas, trade, and modern methods of transport operated

24

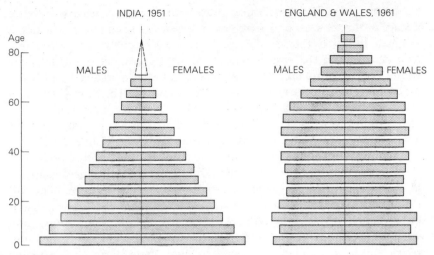

Fig. 3.
Age and sex distributions

in the same way as in earlier periods of history to spread new diseases, and unfamiliar strains of existing diseases, to populations whose previous partial immunities afforded them no protection. In addition, in some areas such as North America, Australia, etc., the local people were deprived of land which had traditionally been a source of food by the spread of white settlement. Thus in India, as detailed in a later section, foreign contact on a large scale resulted in the spread of tuberculosis and plague, to which the population had not previously been exposed. Similarly, the early period of foreign contacts and the advent of colonial rule in the late nineteenth century in East Africa were accompanied by outbreaks of diseases both among men and cattle, while the main effect of the 1914—18 war there was the appalling mortality from disease among and spread by the native carrier corps recruited by the British and German forces in connection with the East Africa campaign. [10]

At the same time, however, these consequences were being offset by other influences. When peace was established over wider areas than in traditional conditions, when a unified administration was set up, when roads and railways were built, famine relief became possible and the effects of local calamities could be minimized. Scientific investigation into local diseases took place — in East Africa, for instance, research into sleeping sickness began immediately after the establishment of British rule in Uganda, and within a few years appropriate measures were being taken to eliminate the disease. In India, similarly, vigorous action was taken by the British administration against diseases such as smallpox, while famine relief was a high priority of the government and the building of hard roads and railways was pressed forward accordingly.

25

Turning now to the fall in fertility which we have characterized as the onset of stage 3, the reasons for this have been less obvious than the medical and economic factors in the fall of mortality in stage 2; indeed, the process was often described in the past as obscure or mysterious, though sociological studies like those of Banks in England and Alva Myrdal in Sweden give us a reasonably clear understanding of what happened. Thus the practice of family limitation in England occurred first among a prosperous middle class for whom having too many children had come to be seen as a threat to their newly won prosperity, and spread down the social scale. More generally, it is in response to what has been aptly called 'a spirit of prudence' that such developments have occured[11] — when children cease to be regarded as economic assets and become economic liabilities; when children are thought of in terms of cost, as a source of expense and responsibility; when serious questions arise as to the opportunities available for children's future; and when having a large number of children is seen as a threat to living standards, so that the choice comes to be between having a large number and bringing them up 'decently', 'properly', according to standards which have become customary in the society or social class in question.

In these societies, then, life is long, the predominant causes of death are old age itself and the diseases associated with it, in which the death of a child is a rare event (and one viewed as a greater tragedy accordingly); people have only a few children, commonly around two or three per married woman, so that dependency ratios are low, especially in relation to a longer working life. In such a society, greater resources can be devoted to the care of the small number of children in each family. They are better fed, better housed and clothed, and better cared for in sickness, so that they grow up strong and healthy and can look forward to a long life. Whether privately through the family, or publicly through the state, local governments, or other agencies, greater resources are available for the education of these children so that they experience longer schooling — literacy is almost universal in such societies — and a longer period to develop intellectual skills which in adult life will enable them to learn and adapt themselves to the circumstances of a changing world, as well as the actual working skills they need to earn a living when they first begin to work. It is clear that the processes we are outlining here are cumulative and self-reinforcing. The fewer the children of each family, the better their health and education, the greater the likelihood that they will limit the number of children in turn. Once again, in the new balance of low mortality and low fertility, the two cannot be seen in isolation from one another. We have, indeed, rather strong grounds for suggesting that the fall in fertility in highly industrial societies is not some kind of mysterious side-effect of a rising standard of living; it is an integral part of the whole process, an indispensable condition for the raising of the standard of living as industrial development proceeds. To put it as bluntly as possible, poverty and

26

large families go together in the world as a whole just as they do within national communities. It is precisely when and where people limit the number of children they have that they, and their children, enjoy the higher standards that an industrial technology is capable of affording.

Different industrial societies differ widely, in fact, in the historical circumstances in which that fall in fertility has taken place, and in the methods used to achieve it; and some fuller details are given in the case-studies at the end of this chapter which emphasize these differences and the difficulty of generalizing about this particular process. There are differences also in the length of the time-lag between the onset of stage 2 and stage 3. The experiences of England and France are at opposite extremes in this respect: in England and Wales the time-lag was very long, so that stage 2, involving accelerating population growth, was also very long; some 120 years elapsed between the beginning of the fall in the death-rate, in about 1750, and the Bradlaugh—Besant trials in 1876—7 from which stage 3 can confidently be dated. By contrast, in France the birth-rate fell concurrently with the death-rate, there was no time-lag, stages 2 and 3 coincided, and there was no period of rapid, 'runaway' population growth.[12]

Stage 2, then, though it may be long or short, represents the period in which population growth proceeds rapidly and at an accelerating pace — a population explosion. In stage 3, though growth continues, the rate of increase slows until the practice of family limitation has become general throughout the population. Stage 4, which represents the condition of the fully industrialized societies today, may accordingly be seen as a new balance, this time with low fertility and low mortality. At the time of writing, indeed, the latest figures indicate virtually zero population growth in some major industrial countries including Germany, Belgium, the United Kingdom, and Hungary.

There is indeed a striking contrast in the ways in which the birth-rate and the death-rate are determined. The death-rate is almost entirely a matter of collective action and decision by public bodies, especially in the field of public health. By contrast, the birth-rate is determined by decisions made by large numbers of people, married men and their wives, paying scant regard in many cases to the policies and exhortations of state, church, and other large organizations. For that reason, the family limitation movement has been described as 'spontaneous', though the term is not entirely satisfactory; why should decisions by large numbers of people in their roles as parents be regarded as any more 'spontaneous' than decisions by a few in their roles as government ministers, senior civil servants, bishops, or medical practitioners? Indeed, in nearly every case the fall in fertility has taken place despite the hostility of persons in authority. The first government to adopt a policy of promoting birth control was that of India in the 1950s. In all the western industrial countries, governments, churches, and the medical profession alike were hostile to the notion, and placed obstacles in the way of the spread of the relevant knowledge and the availability of the necessary materials and appliances. In some cases this was in response to ideas concerning public decency and propriety, or what is usually, if inaccurately, termed 'morality'. Sometimes there have been implications of a 'cannon fodder' attitude on the part of some in authority. No government in an industrial country has ever gone beyond a position of neutrality on this issue so far as its own people are concerned, and it is distinctly ironic that some such governments and influential persons in those countries should now be outspoken about the merits of birth control for others, and adopt a more favourable attitude in the context of aid to the poor nations.[13]

Organized religious bodies have been similarly hostile. The Roman Catholic church, indeed, maintains an attitude of hostility to practices of contraception involving the use of physical or chemical barriers, and is strongly opposed to the legalization of abortion; and in countries in which that church is an important political force, the law and administrative practices operate with some effectiveness in limiting the spread of the knowledge and practices in question. However, while there has been a change of doctrine on the part of Protestant churches on these issues, this has occurred at a comparatively recent date, and long after the practices of contraception had become widespread among the people to whom these churches have ministered. In the case of the Anglican church, for example, though some individual clergy were already changing their attitudes, formal recognition was not given till the Lambeth Conference of 1958 to the propriety of implementing responsible decisions about family size by methods not involving a hindrance to married love.

The way in which the family limitation movement has occurred despite official and religious disapproval is reflected in the variety of the methods employed to limit the size of families. In nineteenth-century France, apparently, married couples practised coitus interruptus or slept apart; in England people used contraceptives, though apparently not at first the condom; in Ireland, as mentioned above, population growth has been limited by late marriage and a high proportion of the population who never marry; in Japan, there was a mass resort to abortion during the early 1950s, followed by a rather rapid spread of contraception and coitus interruptus; these represent the range of methods used in the early stages of the fall in fertility, while, of course, in recent years with the development of 'the pill', vasectomy, the intra-uterine contraceptive device, and other methods a wider range of techniques is now available. What is important is clearly not the method but the motive. Where there's a will, there's a way; when people find that it is necessary or desirable to limit the number of children they have, they will find a way of doing so, whether or not state or church approve. These considerations are clearly of the greatest relevance to the question, considered below, of whether, and if so when, the present-day developing countries will experience a decline in fertility similar to that experienced in the past by those already industrialized. I return to this question at the end of this chapter.

World population *circa* 1970: the poor countries and the population explosion

If we contrast pre-industrial and industrial societies, the one, corresponding to stage 1 of fig. 2, has a balance of high fertility and high mortality; the other, corresponding to stage 4, a balance of low rates. The contrast is brought out extremely clearly in fig. 3 in terms of the contrast between the age-structures of the population in the two types of society, represented respectively by England and Wales in 1961 and India in 1951.

That said, however, it is in fact virtually impossible at the present time to find a human population in which the balance of high rates still prevails. During the last two or three decades, death-rates have tumbled all around the non-industrial world, so that whereas a high death-rate used to be thought of as one of 40 or more, the highest rates are now those around 25–6 in some West African countries. In terms of the succession of stages outlined above, there are no pre-industrial societies left. Most of the poor countries have clearly passed into stage 2, that of falling death-rates, while their birth-rates remain high, so that they are experiencing population growth which is not only rapid but accelerating.

The rapid current increase of population is in fact accentuated by the very rapidity of the fall in death-rates, reflecting a rapid improvement in mortality conditions in which, however, the populations of many poor countries still exhibit the 'youthful' age-structure with which they emerged from the earlier stage. These improved conditions naturally take their first and most dramatic effect on the mortality of children and young adults; combating the diseases of old age is a slower process, and it is the young who benefit more from measures such as the control of malaria and the improvement of midwifery. The main improvement in mortality conditions, accordingly, is felt just in those age-groups which are most numerous; in arithmetical terms, the most reduced mortality-rates are multiplied by the biggest age-groups in the reckoning of overall mortality and the summing which produces the death-rate for the population as a whole, the so-called 'crude' death-rate.

As a simple calculation will show, a stable population in which every baby born lives to the age of exactly 100 years will have a death-rate of 10 per thousand. Needless to say, no country has ever approached such favourable mortality conditions as that, and countries like Britain and Sweden with highly developed public health services backed by adequate resources have a hard time getting their death rates below 12 per thousand in populations which include a due proportion of old people. But in many poor countries to-day, where the age-structure of the population is a 'youthful' one as a result of past high mortality and present increase, a comparatively modest improvement in mortality conditions enables the crude death-rate to be brought well below 10; while in newly industrialized Japan the almost incredibly low death-rate of 6 per thousand has been attained despite mortality conditions which, age for age, are still not quite as favourable as those in western Europe. Such rates could indeed be regarded as 'artificially' low, and they are likely to rise again in decades to come as the age-structure of the population matures — that is, as the big age-groups now young in those populations survive into old age and fill out the numbers in the older age-groups. Meanwhile, though, the extremely low death-rates in many non-industrial and recently industrialized countries constitute one important factor in the current rapid population growth in the world as a whole, commonly called the population explosion.

The other factor is, of course, fertility. It has to be stressed that Blacker's stages do not constitute a natural law, and there is nothing inevitable about them. It is an open question whether, and if so when, fertility will fall in to-day's poor countries as it did in countries like England and Wales after 1876—7, or Japan after 1949.

The crucial nature of this question is now well recognized. Thus Lord Blackett has written of 'the extreme importance for the economic advance of the developing countries of reducing drastically the now high population increases', and on the basis of calculations for a typical 'model' country has estimated that it would pay the government of such a country to spend up to $150 to prevent one birth from taking place.[14] Other authorities have estimated that birth prevention is by far the best possible form of investment: 'The addition to income per head in a poor country caused by spending £100 on birth prevention is, at very least, fifteen times the addition to income per head from the best alternative use of £100.'[15] From this kind of calculation, many authorities on economic planning have been led to urge the desirability of birth-control programmes, seeing the success or failure of such programmes as a major factor in trends of income per head.[16] In particular, the the World Bank, for many years aware of the problem, adopted a more vigorous approach when Mr Robert S. McNamara became its President in 1968;[17] and the Pearson commission, reporting to the Bank of 1969, regarded the 'staggering growth of population' as a major cause of the discrepancy between rich and poor countries. The direct difficulties created by very rapid population growth included sharp increases in budget expenditures on education, health, housing, water supply, and so forth, and a threat to the quality of the next generation. 'There is a strong inverse correlation between child health and family size. Rapid growth of the child population also delays educational improvement.' The burden of dependency was increased, to the detriment of resources that could be devoted to raising living standards. More aid was needed. Inequality tended to increase, as a result of developments such as the raising of land values and rents; and severe urban problems arose. The controversial nature of the matter was recognized, and much was to be left to the initiative of the poor countries themselves; the need for more research was recognized, and there was recognition of the need for information to spread freely. 'To make the knowledge and means of family planning available to all is an enormous task in societies where communication and commercial distribution channels are highly imperfect.'

As reported by the Pearson commission, the governments of a number of poor countries have in the last few years followed the initiative of India in adopting policies favourable to family planning:

There has been a remarkable awakening to the acute problems posed by this population explosion. In only a few years, ambitious policies to spread family planning have been introduced in countries representing over 70% of the population of the developing world. The development of intra-uterine contraceptive devices (IUD's) and of oral pills has amounted to a major breakthrough in family planning techniques.[18]

Besides India, such countries now include Pakistan, Indonesia, the Philippines, and South Korea, and in Africa Morocco and Kenya; while in some other countries again government assistance is in fact given to family planning without there being an official population policy, including Nigeria, Botswana, and a number of Latin American countries.[19] However, in his 1970 report the President of the World Bank stated:

Are the 'ominous implications of uncontrolled population growth' being acted on effectively? If one is to be candid, the answer would have to be *no*. With the exception of Singapore and Hong Kong, which are special cases, in only two developing countries, Taiwan and Korea, is there clear evidence that the rate of population growth has been significantly reduced by family planning programmes.*

Such a conclusion, however, must be regarded as neither surprising nor disappointing in the light of the foregoing analysis. If the experience of the already industrialized countries, and some other western societies, is any guide, then trends in fertility simply do not occur in direct response to the 'success' or 'failure' of government campaigns. On the contrary, this is an aspect of human behaviour in which government activity seems to be almost totally ineffective one way or the other. People in countries like England and

---

* And there is even some doubt about Taiwan. Lipton, in Seers and Joy, *Development in a Divided World*, 1971, p. 50, cites an unpublished study by Harkary concluding that fertility decline there had already begun before the family-planning programme, which was seen as an effort to accelerate rather than initiate it. Kingsley Davis (*Science*, 10 November 1967, pp. 730–9) also argues very persuasively that fertility in both Taiwan and South Korea was already declining.

Wales, or Sweden, decided to limit their families despite the heavy disapproval and discouragement of the authorities of state, church, and the
medical profession, official attitudes symbolized in the trials respectively
of Bradlaugh and Besant and of Knut Wicksell. On the other hand, despite
the encouragement of the government and the neutrality of religious opinion
in India, most people do not as yet seem to be limiting their families. I have
suggested that people decide to stop having more children than two or three
when two conditions are satisfied: when having more is seen as a threat to a
standard of living which has become customary and expected in a given
social *milieu*, and when the infant-mortality level falls below a certain level
(exactly what level clearly cannot be specified) so that people expect that
most of their children will survive. As the Pearson commission put it,

In the developing world many parents want large families for good and valid
economic reasons; not because they are ignorant or improvident. In such cases,
access to family-planning information and facilities will not make much difference.
When child labour makes a significant contribution to family income and when
parents are dependent on a large family for protection and security in old age, there
will be few incentives to reduce fertility, no matter what the social cost of a rapidly
expanding population ...

'Actually, however, many of the children born today are unwanted. Numerous
field surveys of parents in developing countries indicate that birth rates would be
reduced by one-third if parents had the knowledge and the means to plan the size of
their families. (The incidence of illegal abortions, and of maternal deaths from such
abortions, is high enough to be a serious problem in Latin America and elsewhere. As
a consequence of the sudden decline in infant mortality, families tend to be larger
than their traditional size and larger than parents can afford.) In short, there is in
many parts of the world a silent demand for family planning.'[20]

Although people will probably be resistant to direct persuasion to limit
their families, there is much that governments can do indirectly to bring
about a state of affairs in which people want to avoid pregnancies and have
access to the means of avoiding them. One highly important set of measures
in this context are those directed to reducing the infant-mortality rate. Such
measures are clearly justified as an end in themselves in countries where
many children die — where, indeed, in many cases child deaths outnumber
adult deaths — on humanitarian grounds alone, needing no other justification.
In these countries, methods of child care and nutrition frequently leave
much to be desired, and the education of mothers (together with midwives,
grandmothers, and indeed all who are concerned in the birth of children and
their early care) is to be seen as an urgent task whose reward will be healthier
people in the next generation. This view in turn has suggested a high priority for mother-and-baby clinics in the general development of public health
services. Once such clinics have been set up, and gained the confidence of
mothers and fathers, then it is believed that they can become the agencies

through which knowledge of contraception can spread, and where people can get the necessary devices, undergo fitting, etc., when they decide that, having got enough healthy children, they will not have any more. Family planning has accordingly come to be generally regarded as the concern of Ministries of Health in poor countries, and to be an activity carried on in clinics staffed by medical and nursing personnel.

This view has, however, come under attack on several grounds, and there is now much controversy about the effectiveness of different approaches to family planning. It is argued that the medical approach is expensive in terms of the time and energy of extremely scarce and highly rewarded professional people. Further, it is represented that it is a mistake to put about the idea that family planning is something that requires all the solemnity of a visit to a clinic, possibly many miles away. The middle-class parents of Britain in the 1870s did not accomplish family planning by visiting clinics, nor do a great many people in industrial countries today; they buy contraceptives in shops, for example in Britain the barber's. It was, indeed, something of a historical accident that family-planning clinics were set up in countries like Britain and America at all, and some authorities think that they have been a relatively ineffective and expensive expedient there too. According to this view, the governments of poor countries should concentrate less on clinics and personnel in their family-planning programmes, and more on making contraceptives available, possibly at subsidized prices, through ordinary trade networks like the village store and the itinerant trader.[21] Certainly, in so far as people are already in situations which lead them to want to avoid pregnancy, the least that governments can do is to ensure that their people have unrestricted access to knowledge about the humane methods of fertility control, and unimpeded access also to the requisite appliances. In so far, that is, as a 'silent demand for family planning' exists, then freedom of access to contraception will do something to avert a resort to the more dangerous and cruel methods of abortion or infanticide.

Case-study 1: India

India has a particular interest for the study of population trends in poor countries on two counts. First, it represents a well-nigh unique case of a country in which adequately reliable estimates exist of the birth- and death-rates in pre-industrial conditions of high mortality. These are afforded by the analysis carried out by Kingsley Davis of the census data gathered under British rule between 1881 (when the first census was taken) and 1947. They refer to the old undivided India, including the parts which are now Pakistan and Bangladesh, but only to those provinces which were under direct rule, and excluding the princely states. Fig. 4 shows the high fluctuating birth- and death-rates around 40–50 per thousand before 1920, and in particular

33

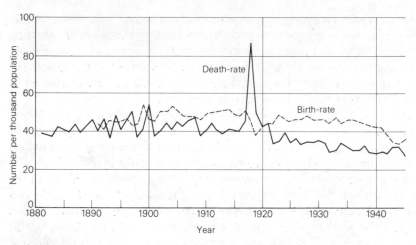

Fig. 4.
Estimated birth- and death-rates, India
(Source: Figure 'Estimated Annual Birth and Death Rates in India, 1881—1946',
in Kingsley Davis, *The Population of India and Pakistan* (copyright 1951 by Princeton
University Press), p. 37. Reprinted by permission of Princeton University Press.)

the appalling catastrophe of the 1919 influenza epidemic, which almost
literally decimated the population of the subcontinent. After 1920, with
a falling death-rate and a birth-rate which remained above 40, this population may clearly be regarded as having entered Blacker's stage 2; but right
up to the time of independence in 1947 no one could be sure that famine and
catastrophe might not return. The British administration's main concern
accordingly was to prevent such calamities by means which Davis describes
in detail — the development of irrigation, transport for famine relief if it
should be necessary, and health measures.[1] It was not until after the separate
independence of India and Pakistan that a problem was recognized of rapid
population growth, and as described by Myrdal the new government of India
in successive Five-Year Plans became the first government in the world to
adopt a policy positively favourable to family limitation.[2] This is India's
second chief interest accordingly, though how effective the policy has been
is more doubtful; while the death-rate in the Republic of India fell to 13
in the 1960s, the birth-rate when last estimated was 42. In December 1973
it was reported that 14 million couples between the ages of 15 and 44 were
using some method of birth control — an impressive number, but far short
of the 100 million that had been hoped for by 1980.[3]

Case-study 2: England and Wales

Our knowledge of the pre-industrial population history of this country is
sketchy, and before the census of 1801 and civil registration of births and

deaths in 1837 there are only parish registers, not all of which were ever complete, and many of which have been lost. Parish register material, however, has enabled estimates to be made of national birth- and death-rates from about 1700 onwards,[1] while the detailed analysis of one register – that of Colyton in Devon[2] – affords strong presumptive evidence of family-limitation practices during the hard times from about 1650 to 1780. Men married late, around 26–7; they married women older than themselves, often nearing 30 and more than half-way through their childbearing period; and births were widely spaced, though we can only guess at how this was done.

Nationally the death-rate, which was probably rising during the early eighteenth century, fell after about 1750. There has been much controversy about whether the birth-rate rose or merely remained high,[3] but the balance of evidence now suggests that it rose in response to new opportunities in rising industries, with earlier marriages and the abandonment of old family-limitation practices. Large families were accordingly a response to industrialization, rather than a traditional pattern.

The fall in the death-rate, however, was arrested by the 'health of towns problem' in the early Victorian era, and it hesitated around 20 to 21 from about 1820 to 1880 until the sanitary reforms which were the achievement of that unsung hero of English history Edwin Chadwick.[4] That long hesitation was a special feature of the experience of this country, part no doubt of the penalty of being the first industrial country, and not repeated elsewhere.

The circumstances in which the birth-rate began to fall in the late 1870s are now fairly well understood.[5] Following Malthus' work, published in 1798, there had been some advocacy of family limitation, especially by the early radical Francis Place, but it had fallen on deaf ears.[6] By 1870, however, the rising middle class were experiencing a number of checks to their standard of living – falling prices which disproportionately reduced profits and investment,[7] and an absolute shortage of domestic servants – along with other

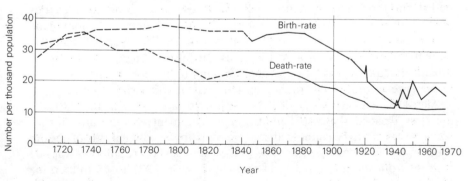

Fig. 5.
Birth- and death-rates, England and Wales
(Source: A. M. Carr-Saunders, *World Population*, to 1936. Earlier data averaged and smoothed.)

35

changes that made children a source of new expense, such as the introduction of examinations for the civil service, Army, Navy, and other professions, the concurrent rise of the so-called Public Schools (actually private and very expensive), and some minor changes like the custom of taking holidays by the sea. At the time when the middle classes were motivated to limit their families, the trial of Charles Bradlaugh and Annie Besant in 1876—7 on charges of obscenity arising from a book on birth control, and the wide publicity it received in the press, gave them a knowledge of the means. The use of contraceptives, beginning among the well-to-do, spread down the social scale and by the 1950s was widespread throughout the population.[8] The death-rate meanwhile had levelled at around 12 per thousand. Since the second world war there have been 'baby booms' when the birth-rate has risen, but no higher than 18, while at other times it has fallen almost to the level of the death-rate. Population growth has accordingly been slow, if irregular, at rates well below 10 per thousand or 1 per cent.

Blacker's four stages, then, may be seen as having occurred in this country as follows: the first before 1750; the second from 1750 to 1877; the third from 1877 to 1940; and the fourth since the second world war. The other main feature of the experience of this country lies in the extreme slowness of the changes, which took over two centuries here in contrast to the way they have been telescoped in some later-developing countries into scarcely more than two or three decades.

Case-study 3: Japan

For over two hundred years, from the gradual expulsion of foreigners in 1615—28 to the incursion of Commodore Perry in 1852, Japan was completely secluded from the rest of the world by the deliberate policy of the ruling Tokugawa shogunate. Censuses were taken at frequent intervals during this period, and though these enumerated only the commoners and excluded the nobles, samurai, and rich merchants they show a variation of no more than 10 per cent. The checks which kept population so remarkably stable included natural disasters like volcanic eruptions, but also deliberate measures — infanticide among peasants, and abortion among the nobility and gentry — to preserve a limited inheritance on land which was visibly limited.

After 1852, and especially after the Meiji Restoration of 1868, the new ruling class decided that rapid industrial development was essential if the country was not to be conquered and subjected to the colonial rule of one or other of the European powers. The immediate effect on population was an increase from its Tokugawa level of 35 million in 1873 to 55 million in 1918. It is not known exactly how this occurred; certainly the death-rate fell, but its fall may not have been immediate, while the birth-rate may well have risen with the abandonment of traditional family-limitation practices in res-

36

ponse to the rise of new opportunities and the migration to the new industrial towns.

Modern vital statistics were instituted in 1920, from which date we have a clearer picture of trends. Fig. 6 shows that the fall in the death-rate from 25 in 1920 to 11 in 1950, comparable to that which took 130 years in England and Wales (*c.* 1810 to 1940), was achieved in Japan in thirty. Meanwhile the birth-rate remained high at first, though with a suggestive slight drop in the late thirties. Population growth was fairly rapid accordingly at around 15 per thousand or 1.5 per cent, from 55 million in 1918 to 73 million in 1940.

At this time it began to be recognized that population growth was a problem, and a government commission in 1927–30 recommended that planned parenthood should be encouraged and there should be a reasonable diffusion of birth control. The government rejected this report; in the then climate of opinion, the obvious answers to population growth lay rather in agricultural improvement at home and imperial expansion abroad. However, some influential people continued to believe in the desirability of birth control, and the government did not interfere with the sale of contraceptives and the spread of information.

But the decisive events took place in 1948 with the passing, amid great

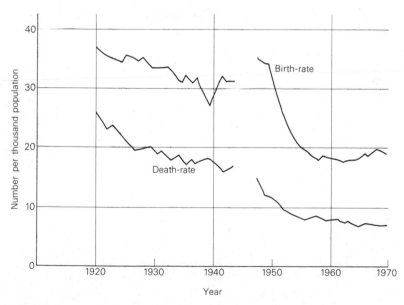

Fig. 6.
Birth- and death-rates, Japan, 1920–1970
(Sources: Irene B. Taeuber, *The Population of Japan*, to 1955; U.N. *Demographic Yearbooks*.)

political confusion, of the Eugenic Protection Law, which came into force in 1949 and in effect legalized abortion. The effect was dramatic. By the early 1950s well over a million abortions were performed annually in Japan, something like one to every two live births; and the birth-rate fell with unparalleled rapidity from 34 in 1947 to 17 in 1957.[1]

The great wave of abortions at that time has been followed by a quieter spread of the knowledge and use of contraceptive methods, and as in other industrial countries the birth-rate now fluctuates at levels well below 20 per thousand. Meanwhile the death-rate has fallen to the extremely low level of 6—7, for reasons analysed above; so that population growth continues at around one per cent — a rate of increase, however, that does not appear to be beyond the capacity of a country whose industrial growth rate has reached 10 per cent in recent years. Moreover, as already indicated, the death-rate must rise in decades to come as the older age-groups fill out, and unless Japanese attitudes to family size change once more it is likely that the population will stabilize over about the next thirty years.

SUGGESTION FOR FURTHER READING

Carlo M. Cipolla, *The Economic History of World Population*, revised edition, Harmondsworth: Penguin, 1964—70

3 The colonial episode and the race question

Most of the poor countries of the present day underwent at some time the experience of colonial rule. A few indeed are still colonies. Many, including some major states with large populations, became independent comparatively recently; in South Asia there was a rush to independence shortly after 1945, while in Africa there was a similar rush around the so-called 'year of Africa', 1960. Others have been politically independent since the early nineteenth century, such as the South American countries — the former Spanish colonies became independent republics in 1810, and Brazil effectively asserted its independence from Portugal in 1822. In some countries, however, political independence was attained by 'white' communities who continued to dominate populations of non-European descent. In this way a colonial situation has become internalized, as it were, in countries like South Africa and the southern states of the U.S.A., while at an earlier period the independence of Brazil and other South American countries may be seen in a somewhat similar light. Finally, the giant state of China, though never completely subjugated to colonial rule, experienced a strong assertion of the power of European states during the nineteenth century, when Europeans in China enjoyed extra-territorial rights and immunity from the processes of Chinese law, and a number of territorial concessions were made which produced enclaves of foreign rule on Chinese soil, including a number of important sea ports, one of which, Hong Kong, remains as the last survivor of that period.

Look at the globe of, say, 1914. This . . . was the jingo world, the Imperial Ice Age. See how the European burst his borders, sprawled out over the Americas, gobbled a continent in Australasia. The glacier of white supremacy flows across all Asia (including Siberia and Kazakstan) to Shanghai. Only four brown peaks thrust up through the suffocating mantle: Ethiopia, Thailand, Afghanistan, Japan.

Jump forward fifty-one years and, on the globe of today, the great glacier is in rapid retreat. But the experience of surviving the ice age was something reserved to yellow, brown, and black men — those who wear what was once cruelly called 'the badge of servitude'. It is doubtful if those of us whose skins are pinkish-white can ever hope to comprehend the thing emotionally.[1]

The expansion of Europe, that is, created over large areas of the globe situations in which people of 'white' appearance and European descent

39

dominated 'native' or 'coloured' populations. Even though that state of affairs has largely come to an end, an awareness of the colonial past is an important factor in the modern world. For purposes like those of the present book, the past must often be considered at two distinct levels — what actually happened, and the way in which people now perceive, evaluate, reflect upon, and react to their perception of what happened. We are concerned, that is, with the colonial past both as history and as myth. Both are facts; what actually happened is of course fact at one level, but at another level the social facts of present situations include people's ideas about what happened in the past, even though those ideas may be selected, distorted or in part just plain wrong.

A short history of the world 'colony'

A colony is defined by the O.E.D. as 'a settlement in a new country; a body of people who settle in a new locality, forming a community subject to or connected with their parent state; the community so formed, consisting of the original settlers and their descendants and successors, as long as the connexion with the parent state is kept up ... The territory peopled by such a community.' Thus the world could be applied in its literal dictionary sense, for example, to the thirteen colonies on the North American continent which became independent in the late eighteenth century, and similarly to the British and French communities in Canada, or the British settlers in Australia and New Zealand. During the nineteenth and early twentieth centuries, some of the colonies which retained a connexion with Britain grew in size and importance, and attained a good deal of local autonomy, so that after the first world war a new term for them gained official usage, and they became known as the Dominions. At the same time, however, areas like Jamaica or Kenya, which were more directly administered from London, were known as Colonies, even though the European populations there were small and the great majority of their peoples were not, in the dictionary sense, colonists or colonials at all. At that period, then, there occurred a curious inversion; countries which were in the dictionary sense colonies were called Dominions, while countries where most people were not of European descent, but which were under British rule and could properly have been called British dominions accordingly, were in fact called Colonies. And the usage has persisted, not only officially, but also in common speech, so that 'colonial rule' and 'colonialism' have come to be used in the way I have done at the beginning of this chapter.

A thumbnail sketch of colonial history, c. 1500 to 1960

The age of European expansion falls into two major periods. During the first, from about 1500 to the early nineteenth century, Europeans conquered the Americas and wholly occupied many islands around the world; they remained

40

confined, however, to small enclaves on the coasts of the Asian and African continents. From about the middle of the nineteenth century, they occupied the whole of Africa and parcelled out between them most of the continent of Asia.

1 Sixteenth to early nineteenth centuries

During this first period the technological superiority of western European civilization was narrow, and limited in Cipolla's apt phrase to 'guns and sails'. The revolutionary characteristics of their man-of-war enabled Europeans to establish absolute predominance over the oceans in only a few decades, yet for almost three centuries it was confined to the seas. No serious attempt was made to extend territorial conquest inside Asia, while Africa long resisted European inroads by its lethal diseases and as late as 1876 only 10 per cent of the continent was under white occupation. The Americas were different, being inhabited by sparse populations of technologically very primitive peoples, whose meagre resistance was further reduced by their susceptibility to European infectious diseases. Even there, however, until the eighteenth century the areas under effective European control — as distinct from nominal sovereignty — with few exceptions were close to the sea.[2]

During this period, colonies (in the original sense of the word) of European traders were established accordingly in small enclaves around the coasts of India and Africa, and on islands like those of the East and West Indies. Trade with the local inhabitants in tropical products and specialized handicrafts was the main object. During this period, for instance, South African history began in an unpretentious way with the settlement at the Cape of a small colony of Dutch servants of the Netherlands East India Company, to establish what a leading South African historian called 'a cabbage patch on the way to India'.[3] Most of the original colonies, in fact, were established for the purpose of trade, while a few such as St Helena, the Cape, and Ascension were acquired as supply and repair depots for the sailing ships which carried on the trade.

Some places where the Europeans established themselves were uninhabited before (for example, Mauritius, the Seychelles, St Helena, the Falkland Islands), while in others the former native population became extinct, or was extinguished (for example, Tasmania, the Caribbean islands). In some such places the present-day population is wholly of European descent, the society is a transplanted version of a European society, and the colonial situation in the later sense of the word does not exist; Tasmania and the Falkland Islands are cases in point. Elsewhere, however, the European settlers introduced an imported labouring class from an African or Asiatic mainland. In Mauritius, for example, the French settlers brought in indentured labour from India, while later immigrations added 'Creoles' (of mixed descent including African ancestry) as clerks and skilled workers, and Chinese shopkeepers, to make

41

the present-day plural society.[4] Similarly, in the West Indies and some enclaves on the mainland of tropical America, such as the colonies of Guiana,
Indian labourers were brought in under indenture agreement to work on the
plantations. But by far the biggest movement of population of this period
resulted from the trade in African slaves.

This trade began in a small way about the middle of the sixteenth century,
when slaves captured in the hinterland of the Portuguese possessions of
Guinea, São Tomé, and Angola on the west coast of Africa were shipped to
the Americas, at first mainly the Portuguese colonies on the Brazilian coast.
People of other European nationalities soon joined in the trade, including
French, British, and Dutch; the first twenty black slaves in North America,
for example, were sold from a Dutch warship to Virginia settlers in 1619.
There was a spurt in the trade about the middle of the seventeenth century;
this occurred in relation to a number of developments on the American continents, including action by the Portuguese administration in Brazil (under
Jesuit missionary pressure) to stop the enslavement of native Indians, which
led to an increase in the demand for African slaves. Further north, plantations on the British and French islands of the West Indies also provided a
market for British slave traders. At that period, too, the West Indies became
important for supplying to the plantations of the southern United States
workers who were born into slavery and did not require 'breaking in' — for,
contrary to popular belief, few slaves were ever imported into the United
States directly from Africa, a fact which has been held to explain the lack of
African culture elements in the traditions of the black population of North
America. For a time, however, the scale of the trade was limited by limitations in the demand for agricultural exports from the plantations of the New
World — tobacco, rice, sugar, indigo, and 'naval stores' — ropes, etc. — used
by the ships themselves. The period when the trade appears to have reached
its greatest volume lasted from the middle of the eighteenth century till it
ceased abruptly in 1807—8. This was a period of brisk demand for plantation
goods; the number of slaves rose rapidly — there were 700,000 in the United
States at the time of the first census in 1790 — and there was a vast influx
into South America also at this time, drawing in Mozambique as a source of
supply as well as the west coast colonies.

Those who carried on the trade included African chiefs and merchants,
and on the east coast of Africa Arabs were also involved. Slavery was a
traditional institution of many African societies, and the circumstances of
European contacts at the coast put a premium on chiefs' making war on
their neighbours, taking captives, selling them as slaves, and buying guns
to make further wars. Europeans were not generally involved in the actual
enslavement, but came in at a later stage. In the case of British merchants,
a complicating factor was that slavery was not an indigenous British institution, and any doubts as to its illegality were dispelled by a famous judgment

of Lord Justice Mansfield in 1771. Slaves could not be brought to England, or they would have become free automatically, and the shipowners of Liverpool, Bristol, and London who engaged in the trade had to make use of the notorious 'black triangle' — out with trade goods (cloth, etc.) to West Africa, across with slaves to the West Indies, and home with plantation goods.[5]

If some British, and other Europeans, were involved in the trade, however, it was also British and other Europeans who suppressed it. Many influential voices were raised in Britain against it during the eighteenth century, including those of Dr Samuel Johnson and Horace Walpole. By the end of the century, the slave trade and its abolition had become a major issue in British politics. The anti-slavery movement was spearheaded by men of genuinely humanitarian convictions, especially Clarkson; it was supported also on other grounds by opponents of the West India plantation magnates, who played an influential role in the politics of the time and whose monopolies had been discredited by the rising school of laissez-faire economists. Free trade, economic individualism, and the abolition of slavery were inter-related aspects of a new set of social, political, and economic principles, and early in the nineteenth century the anti-slavery movement achieved its two prime objects — the prohibition of the slave trade in 1807, and the liberation of all slaves in the British empire in 1833, the year of Wilberforce's death.[6]

Nor did the movement stop there. The United States too outlawed the foreign slave trade in 1808, though slavery remained a domestic institution until after the civil war in the mid-1860s. During the early nineteenth century, the British government took the initiative in securing international agreements to prohibit the trade in slaves. In doing so, it was again subject to the pressure of converging interests, with the anti-slavery humanitarians joining forces with British plantation-owners who, having been forced to give up slave labour themselves, did not see why their competitors of other nationalities should still have that advantage. Thus it was in a treaty with Britain that the newly independent government of Brazil agreed in 1831 to outlaw the slave trade, though it was twenty years before it was effectively stopped, and not until 1888 that slave status was abolished in Brazil itself. Meanwhile, the Royal Navy maintained anti-slave patrols round the coast of Africa from 1807 to 1869, and consignments of slaves intercepted by these patrols were put ashore at settlements like Freetown in Sierra Leone, Nasik near Bombay, Zanzibar, the Seychelles, and later Freretown near Mombasa (named after Sir Bartle Frere, a British commissioner specially appointed to deal with the suppression of the East African slave trade in 1872). The establishment of a British consul at Zanzibar in 1841, partly in order to look after the interests of British Indian subjects, was also intended as a means to bring pressure to bear on the sultan to curb his subjects' slave-trading activities on the mainland. The hero-worship accorded by British public

43

opinion to Dr David Livingstone owed a good deal to his unceasing campaigns against the continuing slave trade on the mainland of eastern Africa, and the conclusion which some drew from his life and death there was that it would never be finally stopped until large areas of Africa were brought under direct British control.[7]

This first period of European expansion, then, ended in the early nineteenth century with the independence of the white-dominated societies of the Americas, and the suppression of the slave trade.

2 Mid-nineteenth century to c. 1960

During this period, European expansion continued as substantial areas of the major continents, away from the sea, were brought under the control and administration of European states. This was a new development, and was made possible by a cluster of technological innovations. Notably these included the railway, and later the internal combustion engine, in inland transport; at sea, the steamship, both in its mercantile application and the steam-powered ironclad warship; and some crucial medical discoveries, notably quinine, which enabled Europeans to survive despite exposure to the diseases of Africa and Asia.

It is important to emphasize the comparatively recent dates at which some major countries came under European colonial rule. In India, for example, though coastal settlements and enclaves were already being extended during the eighteenth century, and the British East India Company and its counterparts were being drawn increasingly into administration as well as trade, the process of European — especially British — conquest inland continued well into the nineteenth century, and it was not until the 1860s that most of India was under either direct British administration, or indirect rule through the princes. Burma was annexed in two bites in 1852 and 1886. A British trading base was established at Singapore in 1819, but it was not for several decades afterwards that a British sphere of influence over Malaya, though recognized by the rival French and Dutch, was implemented in the form of actual administration. Similarly, the 'white Raja' Brooke acquired Sarawak in 1841, but it was not for decades after that date that North Borneo and Brunei came under British protection. It was in the middle of the nineteenth century too that the French and Dutch were consolidating their 'spheres' in Indo-China and Indonesia respectively.[8] As for Africa, even the basic geography of the sources and courses of the great rivers was not known to Europeans till the explorations of Burton, Speke, Livingstone, Baker, and Stanley in the 1860s and 1870s. The 'scramble for Africa' took place after 1870, spheres of influence between the British, German, French, and Belgian governments were not settled till the late 1880s, and actual administration in some of the remoter areas was not a reality till after the first world war.[9]

In the passage quoted above, then, Patrick Keatley did well to choose the date 1914 as representing the time when 'the Imperial Ice Age' reached its greatest extent. Between the two world wars of 1914—18 and 1939—45, some parts of the European empires were already becoming more independent in fact, and there were the beginnings of movements of resistance to European rule especially in India. The Cripps mission of 1943 made Indian independence certain as soon as the war was over, and once India was independent there was no holding the rest of the Asian empires. With many former Asian colonies independent, 'freedom' movements in African colonies could hardly be denied their independence; and so, by what seemed an irresistible logic of events, soon after 1960 and with the exceptions already mentioned colonial rule was a thing of the past. It remains to emphasize how short was this second period of European expansion, involving colonial rule in what we have come to think of as the modern sense — little more than a century at most, and in many countries no more than sixty or seventy years, or a rather long lifetime. Thus the memory of a man like Harry Thuku, honoured at the independence ceremonies in Kenya in 1963, extended back to the days before the white man came.[10]

The nature of colonial society

Economic institutions

The salient feature of colonial society was that most, if not all, of the institutions of modern life were first initiated and then controlled by foreigners, and predominantly by Europeans. This was true of the organizations concerned with three main areas of activity: economic institutions, Christian missions, and government.

Not all colonies were acquired in the direct prospect or even hope of economic gain. On the contrary, for example, a reluctant Liberal cabinet was persuaded to annex Uganda partly to forestall German control of the source of the Nile, and partly by a campaign in the churches to protect the missions and their converts there.[11] Whatever the motives for its original acquisition, however, there was clearly an advantage if the colony could in some way be made to pay the costs incurred in establishing and administering it, and withdrawing any subsidy from the exchequer of the metropolitan nation as soon as possible. To this extent at least all colonial regimes were concerned in economic development; they sought to promote economic activity which could serve as a tax base. In some cases, trade with the local people continued to be an acceptable, practicable economic base, whether the trade were minerals, tropical agricultural products, or local handicrafts. In such cases it was the institutions of marketing, finance, transport, shipping, etc. which

45

were under European control, rather than the enterprises engaged in primary production. Another possibility, especially where tropical agricultrual products were concerned, was to encourage the local people to grow them as cash crops in addition to their indigenous subsistence crops. It was in this way, for example, that cotton and later coffee were introduced into Uganda by the combined efforts of the British administration, the Anglican mission, and the local African chiefs. The development of cash-crop production by the indigenous peasantry was, indeed, a well-nigh universal feature of African and Asiatic countries under colonial rule.

In many places and at different periods, however, reliance on native sources of supply came to be regarded as unsatisfactory — the goods required were not available in sufficient quantity, their quality was variable and uncontrolled, and so forth — so that there was always a tendency for European and other foreign enterprises to try to secure sources of supply under their own control. This they did by establishing productive enterprises such as mines (which were almost always foreign enterprises), or plantations or farms in the case of agricultural production. Important differences arose between different colonies according to the balance which was struck between cash-crop production by the local inhabitants on the one hand, and the establishment of European-controlled agriculture on the other; if the latter, then it made a big difference whether family farms or plantations predominated. These variables alone have made for wide diversities in the actual experience which different countries had of colonial rule, and their situations today.

In some places, the soil and climate or the sparseness of the native population made farming appear to be the most suitable use of the areas brought under control. This occurred, for instance, in the more northerly of the original colonies on the North American coast, in contrast to the plantation economy further south; thus the United States were long divided between those in which the family farm, employing only a few free white labourers or relying entirely on family labour, was the dominant form of agriculture, and the southern states where large plantations worked by black slaves were more characteristic, and conflicts between the economic interests of the two types of agriculture were powerful factors in bringing about the civil war, with effects which persist to this day. Elsewhere, farming as distinct from planting was the predominant form of settlement in Australia and New Zealand, where the native populations were small and greatly outnumbered at an early stage by the settlers. In these countries there is accordingly a 'colonial situation' to a limited extent; thus large stock farms in Australia rely on the services of stockmen of aboriginal or mixed descent, while in New Zealand there were Maori wars in the nineteenth century and there is a certain amount of tension today. However, Australia and New Zealand are not poor countries and so come into the scope of this book only peripherally. In

Africa, settlement by farmers of European descent characterized southern Africa (South Africa and Rhodesia), Algeria, and Kenya, and to a more limited extent other territories.

European settler-farmers, pioneering modern agriculture in difficult country, clearing and tilling new land in remote areas with their own and family labour (together with some native labour in many cases) tended to become extremely possessive about their land and their rights in it. This was not simply a matter of economic self-interest. Their attitudes included a pride in their achievements which was in many cases entirely justified; for example, in Kenya it was widely agreed that farming standards in the former White Highlands were high, and many white farmers devoted resources of knowledge painfully acquired in unfamiliar conditions, of skill, and of economic enterprise to developing methods of cultivation which were productive and yet improved rather than reduced soil fertility. Moreover, many such men combined practical skill with an appreciation of the beauties of the country in which they had settled, and when to such attitudes was added a determination that their children should share in such a goodly inheritance it is not difficult to understand the special tone of robust yet highly emotional self-assertiveness with which white-settler communities characteristically conducted their relations with the rest of the world.[12] Throughout colonial history, indeed, settler communities were at loggerheads with the administrative officials whom home governments sent out to govern them. In addition to the contempt with which rugged practical men always view those whom they stigmatize as 'bureaucrats', in the particular colonial situation the administrator was almost always regarded as fatally 'soft on the natives'. It was partly over this issue, indeed, that the American colonists rebelled in the eighteenth and nineteenth centuries against British, Spanish, and Portuguese rule. Similarly, though British governors in Australia enjoined settlers to 'live in amity and kindness with' the aborigines, they had the greatest difficulty in restraining them from 'punitive expeditions' which sometimes degenerated into cruel and indiscriminate shooting.[13] Similar examples of settler resentment against rule from a remote capital in the home country will no doubt spring to mind. Possessiveness about their rights and a sense of their national identity led to settler communities' being the most intransigent of all towards the extension of political rights to Africans, or other non-white peoples. In some cases this led in turn to an insistence that the colony should remain a colony; hence 'Algérie française!', or the long-continued insistence of the Rhodesian settlers on being British. Sometimes, indeed, such a sense of national identity was linked with images of the 'home' country which became steadily more unrelated to realities; settlers dreamed of belonging to an England or France that never really was, and which modern changes since the settlers or their forebears left it have made less and less like their dream. In other cases, if the dream has finally been shattered, then there has been an abrupt swing; disillusionment, a sense that the home government seemed determined to betray their own kith and kin, has seemed to make it clear that the only hope for maintaining a 'civilized' state of affairs lay in independence with white minority rule.

Settlement by white-settler farmers depended, of course, on the ability of the colonial regime to alienate land to them in perpetuity, or at least on leases long enough to afford them the security of tenure which was necessary if they were to invest their lives and fortunes in their farms. In Kenya, for example, most of the White Highlands was held on leases of 999 years. In some places the land made available for white-settler farmers was empty; in others it might be subject only to grazing or hunting sporadically by a sparse, scattered native population; or it might be land that had been cultivated and abandoned to bush fallow, and regarded by natives as reserve land to which they might one day return; or, at the other extreme, natives might be actually evicted to make way for settlers. In almost every case there was clearly likely to be resentment on the part of the natives. Thus although land in Australia was used only for hunting and food-gathering, and although the much more intensive and productive use to which it was put by settler farmers represented a clear gain from a world point of view, yet aboriginal resentment at intrusions on their hunting grounds led to cattle-raids and crop thefts which in turn provoked the punitive reprisals already mentioned. In the same way, although most of the land which was alienated to settlers in Kenya was used only for occasional grazing by the pastoral Masai, some land was alienated to which, though it was unoccupied at the time, there were valid claims by the agricultural Kikuyu, and this resulted in a bitter conflict which dominated Kenya's history up till independence. Moreover, even if land alienated for white settlers was empty at the time, the subsequent growth of native populations (a result, very often, of medical and sanitary improvements resulting from colonial rule) created situations in which land-hungry peasants on dwindling holdings afflicted by soil erosion as a result of over-intensive cropping confronted, across a strand of barbed wire, the prosperous wide fields of the white farmers. In situations like this it often seemed impossible to reconcile the claims of social justice on the one hand with those of efficient and productive agriculture, in a hungry world, on the other; and dilemmas such as these have been bequeathed, along with race tensions, to the new governments of those countries with a white-settler population which have become independent under black majority rule.

Where the predominant form of agricultural enterprise initiated and controlled by Europeans was the plantation rather than the farm, rather different situations were created. Here Europeans were a small minority who tended to be the salaried officials of large companies incorporated in the home countries; they came and went on leave and retirement, and they did not put down roots in the country in the same way as did settler farmers. Their attitudes tended accordingly to be less emotionally possessive towards the country in which they spent their working lives, and they have not been the source of such bitter conflicts as those which have characterized countries with a substantial settler minority. The nature of the economy and society of plantations in South Asia has been acutely analysed by Myrdal, who points out that their alien control and management led to dividends and a large part of salaries being remitted abroad or used to purchase foreign goods rather than to stimulate demand on the local market. They were extensions of the metropolitan countries, stimulating demand there much more than in South Asia. Not only did the higher salaries go to alien managers; skilled workers, foremen, and even some unskilled workers were brought in from other South Asian countries. The gulf between the European upper caste and the masses of unskilled workers was widened by the use of middlemen, who were very often 'Oriental aliens', and by the system of 'managing agencies'. Relations between European managers and these intermediaries or 'jobbers' might be somewhat antagonistic, and managers might from time to time become aware of grievances against the 'jobbers' on the part of the workers, yet be too dependent on them to be able to take action.

As Myrdal points out, plantations as a form of 'industrialized agriculture' played an indispensable part in economic development, raising average income levels (though not everyone shared in the increase) and stimulating investment in the infra-structure of buildings, roads, ports, and railways. Even though these, like the associated commercial and financial institutions, were geared to the foreign-dominated export sector, they could become part of the local scene and be used for wider purposes. And on the whole the independent governments of South Asia have left them alone. Threats to nationalize them, as in Sri Lanka, or actual nationalization, as in Indonesia, were on the whole disastrous; the threats scared off new foreign capital, while the actuality led to inefficiency, graft, and corruption.[14]

Except where they have been nationalized, many plantations in poor countries today are owned or managed by large international corporations. They tend accordingly to exemplify the 'big firm, small country' syndrome which is referred to in chapter 4 below, and from the economic point of view to be a somewhat inassimilable legacy of the colonial period. From a social and political point of view the legacy of plantation agriculture was possibly less awkward than that of farming by European settlers. Plantations and mining, however, depended even more than did settler farming on a plentiful supply of cheap labour. Not that all settlers lived up to their proud boast that they alone among European expatriates were not afraid to get their hands dirty; although some farmers in countries like South Africa, Algeria, and Kenya depended mainly on family labour, there was also widespread reliance on the services of native African farm workers. But the dependence of mines and plantations on native labour was total. In the earlier period of colonial history, as has been emphasized, this was largely provided by slaves. After the abolition of the slave trade, and the later abolition of slave status, recourse was had to other methods of recruitment.

In many societies which came under colonial rule, there were already indigenous systems of forced labour. In most cases these involved only a few days or weeks each year, and people were required to work for public purposes. Thus in many Asian societies there were traditional obligations upon cultivators in irrigated areas to turn out when required to repair and maintain the irrigation canals, dams, embankments, and similar works. In many African societies, subjection to a chief carried with it the duty to mend his fence or work on his fields, which yielded food which was used to feed councillors, litigants having their cases heard, and so forth, and which served as a famine reserve for the chief's subjects at large. In some cases it was possible to maintain these customary obligations, and turn them into useful instruments for modernization; for example in the kingdom of Buganda people had to turn out for a few days a year to do *bulungi bwansi* (literally 'good works underfoot') maintaining minor roads and village tracks. Such customs amounted in effect to a tax payable in labour rather than in money, though it was difficult to enforce such obligations in law after the international convention against forced labour in 1926. There were, however, also instances where forced labour was raised, not for public purposes, but for private employers, and not for a few days but for long periods.[15] Thus Myrdal recounts how the indigenous systems of forced labour which colonial rule inherited in South Asian countries were adapted to induce large-scale movements of labour. Often, particularly in earlier times, the inducement was of a type that implied compulsion. Even when there were some elements of 'voluntariness', there were severe restrictions on the freedom of movement of workers recruited from distant places, for example, the Indian and Chinese labourers respectively in the rubber plantations and tin mines of Malaya, Indian workers in Burma and Ceylon, and the Chinese brought into Java both as coolies on the tobacco plantations and as intermediaries between the government and the indigenous population.

Foreign labourers, isolated in unfamiliar surroundings, were more docile, more easily organized for effective work, and more permanently attached ... Secondly ... the difficulties in attracting local people to wage employment were serious — though again we must remember that the matter was never considered on any assumption other than an extremely low level of wages. And thirdly, no one who had any say in policy saw anything wrong in bringing in foreign labour.

Myrdal emphasizes that it was private employers who complained of labour shortage and tried to get the colonial governments to do something about it. Those governments themselves do not seem to have had the same problem: 'At the same time it is striking that some very large undertakings, such as the construction of railways and public works in India after 1860, seldom suffered seriously from labour shortage, though wages rose conspicuously as the demand for labour increased.'[16]

As Myrdal indicates, there were various ways in which colonial governments might 'induce' a plentiful supply of cheap labour. Outright compulsion under a public law or official order might well be challenged by missionary interests and made the subject of campaigns in the home country; thus in Kenya the activities of the government in the early days of British administration were successfully publicized and discredited by the writings of J. H. Oldham and other missionaries, and the government was forced to abandon formal compulsion of Africans to work on the settlers' farms in 1921.[17] Moreover, as already mentioned, forced labour was officially proscribed by international agreement in 1926. Informal pressures, however, might still be brought to bear on native chiefs to 'persuade' or 'induce' their subjects to come forward for wage work.

Another form of pressure upon men to work took the form of imposing money taxes in circumstances when there was little option but to earn the money by working for the settlers, or in the mines, at whatever wages were offered — and clearly such a situation tended to put the native workers at a disadvantage in bargaining, and to depress the level of wages. In South Africa, in a situation of 'internalized colonialism', similar conditions continue to prevail. The limited amount of land available for African occupation leaves most men little alternative to working in the towns or mines, especially as non-Bantu investment in African areas is heavily discouraged, and employment opportunities are restricted there in consequence.[18] In towns, however, opportunities for African advancement are restricted by job reservation orders, and the bargaining power of African workers is further reduced by various difficulties placed in the way of trade-union activity.

European enterprises, then, were established in colonial territories in order to produce goods — mainly raw materials — which were wanted in trade with the home countries in Europe, and in relation to an international market generally. It remains to mention that in assocation with these productive enterprises — farms, plantations, and mines — there were, of course, other economic enterprises and institutions concerned with transport, marketing, shipping, finance, insurance, and similar services; and that for the most part these organizations, too, were controlled by Europeans. The nature of many of these organizations, too, was such as to reinforce the point made by Myrdal that they made the colonies into extensions of the economy of the home country in Europe. Thus, for example, the railways built in colonies in Africa linked the mines, the plantations, or the white-settled farming areas to the sea, where the raw materials produced in the colony were exported and the products of the industrialized countries imported. Similarly the telegraph lines linked the colonial capital to that of the mother country. The lines of transport and communication thus set up did not constitute a network; in particular, they were very defective in providing lines of communication from one African country to another.[19] Though an infra-structure was certainly built up, then, it may not have been the precise infra-structure that the present independent governments would have preferred. In the same way, banking in the colonies was in the hands mainly of subsidiaries of the major banks in the home countries of Europe, the currencies which the new governments inherited were linked to those of the European nations, systems of weights and measurements (metric or other), and even such things as driving on the right or the left, represented an extension of the former metropolitan country's practices.

Missions

Christian missionary activity was integrally concerned in the whole history of European expansion, and the missions constituted important and influential interest groups among the Europeans in colonies. In the most obvious and direct way, missionaries initiated new organizations in the branches which they founded of the churches which had sent them; and, once initiated, these ecclesiastical organizations were for long dominated by Europeans, in the sense that the white missionary clergy and bishops, ministers, etc. tended to be replaced only slowly by native clergy locally born and educated. But missionaries were concerned with many more activities than preaching the gospel, central and primary though that task might be. They concerned themselves with healing bodies as well as saving souls — indeed, both often seemed equally urgent tasks for men of goodwill and Christian charity; so that in association with mission stations there grew up dispensaries and hospitals, followed shortly afterwards by schools for training nurses and dressers, and other medical personnel. Here the medical side of missionary work coincided with a third vitally important side, the education task, so to churches and hospitals were added schools. Schools needed books and other equipment, so that the work of missions was further extended, now into the industrial and commercial field, and in many places missions initiated and controlled printing works, bookshops, and workshops where educational materials (such as school furniture) were manufactured. And in some places it came to be felt that an economic underpinning was necessary if native converts were to be able to lead a Christian family life. To care properly for a family, a man had to be able to afford a house with minimum sanitary and hygienic arrangements, such as soap and mosquito nets; to do this required a command over resources well above the subsistence level of a traditional economy; so that many missions became involved in what they termed an 'industrial' side, with training men to be skilled craftsmen and so to command a better wage, and with introducing cash crops so that peasants could earn money to buy bibles and clothes, afford school fees for their children, and so

52

on. For example, the Church Missionary Society in Uganda (an Anglican mission) developed an industrial side under a Mr Borup, who in partnership with officers of the government was largely responsible for introducing the growing of cotton as a cash crop in that country. Moreover, the commercial organization which was set up originally by the C.M.S. grew into a major commercial and industrial firm, the Uganda Company, established in 1903 with capital raised in Britain largely from wealthy Christian philanthropists, and which offered very little for many years in the way of dividends. This company dominated the processing and export of African-grown cotton in Uganda, and also developed a many-sided trading and industrial business while long retaining its character as a philanthropic organization with missionary roots.[20]

In Africa, a large mission station might come to resemble a whole town, with its hospital, schools, seminary, workshops, bookstore, and numerous houses of foreign missionaries and native adherents, all centred of course on a large church or cathedral. Indeed, in a few cases the resemblance to a medieval European town was heightened by the presence of a fortified wall surrounding the whole, for there were times in the early days when missionary penetration antedated that of colonial administration and when so tempting a target for envious attack by surrounding tribes had to be defended by force of arms.

Mission stations thus afforded a refuge for people who needed protection; for example, many freed slaves found safety in stations like that at Freretown near Mombasa on the Kenya coast, while during the female circumcision crisis of the 1920s the Protestant missions similarly extended protection to girls who refused clitoridectomy. Such circumstances further heightened their character as settled communities with an economic base, clearly different from the surrounding areas and acting as change agents in relation to the life of those areas.

Throughout colonial history, the Christian missions tended to act as champions of the rights of the natives against exploitation by European enterprises or unjust treatment by government officials. For example, Jesuit missionaries in Brazil played a leading part in the struggle to stop the enslavement of the native Indians, establishing stations at strategic river confluences to stop slave raiders penetrating upstream, to intercept convoys coming down-river, and to settle the freed captives on land where they could live and be evangelized.[21] Similarly, the part played by the missions in changing the practices of the Kenya government in relation to forced labour have already been mentioned.

Missionaries, however, did not always make themselves popular with the native peoples of colonial territories. Despite their concern for the local people's welfare, they were necessarily deeply committed to changing many aspects of the indigenous cultures. Naturally these aspects included supernatural beliefs; the local deities were seen as heathen gods, to be abjured by the convert, along with many customs and practices which from a Christian point of view were immoral. In some cases the practices which were frowned on appear to us to be comparatively harmless, and missionaries were not always able to distinguish in their own minds between the essential core of Christian teaching and some of their own cultural preconceptions; forms of dress and dancing were stigmatized as indecent, for example, by Victorian missionaries which by today's standards seem inoffensive enough. Not all the alien practices which were condemned were so innocent, however. A particularly interesting case was the storm which occurred in Kenya over clitoridectomy, a traditional practice of the Kikuyu in initiating young women into adult status. The objection the missionaries raised to this operation was not only the way it was done, which was dangerously unhygienic; the same objection to the native method of male circumcision could be met by having it done in a hospital or dispensary by a trained medical assistant, and this was sometimes done in Christianized versions of the traditional rites. 'Female circumcision' was a different matter; the operation was found to have lasting harmful results, and a mission doctor who honestly and in good faith allowed one to be done in his hospital found that it was quite incompatible with his Hippocratic oath, let alone his sense of Christian vocation. From the Kikuyu point of view, however, the missionaries' action in urging their adult converts not to allow their daughters to be circumcised, and in giving protection in mission stations (as already mentioned) to those who refused to follow the custom, seemed to be a totally unwarranted interference in an integral part of their traditional life. In the acute conflict which ensued between the missions and the Kikuyu, the government administrators who not long ago had been under missionary pressure to stop forced labour now found themselves having to lead forces of police to protect the lives and property of missionaries who, as it appeared, had made themselves quite gratuitously unpopular by their tactless handling of the matter.[22]

And there was also resentment at the long-continued occupancy of the positions of higher authority in the churches by European foreigners. Protestant and Catholic churches differed somewhat in their approaches to this problem, and different Protestant bodies from one another. The Roman Catholic missions soon established schools from which a few young men with the necessary high qualities of intelligence and vocation might pass on through the long and exacting training of a seminary and eventually be ordained; they were few, the proportion who dropped out was high (though failed seminarians were an important source of educated manpower, as teachers and in the middle ranks of the government service), and the process appeared painfully slow. Once ordained, however, absolutely no distinctions were made between local and expatriate priests, and when there were enough of the latter a whole diocese might eventually pass from the original mission order to a local secular clergy. Among Protestant missions, emphasis on worship in the vernacular and the free availability of the scriptures to all men made for a greater emphasis on mass literacy and primary education. The standard of literacy among Protestant converts tended to be higher, accordingly, and general education more advanced. Some Protestant missions also took higher education and the training of clergy seriously, and ordained substantial numbers of local men; however, the Anglican method in particular was to maintain a distinction between the mission, financed from donations in England, and the native daughter church — 'Native Anglican Church' was a term often used — which was financed from local sources. Native Anglican clergy were accordingly much poorer materially, which tended to cause a certain amount of feeling within the church. Other Protestant denominations varied, but many tended to be slow to ordain local men, thus giving an appearance of trying to keep control of church affairs in white hands.[23]

Reactions to this situation were accordingly in part a simple resentment of foreign domination, analogous to that in the political and economic fields. It took the form of movements to set up indigenous churches, of which there was (and continues to be) a great variety; I return to this point in chapter 11 below.

Government

It was under colonial rule that many of the present-day poor countries came under modern systems of administration. They differed widely in the extent to which indigenous cultures had developed writing, money, and systems of administration which could be modernized rather than a complete blank in which administration had to be created out of nothing. Thus at one extreme, Indian civilization included traditional scripts and literatures, money, and even banking and credit institutions; so that money taxes and written records were no innovation when India came under British rule. At the other, the social and political organization of many African tribes was of a nature that was not recognized as 'government' at all by the early European explorers, missionaries, and government officers; there was no indigenous writing, while money was little developed and had been introduced only recently (by Arab slave traders) and in only a few areas. Clearly modern administration had to start from the beginning in such places, and there are records of the well-nigh comic confusion that sometimes occurred when the first attempts were made to introduce taxation in kind before money was sufficiently familiar and widespread.[24] African traditional societies, however, differed widely in their forms of political organization, and in places such as the emirates of northern Nigeria or the interlacustrine kingdoms of Uganda despotic monarchies with a rudimentary system of bureaucracy in appointed chiefs and courtiers were recognizable as 'government' by nineteenth-century

Europeans. In all cases, then, colonial regimes introduced modern administration and exercised law-and-order functions, though in some places those
involved more abrupt innovation than others.

The government of colonies was characteristically regarded as a matter of
administration rather than of politics. The positions of greatest power in a
colony — the Governor or Viceroy and his principal officers, the Provincial
and District Commissioners — were held by officials of the metropolitan
country, and they were ultimately responsible to the government of that
country rather than to any local body. Local legislatures were, it is true, set up
with the object of distinguishing between when the Governor was giving an
order and when he was making a law. In most cases, however, membership
of a legislative council was by nomination rather than election, and those
appointed were mostly local white 'unofficials' whom the government
wished to placate and conciliate by associating them with the process of law-
making. Even so, white settlers frequently complained that since the government of the colony was not responsible to the legislative council, in the same
way as the home government was responsible to Parliament, they had little
power to influence its decisions, and the appearance of senior government
officials in 'Legco' to answer for their actions was a mere formality. Further,
in some British colonies this situation was held to be a denial of the basic
democratic rights of Englishmen; and the argument was used to sustain a
claim for making government responsible to a very undemocratic electorate,
namely that of the local white minority. Generally speaking, it was only in
the later stages of colonial rule that non-whites were nominated to membership of legislative councils, and only on the eve of independence that they
were elected by popular vote. Meanwhile, administering a colony was
viewed as an art comparable to administering a government department at
home — a matter of making sensible rules and seeing that they were obeyed,
collecting revenues and using them efficiently for approved purposes to the
satisfaction of a government auditor, and generally attending to the business
of government in an orderly manner. It remains to add that many colonial
governments, and many individual officials, were both well intentioned and
sensitive to local conditions, and their numbers included intelligent men who
were at pains to learn local languages and cultivate an appreciation of local
cultures — as well as many who did not.[25]

In areas where colonial rule was established over (in the narrow sense) a
native population and society, some account had to be taken of the indigenous system of law. On the one hand, the colonial administration existed precisely in order to ensure that European lives and property came under the
same kind of protection as they might at home, and that contracts to which
Europeans were parties could be relied on, if necessary, for enforcement in
the setting of a congenial legal system. On the other hand, however, where
there was a native population which already had its own set of rules for deal-

ing with offences and for settling civil disputes, there might be little need to interfere, and a good deal to be said for leaving well alone. Thus a very characteristic development was for the courts of the European administration to enforce 'native customary law' (or whatever term was used) in cases in which all the parties were native, while applying the law of the European mother country or some local modification of it, to cases in which one or both parties were European. In such situations, however, the colonial powers' administrations generally bound themselves to recognize native law only in so far as it did not conflict with 'natural justice' or some such concept, meaning the fundamental preconceptions of the European law concerned.

In some places, too, native legal institutions were recognized, or modified, or even created to administer native customary law in civil cases in which both parties were native, or in minor criminal cases in which the accused was a native. Thus there might be a dual system both of law and of courts, though the courts of the European administration were clearly superior to the other, dealing with all civil cases in which one or both parties were Europeans and criminal cases in which the accused was a European, and also reserving for their own jurisdiction the more serious criminal cases (usually defined by the penalty involved — thus the colonial courts alone would be able to order the death penalty or long terms of imprisonment) as well as, very often, other criminal cases committed in areas under wholly European control like townships or land alienated to European settlers. Where such a dual system existed, efforts were in many cases made to modernize the native courts and the law they administered, for example, by attaching literate persons to gazetted native courts to keep records, thus establishing a new basis for precedent, and by attempts to codify native customary law, which in Africa was of course formerly unwritten and a matter of the traditional judgment of chiefs and elders. And the colonial courts were superior to the native courts in reserving the right to hear cases from them on appeal. This, in general terms, was the situation which prevailed in most of colonial Africa.

Where such a situation existed, its effect was both to sharpen the distinctions between Europeans and natives, and to give legal sanction to them. This was because, where two systems of law existed enforced by two systems of courts, the question of who was subject to which had clearly to be made a matter of legal definition. Thus the laws of the East African territories under British rule included a definition of an '"African" or "native"' as a person who is a member of, or one of whose parents is or was a member of an indigenous African tribe or community. Persons whose legal status was defined as '"African" or "native"' in this way were subject to the jurisdiction of officially appointed or recognized chiefs, and had to obey their lawful orders in matters like health control, soil conservation, drinking, and the brewing of local beer. 'Non-natives' were not subject to the jurisdiction of African chiefs, but they did pay more tax. In East Africa, legal definitions were restricted to

57

the distinction between native and non-native; distinctions between non-natives of European and Asian descent were made as a matter of administration, rather than of law.[26]

All colonial governments, then, exercised law-and-order functions, collected taxes, and set up a framework of modern administration. In addition, to differing extents some promoted economic development and introduced modern social services in fields such as health and education.

As already mentioned, most contributed to the infra-structure for economic development — harbours, roads, railways, government buildings, and similar forms of public investment — and this aspect of their legacy is obvious and visible today even in such minor details as police uniforms and the rule of the road.

All colonial governments left another legacy, that of a European language. Whatever the variety of local vernaculars, at least some people in a colony learned to speak and to write English or French, or some other language with a wider currency in the world. Thus at least an elite were left with the key to a wider world of knowledge, culture, and political and commercial opportunity than the local languages in most cases afforded. The structure of that opportunity was, of course, skewed in favour of the former metropolitan country; thus the educated elites of former British colonies feel more at home in the English language and tend to have closer and easier communication with English-speakers, while the elites of former French and Belgian colonies in Africa have tended to be more assimilated into the life and culture of the French-speaking world. Africa is indeed divided at present between Anglophone and Francophone countries, in the same way and along the same lines as it is divided by those railways that run straight to the sea and not to neighbouring African countries. I return to the question of language in chapter 9.

Under colonial rule in virtually every case at least some beginning was made on the building up of a system of education, in the sense in which it is understood in western countries — the establishment of schools in which children are taught by specialist teachers to read and write, the skills of numeracy, and a body of modern knowledge of science, history, and similar basic subjects. (It can of course be maintained that no society lacks a system of education, in the sense that all prepare and socialize their young people for their adult roles in some way; not all, however, did it through specialized institutions like the school.) In many colonies the beginnings of education for the natives owed more to missionary than to government initiative, and in many there was at least for a time a partnership between government and missions. Colonies differed rather widely in the extent of the public provision that was made for native education, and in the policy that was pursued. In some, there was a tendency to concentrate on primary schooling and make disproportionately small provision for the higher levels. Such a policy was followed, for example, in the former Belgian Congo, where the educational policy was for long based upon a view that what was needed was to train Africans in the basic skills of modern industrial civilization, for example as craftsmen, railway workers, and the like, while it was assumed that the higher posts would be filled by Europeans for an indefinitely long period in the future. When in the 1950s the last assumption was clearly open to question, the rapid establishment of higher education, including three universities, had all the appearance of a death-bed conversion, and the institutions concerned had had very little effect on the situation when independence eventually broke upon the country. In some colonies, however, governments early assumed a responsibility for native education, and pressed it forward; among British African colonies, Uganda and the Gold Coast were notable in this respect. In some places, the rise of African education took place in a difficult atmosphere as a result of the pressures of white settlers on the colonial administration at the local level. Thus the settlers of Kenya were never very happy about the development of African education; but it would be wrong to conclude that African education in Kenya was actually hampered very much as a result. On the contrary, though it made a late start as a result of the late date at which the country came effectively under British rule, and though settler influence may have slightly delayed matters about the time of the second world war, after 1950 African education went ahead at a pace which outstripped that in Uganda or Tanganyika, the neighbouring territories under British colonial rule.[27]

The great issue of educational policy in all poor countries is the balance which has to be struck between the claims of primary education for the maximum possible number on the one hand, and the needs of the higher levels of education for an elite on the other. On the whole, colonies which were least subject to settler pressure tended to emphasize higher education and the creation of an elite, while those most subject to local European opinion tended to try to keep native education mainly to the primary level. This tendency is shown also in countries where the colonial relation has become internalized. For example, though the South African government has developed Bantu education at the primary level, its support for secondary and higher education for non-whites is more equivocal.[28] In the same way, the question of the Rhodesian government's sincerity in implementing an educational programme to go with a constitutional settlement based on an educational franchise, is one which has been crucial in relations between Britain and Rhodesia both before and after U.D.I.

Another important field of welfare policy is that of the medical service. Western medicine was introduced into colonial territories along with the first Europeans who penetrated them; it was, indeed, a necessary condition of their survival, and the first government medical services arose out of what was essentially an expeditionary situation. In modern times, a mountaineering expedition, for example, to the Himalayas will include a medical man, who may or may not be a climber himself, whose job is to ensure the survival of the members of the expedition, treat them if they are sick or injured, and advise on matters of hygiene, diet, and so forth. He may also practise, to the extent that time and resources permit, among the expedition's porters, and he will be a hard man – and one insensitive to his Hippocratic oath – if he fails to do what he can to relieve sickness and suffering in the villages through which the expedition passes on its way to the mountains; but they are not his primary responsibility. It was in rather similar circumstances that the first government medical officers worked in the early colonial period; the circumstances of their very presence made it necessary for them to take care of the health, first, of the European officials, and then as time and resources allowed to practise among others – European 'unofficials' (missionaries, persons in the employment of commercial firms, banks, shipping firms, etc.); natives employed by the colonial government, as policemen, clerks, etc.; and then the native population at large. Where matters of public health were concerned, the first requirement was to create conditions in which Europeans could survive and work efficiently, so that the original purpose of establishing townships, cantonments, or government stations was to create islands of health control – piped water, modern sanitation and refuse disposal, mosquito control, and the like. The arrangements for the treatment of the sick tended to follow the pattern which followed logically from this situation. Government hospitals for Europeans (initially officials, later non-officials and their families) were separate from those established for the needs of the native population. At the same time, the Christian missions early developed a medical side to their work; indeed, for many notable missionaries, like the redoubtable Dr David Livingstone in Africa, medicine and evangelism were indivisible aspects of the same mission; to heal bodies and to save souls were part of the same process. Medical services accordingly had a dual character, in the same way as schools; some institutions bore marks of their missionary origins while others arose from government initiative.

The European community

Although from the point of view of the 'native' or subject population the Europeans may well have appeared as a united force, in fact, as has been seen, there was considerable diversity of interest between different groups of Europeans, and in many places sharp conflicts occurred. Settlers were often in conflict with the government over land questions and the conditions of native labour; missionaries often played the part of champions of native rights, but made themselves unpopular with natives and government alike; and so on. All the interest groups involved tried to outmanoeuvre one another, not only in the colony itself, but also in the metropolitan country; thus missionaries could appeal to their parent churches for support, while economic interest groups could also bring pressure and persuasion to bear in the home capitals.

But though the European population of a colony might be riven by bitter conflicts of this sort, generally speaking the native population knew little of it. To some extent there might be a conspiracy of silence, a prevalent view that, however deep the disagreements, white prestige and even perhaps survival itself depended on a united front. A sentiment that white men had a duty to stick together and be loyal to one another was assented to accordingly by at least many white people part of the time. Moreover, in British colonies the appearance of white solidarity was accentuated by one special and peculiar institution known as 'The Club', to which insufficient attention is generally paid in studies of the colonial situation.

In a small colonial community the club is a focus of European activities. It usually provides the only library, billiard table, tennis court and golf course for many miles, and members meet there after work for drinks, conversation and games before dinner. Membership is open to both sexes, and the European dances, concerts and amateur dramatics which are organized take place within the clubhouse. In the smallest stations non-membership of the club involves isolating oneself almost entirely from the European community. In the larger centres some opportunities exist for associational activities among Europeans outside the club, but it is considered the 'right' thing to be a club member.

Not all Europeans were acceptable as members of the club, however. Writing of Jinja (Stonetown) during the influx of Europeans working on the Owen Falls dam and hydro-electric station, Sofer and Ross continue:

Ability to pay the entrance fee and monthly subscriptions is only one of several qualifications for club membership, though the expenses in themselves would constitute a serious deterrent to members of Stonetown's lowest income category. Being 'clubbable' seems to depend mainly on being in the correct occupational categories (i.e. government servant, professional or white-collar worker in a private firm), speaking fairly good English and living the appropriate style of life. The characteristics of a large number of the new immigrants assign them to the 'non-clubbable' category.[29]

The exclusiveness of the European club was heightened, that is, by the fact that not even all Europeans were regarded as suitable for membership. The club, accordingly, was the meeting place for the people who exercised authority at the local level — the District Commissioner and his senior assistants and the specialist officers of the government services (medical, education, agriculture, veterinary, police, works, etc.), the bank manager and the senior managers of the oil companies, and the like. Here, in a setting and an atmosphere which reinforced a sense of their national and racial identity, the top people and their families met and mingled informally, in circumstances which gave every plausibility to the suspicion that they could from time to

61

time settle important affairs behind closed doors — closed, as we have seen, even to some Europeans, and certainly closed to all natives. Thus the club as an institution heightened the impression, seen from the outside, of the Europeans as a united force.

Populations of mixed descent

In colonial societies, populations of mixed descent resulted naturally from contacts between the European settlers and the local people and in many ex-colonies these populations constitute distinctive elements in the present-day social structure, for example the Coloureds in South Africa, Anglo-Indians in India, mestizos, mulattos, etc. in Latin America.

In many such societies, sex relations between people of different 'race' — that is, between Europeans and others — were the subject of a somewhat ambiguous disapproval. Ambiguous, because it might well be a sign of manly prowess for a white man to have black mistresses, while sex relations the other way about, between a black man and a white woman, were much more heavily disapproved and penalized as symbolizing the black man getting above his place. Clearly such attitudes represented the extension of the usual 'dual morality' of sex relations into the race-relations situation. A man must gain experience, but equally he must protect his sister's honour; so there are two sorts of women, the virtuous who are good for marriage, and the other sort, who are socially inferior. In a race-conscious society, white men clearly tend to class black women in the latter category.[30]

Colonial societies differed widely, however, in the extent to which such unions might be regarded as legal marriages whose children were legitimate. To some extent the recognition of interracial marriages affected both the number of people of mixed descent and their status. These factors in turn have an important bearing on the present-day situations in former colonies, affecting as they do the extent to which racial categories are closed and rigid on the one hand, or open and flexible on the other. Two contrasting examples will illustrate the point.

Brazil is an example of a racially mixed population in which despite a good deal of both prejudice and discrimination, hard-and-fast colour bars are absent and the situation is relatively flexible and open. From the earliest times of Portuguese settlement, intermarriage and the founding of legitimate families of 'mamelucos' were encouraged both by church and state, since the practice increased the population who were brought up as Catholic Christians and added to the number of loyal subjects of the Crown.[31] Such patterns set up in the beginning have tended to persist. Thus Wagley quotes a study by Hutchinson of a rural community in which only a small minority could trace pure European descent, a minority which included the local planter-aristocracy. A second class of bureaucrats, professionals, technicians, and other specialists included the rest of the pure whites, but otherwise its racial composition was somewhat mixed. A third stratum consisted of fishermen, carpenters, bricklayers, mill hands, plantation workers, and other manual workers, while a fourth consisted of casual workers without a regular income. These two lower groups included a few 'brancos de terra' (of ancestry mainly white but known to be mixed) with mulattos and a majority of Negroes.[32]

Paler skins and European appearance predominate at the higher levels of income, power, and prestige. There is a widespread acceptance of the idea of 'whitening' or 'purification of the blood' through miscegenation, as a result of which the class structure is complex and fluid. Race is only one factor in social status, and other factors such as wealth, occupation, and education also count. Brazilians say that 'a rich Negro is a white man and a poor white is Negro'; people of darker skin colour can hope and strive to better their economic position as individuals. There is in Brazilian usage a rich vocabulary of racial terms — branco, branco de terra, indio, negro, mulatto, mameluco, preto, cabra, cabo verde, caboclo, escuro, pardo, sarara — and this very complexity makes for a fluid situation characterized by ambiguity and vagueness. The flexibility with which people are classified as belonging to one racial category rather than another is shown by the way in which, according to Roger Bastide, 'In regions with a high percentage of Africans, the census officials tend to class Negroes as mulattoes and light-skinned mulattoes as whites. In regions where the European element predominates, mulattoes tend to be classed as Negroes.'

Urban and industrial development may increase race consciousness, however, with a tendency for racially homogeneous quarters to form in towns, while new immigrants from European countries may be grouped together in self-contained 'colonies'. Both prejudices and discrimination are to be found, and Bastide quotes a revealing response by a Brazilian gentleman to a social survey carried out by René Ribeiro:

You know that, as a Catholic intellectual . . . I have not, cannot and must not have any racial prejudices . . . My evidence, however, will not be that of the intellectual . . . brought up in the doctrine of the Church but of the man, the grandson of a *senhor de engenho* who is full of prejudices . . . I have never reacted violently when a coloured man has sat down in the same omnibus, at the same table or in the same cinema as myself. What irritates me is . . . the mulatto's wanting to take the place of a white man, dressing like a white man, wanting to marry a white woman, owning a car . . . Inferior race. Good for work. They have a soul and must be baptized. They must seek salvation and go to Heaven. But be equal with the white man, no . . . I think that it is the Catholic intellectual who is right, but it is the man who actually lives and feels.

As for discrimination, Bastide states epigrammatically: 'A Negro is not refused a post because he is a Negro — he is told that unfortunately it has just been filled; he is not refused promotion — he fails to pass the medical examination.' The interracial etiquette which in Brazil consists in avoiding giving offence to other people by reference to their colour is clearly at variance with the actualities of prejudice and discrimination. Nevertheless, both the practical difficulties of rigidly classifying so mixed a population, and the ideological constraint imposed by the 'official' view of Brazil as a colour-blind society, inhibit the setting up of rigid colour bars as a matter of social practice or overt legal discrimination.[33]

Although not dissimilar in its origins, the situation in South Africa is now clearly at the other extreme from that in Brazil. The early Dutch settlers at the Cape brought in slaves from Madagascar, Mozambique, and the East Indies, besides assimilating the indigenous Hottentot population into a condition of serfdom. Unions between the settlers and the women of these slave communities had in some cases the status of marriage, especially if the woman had been baptized; as time went on however, they were regarded as concubinages, and the woman's children however begotten were slaves, until the general abolition of slavery in all British dominions in 1834. In the later stages of South African history the attitudes of white people to unions with non-whites changed completely, becoming more and more unfavourable; and such attitudes, now strongly entrenched as a part of South African white culture which is thought of as central and vital to their way of life, have found expression in laws which deny the status of marriage to any union between a white and a non-white person (Prohibition of Mixed Marriages Act, 1949), and render sex relations between such persons a punishable offence under an Immorality Act (1927, amended 1950 and 1957). Thus although subsequent miscegenation may have added to the so-called Coloured population of South Africa, the indications are that most of that population are the descendants of the early unions referred to above. The great majority speak Afrikaans as their home language, and some continue to maintain elements of their original culture; this is especially the case with the Malays, who remain Muslims, though otherwise their culture is Afrikaans and western. Thus the Coloured population may well now be largely self-contained as a separate and largely endogamous racial group. Thus, in contrast to the complex and fluid system of racial categories in Brazil, in South Africa there are just four such categories — White, Bantu, Coloured, and Asian. The process of 'whitening' as it is termed in Brazil has its equivalent in 'passing' in South Africa, and may still continue to some extent; but the Population Registration Act of 1950 had the express aim of eliminating passing, and as a result of that and subsequent legislation an administrative framework has been set up in which each person's race is a legally defined status, from which it is very difficult to get reclassified.[34]

Plural societies[35]

Finally, in most cases European colonial expansion created a society of the sort that has been called 'plural' — that is, one in which people think of themselves, and are thought of by others, as belonging to different 'communities' associated with different occupations and social statuses, and marked off by racial appearance and also by cultural features such as language and religious affiliation.

In a colonial society there were always at least two such communities, whites and natives; usually, however, there were more than that. The slave trade took populations of African descent to the Americas, while large-scale migrations of free or indentured labourers took populations of East Indian descent to the Caribbean, Chinese and Indians to many parts of South Asia, Indians to South Africa, and so on. Slave and labour migrations are only part of the story, however; others besides Europeans migrated on their own initiative in search of trade, land, or employment, like the Indians who took part in the opening up of East Africa, or the Chinese in Malaya. In many such places, occupational groups or other economic-interest groups came to be associated with migrant communities of this sort, so that in many of the present-day poor countries a person's identity as a member of one or other of the 'communities' may overshadow his citizenship of the country itself, and matter more to him and to others. Thus among citizens of Malaysia it matters a great deal if a person is counted as a Malay, a Chinese, or an Indian; while to be an Asian in Kenya is both to be, and to be regarded by others as, a quite different kind of person from an African.

Though it is necessary to refer only briefly here to this aspect of the colonial heritage, it is one that has been of the utmost importance in shaping the present-day social structures of many of the poor countries.

The question of exploitation

It is sometimes alleged that the relation between rich and poor countries, both in the colonial past and at the present time, was and is essentially an exploitative one; that the rich countries have made themselves rich by exploiting and impoverishing the poor. In so far as it concerns the colonial past, this may be a suitable point at which to consider the question. Exploitation is a value-laden term, and it is not possible to weigh the question in a completely objective, value-free manner. In what follows, therefore, it is inevitable that my own personal valuations will appear.

The words 'exploit' and 'exploitation' themselves are used in a variety of ways. When applied to things rather than people they are presumably ethically neutral; thus we may speak of exploiting a mineral deposit, meaning to initiate and successfully carry through mining operations to turn it to human use. There may be implications of unwisdom or imprudence here — exhaustion, pollution — but none of injustice. Moreover, when the thing exploited is abstract, as in the case of a scientific discovery, there are no unfavourable overtones; thus discoveries about the behaviour of gases under pressure are

65

exploited to human advantage in the design of refrigerators. When applied to persons, however, the terms do carry moral implications; thus the O.E.D. definition, after giving the first meaning, goes on, 'To utilize for one's own ends, treat selfishly as mere workable material (persons etc.); to "make capital out of" . . . turning to account for selfish purposes, using for one's own profit'. In terms of elementary economic analysis, it is axiomatic that a bargain freely made benefits both parties — or to be exact leaves one better off and the other no worse. The classical welfare economics, indeed, was based on the premiss that a change which benefits one person or group while leaving others no worse off constitutes an increase in welfare. From this point of view, exploitation may be said to occur when the circumstances are such that bargains are not freely made, and economic exchanges take place which make one party better off at the expense of the other. Such circumstances usually involve an element of coercion, but it is also possible for one party to exploit the other through ignorance, gullibility, etc. In this sense, and in the context of colonial history, presumably the grossest possible form of exploitation was practised when slaves were forced to work and given no more than the barest subsistence to enable them to live and breed more slaves. Exploitation also occurred no doubt in forced labour, and in the recruitment practices like those detailed by Myrdal in passages cited above, when although there was a semblance of freedom of contract the bargaining power of workers was reduced by moving them far from home and restricting their freedom of movement. Though from one point of view employers did no more than shop around in the cheapest market for labour, at least it may reasonably be surmised that workers' ignorance and gullibility were exploited when they ventured into the unknown on long-term contracts. However, as Myrdal makes clear, such practices were by no means universal. Certainly by the end of the colonial period, the wages paid by foreign enterprises may well in many cases have considerably exceeded the incomes available to men in alternative occupations, especially staying on the land and continuing to practise traditional subsistence agriculture. Indeed, this is clearly attested in the characteristic phenomenon of many of the present-day poor countries — large numbers of 'unemployed' men who migrate from rural areas in the hope of being among the favoured few to get wage work, and live meanwhile in the shanty towns which surround the large cities. In such countries, indeed, wage workers came to be a privileged minority, and if there is exploitation it is they who are exploiting the peasantry; I develop this point more fully in the next chapter.

Exploitation might also be said to occur when a native population experienced deprivation of, or encroachment upon, land or other resources on which they relied for subsistence, and when they might be left with little or no choice but to make a living by work on settlers' farms, plantations, or other foreign enterprises. As has been seen, in some colonies much land was alienated, in others little or none. In some cases the establishment of plantations or settlers' farms entailed making a more productive use of land than formerly, and was also a source of employment. Thus Myrdal states, 'Of the four main types of agriculture, plantations yield by far the highest returns per unit of land, followed by wet paddy, sedentary dry farming, and shifting cultivation', and he makes it clear that the plantations of South Asian colonies were also 'labour-hungry', though their managements shopped around for the cheapest labour and the employment did not always benefit the local people. In some colonies, paternalistic administrations protected the land rights of the local people; African examples I have referred to are Uganda and Tanganyika, while in South Asia the Netherlands East Indies were another example. In others, conflict might arise, as in Ceylon where, to quote Myrdal again, 'the planters laid their hands on uncultivated land in the hilly districts around the villages, in the very period when an extension of the land under food crops was becoming urgent as population was increasing'. Much the same might be said of areas of white settlement in southern Africa.

In some cases colonial governments used their power to forbid or discourage the native populations from taking part in economic activities in which they might compete with Europeans, either locally or in the home countries. One example of such a practice was the discouragement of textile manufacturing in India during the earlier period of British rule. The export of textile machinery to India was first prohibited, then subject to a duty which was repealed in 1860; and the migration of skilled workmen and technicians was also discouraged. At the same time, import duties were levied on Indian products entering Britain, while British goods manufactured with the aid of power-driven machinery entered India free of duty.[36] Another example is afforded by the restrictions which were placed on the growing of coffee by Africans in Kenya from the early period of British rule to about 1950. The Kenya settlers, indeed, tried to get similar restrictions imposed in Tanganyika; the administration there, however, resisted their pressure, and encouraged native coffee-growing on Kilimanjaro and elsewhere. Later, too, the Kenya administration's former policy was reversed, and it too encouraged Africans to grow coffee.[37]

Another way of looking at the same question is to ask such questions as: Did those European countries which had colonies prosper more than those which did not? Were countries deprived of colonies made noticeably worse off thereby? And are those of the present-day poor countries which missed the colonial experience any better off than ex-colonies? It would appear that the answer to all three of these questions is No. Britain, Holland, Belgium, and France, which had colonies, have not prospered noticeably more than Sweden, Norway, or Denmark, which did not. Germany does not now appear perceptibly worse off for being deprived of colonies after the first world war, while Japan's meteoric rise as a major industrial nation took place only after an expansionist period had been abruptly ended and Japan had been deprived of an overseas empire. As for the United States, the common use of phrases like 'American imperialism' should not hide from us the facts that the United States never had much of an empire, that few people came under American colonial rule and only for short periods, and that the whole tradition and ideology of the United States caused that nation to be regarded as the leading anti-imperialist power in the world, whose representatives frequently chided European nations like Britain and France for the sin of having empires.[38]

And while, as has been emphasized, it is not easy to find countries which escaped European domination altogether, it is not immediately apparent that (say) Afghanistan is now any better off than (say) Pakistan, or that Ethiopia (which preserved its independence apart from a short period of less than ten years of Italian rule) is now noticeably better off than its neighbours in the Sudan, Kenya, or Somalia which were under colonial regimes for some seventy or eighty years.

As Myrdal has pointed out, the gains from colonial rule accrued to a few — shareholders in the metropolitan countries, and European nationals settled in the colonies — while the costs of empire, in so far as they were not borne by the colonies themselves, fell upon the whole nation. National liberation movements in the colonies led to a rise in the costs of policing them, while at the same time the broadening of the franchise in the home countries made it increasingly difficult to persuade a financially disinterested electorate that these costs were justified. In the case of Britain, after the first period of crude exploitation it is probable (says Myrdal) that the colonies were never very profitable; it was free trade with and investment in the areas of white settlement in the temperate zones of the New World, rather than colonialism in tropical Africa and Asia, that laid the basis for British prosperity in the late nineteenth century. So 'the British were cool and rational rather than generous and idealistic in giving up their South Asian colonies ... The French and Dutch acted differently because they did not see their own interests.'[39] Somewhat similarly, if more pungently, Galbraith has said of the 'lucky, lucky British' that perhaps along with the Japanese they were the first people in history positively to benefit from shedding an empire. At the very time when colonies were demanding independence it became economical to let them have it, rather than being saddled with the cost of providing assistance, administration, education, and capital for emerging nations.[40] And Gellner has put the issue in more general terms:

The colonial and imperial set-up was a bit like a global version of an open field system: each political unit was a kind of strip, starting at the centre of the global village (i.e. in developed areas) and stretching outwards to the badlands. As a consequence of nationalism, political boundaries now run at right angles to the previous ones: roughly speaking, they are rather like a system of locks, separating areas with diverse levels of economic development.[41]

As an example of the extent to which the British government was in fact involved in welfare expenditure during the late colonial period, mention may be made of the Colonial Development and Welfare scheme which provided for the provision of grants and loans, but almost entirely grants, to colonial territories for purposes such as rural development and the establishment of university colleges in the then colonies. Most of the activity under the various C. D. and W. acts took place in the 1950s, and between 1946 and the winding up of the scheme in 1970 some £341 million had been made available by the British treasury.[42]

We may therefore conclude that exploitation under colonial rule did occur at some times and in some places, though not everywhere and at all times, and that generally speaking colonial rule became less exploitative as it went on. Despite some exploitation, though, the economic returns from colonial empires were disappointing. There seems no warrant whatever for the assertion that the prosperity of the present-day industrial societies is founded on colonial exploitation, and on the contrary industrial nations have been better off without colonies than with them.

In the foregoing, I have adhered fairly strictly to a view of exploitation as a form of economic arrangement which makes one party better off at the expense of impoverishing the other. If we extend the term, however, we may find situations in which there is an appearance of exploitation even though no exploitation, strictly speaking, is taking place, and to this kind of situation I apply the term 'quasi-exploitation'. For example, well-to-do people with pale complexions may live comfortable lives by employing a number of low-paid domestic servants with darker-coloured skins. Domestic service is not necessarily exploitative; the servants may be under no compulsion or pressure to take jobs of that sort, and the job may represent a better situation in life than any alternative occupation open to them. If servants' wages are better than the returns to subsistence agriculture, in a country where peasants' rights have not been eroded by land alienation; and if domestic service has advantages over (say) factory employment, such as living quarters and perhaps the patronage of an influential employer, then domestic servants' jobs may come to be sought-after prizes, and there is no exploitation, even though there is a situation which looks like rich people making themselves comfortable at the expense of the poor. And this situation was, of course, quite typical of colonial society; thus the Sofers write of

the standard of living or style of life which has in the past been considered appropriate for Europeans. This has included, for instance, the employment of at least one servant ... Phrases such as 'Send your boy', 'I will let the boy do it', 'We let the boys off on Sundays', are characteristic ... On the whole, non-economic factors probably play a greater part in inducing the European immigrant to prolong his stay, or to return to the country, than in motivating his first arrival. It is, for instance, probably only after he comes out to the country that the physical indulgence available through the existence of low-paid domestic service, and the psychological gratification arising from membership of the top status group in the multi-racial society, become realities difficult to relinquish.[43]

Psychological gratification, in the Sofers' phrase, is the basis of a further usage of the term which has been proposed by de Vos, who suggests that in addition to 'instrumental' exploitation of the sort already discussed, there may be 'expressive' exploitation when, as he puts it, 'socially dominant members of a society make ... indirect use of others for a psychological advantage'. Thus a fundamental feature of caste societies is that some people are regarded as elevated, others debased. 'Socially exploited pariahs separated off by "sacred" considerations perform innately polluted acts as part of their occupation ... [which] cannot be cleansed ... [and] persists by blood continuity into offspring.' Racialist attitudes have some similarities to those of caste in this respect. Both are conducive to 'scapegoating', which occurs when a disparaged group has instrumental utility, and dominant groups have feelings of dependency; when they want the out-castes to continue, and cannot practise irretrievable violence upon them. The out-caste groups accordingly become 'necessary for the maintenance of a secure definition of superior social status on the part of the dominant groups.[44]

Expressive exploitation of this sort is clearly not peculiar to colonial societies; as de Vos points out, it characterizes caste societies, especially that of traditional India, and other examples would not be hard to find. It may have had some relevance, though, to colonial situations in the past and present. Some personalities may thrive in a society in which they have someone to despise and patronize, even though their presence and activities there may be doing nothing but good to the despised and patronized; and this may apply, or have applied, in colonies to the more paternalistic sort of missionary, administrator, teacher, or technical officer. In which case, is it not arguable that the psychological needs of such individuals are at least being harnessed in a manner which benefits their fellow-men? Yet though exploitation in this widely extended, almost metaphorical sense may be seen from one point of view as beneficial rather than harmful, nevertheless we may suspect that it was resented by the despised and patronized beneficiaries almost as much as outright, objective, 'instrumental' exploitation. Quasi-exploitation and expressive exploitation, in other words, must take their place among the aspects of the colonial situation which aroused hostility, resentment, and protest, to which I now turn.

The view from below

I have emphasized throughout that there was great diversity in the colonial experience. Some colonial regimes were harshly repressive, alienated much land to white settlers, used forced labour or other methods of ensuring a plentiful supply of cheap labour for European mines, plantations, or farms, and neglected or failed adequately to develop native education, health, or economic development. Others, by contrast, were mild and beneficent, imbued with a 'development and welfare' mentality, alienated little or no land, encouraged native education, and welcomed the emergence of an indigenous elite. Thus among African colonies we may contrast Kenya and Algeria on the one hand with Uganda, Tanganyika, and Senegal on the other.

Whether the regime was harsh or mild, exploitative or beneficent, however, it was always resented by the natives, or non-whites — especially the more intelligent, educated, and urbanized people among them. Tanganyika, indeed, affords an extreme case of a colonial regime whose genuinely beneficent schemes were wrecked by what seemed from above like wanton intransigence on the part of the people whom they were supposed to benefit. Maguire recounts how in Sukumaland, a central area of Tanganyika, government technical officers drawing upon the best available scientific advice devised a scheme for development which, it can scarcely be doubted, would if followed have materially raised the standard of living of the people. The circumstances seemed ideal; the area included a minimum of foreign interests (to be exact, at the edge of the area in question was a large diamond mine, whose activities, however, would not have been affected; apart from that there was just one white settler!), so there was no settler problem as in neighbouring Kenya; the government were anxious to impress, not only public opinion in Britain, but also the United Nations to whom they were responsible as trustees of the territory; and not only were expert technical and scientific services available, but also a thoroughly competent administration and (most unusually) adequate funds for what was intended to be something of a show-piece which should have demonstration effects throughout Tanganyika and even more widely in the British Commonwealth. Yet the scheme foundered, not because it proved impracticable on technical or economic grounds, but because of the political ineptitude with which it was enforced. Plans were at an advanced stage before local opinion was even informed, let alone consulted, so that the Africans who were to conform to the scheme and benefit from it were not consulted at any stage, and took no part in the making of decisions which were intended to affect their whole lives. Moreover, the government combined the scheme for development (which involved livestock improvement, health control, etc.) with an

71

attempt to introduce a new system of local authorities in which elected representatives of the three main races — European, Asian, and African — should have parity of numbers, a pattern which the authorities in Dar es Salaam intended should prevail nationally, and which was thought of as a middle way between what were regarded as the almost equally disastrous excesses of white-settler domination, as in Kenya, and outright black nationalism, as in Ghana. On the proposed county council in Sukumaland, therefore, the Africans who made up the overwhelming majority of the population would have had one-third of the seats. Protests by a few of the more educated and politically conscious Africans were rejected by the administration who characterized them as 'irresponsible politicians' who 'represent nobody except themselves ... discontented and self-seeking men who by malicious propaganda seek to turn public opinion against progressive policies'. Suspicion of both the political and the agricultural schemes focussed on the subordinate African chiefs, who were regarded as failing to represent the people's views to the government, and acting as mere paid agents. Widespread non-cooperation with the government orders, transmitted through the chiefs, for livestock improvement etc., drew from the administration the fatal response that 'sometimes people have to be coerced for their own good', and there followed mass demonstrations, which as usual readily degenerated into ugly scenes of rioting and brutal repression.[45]

What was resented, therefore, was first and foremost foreign rule. In a situation in which the organizations of modern life were almost all controlled by Europeans, the local people were denied participation in decision-making, even as has been seen in the most beneficent schemes. Secondly, colonial rule was associated with exploitation, real or imagined. Thirdly, there was a reaction against what was seen as the disdainful rejection by Europeans of local, indigenous customs, cultures, and ways of living. As we have seen, on this count missionaries were indicted as strongly as others, despite their role in many cases as champions of native rights. And fourthly, people subjected to colonial rule found much to resent in practices like the colour bar and the personal humiliations which accompanied them. In the late colonial period, resentments of this kind began to be expressed in what may be called a literature of protest, as well as in anti-colonial political movements whose aim was freedom or independence from colonial rule. In chapter 12 I deal more fully with the political movements, but it will be appropriate here to review the literature of protest.

The literature of protest: anti-colonial ideologies

It is, of course, a very large literature. Among the earliest instances are the works of Jawaharlal Nehru, including many letters from prison to his daughter and others — ardent in the nationalism that they express, sweeping in the perspective of world history in which they place India, and moving

72

in the balance and moderation of the personality which they reveal.[46] Another early example is Jomo Kenyatta's *Facing Mount Kenya*, an ethnographic text on the Kikuyu which also had a political message: 'To Moigoi and Wamboi and all the dispossessed youth of Africa: for perpetuation of communion with ancestral spirits through the fight for African Freedom, and in the firm faith that the dead, the living, and the unborn will unite to rebuild the destroyed shrines.'[47]

In the 1940s and 1950s the volume of such writing grew, as many men later to become political leaders in the new states of Africa set out their manifestos, often in autobiographical form. A frequent theme is the personal experience of humiliation and frustration which the writer as a black man underwent at the hands of prejudiced whites, whether in his home land under colonial rule, or in Britain or America during his study years. Thus Kenneth Kaunda records his collisions with the colour bar in a chemist's shop in Mufulira,[48] while Kwame Nkrumah relates similar incidents in his first autobiographical book, *Ghana*, and like anecdotes are to be found in the writings of Oginga Odinga and Tom Mboya.[49]

To such a situation there are two possible reactions. One is to assert that 'men of colour' (in Kaunda's phrase) are fully equal to white men, and can perform similar tasks and rise to similar challenges. The other is well exemplified in a famous poem by Aimé Césaire:

> Exult for those who have never invented anything ...
> who have never explored anything
> who have never conquered anything
> but who yield themselves, captivated by the essence of things
> ignorant of appearances ...
> truly the elder sons of the world ...
> spark of the World's sacred fire ...[50]

It is, of course, hard to reconcile the two responses; the more competent the formerly subject peoples show themselves at coping with the modern world, the more it is by acquiring and exercising scientific knowledge, administrative skills, and so forth, which are to say the least not particularly characteristic of the indigenous cultures of 'those who have never invented anything'. This poses deep dilemmas for modern cultural and literary movements like that of *négritude* or 'the African personality', of which indeed perceptive critics of such movements are not unaware. There is, for example, the often reported remark of Wole Soyinka, 'A tiger does not go around proclaiming its tigritude — it just pounces.'[51]

Another theme made much of in the literature of protest is the exploitation which, it is alleged, consistently characterized the relations between white men and others, and continues to do so today. This is the theme of much of the writing of Kwame Nkrumah, especially *Neo-colonialism*,[52] and it is most vehemently expressed by Frantz Fanon:

For centuries the capitalists have behaved in the under-developed world like nothing more than war criminals. Deportations, massacres, forced labour and slavery have been the main methods used by capitalism to increase its wealth, its gold or diamond reserves, and to establish its power . . . For in a very concrete way Europe has stuffed itself inordinately with the gold and raw materials of the colonial countries: Latin America, China and Africa. From all these continents, under whose eyes Europe today raises up her tower of opulence, there has flowed out for centuries diamonds and oil, silk and cotton, wood and exotic products. Europe is literally the creation of the Third World. The wealth which smothers her is that which was stolen from the under-developed peoples. The ports of Holland, the docks of Bordeaux and Liverpool were specialised in the Negro slave-trade, and owe their renown to millions of deported slaves.[53]

Comment on this passage is presumably unnecessary at this point, in view of the discussion of the question earlier in this chapter. Fanon's own life and his personal experiences of colonial rule were in many ways peculiarly unfortunate, and do a good deal to explain the wildness of his accusations and the bitter, intemperate tone in which they were expressed. He was, of course, of black complexion, and at first he might be said to have been a beneficiary of French colonial rule – he studied medicine in France, special- izing in psychiatry, and in accordance with French assimilationists' policies was appointed to the government medical service. After serving for a short time in Normandy he applied for and was appointed to a post in Algeria. Here the horrifying experiences of the war, of which he gives some details in his essay 'Colonial war and mental disorders', led him to resign his post in the French hospital service, and attempt to identify himself with the Muslim rebels, by whom, however, as a black outsider from the Caribbean he seems not to have been accepted.[54]

Fanon's tirades are directed not only against instrumental exploitation, but equally against quasi- and expressive exploitation. Thus, in his letter of resignation to the French resident minister in Algiers, he wrote: 'The events in Algeria are the logical consequence of an abortive attempt to decerebralize a people.' Ridiculous as such an assertion must have appeared to the recipient of the letter, it has to be read against the background, for example, of his long essay on the veil. From his account it appears that the French authorities in Algeria had for many years attempted to liberate (as they saw it) Algerian women from the veil, which they regarded as symbolizing a low social status for women and an attempt by Algerian men to seclude them from participat- ing in the life of the modern world, like French women, on terms approach- ing equality. What from the French point of view was regarded as part of a civilizing mission, however, was resisted by Algerians as tending to strip them of their distinctive culture and identity. During the war, Algerian women who participated actively found a fresh reason for wearing the veil; it was useful for concealing weapons, money, etc., and when carrying them to the guerilla fighters. In this situation they might well be unveiled, literally and not metaphorically and by force and not persuasion, by the French security forces; this practice was seen as an indignity, and led some emancipated Algerian women who had previously given up the veil to resume it as a symbol of their sympathy with the anti-colonial struggle.

Fanon often seems to be taking a similar position to Césaire, in suggesting that it is somehow better to be irrational than rational, vague rather than specific, to fail to make relevant distinctions than to make them; this, for example, is the central theme of his essay 'The North African syndrome'. Nevertheless, he is clear about the meaning of the war against colonial rule, from the point of view of those who were fighting it: 'For three years the Algerian people has not ceased repeating that it proposes to liberate itself for its own sake, that what is important for it is first of all to reconquer its sovereignty, to establish its authority, to achieve its humanization, its economic and political freedom.' French intellectuals and democrats who asked tiresome questions like 'Give us some idea of which direction you expect to take afterwards' were accordingly berated for 'practising this kind of hateful blackmail whereby solidarity is hedged about with all sorts of fundamental restrictions as to our objectives'.

I have paid particular attention to Fanon in this brief reference to the literature of protest, then, for two reasons. First, because of the explicit and articulate way in which he expresses the reaction against colonial rule. The significance of his writing is at the subjective rather than the objective level; this is what it must have felt like, this is what the colonial experience – at least in one extreme and distressing case – did to an intelligent and sensitive mind. Secondly, because since his tragic death at the early age of thirty-six he has become one of the folk-heroes of the New Left, along with Ché Guevara and Herbert Marcuse; and his books are read with approval by intelligent, articulate young people, not least in the poor countries.

And so it was in reaction against colonial rule, with its racial overtones of rule by 'white' people of European descent, that the distinctive ideologies of the poor countries were developed. These are not in the ordinary sense nationalist ideologies; though the tone of the 'literature of protest' is assertive, it is not in assertion of a distinctive nationality or culture, but rather a common consciousness of belonging to the non-'white' majority of men and an assertion that they too are fully human. It is in this setting that phrases like 'the Third World' came to be coined – the poor nations seen as standing outside the quarrels of the cold war between East and West, communist and non-communist industrial nations, yet asserting their common humanity with both. Such ideologies have become important influences in the new states that have been established among the former colonies and other poor countries, and I develop this theme further in chapter 12. They represent a reaction against a state of affairs, and a view of the world, in which in the words of Sartre's epigram, 'Not so very long ago, the earth had two thousand million inhabitants; five hundred million men, and one thousand five hundred million natives.'[55]

SUGGESTIONS FOR FURTHER READING

Philip Mason, *Patterns of Dominance*, Oxford: Oxford University Press, 1970
Peter Worsley, *The Third World*, London: Weidenfeld and Nicolson, 1964, especially the introduction and chapters 1 and 2
Carlo M. Cipolla, *European Culture and Overseas Expansion*, Harmondsworth: Penguin, 1970

4   Economic conditions

Income

The most obvious way of starting to investigate the differences between rich and poor countries, or individuals, is to compare their incomes. As I explain below, there are certain pitfalls in this approach to the differences between rich and poor countries, but up to a point it is a good and useful one.

There are three possible measures of a country's collective income, and of these the one most commonly used is the gross national product, or G.N.P. The *gross domestic product* is the value of all goods and services produced in the country, usually valued 'at factor cost', that is adjusting for indirect taxes and subsidies. *Gross national product* is the gross domestic product at factor cost, plus any balance of income received from abroad. *National income* is gross national product net of depreciation. It represents the resources available for current use after setting aside sufficient to maintain the nation's stock of capital equipment, and is the best measure accordingly; however, it is more difficult to calculate, since it is hard to arrive at estimates, or even a satisfactory definition, of depreciation; and it is not available for as many countries as is G.N.P.[1]

Most countries have statistical departments which calculate and publish an annual estimate of the G.N.P., the chief exceptions being the communist countries. The average for the population, or 'per capita G.N.P.', can be converted into a standard currency (by convention U.S. dollars) at the prevailing rate of exchange; and these calculations enable us to see at a first rough approximation what the average income is in each country and how each stands in relation to others.

When the different countries of the world are ranged in income order, some very clear facts and contrasts emerge, which I have presented in table 4.1. The data for this table are drawn from United Nations statistical publications, and relate to dates around 1968.

At the top of the league stand some twenty rich industrial nations – the United States and Canada, the Scandinavian countries, the then E.E.C. (France, Germany, Italy, Belgium, the Netherlands, and Luxemburg), the United Kingdom, Austria and Switzerland, Australia and New Zealand, Israel, and Japan. All these countries had at that date average incomes of over $1,400.

TABLE 4.1

Class (no.)	Rich countries (20)	Anomalies (5)	Intermediate countries (4)	U.S.S.R. and eastern Europe (10)
G.N.P. per head (range)	Over $1,400	Over $1,000	$750 and under $1,050	
G.N.P. per head (average)	$2,728	$1,426	$813	
Aggregate population (million)	620	5.5	55	366
Birth-rate	17.3	31.8	23.1	17.3
Death rate	9.6	5.3	8.6	8.5
Urban proportion[a] (excluding U.S.A.)	40.6		31.4	27.4
Energy per head (kg of coal equivalent)	5,887	3,403	1,553	4,062
Electrical energy per head (kWh)	4,600	1,694	1,258	2,396
Private cars[b]	244	107	47	Data incomplete
Commercial vehicles[b]	55	26	17	
No. of newspapers[b]	282	68	152	198
No. of cinema seats[b]	32	27	103	33
No. of radios[b]	676	95	191	307
No. of TV sets[b]	277	159	118	114
No. of doctors[c]	136	71	120	199
No. of hospital beds[c]	925	425	510	943

NOTES

[a] Percentage of population living in towns of 100,000 or more inhabitants.
[b] Per 1,000 people.
[c] Per 100,000 people.

TABLE 4.1 (*cont.*)

'Better-off poor' (13)	'Middling poor' (38)	'Poorer' (20)	'Poorest' (34)	China, N. Korea, N. Vietnam, Cuba (4)	Small countries and territories not otherwise classified (64)
$500 and under $750	$200 and under $500	$100 and under $200	Under $100		
$600	$293	$150	$77		
125	365	304	905	783	14
29.3	29.8	33.6	Figures		
8.6	7.0	7.5	unreliable		
25.4	24.5	13.6	7.9		9.4
1,373	415	195	132		
815	286	100	66		
37	10.5	3	1.3		
15	6	2	0.9		
99	37	27	10	19 (China only)	
35	20	5	5.7		
234	73	43	16.8		
56	15	3.5	0.2		
76	35	19	13		
366	217	105	67		

Rich countries: Canada, United States, Iceland, Norway, Sweden, Denmark, Finland, United Kingdom, Netherlands, Belgium, Luxemburg, West Germany, France, Italy, Switzerland, Austria. Israel, Japan. Australia, New Zealand.

Anomalies: Netherlands Antilles, Puerto Rico. Kuwait. Brunei, Libya.

Intermediate countries: Venezuela, Eire, Spain, Greece.

(continued overleaf)

Communist countries apart, the next substantial group of countries start at average income levels of below $750, hardly more than half the lower limit for inclusion in the 'rich men's club' of the first group. Clearly it is here that the significant gap falls. Only four countries — Eire, Greece, Spain, and Venezuela — with average incomes between $750 and $1,050 span the gap, and can be classed as genuinely intermediate countries. Mention must, however, be made of another small group which can only be classed as anomalies; countries with enormously high incomes, due in most cases to a combination of oil revenues and small populations, but no other real claim to be included in the industrial class.

Below $750 come the poor countries, and for present purposes these have been subdivided into four groups — the 'better-off poor' countries with incomes between $500 and $750; the 'middling poor' ($200 and under $500);

NOTES (*cont.*)

U.S.S.R. and eastern Europe: East Germany, Poland, Czechoslovakia, Hungary, Yugoslavia, Albania, Romania, Bulgaria, U.S.S.R., Mongolia.

'*Better-off poor*': Mexico, Panama, Trinidad and Tobago. Chile, Argentina, Uruguay. Portugal, Malta, Cyprus. Lebanon. Singapore. Gabon. South Africa considered as a whole. (In the construction of this table South Africa has been treated as a single country. We have, however, sufficient indications of the distribution between the racial groups there to be able to make rough estimates of their incomes separately. On the basis of these estimates it would appear that the White population could be classed among the rich countries, the Asian and Coloured population among the 'better-off poor', and the Bantu population somewhere around the boundary between the 'middling poor' and the 'poorer' countries.)

'*Middling poor*': Jamaica, Dominican Republic, Barbados, Guatemala, British Honduras, Honduras, El Salvador, Nicaragua, Costa Rica. Colombia, Guyana, Surinam, Ecuador, Peru, Brazil, Paraguay. Morocco, Algeria, Tunisia, Turkey, Iran, Syria, Iraq, Jordan, Saudi Arabia. Malaysia, Philippines, Taiwan, Hong Kong, Ryuku Islands. Senegal, Liberia, Ivory Coast, Ghana, Zambia, Mauritius, Reunion, Fiji.

'*Poorer*': Bolivia. Egypt, South Yemen. Pakistan (before the secession of Bangladesh), Ceylon, Thailand, Cambodia, South Vietnam, Korea. Mauritania, Sierra Leone, Togo, Cameroon, Congo, Central African Republic, Sudan, Kenya, Southern Rhodesia, Swaziland, Madagascar.

'*Poorest*': Haiti. Yemen, Muscat and Oman, Afghanistan. India, Nepal, Bhutan, Burma, Laos, Indonesia, West Irian, Portuguese Timor. Gambia, Portuguese Guinea, Guinea, Mali, Upper Volta, Dahomey, Niger, Nigeria, Chad, Congo (Kinshasa — now Zaïre), Angola, Ethiopia, Somalia, Uganda, Rwanda, Burundi, Tanzania, Malawi, Mozambique, Botswana, Lesotho, Comoro Islands.

China, North Korea, North Vietnam, Cuba.

Small countries and territories not otherwise classified, and for which no G.N.P. is available: these include American Samoa, Andorra, Cape Verde Islands, Greenland, West Berlin, East Berlin, Liechtenstein, Holy See, Isle of Man, Qatar, Sikkim, St Vincent.

Data relate as far as possible to 1968 or 1969, otherwise latest available year.

Sources: *United Nations Statistical Yearbook* for 1969
        United Nations Demographic Yearbook for 1969 and 1963

the 'poorer' countries ($100 and under $200); and the 'poorest', with average incomes of under $100. The individual countries in each class are listed in the notes to table 4.1.

As will be seen, the 'better-off poor' countries include some at the fringe of Europe — Portugal, Malta, Cyprus — and a few Central and South American countries, but only three rather exceptional countries of Africa and Asia, namely South Africa, Gabon, and Singapore. The 'middling poor' group of countries includes much of Central and South America, and much also of that broad band of countries which runs along North Africa and the Middle East into Arabia and south-west Asia — from Morocco through Turkey to Iraq and Saudi Arabia. Some of the better-off African and Asian countries also come into this group, including Ghana, Zambia, and Malaysia. The 'poorest' countries are almost wholly in Asia and Africa, and they most notably include India and a band of neighbouring states stretching through Burma to Indonesia. Most of the new states of Africa also come into this category, including Nigeria, Ethiopia, Uganda, Tanzania, and Malawi.

Africa and Asia thus emerge as the poorest continents. Relatively poor as they are, most of the countries of South and Central America are better off than most Asian and African countries, and the same could be said of the countries of what may be broadly termed the Muslim world — North Africa, south-west Asia, and Arabia. The great divide, however, is between all of those countries on the one hand and those of North America and Europe on the other. Only the poorest European countries like Portugal overlap the most prosperous countries of Central and South America, Africa, Asia, and the Muslim world.

For the purposes of the table, the communist countries have been divided into two groups. For the U.S.S.R. and eastern Europe, and also Mongolia, although there is no national income figure there is a good deal of other statistical information which can be compared with that published by other countries. At a first rough guess one would be inclined to class this group of countries, on the basis of their material standard of living, between the rich industrial nations and the 'better-off poor', and when we do so we seem to find that this hunch is confirmed by the levels of consumption of real goods and services like electrical energy. They occupy that place in the table accordingly. The other group of countries consists mainly of China, to which for convenience may be added North Korea and North Vietnam. For these countries almost the only information relevant to this study which is available is the proportion of the population who live in towns, a figure which is important for the next chapter. Cuba, although it publishes more statistical information, has also been included with this group. Finally, there is a large number of countries, territories, and islands with very small populations (from Greenland to the Holy See) for which estimates of the G.N.P. are not available. The total population of these sixty-four countries and territories, listed separately in U.N. sources, is only fourteen million, and again the only relevant information about them is the urban proportion; they are included otherwise only for completeness.

The importance of table 4.1, therefore, is two-fold. First, it demonstrates how clear-cut and wide is the gap between the rich nations and the poor. Secondly, it shows that the 'league table' which results when countries are ranged in groups in order of income corresponds closely to their material resources in things like energy, transport, communications, and health services; the countries with the highest incomes have the greatest resources in real terms and vice versa.

The limitations of the G.N.P. measure

Published figures of G.N.P. per head are only useful as a first approximation. If taken too literally they can be misleading; besides obvious sources of inaccuracy and error, they are subject to reservations on a number of grounds. On the whole there are reasons to think that they exaggerate the real differences of living standards between rich and poor countries — wide though these are, they are not as wide as the figures, taken literally, would lead us to think.

First, it must always be remembered that they are average figures. They conceal the differences in income levels between rich and poor people within countries; and as indicated later in this chapter, these differences are particularly wide within many poor countries.

Secondly, they are apt to mislead because of the vagaries of rates of exchange between currencies. In compiling the statistics, figures computed initially in the national currency (rupees, etc.) have then to be converted to a common standard, which by convention is taken to be the U.S. dollar at the prevailing rate of exchange. As is well known, however, official rates of exchange are not a good indication of the 'purchasing power parity' of currencies. They change suddenly, for example when a country's government devalues its currency; thus, for example, the standard of living of the British people did not suddenly fall by 17 per cent when in 1966 the pound was devalued by that amount. Some governments maintain particular rates of exchange for particular purposes, and may even have more than one rate at a time; for instance, a country with a centrally planned economy might have an 'official' rate making it expensive for foreign governments to maintain embassies and consulates in the country, and a different 'tourist' rate with the opposite aim at attracting foreign tourists by making it cheap for them to visit the country. (This is one reason why G.N.P. figures are not available for communist countries.) Most significantly, official rates of exchange tend to place a relatively low value on the currencies of poor countries, because they reflect mainly the supply and demand situation of a small number of key exports in which the bulk of dealings in those currencies takes place. In recent times, the primary products of poor countries (like cotton, copper, cocoa, rubber, coffee, and tea) have had to be exported in a highly competitive world market in which they have faced competition from modern industrial substitutes. Their demand for imports, however, has been inelastic, since their imports consist mainly of industrial products for which there are no close substitutes, including the capital goods — machinery and the like — for economic development. In the case of a country like India, therefore, much-needed capital goods from the industrial countries have had to be bought with foreign exchange earned by the sale of goods like tea, cotton, and jute in a difficult and unstable market. In the balance of payments difficulties that tend to result from a situation like this, repeated devaluations of the rupee have clearly been the proper course (according to the practices established since the Bretton Woods agreement at the end of the second world war); and as a consequence, currencies like the rupee have been relatively cheap to acquire by foreigners, especially from rich industrial nations, who when they visit India find the prices of everyday goods and services extremely low when valued in terms of their own money (pounds, dollars, etc.), converted at the prevailing rate of exchange.

Thirdly, the national income or G.N.P. statistics in the poor countries themselves probably tend, on the whole, to undervalue goods and services which are locally produced and consumed and which, in many cases, do not go through a marketing process at all. As is seen below, a leading characteristic of the economies of the poor countries is the importance of the subsistence, non-monetary sector. Peasant families living on the land may well produce most of the goods and services which they consume themselves, with family labour and the occasional help of neighbours or kin, without any money changing hands. Food is grown and stored, cooked and served; houses are built and repaired; even simple clothing may be hand-made. For many millions of people in the poor countries, money transactions are the exception rather than the rule, and they are confined to wage work for the minority who, at any one time, are working for wages in the 'modern' monetary sector; taxes; school fees and church dues, or other gifts for religious purposes; and a few purchases of goods like cloth, paraffin, sugar, and tea. To accumulate enough money capital to buy a bicycle or some corrugated metal sheets for the roof may be a long-term undertaking. It is true that in most such countries an attempt is made by the government statistical office to put a money value on subsistence-sector production; for example, the agricultural department's reports of the acreages and yields of subsistence crops may be valued at local market prices. Such estimates are, however, vitiated by the very fact that the greater part of such production does not in reality go through the local market. To imagine what would happen to prices if it did would involve making assumptions, highly speculative in nature, about the whole structure of marketing and price determination, which in their

83

very nature would be unrealistic, for things are in fact otherwise. However, there is reason to think that the net effect is to undervalue the subsistence sector. If a farmer and his family live mainly on bananas, and sell a few bananas occasionally when they need a little money for some specific purpose, the general effect is likely to be that the price to the producer will be very low. Farm prices tend to be much higher in countries like those of Europe, where most production is for sale and the farmers buy most of what they consume.

The fourth difficulty is, in a sense, the obverse of the third. In the highly sophisticated and comprehensive social accounting systems of industrial countries, all goods and services are included which are in fact produced and which people (privately or through governments) in fact pay for. Thus soldiers' services are 'produced' by the soldier and paid for by the government, whether or not they can be regarded as raising people's standard of living. (This is, of course, true in poor countries too, and may well lead to their officially estimated G.N.P. rising as they get bigger armies; whether this can be called an improvement in living standards, though, is a different matter.) In an industrial economy, many goods and services are bought and sold which are not thought of as 'life-enhancing' at all, but often rather as a cost than a benefit. An example often given in this context is the journey to work. The size of modern cities and the complexity of the division of labour within them make it necessary for many people to travel considerable distances to work each day. The cost of doing so (fares on bus or rail, petrol and running costs of private cars, etc.) enters into the national accounts, for the relevant goods and services are produced and consumed, bought and paid for. Yet most people undoubtedly consider daily travel a tiresome chore rather than a form of consumption they desire, a cost rather than a part of a high standard of living. Another example would be the food-packaging and retail distribution industry; this has little or no counterpart in a poor community where people eat their yams straight from the earth, their bananas straight from the plantain, and their milk (however unhygienically) straight from the cow or goat. Food is no more nutritious, and tastes no better, for being packed in polythene, sold in a supermarket, and carried home in a car; yet the cost of packing, retailing, and transport figures in the national income accounts.

For these reasons, then, it seems probable that the ordinary estimates of G.N.P. per head, in money terms, converted into U.S. dollars, exaggerate the true contrasts between living standards of people in rich and poor countries. One attempt to discount these errors has been made by Hagen. He states that 'the calculation which shows that people live at average incomes one-thirtieth or one-fortieth of that of the United States is a statistical mirage', and concluded that the average income of the poorest countries (those with less than $125 per head per year in his analysis) should be multiplied by three to give a true comparison. When that was done, the lowest-income countries were shown as having incomes, on the average, about one-ninth that in the United States or a fifth that of Western European countries, ratios which, as he says, are 'believable'.[2]

However, while G.N.P. per head is not a good measurement scale, it is probably still of some use as an ordinal scale. In other words, while it may be rather nonsensical to suggest that the inhabitants of the rich countries are in any real or absolute way thirty-five times as well off as the inhabitants of the poorest countries, no one seriously doubts that when we range countries in order according to their G.N.P. per head we are doing almost if not quite the same thing as to range them in order from better off to worse off.

Real indicators

Besides comparing incomes, therefore, it is necessary to compare rich and poor countries in terms of 'real' consumption – the availability of particular goods and services. Some of the material for making comparisons of this sort is available for enough countries, and in a reliable enough form, to be included in table 4.1. For other types of data we must rely on illustrative examples from particular countries. Ideally an index number for all consumption in real terms would be the measure we should prefer; but this is impracticable. Even changes in the standard of living in one country at different periods are made difficult when patterns of consumption change, so that people do not consume the same things as they did, and a comparison of prices and quantities does not give an accurate impression. Such difficulties are multiplied when people in different countries meet the same needs by consuming different things. Comparisons become meaningless when the price of (say) rice in India has to be compared with that of wheat in Europe, and maize, potatoes, and bananas in other parts of the world.

Further, it must be emphasized that here too we are dealing with average figures for national populations, and such figures do not take account of the wide disparities within the poor countries themselves.

Diet

It is not surprising to find that on the whole people in the rich countries eat more and better food than in the poor; but the differences are less striking and less clear-cut than in the case of other aspects of real consumption. For many countries, United Nations sources give three measures – the average number of calories per day, the percentage of calorie input that is derived from animal sources, and the number of grams of protein. However, these figures are not comprehensive enough to make it possible to aggregate and average them over groups of countries, so they are not included in table 4.1. In most of the twenty rich countries the average diet is around 3,000 calories a day, though somewhat lower in Japan at 2,460. The proportion derived

85

from animal sources ranges from as much as half in New Zealand and Canada to 18 per cent in Italy and 13 per cent in Japan. Protein intakes range from 107 grams a day in New Zealand to 75 in Japan. Not many communist industrial countries give statistics, but in those that do — Hungary, Poland, Romania, and Yugoslavia — diets are fully comparable to those in the West.

At the other end of the scale, in the poorest countries the average diet is of around 2,000 calories a day, while in India it is only 1,810. As little as 5 per cent of this may be of animal origin, and protein intakes are commonly around 50 grams a day. India apart, the poorest diets are those in African countries, where the proportion of the diet which is of animal origin ranges around 3 to 5 per cent and protein intakes are low.

In between the richest countries and the poorest, however, there are many variations, and diets are not as closely associated with national incomes as might be supposed. Thus South American countries generally fare better than might be expected; a typical country here is Mexico, with 2,570 calories, 11 per cent of animal origin, and 66 grams of protein, while Argentina's national diet is as good as that of the rich countries. Elsewhere, Turkey has a diet far better than would be expected from its G.N.P. of $380 — 3,110 calories, 10 per cent of animal origin, and no less than 98 grams of protein.

Generalizing very broadly, then, we may say that the inhabitants of rich countries eat about half as much food again as those of the poorest countries, including nearly twice as much protein. But a high G.N.P. is not a necessary condition of an adequate diet, and in suitable conditions people in quite poor countries can nevertheless eat reasonably well.

Many factors affect what people eat, among them being their tastes and preferences, the methods of agriculture and stock-keeping, and the resources of land and labour available for producing food. Traditional diets in many poor countries consist of a basic carbohydrate source eaten in enormous quantity once a day, after cooking usually by boiling in the form of a paste or porridge. The basic source may be rice, as in many part of Asia, or wheat, maize, or other grains, a root crop such as the yam, or the plantain or banana. Other foods may be taken in small quantities as a relish or sauce, but the overall effect is monotonous as well as lacking in the other dietary constituents besides calories — protein, vitamins, minerals — which in the light of modern nutritional science we know to be necessary for maintaining the human body in full health and energy as distinct from mere survival.

Broadly speaking it is the rice- and wheat-eaters who fare best, for these food grains are reasonably good sources of vegetable protein, while the same could have been said of those African peoples who traditionally cultivated the grains known collectively as the millets. In recent times, however, millets have tended to be displaced by the high-yielding exotic maize, whose protein profile lacks certain essential amino-acids. Maize should accordingly be supplemented with good animal protein such as meat and milk; but the same

86

population pressures and local land shortages which have been associated with the change to maize have also resulted in more land being used to grow the basic carbohydrate crop and less being available for grazing – an instance of a problem which is found in many poor countries. Not all climates and vegetations are suitable for cattle, while in addition to shortages of resources there are also cases where local food taboos, or even mere tastes and preferences strongly ingrained in local cultures, work against an adequate protein intake. For example, religious prohibitions on the eating of meat seriously affect the diets of people in many countries of South Asia; while an F.A.O. report on Siam (Thailand) stated that 'Milk, unfortunately, is not relished, and even children get little of it',[3] and many Africans detest the smell and taste of cheese. Diets based on the potato are vulnerable to disaster, as the experience of the Irish in 1848 showed; yet, according to Connell, even the potato was able to provide an adequate basis for the diet if eaten in sufficient quantity, and if supplemented by high-grade protein from milk.[4] Probably the worst diets of all are those based on the plantain. Plantain diets, such as those of the peoples around Lake Victoria in central Africa, have become notorious as a result of the gross protein deficiency associated with them. The disease, or condition, known in the Ga language as kwashiorkor was identified in the 1930s as a clinical syndrome almost simultaneously in West and East Africa, where it was found that children who at weaning were put straight onto the almost protein-free local diet showed a well-marked set of symptoms, including a lack of the black pigment melanin which led to their skin colour being pale reddish-brown rather than black, and the hair pale and loose rather than black and tightly curled. Kwashiorkor has since been recognized as a very widespread deficiency in many tropical and sub-tropical areas, and since children need protein for growth where adults need it only for replacement, it is in the nutrition of children that the starkest contrasts appear between the diets of rich and poor countries.[5] Deficient diets in childhood undoubtedly contribute much to the high rates of infant and child mortality which characterize the poor countries. By adversely affecting growth, they must also contribute indirectly to diseases and deficiencies later in life.

In these circumstances, to raise levels of nutrition may be seen not only as a worth-while end in itself, but also as having instrumental value in increasing people's working capacity and efficiency, or in economists' terms 'labour input'. It has been strongly urged by Myrdal accordingly that it is wrong to regard expenditure on food in poor countries merely in terms of consumption or expenditure; rather, it should be thought of as investment.[6]

Clothes, housing, and sanitation

Although quantitative data about clothes, housing, and sanitary standards in different countries are hard to find and subject to serious difficulties of definition and comparison, it is clear that there are wide inequalities both between countries and within them in these respects.

In the case of clothing, some indication of the range of inequality may be gained from statistics like those given by Myrdal for the consumption of textiles. In South Asian countries in the late 1950s the consumption of all textiles was around 2 kilograms per head, compared with 10-11 in Sweden and the U.K. and 15 in the U.S.A. In South Asia, too, a high proportion of all textiles consisted of cotton — over 90 per cent in India, Pakistan, and Burma — where in rich countries the proportion was around a half to two-thirds. Some of this is due to climatic differences, but 'the monotony observed in South Asian diet carries over into clothing'; many people have only one set of clothes, with hygienic consequences which are easy to imagine.[7] Lack of shoes or even sandals, especially among the poorer classes, is not just a matter of comfort; it is serious for health, since bare feet are exposed to a number of pests ranging from the minor nuisance of jiggers to the serious infection of hookworm, the latter especially in countries where sanitation is lacking.

Turning to housing, it is even more difficult to cite statistics. The subject is, indeed, one of intrinsic difficulty, and even in advanced societies there are complex problems for statistical departments in defining such terms as a room, a window, or 'permanent materials'. In poor countries there are virtually no statistics at all. Nevertheless, the contrasts are wide and obvious. In the rich industrial countries, the great majority of the population live in houses constructed of brick, stone, concrete, or similar material, with roofs of slate or tile, floors of wood or cement (and usually with a floor covering for ease of cleaning as well as comfort), with a kitchen equipped with running water, inside water-borne sanitation, and in most cases a bathroom. When censuses or housing surveys in such countries reveal that a proportion of the population are living in houses which are not equipped with all these amenities, the reaction is one of shame and outrage, a matter for campaigns by charitable associations and political pressure groups. By contrast, in poor countries it is far more typical to find that the great majority of people live in houses built of dried mud, with grass-thatch roofs and earth floors. Water may be carried from a well, spring, or pond for distances of up to a mile or more, cooking is done either inside the main living room, or outside, sometimes in a separate out-house, and excretion is performed at best into a deep earth pit — or failing that, a shallow pit or out in the open.

While such conditions may be tolerable in rural areas, serious sanitary troubles arise (as they did in nineteenth-century Europe) when the traditional building methods and sanitary habits are attempted in the slum areas of the new industrial towns. It is in these areas that the conditions of extreme squalor are found, such as the 'bustees' of Calcutta, the shanty towns of Africa, and the favelas of South America.

Health and vital statistics

Referring back to the discussion in chapter 2, it is of interest to note in table 4.1 how the richer countries have the lower birth-rates. (These figures are for years around 1967–9.) There is indeed a clear jump from the average figure of 17.3 for the rich capitalist countries, and the average for the Soviet countries which also happens to be 17.3, to the levels of around 30 and above in the first three groups of poor countries. The data for the poorest countries are too unreliable and incomplete to be included, but there are indications of very high birth-rates indeed in some of them.

There is, however, not much difference in death-rates, and even a slight tendency for the poorer countries to have the lower death-rates. In part this may well be due to incomplete reporting (which may well also make the poor countries' reported birth-rates lower than they are in reality); in part it is due to the effect of a sudden recent improvement in mortality conditions, which as explained in chapter 2 leaves these countries with a 'youthful' age structure. As the older age-groups fill out over the next thirty to fifty years, death-rates may be expected to rise somewhat. For the present, though, the faster-increasing populations are clearly those in the poorer countries.

It would be most desirable to compare the infant mortality-rates in the different groups of countries, but unfortunately the available data are too incomplete and too unreliable. The rich countries are those with the most reliable statistics, as well as the best diets and the most favourable conditions of hygiene, maternity care, etc., so that we know with some accuracy what the low infant mortality-rates are; they range from 12.9 in Sweden and levels around 20–1 in North America, Eire, and East Germany to around 30 in Italy, Spain, and Bulgaria. The rate in this country was 18.8 when last reported, and in the Soviet Union 26.4. Among the 'better-off poor' countries, Portugal has an infant mortality-rate of 61; among the 'poorer', Pakistan reports a rate of 142, while among the 'poorest' countries a fairly reliable estimate for Tanzania (based on census data rather than registration) is around 160 to 165. The infant mortality-rate, or to put it bluntly the rate at which a society lets its babies die, is from one point of view a critical test of a country's state of civilization. While it is unfortunate that we do not have more reliable data, it is in the nature of things; and the wide contrasts between countries at different income levels are clearly enough apparent. Even disregarding the lowest rates in some smaller countries with exceptionally good health services, such 'average' industrial countries as the United States, the Soviet Union, or Britain lost only some 20 to 25 babies out of every thousand, where poorer countries may lose 150.

United Nations sources indicate also the level of provision for the care of the sick in the number of medical practitioners and the number of hospital beds per 100,000 people, and these figures are shown in table 4.1. They show a clear and regular sequence, with the best-provided countries being the

Soviet Union and eastern Europe, followed by the rich capitalist countries. Among the poor countries, the level of provision falls from about a third to one-fifteenth of that in the richer countries as we move down the income scale. Among the poorest countries, India is relatively well provided, and the provision in many other countries is below even the low average figures for this group given in the table. For example, in Nigeria there are 31,000 people to each qualified medical practitioner, and Nigeria is by no means the worst-provided country in Africa.

Energy

By far the best real indicator of the disparity between rich and poor countries is that afforded by their consumption of energy. As has been stressed throughout this book, the industrial revolution was basically the change from an economy based mainly on muscle-power, human and animal, with a little use of wind and water, to one with machines powered mainly by heat engines burning fossil fuels. As in the historical development of the industrial countries, so in the contemporary contrast between industrial and non-industrial countries this is the key factor. Table 4.1 sets out the United Nations data for the late 1960s, aggregated as before by groups of countries, for two measures — total energy per head, measured in kilograms of coal equivalent per head, and electrical energy per head, in kilowatt hours. There are great advantages in using such measures, since they are internationally standard and raise no 'rate of exchange' problems; moreover, they are available for nearly all countries except China.

The relation between income and energy is clear, close, and striking. The richest nations have the most energy available. The intermediate position of the Soviet countries is shown by their use of energy per head, which is two-thirds that of the rich capitalist countries for all energy and a half for electrical energy. Even the better-off poor countries come a long way behind, while at the level of the poorest countries their inhabitants have available to them about one-forty-fifth as much energy as those of the rich countries, and only about one-seventieth as much electricity.

Transport

Another useful comparison, and one clearly related to energy, is that based on the numbers of private cars and of commercial vehicles in each country. The statistics are less complete than those for energy, and in particular no figures are available for the Soviet Union. The broad correspondence between income and transport is clear, however, from table 4.1; and the contrast between rich countries and poor is even more marked. In the richest countries on the average each 1,000 people have between them the use of 244 cars and 55 commercial vehicles; 1,000 people in the poorest countries have only fractionally over one car and fractionally less than one commercial vehicle. Expressed as ratios, the people of the rich countries are nearly 200 times as well off for cars and 60 times as well off for buses and lorries as the people of the poorest countries.

The proportion living in towns

United Nations sources include data on the population living in towns, and for purposes of international comparison a standard definition is that of capitals together with towns of 100,000 inhabitants or more. (This of course defines the term 'town' somewhat narrowly, and confines it to cities of substantial size; there are difficulties, however, about adopting any other definition, and these are explained more fully in the next chapter.) For most countries there is a reasonably up-to-date figure relating to 1968 or 1969; in some the most recent figure is for a date in the early 1960s, and for a few a date in the 1950s. The urban population is growing rapidly in most countries, and it is accordingly of particular importance for this purpose to have up-to-date figures; in calculating the aggregates and averages for groups of countries for table 4.1, figures earlier than 1966 have been ignored, even though this entailed leaving out the United States, for which the latest figure was for 1960.

There is a figure for China from the census of 1953, at which date 9.7 per cent of the population was living in towns as thus defined. As will be seen from the table, that would put China broadly in accord with the poorer countries in this respect.

As will be seen, the urban proportion drops steadily with income levels, and whereas in the richest countries (apart from the United States) some two people out of every five live in large cities, in the poorest countries fewer than one out of ten do so. The significance of these figures is more fully discussed in chapter 5.

Communications and the mass media

Finally, we may note in passing the data in table 4.1 on the mass media of communication, which are important in the context of chapter 9. The data are somewhat incomplete, though not seriously so; although some countries do not give all the relevant information, all the really big ones do so, including the U.S.S.R. and India, so that the averages given for each level of income are representative of the countries with at least two-thirds of the total population in each group. Most of the data are for 1967 or 1968, though in a few cases they are for earlier dates in the 1960s.

The relation between G.N.P. and the information media is clearest in the case of newspapers, where table 4.1 shows a steady fall from 282 per 1,000 people in the richest countries to 10 per 1,000 in the poorest. Such statistics take no account of size; a 40-page American daily and a 4-page vernacular news-sheet in Africa or Asia are alike counted as newspapers. Nor can the

91

quality, accuracy, reliability, and balance of the reporting form part of the official statistics. The contrasts are less sharp in the case of the cinema, and the richest countries actually have fewer cinema seats per 1,000 people than either the Soviet countries or the 'better-off poor'; presumably this illustrates the extent to which television has replaced the cinema as a prime source of visual entertainment in affluent countries. At the same time the relatively high figure of 5.7 cinema seats per 1,000 people in the 'poorest' countries reflects the importance of the film as a vernacular art form and industry in the biggest of those countries, India.

Summary

It may be useful at this stage to sum up the range of inequalities which exist between the richest group of countries and the poorest – the 'top twenty' industrial nations with G.N.P. of over $1,400 per head and the poorest thirty-four countries of Africa and Asia with G.N.P.s of less than $100 per head.

Roughly speaking, the inhabitants of the richest countries on the average
– eat half as much food again, including nearly twice as much protein, as the inhabitants of the poorest countries
– derive between a third and half of their food from animal sources, compared with around a tenth
– use about 5 to 7 times as much clothing
– are markedly better-housed and better provided with sanitation
– lose about 1 in 50 of their new-born babies, compared with about 1 in 6
– have about 45 times as much energy available to them, and about 70 times as much electricity
– have about 10 times as many doctors and 15 times as many hospital beds available to them
– have 200 times as many cars and 60 times as many buses and lorries
– have 28 times as many newspapers, about 40 times as many radios, and 6 times as many cinema seats
– and they have television

The economic characteristics of poor countries

The most obvious economic characteristic of poor countries is their poverty, and the vicious circle of poverty in which they often seem to be trapped. For example, inadequate diets lead to physical weakness and susceptibility to disease, hence to low levels of labour input to all activities including agriculture, hence poor returns from agriculture and poor diets. Or again, low incomes entail a low capacity to save, low rates of investment, a deficiency of productive capital, and hence low incomes.

In the preceding sections the attempt has been to set out the disparities between countries in quantitative terms. In the sections that follow, the discussion is more qualitative, and the aim is two-fold: first, to analyse some of the economic characteristics of poor countries, and secondly, to enlarge upon the theme of their internal disparities.

The dual economy

As a first rough approximation we may characterize the economies of poor countries as being divided between the 'subsistence' sector and the 'cash' sector. In the former, most people work, cooperate, and to a limited extent exchange the products of their labour within a rather small world. Typically this world is limited to kinsfolk and neighbours, a few score or a few hundred people within a radius of a few miles. Within it, much production is carried on with family labour; crops are grown and stored, food cooked and prepared within kin groups such as an extended household, while some tasks may be carried out by groups of men (hunting, fishing) and others by neighbours. For example, commonly in Africa a house is built in a day by kinsfolk and neighbours who come and help, and the occasion resembles a social gathering such as a wedding or funeral — the first task, indeed, may be to brew the beer. In this sector, many needs are met (however inadequately) without the intervention of money, while in other cases money may play a secondary or subordinate role.

By contrast, the modern cash economy in poor countries is commonly represented by such institutions as mines, factories, banks, and commercial offices, pervaded by a thoroughly businesslike outlook and the fullest use of money, credit, and international exchange. At least one commodity or product in each of the poor countries is thoroughly modern in this way — copper in Zambia, cotton in Uganda, the tourist trade in Kenya, or in India such sectors as the iron and steel complex at Jamshedpur, the commercial centre of Calcutta, or the Bombay stock exchange. Often such sectors appear as enclaves or islands of economic and technological modernity in contrast to the life that surrounds them.

The very prosperity of such sectors or enclaves tends to heighten the disparity between them and the rest of the economy and society. To some extent such 'growth poles' generate economic growth in nearby sectors. For example, industrial or mining development in one part of an African country may stimulate food-growing as a cash crop in nearby rural areas, and some of the earnings of workers in mine or factory may generate increased incomes among peasant farmers. Further afield, however, the migration of men to the mines may result in depressed conditions in the rural tribal areas as those left behind — women, old people, children, the sick and handicapped — struggle to maintain themselves and their dependants by traditional methods on the land. As with men, so with capital; even one

93

with quite a modest capital to invest, such as a small shopkeeper, may rate his prospects better in the thriving industrial area than in the impoverished countryside. Such effects cumulate and reinforce one another. So, in the language of development economics, while a 'leading sector' is generating 'spread effects' in neighbouring sectors, those more distant may be experiencing 'backwash' or 'polarization'. A leading sector may be an industry, such as cotton or railways. Or it may be thought of in geographical terms as a town and its hinterland, while the areas experiencing backwash are more distant rural areas. Or the leading sector may be a minority — a class, a racial group, or one of the communities in a plural society like the Asians in East Africa or the Chinese in Malaya. Economic development by its very nature seems prone to engender regional, class, and communal disparities. These have serious political and other repercussions, and I revert to this important point in subsequent chapters.

The precariousness of the cash sector

The modern cash sector of the economy of poor countries, however, tends to have a narrow and precarious base. A small number of goods or services heavily predominate, in particular, the exports of such countries. Thus the mainstays of India are tea, cotton, and jute, which account between them for nearly half of all exports. Tea looms large in the exports of Sri Lanka, and rubber in those of Malaya.[8] Brazil produces about a third of the world's coffee, while Uganda depends heavily on cotton, coffee, and copper, and Zambia is for all practical purposes totally dependent for its prosperity (considerable though that is by African standards) on copper. Similarly, Ghana's dependence on cocoa is well known. Moreover, not only is the foreign trade of such countries often dependent on a few exports; the whole economy is often heavily dependent on foreign trade. Thus the Pearson commission reported that, in Africa alone, 'Calculations for 1965 in 28 countries put the primary export/GDP ratio at over 10 per cent in 19 countries, over 25 per cent in seven, and over 50 per cent in the extreme cases of Libya and Zambia.'[9]

Many such primary products have in recent decades been exported into world markets which have been highly unstable and competitive, and their prices have fluctuated far more widely than those of industrial products. Countries exporting vegetable or animal fibres, like jute and cotton, have had not only to compete with one another (for example, India with Pakistan in the jute market, and with Egypt and Uganda in the cotton market), but also with the man-made fibres such as nylon produced in the industrial countries. In economists' terms the demand for such goods is said to be price-elastic — a small rise in price results in a large diminution in demand. Another example is that of copper, whose producers in Zambia and elsewhere tried for many years to keep price *down* for fear of competition from aluminium, which is produced mainly in industrial countries with an ample

94

supply of electric power.[10] More recently, however, copper has been subject
to wide and rapid fluctuations in price.[11]

In the case of agricultural commodities like tea, coffee, cocoa, and rubber,
the vagaries of the weather lead to variations in the supply, while the period
of years between planting and marketing may lead to excessive swings in
price. Producers who respond to high prices by planting may thereby bring
about a glut in which prices tumble — an effect known to students of
economics as the 'cobweb theorem'. Moreover, some agricultural products
produced by poor countries can be stored, so that buyers in rich countries
with stocks in hand may be able to afford to wait until prices have gone really
low before buying again. In the world market for products of this nature,
much dealing is in fact done in futures, which tends to bring about an over-
sensitive market, liable to precisely the fluctuations against which the consumers (who largely are the big manufacturing concerns in the rich countries)
are trying to protect themselves.

Fig. 7 (reproduced from *The Economist*) vividly illustrates the matter by
comparing price movements from 1951 to 1970 in tea, cocoa, and rubber,
with the index for manufactured exports, representing the goods which
poor countries most need to buy from the rich.[12] The wider economic and

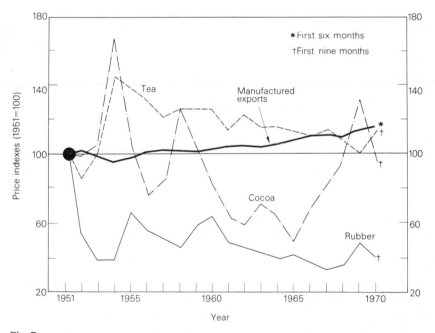

Fig. 7.
The Big Dipper
(Source: *The Economist*, 3 October 1970.)

95

political repercussions of such price fluctuations are well exemplified by the fall in the price of cocoa in 1970—1, which led the government of Ghana — burdened as it was by debts inherited from the regime of President Nkrumah — to devalue the currency by 48 per cent. This caused an immediate sharp rise in the price of imported goods (as indeed it was intended to do), thereby setting up political discontents which played their part in the overthrow of Dr Busia's government by a military coup in January 1972.[13]

In such circumstances, involvement in the modern cash sector of the economy is clearly a risky business, and subsistence production in the non-monetary sector may well continue to have its attractions if only as an insurance against failure in the other.

'Big firm, small country'

Another aspect of the modern international economy which makes it precarious and uncontrollable from the point of view of poor countries, and especially of their governments, is what may be termed the 'big firm, small country' syndrome. Much of the modern-sector activity in poor countries tends to be in the hands of large firms — the so-called 'multi-national corporations' — whose economic resources tower above those of all but the biggest and richest states in the world. If even the more powerful states sometimes have a hard time bringing some of these corporations' activities into line with their domestic economic policies, it may well be appreciated how little influence a small state in a poor country can exert over the activities of the giants.

This aspect is well brought out in a study by Beckford of plantation agriculture in the Caribbean area. Beckford's analysis is similar to that of Myrdal in characterizing plantations as extensions in poor countries of the economic activities of firms based in rich countries. Besides their metropolitan ownership and control, these firms have three other important characteristics. The first is the high degree of vertical integration which they exhibit. Their plantation activities are for them only a part of the enterprise as a whole, and it is the profitability of the whole which matters rather than the most efficient use of resources at the plantation level of its operations. Particularly where a firm produces some of the raw material (e.g. fruit or sugar cane) in its own plantations, and buys and processes some from local independent suppliers, lower profits on the agricultural side may result in higher overall profits.

Secondly, such firms spread their agricultural operations out among a number of countries, and so minimize the risk of losses, not only from natural causes such as weather and plant diseases, but also from political hazards, labour troubles, and the like. This, says Beckford, 'leads to perverse supply responses for individual countries. For although the firm may increase overall acreage and output in response to an increase in the relative price of its output, it may, in the process, contract acreage and output in a particular country.' The response to price changes may be rational from the point of view of the multi-national firm, but may at the same time fail to take the best advantage of the situation from the point of view of the agricultural sector of each country. Clearly, too, for a firm to contract its scale of production at a time of rising prices constitutes exasperatingly capricious behaviour from the point of view of the government of the country concerned.

Thirdly, a large firm may control a significant share — often, indeed, the bulk — of the export production of a particular commodity in an individual state. For example, according to Beckford, in 1966 the United Fruit Company controlled 100 per cent of export banana acreage in Guatemala, 70 per cent in Costa Rica and Panama, and 56 per cent in Honduras, in addition to which it purchased and handled for export slightly more fruit than it produced in its own plantations. In such cases, the land area covered by the plantation enterprise may be so vast that it may be the only source of employment for people living in substantial parts of the country concerned. A combination of rising productivity due to technical improvement and trade union activity may result in wages being paid which are not unduly low (although at the cost of unemployment, a theme to which I turn below); but the dependence of the country, both in economic and political terms, on the firm is clearly great.[14]

On the side of manufacturing industry, the technological factor is one which works in a somewhat similar way to maintain the 'big firm, small country' syndrome. In this respect the situation of the present-day poor countries differs fundamentally from that of the industrial countries at an early stage in their development; the poor countries' situation includes the rich industrial countries, with whose highly developed technology they are hard put to it to compete. To take hypothetical examples, it is not much use a firm in (say) Hong Kong being able to make plastics, or a firm in (say) Chile being able to make automobiles, unless they can do it cheaper or better than I.C.I. or Ford. In the past it was enough for one country, or even one firm, to develop the appropriate technology at all; now a newly developing country has to go one better if it is to make its way. It is true that tariff protection may sometimes enable 'infant industries' to make a start in poor countries, and this indeed is one of the classic arguments in its favour. But these are small countries most of whose inhabitants are poor, and their internal markets are accordingly small. This makes tariff protection of use only in the simpler sorts of manufacture in which there are no large-scale indivisibilities. Generally speaking it seems likely that major industrial development in the modern world will involve such indivisibilities, demanding large markets to secure economies of scale. Major industrial developments, that is, involve competing in world markets with the giant industrial corporations. And these giants not only possess the technological 'know-how' that

97

supplies of energy in this form, and were seen also as an attempt to redress the balance of the world's wealth by forcing the rich countries to pay them their proper due. However, as Peter Odell had pointed out more than two years before the event, raising the price of oil certainly penalized the rich countries, but it seems likely to benefit scarcely any of the really poor, while it makes the great majority — those which, notably including India, lack oil deposits — pay more than they otherwise would for the energy they need for their development.[18]

Labour, migration, and earnings

As a first approximation we may think of the inhabitants of many of the poor countries as living and moving between two worlds, the 'traditional' and the 'modern' and becoming to differing extents involved in both. In many cases the separation is accentuated by distance in space; it may be necessary to go on a journey, perhaps of hundreds of miles, to get a job in a factory or mine in order to earn some money to pay taxes, buy the consumption goods of the 'modern' sector, and after a shorter or longer time return. In many poor countries, that is, labour migration is important. People — mainly men — who work in the growing modern sector commonly come from considerable distances, and form part of a labour force which is of widely different origins.[19] Thus there may not be a common language, and communications at the work place may be ineffective accordingly. Sometimes this difficulty is partly overcome by the rise of a pidgin or lingua franca; however, since this is usually the mother tongue of none of the people who speak it, communication tends to be rudimentary and not particularly conducive to industrial efficiency. The socialization of an industrial worker, indeed, may involve a far more fundamental and thoroughgoing process than in an industrial country. Besides unfamiliarity with the language, new workers may have to overcome unfamiliarity with many commonplace features of life in an industrial society; even such trivial things as switching on an electric light, opening a door with a handle, or walking up stairs, may have to be learned.[20] Where the pattern is one of a short stay at work and a rapid turnover of migrant labourers, industrial training of this rather fundamental sort may seem from the point of view of the management of enterprises an onerous and even unrewarding necessity. Moreover, the clumsy use of modern machinery may lead to high rates of breakage in countries where spares and expert servicing may be hard to get. It is partly for reasons of this sort that there is sometimes an apparent paradox of firms importing and installing the most modern labour-saving machinery and methods in countries where, on the face of it, labour is plentiful and cheap, that is, where there are large numbers of men seeking work and prepared to accept low wages. Part of the reason, that is, may lie in a lack of elementary skills in migrant workers, compared with the much smaller number of men who have worked in industry for some years and can be

100

regarded as skilled. The latter may, indeed, be in short supply. In such circumstances, there is an obvious attractiveness about policies of 'stabilizing' labour, like those pursued by the former Belgian administration in the Congo, which sought to limit the numbers of migrant workers absent from the tribal areas while encouraging those who did come to town to stay there and settle with their families.

The lowest levels of wages, and of other earnings in the urban-industrial sector in poor countries, are generally very low indeed by comparison with wage rates in industrial societies, and this has to be seen in relation to the low opportunity cost of labour. This is the case when the majority of people in a poor country live at a subsistence level on the land in a 'traditional', largely non-monetary sector, even supposing the traditional way of life to have been left undisturbed by modern changes. In such a case, men are accordingly ready to move to the urban-industrial sector if they see prospects there of earning somewhat more than they could at home — perhaps 50 per cent or half as much again being a sufficient margin to compensate them for the travelling costs and loss of amenities which they experience in the process. In fact in some poor countries the lowest earnings outside traditional agriculture are found to be at around that kind of level, whether they be wages in industry, earnings from other work in towns like hawking or domestic service, or wages in large-scale agricultural enterprises which could be regarded as 'industrial' though not 'urban'.

In many poor countries, however, the traditional way of life on the land has not been left undisturbed. In some former colonies, as was seen in chapter 3, land was alienated to white settlers, and population growth has also contributed to land shortages which make subsistence agriculture by traditional methods less and less attractive even where it is still possible at all. In some other areas, especially those of South and south-east Asia, another set of factors tending to push people off the land have been those collectively called the 'green revolution'. New methods of agriculture, based on improved and higher-yielding strains of rice, require also fertilizers and control over water, and lend themselves to mechanized farming. It is the better-off farmers who have profited from these new developments accordingly, while the poorer peasants have been unable to mobilize the necessary resources. Moreover, the bigger landowning farmers have been anxious to gain control over larger acreages to make (say) the use of a tractor economic; and they have less use for seasonal labour, such as was formerly provided by their share-cropper tenants. So a lot of people lose their land and their livelihood while a few prosper.[21]

We can in fact see forces at work here which are quite general in their application. Technical improvements in agriculture raise the productivity of labour; enough food for all can be grown by fewer people on the land; and the results are higher incomes for farmers, rural unemployment, and migration

101

to the urban-industrial sector. The same basic economic forces which operated in England in the age of the inclosures and the industrial revolution can be seen again in the history of the 'White Highlands' in Kenya, and are now at work in the 'green revolution', in agricultural improvements in Latin America, and elsewhere in the Third World.

'Development without employment'

In the modern world, however, the situation is different in one important respect from the classical industrial revolution of the eighteenth and nineteenth centuries in Europe. The dominant technology in industry is now also highly developed and capital-intensive; it provides work for a few highly paid workers, in contrast to the masses of unskilled workers who in former times dug the canals, laid the railways, and hewed coal by hand. In the urban-industrial sector of the present day developing countries accordingly, some wages tend to be well above the 'subsistence-plus' level which would in theory characterize an economy in which there was development with unlimited supplies of labour.[22] Indeed, it is with only slight and pardonable exaggeration that Meier has coined the phrase 'development without employment' to characterize the present situation.[23]

According to Meier, in the 'less developed countries' taken as a whole, in the period from 1948 to 1961 industrial output grew at approximately 7.5 per cent annually, employment in industry by only 3.5 per cent, while at the same time the urban population was growing at the rate of 4.6 per cent. The trend was particularly striking in Latin America, where for instance in Venezuela during the 1950s G.N.P. more than doubled but employment increased by only 37 per cent. In some countries in Africa the numbers employed actually fell slightly during the ten years from 1955 to 1964, though non-agricultural production rose. The proportion of a growing population who were engaged in paid employment actually fell, therefore. These trends do much to explain the extremely high rates of open unemployment in urban areas in poor countries — commonly as high as 15–25 per cent, quite apart from any questions of 'disguised unemployment' or 'underemployment' of people still living in rural areas. Men clearly move into towns in the hope of being among the favoured few who get work and earn wages which are sometimes as much as twice or three times the income of a whole family in the traditional subsistence sector. Accordingly, 'the inflow of labour to the modern sector has actually been "more than it can handle"'.

In these circumstances, Sir Arthur Lewis has warned of the consequences of what he terms 'premature decasualization':

It is normal in an underdeveloped country for certain sectors to live by employing casual labour, most notably the docks, the building industry, some factories, some personal service trades, motor trucking (and in the countryside, the mines and plantation agriculture). If hourly wages are high enough, a man can earn enough to live on

102

with a few days of casual labour a month. As more men attach themselves to these trades, the number of days' work per man declines. Pressure develops for higher wages, which in turn attract still more, in a cumulative process.

Premature decasualization intensifies unemployment. Modern personnel theory is against casual labour. Men on the permanent staff feed better, work more effectively, have a higher morale, and cause less trouble. Unions also object to casual labour, because it is more difficult to organize. Decasualization does not increase the average level of unemployment, but it makes unemployment less supportable. If 100 men each work 3 days a week they can all live. When 60 work 5 days a week and 40 become continuously unemployed, one faces a major social problem. High wages stimulate decasualization, since the employer seeks to get best value from those he employs; and also because high wages make him put in machines, which require him to train a staff and keep it.[24]

In a capital-intensive industry with a few relatively skilled workers, wages play a comparatively small part in total costs and management have little reason to resist wage claims when they are pressed by a well-organized trade union. The governments of poor countries, too, may favour the payment of high wages especially by big foreign enterprises; high wages may be viewed as a kind of 'tax', limiting repatriated profits and making more of the benefits available locally. Similar considerations may apply to generous fringe benefits. Local pressures both by governments and unions for such benefits may in turn predispose enterprises to invest in capital-intensive methods, importing the necessary machinery. At the same time, the policies of some governments in poor countries in relation to the wages they themselves pay in the public sector may accentuate the tendency to high wages, and such policies have a 'pace-setting' effect in the private sector also. For example, in Kenya between 1954 and 1964 public-sector wages rose by an annual average rate of nearly 11 per cent and wages generally by nearly 10 per cent, at a period when population was growing by 3 per cent annually and employment was increasing not at all.

A recent statement by Lord Campbell further illustrates the same point:

I first became connected with the sugar industry in 1934 in what was then British Guiana. Then, there were over fifty factories producing 160,000 tons of sugar a year and employing something like 60,000 people. Now, there are less than ten factories producing nearly 400,000 tons of sugar a year and employing only 30,000 people. Of course, sugar-workers are now paid much higher wages, and the mechanical bulldozer may do the work of gangs of five hundred men — what happens to the four hundred and ninety-nine men who aren't driving the bulldozer?[25]

'Unemployment' is, however, too simple a term for the situation in most poor countries. Outside the favoured ranks of those fortunate enough to hold the highly paid jobs in the modern sector of industry — the 'aristocracy of labour', as some writers call them[26] — people are not on the whole found to be sitting hopelessly about doing nothing. On the contrary, their energies tend to

103

be absorbed in labour-intensive activities in other sectors, especially that which might be called the 'indigenous private sector' — the myriad tiny businessmen and self-employed individuals who in poor countries carry on small-scale manufacture by handicraft methods, food processing, small shop-keepers, street hawkers, and the like. Another related occupation is domestic service, to which I refer in more detail below. The existence of this sector, neither completely traditional nor fully modern, does much to blur the distinction between the two, useful though that is as a first approximation.

Trends of this nature clearly have implications for town life in the poor countries, which are taken up in the next chapter. The immediate point to bring out is that for this reason too involvement in the modern sector is a chancy business. By going to town a man puts himself in the way of a well-paid job, but he also risks long periods of unemployment when there is nothing much he can do but throw himself on the mercy of kinsmen for accommodation, food, and an introduction to the foreman. Going to town may therefore be seen as a hazardous enterprise, appealing to a sense of adventure, and this will be enhanced if the sought-after job is an arduous and dangerous one like mining. Despite the lure of the bright lights, wage work may accordingly be seen as an adventurous and testing episode in the life of a young man rather than as a lifelong necessity or commitment.

Not that everybody reacts in the same way to the same situation. In the present context, people in fact differ rather widely in the balance which they strike between their involvements in the two worlds. Some men, and many — usually most — women stay at home as much as possible in the familiar 'traditional' world and enter the 'modern' world only when they have to. At the other extreme, a few may cut their ties with the traditional or tribal world almost completely, and commit themselves entirely to the new, taking up permanent residence in town and losing touch with relatives to the extent that people at home regard them as 'lost'.[27] Some may try to keep a foot in both worlds, for example by sending money home while working in the monetary sector. In these circumstances, the degree of assimilation of a person respectively to the 'traditional' and the 'modern' worlds is not to be measured by any crude or simple index such as length of residence in town or length of time spent in wage work. For example, van Velsen found that men of the Tonga tribe might spend as long as twenty years in employment at the mines, rising to positions of considerable responsibility and becoming outwardly very 'westernized' (in terms of fluency in English, style of dress, etc.), and then on retirement return to their native village communities to set up in the completely traditional role of household head and (hopefully) village head-man.[28] A concept such as 'detribalization' is clearly only confusing in such a situation, and I return below to the sociological implications of the division between 'traditional' and 'modern'.

104

Corruption

Corruption is widespread in most poor countries. In the nature of things it is not possible to enlarge very much on that simple statement; circumstantial accounts of corruption are usually politically sensitive if not legally action able, and for obvious reasons, as Myrdal says, this is 'almost taboo as a research topic', though he himself devotes a chapter to it in his study of South Asia,[29] and there are also a few other general accounts. To some extent it is a matter of tradition; lavish hospitality, gifts to superiors, and the discharge of kinship obligations, traditional in some cultures, may be regarded in others as bribery or nepotism. Cultural relativity on this topic can be exaggerated, however. New situations arising as a result of modern economic activity create new opportunities for, and new forms of, corruption, in ways for which there may be little or no traditional sanction, such as bribing a tax inspector to accept a low return of one's income, or an airport official to overlook excess baggage. It is simply not the case that corruption is condemned only by the codes of modern western democracies. On the contrary, it is condemned everywhere. Indeed, whenever there is a military coup in one of the new states of Asia or Africa, one of the justifications that are invariably advanced is the corruption of the former regime.

Nor is it suggested that corruption is absent from the life of the rich industrial nations, as occasional and well-publicized incidents show. Communist states, however, both industrial and non-industrial, have proved able to reduce corruption to very small proportions if not to abolish it altogether. What is suggested here accordingly is that there is a difference in degree rather than in kind, and that corruption is much more widespread and per-- vasive in the poorer non-communist countries than it is either in the West or the communist world. I return in chapter 12 to the political aspects of this matter, and concentrate here on the economic effects.

These have been well analysed by M. J. Sharpston, who distinguishes between 'efficient' corruption which occurs when scarce resources command an illicit price which corresponds to their scarcity value, and 'inefficient' when the price is lower. From an economic point of view, efficient corruption has the same effect as a complete absence of corruption in rationing scarce resources for which a government licence or permit is required, though it tends to put the proceeds of the sale of those licences or permits into private hands rather than the public exchequer. It may happen, though, that corruption is inefficient because people, including officials, are 'naturally obliging, and more inclined to give you the stamp you need on your document than not'.

Generally speaking, high rates of customs duty, and complex and stringent controls on economic life, combined with 'inefficient' corruption, make for the widespread evasion of laws and regulations. Thus smuggling will be commonly practised if rates of duty are high but customs officers do not ask for large bribes; if the rate of duty is lower, it may be as cheap, or almost as cheap, to pay it. Corruption may 'oil the wheels', for example in securing the prompt import of a vital spare part without which much production is being lost. In some circumstances, too, it may stimulate investment by affording a means for the accumulation of capital; for example, corrupt politicians may invest their ill-gotten gains in bus companies or similar enterprises with a local development potential — though they may also invest them in Switzerland or Wall Street.

On the other hand, corruption may well lead to 'the diversion of resources — particularly that really scarce resource, practical and intelligent manpower — into "fixing" rather than producing'. Secondly, corruption tends to lower the standard of the services provided by all parts of the public sector. If officials are overworked but corruptible, so that a small bribe will lead to prompt attention to important papers while others wait, then the temptation will be to introduce delays in order to attract bribes for circumventing them, and the level of the bribe needed will tend to rise. Though this may be a way of rationing scarce resources like officials' time, it is not one that affords them an incentive for the prompt and efficient despatch of business. On the contrary, it is a way which introduces delays and inefficiency and hence costs to the economy generally. At higher levels of decision-making, planning and policy may be affected in a manner that does not make for the greatest good of the greatest number, for example when 'a few local industrialists may obtain effective control of government policy in so far as it affects their industries', and tariffs, government contracts, tax laws, and the like may be manipulated accordingly. And these effects may be compounded when it is not local industrialists who are primarily concerned, but large foreign firms. 'In an extreme case, . . . foreign interests with large investments in a developing country may virtually buy up the government and run the country as an unconsolidated subsidiary.'[30]

On balance, we may surmise that corruption probably tends to enhance inequality. The effects will not be all one way, and corruption may also have some redistributive effects, especially by spreading the benefits of office among the wider kinsfolk of the official. In some statements by educated men in East Africa which I collected in the course of a study of the educated elite there, it was suggested that the demands of kinsfolk for a return on the 'investment' which they considered they had put into his education might be one of the factors leading a government official to accept bribes if they were offered, and the same would apply to other educated men such as teachers.[31] Turning to an example from modern African fiction, one of Chinua Achebe's characters was blamed by his uncles for not demanding big enough bribes.[32] However, the redistributive effects of this nature probably only partly offset the tendency for persons in positions of power and influence, who are in most cases already well rewarded in overt and legitimate incomes from salaries and the like, to command a covert, illegitimate extra price for their services.

106

To quote Sharpston again, 'effective tax rates will be lower, especially on high incomes, and . . . with a corrupt government money can breed money in a very direct way; government contracts, grants, concessions, exemptions and subsidies go to those who can pay for them'.

Domestic service

Another feature of the life of poor countries, which is little noted in the literature, is domestic service. On general grounds we would expect this to be a widespread institution in countries where the inequalities of income are wide, and indeed it seems to serve as a kind of sensitive indicator of inequality. In modern industrial societies, the income of a well-to-do business or professional man may be something like four or five times that of an unskilled manual worker, and in these circumstances it is unlikely that many such men will choose to spend 20—25 per cent of their income on one full-time domestic. In rich countries, indeed, machines are cheaper than people, and we usually find that the better-off prefer to invest in domestic labour saving appliances (washing machine, car, dish-washer, fabrics that do not need ironing, automatically controlled central heating, etc.) rather than pay for scarce and expensive labour services. In countries where the ratio between the incomes of the well-to-do and unskilled manual workers may be something like forty or fifty to one, however, clearly the situation is different, and the households of the well-to-do are likely to include two to three servants. Around 10 per cent is probably a critical proportion, representing the limit of what people will pay for domestic help. Where the 'inequality factor' (as I have loosely used it above) is greater than ten to one, people employ servants; where it is less, they do without.

One study which, exceptionally, gives due weight to this subject is that by S. N. Sen of the city of Calcutta. I quote from this study in the next chapter.[33] Another economist who is aware of its importance is Sir Arthur Lewis, who has said: 'One can tell how prosperous a country is by listening to the conversations of middle-class wives at cocktail parties; if they are complaining bitterly how scarce and expensive the servants are, you know that economic development is going rather well.'[34] The relations between servants and the households employing them differ a good deal in different cultures. In some cases, such relations are strictly contractual, and there is a market for domestic labour operating in a relatively impersonal way, with letters of recommendation from employers of known prestige and standing acting as the means to secure better and more highly paid positions. This was the situation in our own society in the period when domestic service was widespread; the well-to-do in England never employed their own relatives, and servants had the status of outsiders in the employing households. In other cases, the servants may be poor relations of the employer, accepting hospitality in his household in exchange for services such as cooking and other domestic chores, and helping to look after the children. Although definite information on this subject

107

is lacking, I think this may be a more prevalent pattern in modern Africa. In particular, it may be by such means that the small minority of educated African women manage to continue their careers during the infancy of their children.

Domestic service, expressed as a percentage of the working population, seems to rise during the early stages of industrialization and then fall in the later stages as household work too becomes mechanized and wages rise. In Britain, for example, the rise of the middle class during the nineteenth century was accompanied by a corresponding rise in the numbers of domestics, to the point at which in 1881 they constituted the largest single occupation. By the end of the nineteenth century there simply were not enough working-class men and women to go round at the conventional rate of three servants to each middle-class household — groom, cook, and maid. Wages tended to rise accordingly, while other occupations (textiles, office work) drew girls away; hence 'the servant problem' as perceived by the middle class.[35] After 1900 the substitution of the motor-car for horse-drawn carriage made the groom unnecessary, while two world wars also helped to strip the middle class of their servants, and the ordinary middle-class home today is equipped with domestic machinery rather than staffed with servants.

The experience of one country, of course, need not necessarily be followed by others, and there may be factors in the situation of today's poor countries which will lead events to take a different course. One such factor has already been mentioned; in England it was most unusual (indeed, one could say it hardly ever happened) for a middle-class family to employ its own relatives as servants, whereas in some poor countries today it seems possible that this may be a more usual practice. Another relevant factor is ideological; countries with a strongly egalitarian, socialist commitment may be expected to discourage the growth of the private employment of domestic servants, though even in such countries the institution may creep in under other guises, for example, the attachment of military personnel to the households of important persons to serve as 'batmen', drivers, gardeners, and even children's nurses; for example, in Stalin's Russia, where Svetlana's nanny had the rank of sergeant.[36] A third factor in some countries may be that of the tourist trade. A poor country with a favourable situation and climate, and a plentiful supply of domestic labour, is in an advantageous position in this respect compared with rich industrial countries where hotel accommodation tends to be prohibitively expensive and the service poor. Some Mediterranean and Caribbean countries seem to be making the tourist trade the leading sector of their economic development accordingly.

Disparities within poor countries

It has been emphasized throughout that economic development engenders disparities, whether between persons, classes, regions, or communal groups.

In the dual economy which characterizes poor countries, broadly speaking the greater a person's involvement in the 'modern monetary' sector the higher his income. Incomes in the 'subsistence' sector are low, even though they may be somewhat undervalued for the reasons mentioned above (pp. 83–4).

At the top of the scale, a small minority of people involved at the highest levels in the 'modern' sector are generally remunerated accordingly. Thus the local executive of a major international company will have the same kind of salary as his European or American counterpart in the same company; he too will have the use of the firm's car, office facilities, air travel on business, hotel expenses paid at the best hotels, etc.; and his income will reflect this. So much is obvious. What is not quite so obvious is that people whose involvement is at a comparatively humble level — manual workers in industry, for example, or school teachers — may in a poor country represent a small and relatively privileged elite. No one, for example, would suggest that labourers in India are well off, yet according to Myrdal the remuneration of industrial labourers in towns there is about twice that of agricultural labour.[37] Generally speaking too, town incomes are substantially above those in the country, despite the intense squalor of many Indian towns. Moreover, manual workers in wage work are commonly not only a small group, but one whose relative privilege is increasing. Thus Jolly, referring to tendencies throughout the developing world, states: 'Increases in money wages of 7–10% per year have not been uncommon over periods when prices have risen by only 2 or 3% and when agricultural prices (which largely determine rural incomes) have fallen or remained constant.' Such inequality is, of course, liable to be increased by trade-union activity, which accordingly must be viewed in a quite different light from that appropriate in industrial countries: 'Far from defending the right of the underdog to a reasonable share of the national income, the unions are a pressure group for the already privileged, against the interests of both the unemployed and those in rural areas.' On teachers' remuneration in particular, Jolly reports:

In Uganda, for instance, a typical primary teacher earns £150 to £325 per year. This may seem little enough but it is in fact between 6 and 13 times the average national income of £25. A typical secondary teacher in Uganda earns between 25 and 40 times the average national income and a university teacher up to 125 times. African contrasts are rather extreme, but even in India the corresponding figures run from $2\frac{1}{2}$ to $4\frac{1}{2}$ times average national incomes for primary and secondary school teachers and from $9\frac{1}{2}$ to 15 times for university teachers, significantly higher than the proportions in rich countries where the primary or secondary teacher rarely earns more than 3 times average income and often less than twice.[38]

Comprehensive data on the distribution of incomes in poor countries are lacking, but there are strong indications that disparities are wide. Thanks

109

to Myrdal, we have a full summary of the evidence for South Asian countries, especially India and Sri Lanka, which, as he puts it, 'support the general impression of greater inequality in the under-developed regions'. The top 5 and 10 per cent of people in those countries had a larger share of the national income than their counterparts in Britain and the U.S.A., even though of course South Asian countries are much poorer. Moreover the share of that top 5 or 10 per cent had increased substantially. And there was little if any redistribution through the tax system. In only the two richest countries of the region, Malaya and Sri Lanka, were as many as 2 per cent of households liable to income tax; elsewhere the proportion was less than one per cent. Even so, tax rates were moderate except at the very highest levels of income, where those liable were largely Westerners and 'Oriental aliens'. And the tax was largely ineffective as a result of avoidance and evasion. Despite greater inequality in these poor countries than in rich countries like Britain and America, then, there was less redistribution through a progressive income tax, and the well-to-do minorities of the local populations enjoyed their wealth without significant inroads by the tax inspector.

While we do not know the facts about other areas in such detail, it would seem that in this respect the countries of South Asia are not untypical, and that extreme inequalities are a very common characteristic of poor countries in general. This must accordingly be borne in mind when considering the data presented earlier in this chapter. Average figures of income per head, low as they are in the poor countries, may yet be misleading, since the great majority of people in those countries receive incomes much below the average. In the same way, even if the average diet in a particular country may be adequate, the food of large proportions of the people may fall well below the standard necessary for health and efficiency. Thus Myrdal quotes Indian reports stating that, even in the relatively well-off towns in Pakistan, hardly 10 per cent of the population get enough food to maintain good health, while some 50 per cent of Pakistani students examined medically were found to suffer from malnutrition or from deficiency diseases, and among Bombay factory workers, who are probably better off than most Indians, the incidence of anaemia was over 50 per cent and protein intake was much too low. In the same way, of the 31,000 people to each doctor in Nigeria, we may surmise that only a few hundreds can really get adequate medical care when they need it, still less the regular routine examination and advice which are regarded as ideal in industrial countries. The rest may well scarcely ever see a doctor (in the sense of a person adequately trained in what we in the West recognize as medicine), and rely instead on practitioners of some pre-scientific traditional form of healing. Or, to quote Myrdal once more,

Only the more affluent persons — frequently Europeans — can afford the luxury of, say, an automobile; it is still 'an article of fashion, the privilege of the upper middle class and the plaything of the rich'. Generally, not only the greater number but also the highest quality of radio receivers and telephones are in the possession of the upper income groups, mainly city dwellers. Whole villages count themselves fortunate to have a single radio; and in the absence of widespread rural electrification, telephones, adequate lighting, and so on are not possible.[39]

Thus in the poor countries generally, at one end of the social scale the vast majority of people continue to live at, or little above, the level of subsistence afforded by a neolithic technology. As has been seen, even unskilled wage workers do substantially better than this, but their earnings are pinned down to a level not far above subsistence by the opportunity—cost situation, the smallness of the capital-intensive 'modern' sector, and the existence of a 'reserve army' on the land. Above this level again, the pyramid of earnings rises sharp and narrow, through the small elites of school teachers, government servants, and other professional men, to a lofty but tiny pinnacle on which a small number of men (and their immediate families) enjoy living standards and amenities comparable with those of the rich and powerful in any country. At these high levels, indeed, incomes are probably to some extent sustained by the fact that the most highly rewarded few are internationally mobile. Among professional men, for example, the tendency of medical practitioners to join the 'brain drain' from countries like India to countries like the United Kingdom is well known, while a similar international mobility is enjoyed by many university teachers (encouraged, indeed, by a strong strain of internationalism in the academic sub-culture in many countries). In the same way, the ablest government administrators may, if they are dissatisfied with pay and conditions at home, turn up as administrators in the service of the United Nations or other international organizations; indeed, their nationality often makes them particularly desirable for service in such bodies. In a word, the reference group for the topmost levels of society in poor countries is an international elite whose material standards are those of the rich countries. Here as always we have to think of disparities not in merely local terms but in the setting of a world system of economic and social relations.

SUGGESTIONS FOR FURTHER READING

Dudley Seers and Leonard Joy (eds.), *Development in a Divided World*, Harmondsworth: Penguin, 1971; see especially chapter 4, 'How Poor are the Poor Countries?', by Paul Streeten

Everett E. Hagen, *The Economics of Development*, Homewood, Ill.: Richard D. Irwin, 1968, especially chapter 1

Gunnar Myrdal, *Asian Drama: An Inquiry into the Poverty of Nations*, 3 vols., New York and Harmondsworth: Twentieth Century Fund/Random House/Penguin, 1968, especially chapter 12

Partners in Development: Report of the Commission on International Development (the Pearson report), London: Pall Mall Press, 1969

5   The rise of towns

Town life is not new; indeed, it is more than just a play on words to say that town life is as old as civilization. However, while hunting and food-gathering people have no towns, and the neolithic culture which was the basis of the pre-industrial civilizations supported an urban minority, the rise of industry has been associated with a process of urban growth in which most people in industrial countries have come to live in towns. Although in the present-day poor countries the urban proportion is smaller, it is growing, and indeed one of the most obvious changes that are taking place in these countries is a world-wide movement of people from the country to towns which are experiencing rapid, even headlong growth. But in a world in which the dominant technology is capital-intensive, that migration is not generally matched by a corresponding expansion in employment opportunities in modern industry. It is this which gives contemporary urbanization in the poor countries its special character, and many of its special problems.

Urban development in historical perspective

The first towns, such as Ur of the Chaldees and Mohenjo-Daro, in India, seem to have arisen before 4000 B.C., and their life was clearly related to aspects of neolithic technology. Agriculture made it possible to accumulate stores of food, and this enabled some men to live by working at crafts other than agriculture and selling the products for food. At the heart of every town, indeed, then as now, is a food market. Stocks of food could, in particular, be accumulated by persons or groups possessing political power; taxes or tribute from the surrounding countryside stimulated the development of writing and counting, and enabled the rulers to employ bureaucrats, soldiers, and servants, as well as to pay men to build their palaces and temples, dress them in fine clothes and deck them with jewels traded by caravans across the deserts from distant places. And so the 'services' which the town 'exported' to the surrounding countryside, in exchange for food, included political services or administration, and also religion; for it seems likely from the excavations that have been made of ancient cities that their rulers in many cases owed their power at least in part to beliefs that they were of divine origin, or priest-kings uniquely able to perform ceremonies thought vital for the fertility of the land and the survival of men. Thus among the contributions to human culture of the neolithic cities must be counted organized religion, bureaucracy, and organized military forces, the last being necessary to keep order within the city-state and repel the envious nomads prowling round its outskirts. As Keyfitz has pointed out, the relation between these early cities and the surrounding countryside was probably highly exploitative, based as it was on force, bureaucratic organization, and legitimate power. In later civilizations there was more of a balance, with the city dominating its region in an ecological and cultural rather than a political sense, the scene of an uncontrolled market exchange of goods and services which find their own price. Later still, in the most advanced civilizations, cities' taxes may actually subsidize the countryside through agricultural price-support schemes and the like. In the non-industrial societies today, however, it is more likely that the taxation of the peasant generates the capital for industrial development, for example through import duties on consumer goods. Eventually the peasants may be expected to benefit, but after how long?[1]

The greatest cities of the ancient world had populations of perhaps as many as a million, and in the most highly developed pre-industrial civilizations 10 per cent or even more of the population lived in towns. Probably the most highly urbanized of the ancient civilizations was the Roman empire; the city of Rome itself may have had a million inhabitants at the time of Christ or shortly after, while Alexandria had a population of perhaps 750,000, Seleucia 600,000, Antioch and Carthage each 250,000, and there may have been half a dozen cities of over 100,000 in Asia Minor. Of the empire's total population of perhaps 100 million, possibly 10 million lived in cities of substantial size.[2] The collapse of the Roman empire resulted in Rome and other cities being greatly reduced; by the ninth century Rome's population is thought to have dwindled to less than 20,000, and it is only in modern times that Rome has again reached the million mark — still depending, incidentally, on the sewers that were laid down in the classical period.

A figure of 10 per cent for pre-industrial civilizations agrees well enough with the early census data for India, where the population classed as urban was a little over 10 per cent in 1901 and 1911, rising to 17 per cent in 1951 and 18 per cent in 1961. The 1953 census of China too showed 13 per cent living in places classed as urban, but that is thought to have been an uncharacteristically low proportion. It had been higher during the Kuomintang republic — perhaps between 20 per cent and 30 per cent — and the 1953 census was taken at a period when, following the disorganization of the Sino-Japanese war and the coming to power of the communist regime, the authorities were making a strong effort to discourage migration from country to town and encouraged people to go back to the land. By the end of the 1950s, industrial development made it possible to relax these pressures and the urban population probably grew rapidly accordingly.[3] Estimates for earlier periods are, of course, not precise, but it has been suggested that in the prosperous times of the eighteenth century as much as 20 per cent of the population of China lived in towns — a markedly higher proportion than in Europe; and Kracke writes of cities of well over a million inhabitants in the thirteenth century, far bigger than any in Europe at the time.[4]

The first census in this country was, of course, taken when the industrial revolution was well under way, and does not represent a pre-industrial society. In 1801 nearly 10 per cent of the population of England and Wales lived in London, while just over a further 7 per cent lived in other towns of 20,000 people or more.[5]

Rapid increases in the size and importance of towns first affected the early industrializing societies; as Kingsley Davis puts it, 'Before 1850 no society could be described as predominantly urbanized, and by 1900 only one — Great Britain — could be so regarded.'[6] The 1851 census, which for the first time showed more people living in towns than in the country, was a landmark in human history, not merely that of this country. Since 1900 the proportion of the population classed as urban has risen to around 80 per cent, stabilizing and even falling a little from that level in the most recent decades as people find it possible with modern transport to live in the country while keeping their jobs in the town. Britain, indeed, has a good claim to be regarded as the first fully urbanized society. It is in one sense a special case; so important has industry become that the country as a whole imports roughly half its food, exporting industrial products in exchange; there was a time, perhaps, when Britain could be called 'the town of the world', though that was before the rise of industry in Europe and America. Doubtless even higher urban proportions can be cited in more extreme cases such as Belgium or Hong Kong, smaller countries even more dependent upon imported food. But even if we disregard such extreme cases, and consider a fully industrialized country which nevertheless also (broadly speaking) feeds itself from its own agricultural production, namely the United States, we again find the proportion classed as urban rising to over 60 per cent in recent decades.

In making comparisons between countries, and assessing trends over time, we run into statistical difficulties and problems of definition, to which reference must now be made. One measure of urbanization is the proportion of the population who are classed as urban by the authorities of the country concerned. Governments usually define towns either as places with an urban form of local government, or as communities with more than a certain number of inhabitants. Thus the urban proportions of 80 per cent for this country, quoted above, refer to county and non-county boroughs, Scottish burghs, and urban districts, while in China urban places are defined as those with 2,000 inhabitants or more, of whom at least half are engaged in occupations other than agriculture, and in certain conditions places of 1,000–2,000 inhabitants also. In some ways this is the most satisfactory way of defining

114

towns, since each country will presumably adopt a definition suited to its own conditions. However, every country defines towns differently, and this clearly makes it difficult to aggregate or even compare the statistics for different countries. The other way is to adopt a standard definition and apply it to all countries, and this is what the United Nations statisticians do; U.N. sources tabulate the populations of capital cities and towns of 100,000 population or more. This gives figures which are internationally comparable, but yields proportions which are low compared with the true figures for urbanization; 100,000 is, after all, a large town, and many people living in small and moderate-sized towns are omitted from this definition. For example, in this country about 80 per cent live in areas classed as urban, while the proportion living in towns of 100,000 or more is 51 per cent.

However, if we adopt the U.N. definition, we are able to see the sudden recent rise of towns in a dramatic perspective. In 1800, 1.7 per cent of the world population of 906 million lived in towns of 100,000 or more. By 1960, close on 20 per cent of a world population of 2,962 million lived in such towns. Thus while the total population of the world increased rather more than three-fold, the population of large towns increased nearly forty-fold — from 15.5 million to 590 million. Most of the increase, too, took place after 1900.[7]

The character of urban growth

In the historical development of the present-day industrial societies, towns that had traditionally been based on handicrafts and trade grew rapidly as they became the centres of the new large-scale industries based on mechanical energy, while some new towns were created in what were previously rural areas. There was a great influx of workers, displaced in many cases from their peasant holdings by agricultural improvement, and living in poor and squalid conditions since neither the capital nor the knowledge was available at that time to house them in decent and sanitary conditions.

In many respects this process is now being paralleled in the poorer countries. Here too some industrial centres, large and small, have arisen out of nothing (for example, Nairobi), while there has been a rapid growth of some existing towns accompanied by a change in their character (for example, Mombasa) and the rise of some industrial conurbations (for example, the Copperbelt and the Witwatersrand). Migration from country to town brings into dense urban settlements large numbers of people who are not used to the conditions of town life. The rapidity of the influx, and the lack of resources, have meant that building to modern standards has not kept pace with the growth of the urban population, and the provision of essential services like water, drainage, and electricity supply lags behind.

In the recent industrial and urban development of one country, it is true,

115

these problems have been avoided, namely the Soviet Union. There migration to the towns is controlled so that it keeps pace with the building of workers' housing and the availability of jobs in industry, and this is achieved by means of controls on residence. Although citizens of the Soviet Union are free, broadly speaking, to travel and visit within its borders, change of residence requires official permission, and people are not free to migrate from country to town on the chance of finding work. This, of course, entails a restriction on individual freedom which would not be acceptable in countries with a different ideology; and it also requires an administrative efficiency beyond the capacity of most of the poor countries today. It is for this reason that, despite its high level of industrial development, the Soviet Union still has so large a proportion of its population living in the country.

In the urban areas of the poor countries generally, however, living conditions are often extremely squalid, and large numbers of people live in 'shanty towns' in shelters which they have made for themselves out of makeshift materials. The official agencies of administration and law and order in such urban areas are often ineffective, partly because of inadequate resources and partly because in many cases they are mistrusted by the people. In such areas there is accordingly a good deal of crime and 'vice' — prostitution, illegal manufacture and sale of liquor, extortion rackets, confidence trickery, and the like. People accordingly tend to rely for help and protection on networks of social obligation which they formed in the country areas. Kinship is used as a source of benefits — help in finding a job, accommodation, money and credit — while people of similar ethnic origin and language tend to stick together and make common cause against others, and create networks of nepotism and patronage, so that some trades may come to be regarded as the preserve of particular ethnic groups, who introduce one another to employers and their agents, and use various devices to exclude others, or get rid of them if they intrude into their preserve. Geographical areas of the city, too, may come to be associated with particular ethnic groups, who take up residence near others speaking the same language, practising the same religion, and using common facilities like shops which sell their particular types of food. Once created, such areas may acquire a life and character of their own. If closed in upon themselves by the hostility of others, they may become 'ghettos' — the name originally applied to the Jewish quarter of European cities in the Middle Ages, and now extended to, for example, the black quarters of American cities. If, however, the structure of opportunity is relatively open, people may migrate out of the ghetto into better-class residential districts as they become more prosperous and there may be an urban succession in which, for example, the Jews move out and some other group of poor immigrants move in. The nature of the migration from country to town differs, though, between different towns. Sometimes it is a once-for-all movement in which the new townsmen stay and take up permanent residence. In

116

other cases there may be a circular migration, with some people moving out of the town and back to the country as others replace them. Chicago in the nineteenth century is the classic example of the first; once people had made the long and expensive sea journey from Europe they stayed in America, though Poles (for example) might move out of the Polish quarter and into the prosperous outer suburbs as they made money and became more Americanized. The towns of Africa afford examples of the second case, with a good deal of circulation between town and country and a rather small number who settle in town and become permanently urbanized.

In this highly general description we might as well be referring to nineteenth-century Liverpool or Chicago as the twentieth-century cities in Asia, Africa, or South America. There are, however, some important differences. When the first of the new industrial urban areas grew up in the nineteenth century, their rise was unprecedented; never before had there been anything like them, and there was no previous experience to draw on. I have already referred, in particular, to the 'health of towns' problem in Victorian England, and the way in which modern systems of drainage and water supply had to be thought out from the beginning. As Kingsley Davis puts it: 'During the 19th century the urbanizing nations were learning how to keep crowded populations in cities from dying like flies. Now the lesson has been learned, and it is being applied to cities even in countries just emerging from tribalism. In fact, a disproportionate share of public health funds goes into cities.'[8] Disproportionate, one would add, from the point of view of the people in the rural areas in the poorer countries — scarcely so in relation to the sanitary needs of the cities.

Health expenditure, though vital, represents only one of the ways in which the industrial cities and conurbations of the West serve as models of urban life, to follow which becomes a point of emulation and of pride for the cities of the newly developing countries. Grandiose municipal and government buildings, stately avenues, skyscraper blocks, sports arenas, and theatres become legitimate objects of municipal aspiration; Manaos has to have its opera house, with performances by Caruso and Melba. The aspirations, like the economies, of the poor countries tend to be oriented to a world market dominated by the West, and these aspirations take concrete architectural form in the buildings and planning of their cities.

It was remarked in chapter 4 that a feature of the economic life of the present-day poor countries is what has been called 'development without employment', and this is nowhere more vividly to be seen than in the new cities of the Third World. The capital-intensive nature of modern industrial development, which has already been noted, means that industry can grow and produce more goods without employing many more workers, and in fact it is the usual experience in these cities for their industrial employment to grow much less fast than their population. This gives rise to situations

117

which, as a first approximation, are often described as unemployment, though the term is too simple and the situation too different for this word to be readily transferred from a western industrial context. More precisely, the economy of new cities can often be regarded as made up of three major sectors. First, large-scale modern capital-intensive industry, with the capital most often largely foreign-owned and the management, if not actually conducted by foreigners, carried out along lines similar to those of large western capitalist enterprises, which are often indeed the parent companies. In this sector wages tend to be high by local standards, for the reasons which have been dealt with in chapter 4. Secondly, there is another large-scale sector, this time wholly indigenous — the government bureaucracies of central and local government and public enterprises. Much of this sector is not particularly capital-intensive, and it employs considerable numbers of workers at wages often nearer the local market rate, for example, as road construction and maintenance workers, street cleaners, construction workers associated with public health administrations, and so forth. Thirdly, there is a large and highly labour-intensive indigenous private sector consisting of the myriad small businesses of self-employed craftsmen, traders and hawkers, and indigenous entrepreneurs employing a small number of workers. Employment especially in the large-scale industrial sector with its high wages is often greatly sought after, but not as a job for life; rather, the object is to save enough over a period of a few years to accumulate the initial capital needed to start up in business as, for example, a plumber, a bicycle repairman, a street trader, a butcher, or a photographer. Profit-sharing and sub-contracting are often features of this sector of the economy, as for instance when a taxi owner leases vehicles out to drivers and leaves them to pocket any fares they earn over and above the daily rent and the necessary petrol, or may have an arrangement which enables drivers to buy their vehicles over a period and so set up as taxi-owners themselves.

High wages or other earnings, moreover, do not necessarily go with high standards of living, and the tendency for the rewards of industrial employment to diffuse outwards through the kinship network must be borne in mind. Thus the average town worker may be earning several times as much as his counterpart in the country, but this may be largely offset by remittances to relatives at home and by hospitality to kinsmen who have come to town looking for work, loans to other kinsmen to enable them to pay taxes, school fees for children, and the like.

There may, accordingly, be something in the suggestion that migration from country to town is a response to the 'bright lights' or to beliefs that 'the streets are paved with gold'. A realistic analysis, however, must take into account pushes as well as pulls, reasons why people leave the country as well as reasons why they move to town. In some cases special circumstances may result in an influx of people into a particular town; thus Hong Kong is crowded at least in part with people who for one reason or another are anxious to leave China, while the migration to the towns of some Latin American countries may be at least partly due to the depressed conditions of peasant life on the *haciendas*, large estates whose owners may restrict rather then promote opportunities for economic advancement among their tenants.

Contrasts between riches and poverty, though not new and not peculiar to the cities of the Third World, may nevertheless have a special sharpness there and lead to situations which in chapter 3 I characterized as 'quasi-exploitation'. In the nature of things, the life of the big cities is dominated by the large business corporations, many of them foreign, whose higher executives receive the same kind of incomes as they or their counterparts would in the cities of the West. The way of life and the standard of living of such men, and their families, is that of the international 'jet set', and as emphasized in the last chapter the internal inequalities in the poor countries are characteristically very wide. It is in the cities of these countries that the contrast between the affluent way of life of the modern industrial world, and the extremely low subsistence levels of the migrants in the shanty towns, is seen in its most dramatic and visible form. Here is the world in miniature.

Further, to some extent in all parts of the Third World, the town is seen as a centre of foreign influence; and this is an important difference between those towns and the towns of the already industrialized nations. The dependence of the modern sector on world trade, which I have stressed in the previous chapter, and the importance of large international corporations like the great oil firms, certain banks, and hotel companies with world-wide interests — these are widely pervasive influences giving most of the new cities at least some foreign character. Thus even in Latin America, where modern urbanization began after the countries concerned became politically independent, towns are widely regarded as centres of North American influence and to that extent alien. In Africa south of the Sahara there was little in the way of an indigenous tradition of town life. A few of the towns of modern Africa, like Ibadan and Mombasa, grew from existing historic towns, but even they changed their character very drastically in the process of growth, while most of the present towns of Africa began literally from nothing within the last century, and represent almost entirely the initiative of European and Asian foreigners under colonial rule. Apart from North Africa, with its ancient cities like Alexandria and Tunis, town life in Africa is almost wholly a foreign innovation, and viewed as such. In Asia, though there was an indigenous civilization, it is also the case that town life in the modern sense was an innovation under colonial rule. This is reflected rather obviously in the cities of India; Calcutta and Bombay rose to prominence during British rule, and as a result of activities related to the world economy in the colonial period, as seaports and centres of manufacturing (in the case of Bombay, cotton textiles), while the British found old Delhi unsuitable for their pur-

119

poses and created a fresh capital city in New Delhi. And much the same was true even in China, where Peking represents the only major city which did not owe its origins mainly to the activities of European foreigners. Peking apart, by far the biggest cities, including Shanghai, Tientsin, and Canton, are the former treaty ports, established in the nineteenth century by a partnership of European commercial interests and Chinese merchants, at loggerheads with the mandarinate who wanted to restrict foreign trade. These large port cities owe little to traditional Chinese influences; their streets are broad and straight, suitable for modern transport, in contrast to the winding narrow lanes of the old walled city, and their whole appearance is described as completely un-Chinese. The new commercial district of Fu-Chuo, for example, is two or three miles away from the old walled city, while facing it across the River Min is another new district formerly associated with foreign settlement and established during the nineteenth century when foreigners were not allowed to live in the old city.[9]

Attitudes to urban development

In the light of the foregoing, it is not surprising or unnatural that the growth of towns in the present-day poor countries should be widely regarded in an adverse light, as a source of human problems and suffering and hence as constituting a problem in itself. An anti-urban bias, indeed, is not new, and not confined to the Third World; Morton and Lucia White have reminded us of the distaste for the city which characterized the thought of American intellectuals from Thomas Jefferson to Frank Lloyd Wright,[10] while similar bias might be traced in this country from John Ruskin through Ebenezer Howard to the modern town-planning movement in which the town is seen as an 'insensate growth' to be confined within a green belt and prevented from blighting the countryside.

On the other hand, it can be argued that urbanism is so completely bound up with development that it is impossible to have one without the other. Urbanism, indeed, may be regarded as part of the definition of development; we may recognize one country as being more developed than another if it has a higher proportion of its people living in towns. This is the approach of Lerner, who shows that urbanization is correlated with other aspects of modernity such as literacy, both in statistical terms and as a matter of necessity.[11] On this view, while the social and personal problems associated with the growth of towns are not denied, the town itself is seen not as a problem but as a solution. As Sir Joseph Hutchinson has put it, 'There are certain principles in the relation between agriculture and human development that apply universally . . . They stem from the simple biological circumstance that when a man has enough to eat, he has nothing to gain by eating more.' Improvements in agriculture result accordingly, not in the production of more goods by the same techniques, but in a shift out of agriculture and into other occupations — specialization, 'the aggregation of craftsmen together, and the growth of towns. This has been the main stream of development . . . a steady evolution of urban communities supported by an increasingly productive agriculture.' In Africa the basic problem is the same, to shift from a rural base to an urban base. 'In Uganda I sat on a committee to consider how to stop the drift to the towns. The suggestion that we should stop building the Qwen Falls dam was regarded as irresponsible, or indeed frivolous. The drift to the towns poses all sorts of problems, but the only really important problem is that of creating urban employment fast enough to keep pace with it.'[12]

On the other hand, President Nyerere writes of urban development with great reservations. Only 4 per cent of the people of Tanzania live in towns, and less than 340,000 people work for wages out of not less than five million adults.

Unfortunately, the life of these tiny minorities has become a matter of great envy for the majority. Life in the towns has come to represent opportunities for advancement, a chance of excitement, and the provision of social services, none of which is easily available in the rural areas . . .

But although the goal of individual wealth has been accepted by our people, and despite their belief that this can be attained by wage employment and by life in the towns, the truth is that it is an unrealistic goal, especially in Tanzania. The vast majority even of our town dwellers live extremely poorly, and in most cases they are on the whole worse off, both materially and in the realm of personal satisfaction, than the people in the rural areas could be . . .

For the foreseeable future the vast majority of our people will continue to spend their lives in the rural areas and continue to work on the land. The land is the only basis for Tanzania's development; we have no other . . . This means that we have to build up the countryside in such a way that our people have a better standard of living, while living together in terms of equality and fraternity. It also means that, in the course of time, the advantages of town life in the way of services and personal pleasures and opportunities must become available to those who work in the rural sector as much as those in urban areas.[13]

Accordingly, the Arusha Declaration declares forthrightly that 'We have put too much emphasis on industries', and 'Our emphasis should therefore be on: (a) The Land and Agriculture'; and in his pamphlet *Education for Self-Reliance*, President Nyerere calls for school life to be integrated into, and to prepare people for, life in a predominantly rural society.[14]

A case study — Calcutta

The city of Calcutta itself has a population of about three million, while the total population of the metropolitan district of which it is the centre, with an area of about 400 square miles, is about seven million. Calcutta is accordingly

121

not only the biggest city in India but a major metropolis, comparable in size with London and New York. Its importance for the Indian economy is due to its position, some fifty miles from the sea, on the banks of the Hooghly River, a branch of the Ganges which is wide and deep enough for ocean-going ships. As a seaport Calcutta handles about one-quarter of all imports into India and nearly half its exports; while around the docks, and upstream from them, there is a major industrial complex (shipbuilding and engineering, jute, paper and cotton mills, food processing, and a wide variety of light manu-facturing) and also a major commercial and financial centre where enter-prises like coal mines and tea plantations, though situated far away, are managed and financed by the business houses of the city.

The main source of information on the social and economic conditions of the people of Calcutta consists of a series of surveys carried out by Professor S. N. Sen of the University of Calcutta between June 1954 and June 1958.[15]

The origins of the city are wholly colonial. In 1690 Job Charnock, agent of the British East India Company, declined the Nawab's invitation to set up a factory further downstream, and settled instead on one of three villages — Sutanati (which he called Sootalooty), the others being Govindpur (Gobinda-pore) and Kalighat (Calicut or Calcutta) — which together formed the nucleus of the new city. The villages were formally purchased in 1698, and in 1700 the company set up a presidency of Bengal with Calcutta as its headquarters. Later it became the seat of the British government of the whole of India, and remained so until 1912 when the government moved to New Delhi. The population of the city grew during the eighteenth century from about 10,000 in 1701 to 140,000 in 1801. The 1901 population of the present area of the city proper (some 34 square miles) is put at 949,000. From 1901 to 1921 the population grew very little, and it was not until 1931 that it exceeded a million. During the 1930s there was rather more rapid growth, associated with unemployment and under-employment in the hinterland. Migration into the city was stimulated by the natural disaster of the Bengal famine which occurred during the war of 1939—45, and then by a large-scale influx of refugees from East Pakistan during the troubles following independence and partition in 1947—50. Since 1950, 'normal' migration (that is, apart from emergency situations) has been going on at a somewhat higher rate than in the past, but the city has not been growing particularly fast in recent decades. Sen estimated in the mid-fifties that the growth rate was about 5 per cent, with natural increase just about equal to inward migration; while Nirmal Kumar Bose, writing in 1965, quotes the Registrar-General of India:

It seems incredible that, while West Bengal's population grew by 33% in the last decade, Calcutta's should have grown by only 8%. In the same period Greater Bombay grew by about 39% ... The truth of the matter is indeed a paradox; that in spite of the squalor, the swarming streets and pathways, the bustees bursting and spilling around, Calcutta is not growing fast enough.[16]

A feature of Calcutta's population which has been noted, ever since the first accounts of the city early in the nineteenth century, is the heavy preponderance of males, who outnumber females by nearly two to one overall and more than two to one in the working ages of 15 to 59. Associated with this is the high proportion of single-person households, who make up more than half the total of all households.

During the period of Sen's surveys in the middle 1950s, the national average per capita income in India was 289 rupees. In Calcutta the average income, 560 rupees, was just about double the national average. The barest minimum subsistence wage was put at Rs 25 per month. Very few income earners received as little as that, and by far the biggest group – three-quarters of the single-person householders, 39 per cent of the earners in multi-member households – earned between 31 and 100 rupees a month. Thus there was hardly any primary poverty among the single-person householders, whose average incomes were in fact well above the national average. Poverty was widespread, however, in the multi-person households, where each earner had to support an average of 2.8 dependants; nearly half the population living in such households were at or below the primary poverty line of Rs 25 a month. As Sen puts it, 'Probably those who were fortunate to earn comparatively good incomes had brought their families to the city.' On the other hand, although the migrants mostly lived alone in Calcutta itself, most of them had dependent relatives at home in the country, and Sen found that three out of every four of them were sending regular remittances home, and over 40 per cent were sending over Rs 20 a month.

Distinctions between 'local' and 'migrant' city-dwellers are never easy to make; somewhat arbitrarily, Sen defined as 'original residents' those who had either been born in Calcutta, or moved there before 1935, and thus defined they were a majority of the population. On another indication, Bengali-speakers were also in a majority of about 60 per cent of the population; but they included many immigrants who were Bengali-speakers from the area immediately around Calcutta, and there were substantial numbers of people speaking Hindi or Hindustani (25 per cent), Urdu (6 per cent), and Oriya (2 per cent). 'The conclusion is inevitable,' says Sen, 'that the resident Hindi, Urdu or Oriya-speaking population contain hard cores of migrants who have not brought their families even though they have been staying for a long time in the city.'

A further striking feature of Calcutta's economy proved to be the small number of people employed in manufacturing. Only 2.8 per cent of all earners in Sen's surveys were factory workers, and only 16 per cent were engaged in any kind of manufacturing, even though this was defined extremely widely and included 'such operations as the preparation of sweetmeats in small establishments and the making of such homely (and lowly) food products like fried rice, gramflour, etc.' By far the bigger groups were

123

those engaged in distribution and services, and the two biggest single occupational groups were owners of retail shops (9 per cent) and domestic servants (8.8 per cent). General distributive trades and domestic service were moreover by far the fastest-growing occupations. Sen comments:

It is, of course, not difficult to take to petty trading for a certain period of time. But a reasonable explanation of the rate of expansion in purely domestic employment is rather difficult to find. It may be that people had drifted to these lowly paid occupations for want of better paid jobs. And that indicates a difficult employment market rather than a good one. In that case, the drift to the urban areas has meant for many migrants only a change from a not very productive occupation to a similar or a worse one under extremely unhealthy housing conditions ... This is a rather disquieting feature of the employment position in the city, where it seems that employment has become stagnant, if not declining, in almost all other sectors except in petty trading and domestic services.

Resident domestic servants were found to be kept by families, especially the larger families, to all income levels above Rs 200 a month (and even in a few exceptional cases below that level), though naturally the tendency to keep domestic servants rose with income. About 20 per cent of resident domestics were women, and this form of employment was by far the biggest single group among women earners. Nearly three out of four domestics were migrants, though as has been noted migrants were a minority of the population of the city as a whole. Scarcely any were paid more than Rs 30 a month but with food provided by the employer their average earnings were slightly over Rs 49 a month. Out of all Sen's sample of households, about 500 multi-member households with incomes over Rs 200 a month were employing between them about 350 whole-time domestics, mostly resident. The average monthly income of the servant-employing households was about Rs 530, of which, as has been stated, they were paying out about Rs 50 on servants' food and wages. (Translating that into British terms, this is as if households with incomes of £10 to £11 a week were employing servants at a total cost in food and wages of £1 a week.) The importance of domestic service to Calcutta's economy may be further gauged from Sen's finding that, taking into account also part-time domestics, the aggregate income

TABLE 5.1

Monthly income (rupees)	Households with resident domestics (%)
201–350	6.0
351–750	21.5
751–1200	36.0
over 1200	70.0 (50.0 have two or more)

of domestic servants in the samples as a whole was some 6.6 per cent of the incomes of all gainfully employed persons.

There was a good deal of unemployment, though it fell during the period of Sen's surveys from 10 per cent to 7.6 per cent of all 'work-seekers' (that is, those employed or actively seeking work, excluding housewives, students, etc.). Its incidence was heavy among younger people, with over 40 per cent of the 15–19 age-group out of work in 1954–5, falling to 30 per cent in 1956–7. Migrants had a lower unemployment rate than residents – presumably if they could not get jobs they went home – but the rate among 'displaced migrants' (as Sen calls them – refugees for the most part) was much higher. The unemployment rate was also found to be higher among those with some education, and the inference is that the number of educated men and women was growing faster than employment for them.

The housing conditions of Calcutta are notorious throughout the world. Sen found that only about $7\frac{1}{2}$ per cent of households were living in separate modern accommodation, houses or flats of permanent materials and with exclusive use of such amenities as a water tap, lavatory, separate kitchen, and electricity. The biggest group, about a third of all households, lived in conditions which though adequate from a sanitary point of view were certainly bare – joint houses of permanent materials, nearly all having shared access to an inside water tap and lavatory, and most having electricity, but only 23 per cent with a separate kitchen and less than half a separate bathroom. In what he terms '*kutcha*' dwellings, made of temporary or makeshift materials, about a quarter of all households lived, sharing access to a water tap and a lavatory with a large number of other households (typically from ten to fifty) and, in a few cases, using the public drains. From most points of view the worst-housed group were what he calls 'shop dwellers', households living over (or in some cases under) a retail shop or work place; about a quarter of such households had no lavatory at all, and most shared with a large number of others. This group, however, were rather better off for electricity than the other poorer groups. About a quarter of the whole population were found to live in the slums or 'bustees'. In Calcutta, these areas of greatest squalor are not concentrated in one or a few places (like the old East End of London) but are found everywhere, cheek by jowl with modern apartment blocks and the houses of the well-to-do – indeed, in many cases the bustees house the non-resident domestic staff serving these dwellings. Rents, however, were found to be extremely low, and a large number of people lived rent free – 37 per cent of single-person households, and 32 per cent of all households, had free accommodation from relatives and friends, from employers, or through forcible occupation.

Sen concludes with some estimates of the scale on which capital would be required to raise Calcutta's growing population to adequate modern standards, both of productivity at work and of sanitation at home. He gives

125

a figure of Rs 3,000 for the amount of investment needed to provide a job for one additional worker, and Rs 6,000 for a one-roomed dwelling in a multi-storey building of permanent modern materials (the minimum adequate for the average household of 2.78 persons), giving a further Rs 2,500 for each adult and Rs 1,250 per child. The aggregate investment needed at that time to cope with the prospective growth of the city for a five-year period would have amounted to between 6 per cent and 7 per cent of the total investment, public and private, during the Second Plan period for the whole of India. Clearly sums on such a scale were unlikely to be forthcoming.

Commenting on Sen's findings, the following points may be made. First, people migrate to Calcutta, as to other cities, for the very good reason that they are better off there. As has been seen, migrants to Calcutta could expect to earn something like twice the average income of Indians as a whole, and while the risk of unemployment was appreciable it was less than deterrent when deciding whether to move. In any case, unless they were refugees, migrants could always go home if they failed to find work, and unemployment was heavier among those born or long resident in the city. (Sen's analysis in terms of 'push' and 'pull' factors is somewhat laboured on this point; unemployment at home he counts as a 'push', while better prospects in Calcutta is a 'pull'. All that is needed, surely, is a recognition of a gradient of opportunities or prospects — knowledge or belief that things are better in the city.)

Secondly, the capital-intensive nature of modern technology, and the relatively slow growth of the modern technological sector of manufacturing together with the docks and other modern utilities, has meant that the most highly productive sector of the city's economy has employed relatively few people. Putting it rather crudely, Calcutta could probably perform the same services as it does to the economy of India with half its present population or less. If the population were halved — if, for example, it were possible to prohibit migration so that the jobs available were all done by those born in the city — their wages would be much higher, in relation to the higher productivity of labour in the modern technological sector. (In these circumstances, it is truly remarkable that Calcutta people do not see the immigrant workers from the countryside as undercutting their wages and other earnings, and threatening their prosperity as well as their health. It is a situation fraught, one would think, with the possibility of conflict between residents and immigrants.) What actually happens is that the earnings from the modern technological sector are diffused through a much larger population by the practice of labour-intensive occupations, especially petty retailing and domestic service, and also by kinship and friendship networks. The first — service — means that, poorly off though the people of Calcutta are in terms of goods and services like housing and water supplies, they enjoy what some people in industrial societies might regard as the luxury

126

of plenty of people around to help, for a small charge, in small ways — myriad little shops making available a range of commonplace goods without the necessity to travel far, hawkers bringing goods to houses without the necessity of moving at all, and for families with even a modest degree of prosperity the services of a living-in domestic. The second, networks of kin and friends, are seen in Sen's data in the extremely high proportion of people who live rent free. It is because of this diffusion from a relatively narrow industrial and commercial base to a large population that authorities such as N. K. Bose, already quoted, view Calcutta as a city which has experienced population increase without industrialization on a comparable scale, and call it a 'premature metropolis'.

SUGGESTIONS FOR FURTHER READING

Gerald Breese, *Urbanization in Newly Developing Countries*, New York: Prentice-Hall, 1966

Gerald Breese, (ed.), *The City in Newly Developing Countries: Readings on Urbanism and Urbanization*, New York: Prentice-Hall, 1969

6 The family and kinship in a changing world

In no aspect of culture are the diversities between human societies, which developed during the thousands of years when they were relatively isolated from one another, more striking than in the institutions of the family, marriage, and kinship. In some societies, descent was traced through the father, in others through the mother, in yet others through both parents. In some societies there was polygyny, in others polyandry, in yet others monogamy. Diverse too were the practices concerned with the transfer of possessions and rights over resources from the older to the younger, at marriage and at death. Household size and composition differed somewhat, with some peoples tending to live and have catering arrangements in common between a substantial number of persons related by birth or marriage, while in others people lived in smaller households confined normally to a married couple and their children. Different possible arrangements for meeting the basic human needs of mating, reproduction, the care and upbringing of children, and the care of the aged allow for a large number of permutations and combinations, which make the comparative study of kinship a happy hunting ground for the social anthropologist and constitute an important part of the subject-matter of his science.

The *diversity* of kinship is, indeed, possibly the first and most important lesson which social anthropology has taught us. And the second lesson is the *importance* of kinship. Technologically primitive societies tend to be structurally little differentiated, and there are good reasons why this should be so. Where technology is primitive, what Adam Smith called 'the extent of the market' is small and the division of labour is accordingly limited in scope. There is little possibility for the growth of large and complex organizations like those which characterize the life of large-scale, technologically advanced societies like our own — a generalization that applies to aspects of life beyond the economic realm, such as politics, education, and religion. In small-scale societies, therefore, while it may not be quite exact to say that 'kinship is all', the implication is that it is hard to disentangle kinship from other institutions, and that other roles such as those in the political and economic spheres cannot readily be distinguished from kinship roles. Thus, for example, the discussion of law and order among the Nuer immediately involves, in Evans-Pritchard's classical analysis, a discussion of the lineage system;[1] and many

128

similar examples could be cited from the literature of anthropology. Every society has a kinship system — it must, because kinship is the social institution organized around the universal, biologically determined processes of mating and reproduction. Not every society has highly organized, complex, and relatively autonomous organizations such as the state, schools and universities, the army as a separate institution, industrial enterprises, churches, trade unions, sporting and recreational associations, politics, pressure groups, and so on. As a consequence, many other activities like those which in a complex society we should class as 'political' (for example, standing for election to the local council), 'economic' (such as working in a mine), 'educational', etc. or their appropriate counterparts in other cultures, are subsumed under and carried out as part of the performance of kinship roles. Being a member of a clan may give a man rights to land, which he will exercise in his role as father by co-ordinating the work of his wives and sons in digging, herding cattle, and so forth. Clanship may involve the politics of intrigue against other clans at a royal court in which the highest positions are to some extent hereditary, thus again involving the kinship system. Religion may in part be a kinship matter, especially if there are clan deities or an ancestor cult, or if priestly roles are hereditary or associated with particular clans. We should be careful here to avoid the rigid determinism of some conventional treatments of this subject. It is certainly not suggested here that individuals' behaviour was always determined, or narrowly prescribed, by their kinship roles. For one thing, most individuals occupy several different kinship roles in the same system, so that, for instance, a man is at one and the same time a son, a brother, a husband, a father, a nephew, an uncle, a brother-in-law, etc. If the rules prescribe different behaviour at a wedding, for example, for the relatives of the bride and the groom, then in small-scale societies in which there are many cross-connections it must often be the case that the same man is related to both, and has to choose which set of kin to align himself with. For another thing, small-scale and technologically primitive societies are certainly not immune from conflict; and there may often be situations in which we could equally well characterize some man's action as exploiting his kinship position to further his own ends in a political conflict, and exploiting his political power in order to advance the interest of his own kin. Conflict and choice may result in many situations in which individuals *use* their kinship (and are not dominated by it); we could, however, equally well say that in small-scale societies it is their *kinship* which they use (and not, say, their economic or political position, because the latter are not separate categories).[2] In the absence of clearly defined, autonomous institutions such as representative local government, industrial firms, commercial insurance, and the like, it is kinship which people use to gain their ends, because it is all they have.

When societies undergo the sort of change which is the theme of this book

129

they become more complex. Additional social structures like those of industrial enterprises, the state and local government, and the rest are grafted onto the previously existing social structure in which kinship loomed large. Even if no great change takes place at once in the kinship sphere itself, one consequence of this is that individuals occupy additional roles — as well as being a father, a man is also a miner, a candidate for the local council, a party member, and so on — which are not linked in any inseparable way with the kinship role. Thus if a man gives up his job as a miner and becomes a shopkeeper, ceases to be a party member, etc., he nevertheless remains his children's father. The autonomy and independence which these new institutions enjoy, of kinship and of one another, tend to increase as society becomes more complex. Again, we must beware of taking too simple and absolute a position about this. It is not suggested that the autonomy of institutions is ever, or can ever be, complete. On the contrary, the life of modern industrial enterprises is related at various points to the kinship system — for example, in so far as the family firm retains a place in the industrial life of modern nations, and in so far as it helps to be the managing director's son; when enterprises need the labour of married women, they may find it advantageous to arrange working hours which permit women also to fulfil their roles as mothers, or to provide creches for women workers' young children; and so on. Similarly, an example like the composition of Mr Harold Macmillan's cabinet affords ground for suggesting that the family and kinship are not quite unrelated to politics in a modern industrial society.[3] The autonomy of institutions is at most a relative and contingent autonomy, yet nevertheless the contrast with technologically primitive, small-scale societies is obvious. Perhaps it might be put graphically in the following terms. When an anthropologist has written his book, or books, containing an analytical description of the social life of the society he had studied, a high proportion of it is about kinship, and when he has finished describing and analysing the kinship system there is very little else to tell. By contrast, if we imagine a work devoted to a complete analytical description of British, American, or Soviet society, its nature and scope would be somewhat different. For one thing a single book, or even a small number of books, would be insufficient. While there might well be a volume on the family, marriage, and kinship, there would also have to be several volumes about the economy in all its complex ramifications — industry, mining, agriculture, construction, transport, communications, the banking and financial system; another series on politics — central, local, and regional authorities, the party organization, the bureaucracy; another on the armed forces; yet others on the education system, research, the arts, and at least a volume or two on the religious life, as well as some treatment of sporting, leisure, recreational activities, youth movements, and so on. In this encyclopaedic work, kinship would have an important, and indeed vital place. Its absolute importance as the institution within which people are

130

born, mate, and die is unimpaired by the rise of the modern industrial state in all its complexity; its relative importance, however, would appear to be affected by the fact that there are so many other social structures in addition to the family, and in their way of comparable importance to it.

One of the things that happen in societies which are going through the process of structural differentiation is that people learn to bring their new roles into relation with the roles they occupy in the kinship system. Although it is possible to sum it up in one simple sentence, this is, in fact, an extremely complex process, and there are many ways in which the relation between roles may be sought. Sometimes the adjustment is smooth and free from conflict. For example, a Nigerian peasant may find that he can fulfil his obligation to provide his kin with resources (his wife and children with food and clothing, for example) by growing a cash crop according to the procedures urged upon him by the government agricultural extension officer. From one point of view, such a man would be called an innovator, since he is adopting the technological innovation of growing (say) cocoa or cotton; from another point of view his behaviour is highly traditional, since his motive is the thoroughly old-fashioned one of doing his duty to his family.[4] (This quite realistic and even commonplace example, by the way, does much to invalidate the commonly drawn opposition between 'traditional' and 'modern', as discussed more fully in chapter 10.)

As a second and somewhat more complex instance of a relation between traditional kinship and modern industry, we may take the Tonga of Malawi as described by van Velsen. At the time of his field work in the early 1950s, van Velsen found that between 60 and 75 per cent of adult males were absent, most of them working in the mines in Rhodesia and South Africa. They did not take their wives and children with them, for reasons which, he says, 'are corroborated by the literature on urban conditions for Africans'; and for the same reasons, most men wanted to return home when they retired. Although on the face of it such a system of labour migration might appear grossly disruptive of traditional kinship and village life, van Velsen thought otherwise. Men could rely on their kinsfolk to look after their wives and children, while at the same time they remitted home considerable amounts of their miners' pay for the benefit of their families and kin. They performed services for kinsfolk, especially in the employment situation, by providing them with contacts, introductions to employment, and papers (genuine or forged) to facilitate their entry to South Africa. At the same time, they relied upon their own claims to status and land in the village being kept for them, and took part in the politics of village feuding to that end. 'It is within this framework that Tonga hold gardens, marry, have children, occupy political office, seek for protection of their rights — in brief, expect security in life.'[5]

This brings us to a third point. In the partially differentiated societies with which this book is concerned, although the institutions of the modern world

131

may have begun to take root it may not be possible yet for all to avail themselves of their services. In central Africa in the 1950s, clearly men could not look to a system of state old age pensions to maintain them in old age, for there were none. Nor was commercial life assurance a practicable alternative for them, any more than it is for the working class in a rich industrial society. Although there were certainly banks operating in the region at that time, yet for almost equally obvious reasons it was unusual to say the least for African mine workers to handle their money through a bank account. Similarly, representative local government institutions of a modern sort could hardly be said to exist. As a consequence, people's needs to borrow, save, and mobilize capital, to assert and maintain their rights to land, and to secure their future, were met by exploiting the kinship network rather than through the institutions we think of as typical of a modern society. This particular instance will, perhaps, serve to illustrate the general point made already — that in such societies people use kinship to gain their ends because that is all they have.

So in changing societies there are new demands on the kinship system — which is only a more abstract way of saying that people make new demands on their kinsfolk, and respond to their kinsfolk's demands in new ways and with new resources.

This formulation of the problem, if it is true and fruitful, poses a number of questions to be answered by empirical research in societies undergoing change in the modern world. What is the nature of the new demands which people make of each other, the new needs which they seek to satisfy and the ends they seek to gain through the kinship network? How well or how adequately does the existing kinship system enable people to meet those needs or gain those ends? What new resources have people at their disposal in the fulfilment of old or new expectations in their kinship roles? And how far do these changes promote change in the kinship system itself? The last is the biggest and in some ways the most difficult question. In most of the foregoing, we have assumed that — for the time being at any rate, and in the early stages of industrialization — other institutions grow but the kinship system continues to operate along existing patterns. Broadly this assumption is probably justified, too, as a first approximation, for as a matter of observation it seems to be the case that family and kinship institutions change rather slowly, showing indeed a rather massive continuity compared with the more rapid changes taking place elsewhere in the social system. Nevertheless, changes in the family and kinship do occur, and are an important subject of study.

The family and industrialization in western societies

The relation between the family and industrialization is well illustrated by recent research in the social history of our own society, although, as will appear, this presents certain special features which are different from other societies undergoing industrialization at the present time. The special features of western European kinship, which were, of course, carried by migrants to North America and other areas – Australia, New Zealand, white South Africa – may be characterized as follows. First, kinship is bilateral, that is, descent is traced equally on the father's and the mother's side. Bilateral descent is reflected in kinship terminologies (sets of names for kin, like uncle and cousin) which are symmetrical – for example, in the English language both father's brother and mother's brother are called 'uncle'. Bilateral descent is also associated with an absence of corporate, or potentially corporate, kin-groups such as clans or lineages, which characterize societies in which kinship is reckoned at least for some purposes on one side rather than the other. The set of individuals whom a person in our society recognizes as being (as we say) 'related' to himself is accordingly properly called a kindred; brothers and sisters have the same kindred, but otherwise each individual has a kindred different from other people's including his own relatives. Kindreds are not groups, and cannot become groups or act as groups. Further, in our society marriage is monogamous, and has in all probability always been so, even before the pagan tribes of north-west Europe were converted to Christianity. A monogamous marriage sets up a household in which, by a strong tradition, there is normally only one housewife. Although young married couples may in some cases live in the households of one or other's parents, such an arrangement is regarded as exceptional and temporary, justified only in special circumstances such as housing shortage or a loss of domicile by the young couple in some emergency. The nuclear family household of a married couple and their dependent children is regarded as a more or less independent economic unit, responsible for its own budgeting and catering, and though husband and wife can usually rely from time to time on help from related households, especially in time of emergency, normally they regard themselves as economically independent, and are so regarded by their own kinsfolk. Certainly, related households do not normally pool their resources or regard the income of other households as being at their disposal as a matter of right. It needs to be emphasized how distinctive these patterns are, compared with the kinship systems of other societies.

An emphasis on the right of the nuclear family household to manage its own affairs without too much interference from kinsfolk does not, of course, imply that people in western societies lose touch with their kinsfolk altogether. Even in theory this is an unlikely proposition, for the ties of affection which are formed between parents and their children, and between siblings, persist into adult life; and when the children marry and become parents in their turn, they tend strongly to maintain links with their parents and siblings, who are the grandparents and uncles and aunts of the new generation. Ties between siblings' children, who are all classed as cousins in the English terminology, exist and are recognized, though it may often be the case that

133

parents think their children are in closer touch with their cousins than is in fact the case. As the generations go on, ties between related households tend to become weaker; even first cousins may, in Goode's apt phrase, be little more than 'ascriptive friends',[6] while second cousins may hardly know of each other's existence. Nevertheless, research has shown the importance of kinship ties outside the nuclear family in western societies, and Parsons' phrase about 'the isolation of the nuclear family' was certainly an unfortunate and misleading one.[7] Thus Firth found that households in London typically recognized around 100–200 people as kin, and could name up to 150 of them.[8] The well-known studies of Willmott and Young have shown the importance of visits and contacts, especially between married women and their mothers;[9] while a recent study by Colin Bell has shown the extent of the support, both financial and in help in emergencies, which middle-class families received from their wider kin, especially the spouses' parents,[10] and Townsend's survey indicates that the great majority of old people are looked after by their middle-aged children.[11]

But, though other kin are not lost sight of, and relations with them are important, nevertheless the emphasis is on the monogamous nuclear family as the residential group in daily interaction, with its own independent day-to-day catering and financial provision. As has been suggested in chapter 2, these patterns were associated in the pre-industrial history of our own society with rather small households, late marriage, and small numbers of children. Recent research is further tending to show that scarcely any households in pre-industrial Europe and colonial America were of a 'compound' or 'extended' type, including, for example, the married children and grand-children of the household head, or the widowed parent of the husband or wife. Impressions to the contrary, and suggestions in the older literature that extended or compound family households were common in former times, are now seen to be quite wrong. On the contrary, it is becoming clear that though very little change took place in the average size of the house-hold, if anything it tended to increase, not decrease, during the industrialization period.[12]

Some other features of the pre-industrial family in our own society are those related to the tradition of 'service'. As has been suggested, it seems to be the case that people never employed their own kinsfolk as servants in our society. Accordingly, the families of the well-to-do — the gentry and aristo-cracy in the country, the masters and merchants in towns — employed people of lower social class or 'estate', so that the households of the poor were depleted in numbers as some of their members, especially adolescents and young adults, left home to go into service. In this context, of course, although service included domestic service, it included also many other forms of labour; agricultural workers on the home farm of a landed estate, apprentices and journeymen in a town master's establishment, were alike regarded as 'servants' along with the butler, the cook, and the dairymaid. Further, many western European countries (such as England, Holland, and Iberia) had a maritime tradition, in which for centuries some men ventured in sailing ships on long voyages, lasting in some instances for years. Another form of service involving men in long absences from home was military; men-at-arms, mercenaries, or soldiers of fortune were probably few in number, but the existence of this form of service constituted a possibility for young men and heightened the feeling that leaving home to seek one's fortune was a proper thing for a young man to do. Indeed, some people, especially men, probably spent their whole lives in service. Others might leave it after a while — the women to get married, some men to take up a claim to land vacated by the death or 'retirement' of a father. Nor was 'service' confined to the lower classes. The sons and daughters of well-to-do families might enter more honorific forms of service in households other than their own during their adolescence or early adulthood; this during the Middle Ages the sons of the gentry became pages and later knights in the service of lords other than their own fathers, while at a later period in English history a genteel young lady might become a governess or companion in another household.

The important point is that a tradition of 'service' in pre-industrial western European societies meant that there was a relatively smooth transition to employment in industry. There was certainly nothing new in the West about young men and women leaving home, fending for themselves, seeking their fortune (according to what might be called the Dick Whittington syndrome), establishing themselves before marrying, and assuming responsibility for the finance of their own households when married.

One effect of the rise of industry, which has already been suggested in chapter 2, may well have been to make earlier marriages possible. By increasing the number of children born to each marriage, this may in turn have raised the birth-rate, and it may also be partly responsible for the rise in the average size of households that characterized the industrialization period. It may also have been the case, however, that the rise of industry made it possible for teen-age children to work while still living at home, instead of going out into resident service, and to stay at home until they married.

This is shown particularly clearly in a study by Michael Anderson of family life in the Lancashire cotton town of Preston in the nineteenth century.[13] To judge from contemporary pronouncements in books and in evidence before Parliamentary committees, the conclusion might well be drawn that family life was disintegrating and in danger of imminent collapse under the stresses of industrialization. A particular occasion for alarm was the threat by young people to leave home and move out into lodgings, or share houses with friends — 'that they may be more at liberty to follow their own inclinations', as one witness put it; and to quote another, 'the result of this precocious independence is, of course, the utter relaxation of all bonds of domestic

135

control'. An examination of the census returns, however, showed that the proportion of young persons living at home with their parents was considerably higher in industrial Preston than it was in agricultural villages in Lancashire. The fact seemed to be that young men and women in Preston indeed stayed at home as long as it suited them – they could live more cheaply at home while working in the cotton mills, in contrast to the living-in type of service which was traditional in pre-industrial society, and still the norm in the nearby rural areas. Another way in which people made use of their family relations to meet the new needs of industrial life was the practice of having a grandmother living in as a resident baby-minder while mother went out to work – female labour, of course, being specially important in the textile industry generally. This certainly suited the grandmothers, and it also saved mothers the expense of putting their small children into the care of child-minders who did it for a living.

Anderson demonstrates that in 'critical life situations' generally, there was an almost complete absence of viable alternatives to the kinship system as a source of help. This was true not only of Preston families, but also of migrants, who were seen as making positive efforts to build up and maintain a kinship net in the town – despite, again, the widely held view that migration disrupts kinship bonds.

Some other changes in the family have also taken place in western societies like our own, and have been analysed in the published research. One important area of change is demographic; the lengthening of life in recent decades, the tendency to slightly earlier marriage, and fewer children mean that women may expect motherhood to be an episode rather than a life's work. With longer to live after the last child is married, and with a greater expectation too of the husband's life, the tendency for old people to live in independent households away from their married children is enhanced. Women may moreover look forward to an opportunity to resume work after motherhood ceases to demand their whole time and attention, which is normally when the youngest child starts school. Concurrently with this has been a tendency for women to have a more equal share of responsibility, so that family decisions are made by husband and wife in partnership rather than by an authoritarian husband alone. This is related to an emphasis on individual choice of marriage partner, in a society in which the field of choice is wide. In large-scale industrial societies, young people meet a large number of potential marriage partners – at school, in the neighbourhood, at work, and in the milieu of recreational and leisure activities – and in these circumstances patterns of selection, 'dating' and mating, are seen as a search for the 'right' person, with the expectation of a high standard of mutual compatibility, shared attitudes and tastes, and personal affection, all of which is expressed in the enormously influential cult of 'love'. Marriage partners, that is, expect of each other not only sexual relations and competence in performing traditional

136

household tasks, but also companionship, similar political and religious opinions, similar tastes in leisure activities, and so forth. In marriage, the extent to which men's and women's roles are segregated appears to be somewhat variable, and to depend to some extent on the involvement of husband and wife respectively with networks of social relationships outside the home.[14] On the whole, though, there has probably been an increased acceptance of the need for men to perform household tasks formerly thought of as exclusively women's. Finally, though the last Roman Catholic bastions have yet to fall, most industrial countries have now instituted laws and practices which permit divorce as a safeguard against the breakdown of marital relations in an area of life in which individuals tend to have many eggs — emotional and financial — in one basket; and divorce rates, though not by any means equal in the major industrial countries, do not differ by more than a factor of four between the highest and the lowest.[15]

It would appear, then, that characteristics and trends such as have been described are related to the circumstances and conditions of life in an industrial society. If households are small, then resources are concentrated on a few people, rather than dissipated among a large group of people entitled to share. This favours attitudes of individual thrift and self-help, the accumulation of capital, and the education of children. Family-limitation practices are likely to appeal to people brought up in such traditions; in many cases these appear to have existed in such societies in their pre-industrial history, as already noted in chapter 2, and in all cases they have found acceptance in the modern period. Moreover, the tradition of moving out of the household in search of opportunities for individual self-advancement, which characterized all the early-industrializing societies, is clearly related to the rise of new opportunities for employment in industry, and the need for mobility of labour, especially in the early stages, and especially from country to town.

Is it just coincidence that the particular kinship system which happened to exist in western Europe, and was carried to America and other countries settled by Europeans, was associated with an early industrial revolution in this way? If 'Euramerica' were the only instance, then we might well be inclined to suspect coincidence, for this was in a sense a single culture area, with rather marked similarities in the basic kinship system, and a number of other common cultural features. A case of particular interest here might appear to be that of Israel, which is different from 'Euramerica' or 'the West' in at least one important respect, namely that of religion. However, the settlement of Israel largely by Jews from industrial countries in Europe, and the affinities in both history and doctrine between Judaism and Christianity, would lead us to regard Israel as only a partial exception, and in many important ways a part of the single culture area in question.

But there is one other early-industrializing society whose remoteness from western Europe, previous isolation from the rest of the world, and general cultural dissimilarity in terms of language, religion, and other important institutions make it inconceivable that there could be any connection. That society is, of course, Japan, and the similarity of the Japanese family and kinship system to those of the West, despite wide differences in other aspects of culture, makes it a crucial case giving powerful support to W. J. Goode's thesis that there is a 'fit' between an industrial society and a kinship system of the type I have outlined.

The family and industrialization in Japan

Some of the relevant background factors affecting the family and society in Japan have already been outlined in chapter 2. In the traditional kinship system as described by Chie Nakane, the basic unit was the *ie* or *iye*, a household headed by a man who exercised exclusive control of the household property.[16] The household head was succeeded, in his lifetime as a rule, by one man, normally his son; succession and inheritance were never divided, and there was no joint family or corporate lineage among whom property might be divided or who might exercise joint control. If the household head had no son, then a son-in-law might be designated as successor (a process confusingly called 'adoption' in some of the older literature in the English language); in rare cases an unrelated person such as a servant might be designated as successor. The object was clear; it was to maintain the *ie* as what English lawyers might describe as 'a corporation with perpetual succession', a going concern in economic terms, capable of providing its members with a living, including most importantly its retired members, the former household head and his wife. A sharp distinction was made between the successor son and other sons, and this naturally led to rivalry and jealousy; Nakane quotes a Japanese proverb to the effect that 'a sibling is the beginning of a stranger'. Non-successor sons were expected to fend for themselves and set up new households. They might expect a certain amount of family help in doing so, but among the peasant classes there was very little help that could be given, while among the wealthier classes the share of non-successor sons in the family property was traditionally minimal. The 1947 Civil Code reforms attempted to remedy what had, from a modern point of view, become a source of injustice by giving all children, even daughters, equal rights to inherit. Both Nakane and Fujiko Isono report, however, that the new provisions are fully effective only among urban families with modern ideas; in the country the family land is still in fact transmitted undivided, and non-successor sons in effect waive their rights in order to avoid the fragmentation of holdings which would clearly be uneconomic and disadvantageous to all concerned.[17] In a society undergoing industrialization as rapidly as Japan, it is possible in many cases for non-successor sons to move into towns

138

and get jobs in industry, while many country-dwellers also find non-agricultural work; according to estimates by Mrs Isono, although around 1960 there were six million families on the land, only a quarter of them were living exclusively by agriculture, and for the majority their non-agricultural earnings exceeded their agricultural income.

Traditionally, the households set up by non-successor sons were regarded as 'branches' (an exact translation of the Japanese term *bunke*) of the original 'stem' household (*honke*), and a set of households thus linked called a *dozoku*. (Some confusion occurred here too as a result of the mistranslation of this term as 'lineage'.) The links were apparently partly sentimental, arising from the natural tendency for people to keep in touch with their parents and siblings, and partly ritual, and family reunions occurred in connection with the ancestor cult. Only aristocrats, however, maintained long genealogies, and for most commoner families there were only two ancestral ceremonies — one for the founder of the stem household, the other for that of the branch.

Japanese kinship terminology, moreover, is perfectly bilateral. It is most unusual in this respect, which constitutes a rather striking similarity with western societies. It is, in fact, very rare to find a non-European language into which English kinship terms like 'aunt' and 'cousin' can be directly and accurately translated and vice versa; the only difference, indeed, between Japanese and English in this respect is that Japanese has four terms for siblings, distinguishing elder from younger brothers and sisters, where English has only two. Moreover, the Japanese word *shinrui* signifies the circle of recognized kinsfolk which in sociological terms we call the cognatic kindred — the circle we ourselves recognize and in vernacular English call our 'relatives'. There are no clans or lineages in Japanese society; although, as has been stated, the *dozoku* was at first thought by British and American social anthropologists to be a lineage structure, this is clearly a misapprehension. Its constituent units are households, not individuals. It is not an exogamous group — both parallel-cousin and cross-cousin marriages may take place within it. Servants' households, too, may be included in a *dozoku*, though unrelated.

Moreover, Japanese marriage is monogamous — legally so since 1898, in practice traditionally so before that. The essential rule seems to have been that, just as a household could have only one male head, so it could have only one mistress. Extra-marital sex relations were not unknown, and prostitution was a traditional institution; but though a man might have a mistress, and might father children outside marriage, it seems clear that even if he brought his mistress into his household (and a faithful wife was supposed to submit with fortitude to such behaviour on her husband's part) her status would officially be that of a servant, not a co-wife. The status of the mistress of the household was regarded as unassailable, and traditionally she would exercise a petty tyranny especially over her daughter-in-law, the wife of the successor

139

son. On the retirement of the household head, however, in a simple ceremony of handing over a wooden spoon, that tyranny was brought to an end and the daughter-in-law became the unchallenged mistress of the household in her turn. The strength of traditional feelings on this area of family life may be judged from the controversy over the provisions of the 1898 Meiji Civil Code, which in attempting to modernize the law of marriage and the family prohibited marriages, *inter alia*, of men under thirty and women under twenty-five without their parents' consent. This was bitterly opposed by traditionalists, on the ground that marriage without the parents' consent ought not to be legal at *any* age!

Some changes in Japanese family and kinship have taken place, and continue to take place in the conditions of modern life. Vogel in his study of the urban professional middle class — the 'salary-men' — reports a weakening of the *ie* ideal, though this was a matter of fear and apprehension among old people who wondered who would look after them in their old age, and this was a point also strongly emphasized by Isono. Traditions of arranged marriage were still strong, though opposed by many young people who were seeking the same sort of freedom of choice and search for 'love' as their counterparts in western industrial countries. Isono reports that the understanding parents of a young couple who fall in love might try to disguise a love-match as an arranged marriage, in order to placate older and more traditionally minded relatives. Vogel, however, found that not all young people were really wholehearted in their attachment to 'love' and freedom of choice. While that might suit some, there were others — 'the over-protected, the bashful, the cautious, those with high standards, those with a proud family history, and the "left-overs"' — who might be quite willing to acquiesce in arrangements or suggestions made by their parents. There was, however, a difference; where the old institution was unequivocally one of arranged marriage, the new practices consisted rather of arranged introductions for a formal first meeting or 'interview', after which the young couple find out for themselves whether they will be suitable marriage partners. Isono puts it quite clearly: 'The favourable attitude to the "interview" is not a remnant of traditional mentality, but *a rational utilization of a traditional practice*' (italics mine).

Modern-minded Japanese families were not inclined to take the ancestor cult very seriously, and there was little that a modern household head had that he did not have as a husband and father. Vogel states accordingly that 'the nuclear family has replaced the *ie* as the basic social unit in Mamachi' (a 'salary-man' residential area).[18]

Although Japanese family and kinship organization was different in important respects from that of western Europe, therefore, there were also some striking similarities. In both, descent was bilateral and marriage was in practice monogamous. Although traditionally many Japanese households

140

were of an extended or three-generation composition, with the former head and his wife living on in retirement, they were nevertheless small. There was no joint family, nor was there a clan or lineage structure. Moreover, there was a strong tradition for non-successor sons to move out and fend for themselves, with little or no economic help from the stem family; and their households appear to have been financially independent. Even though there were some differences in detail, then, in essentials the pre-industrial Japanese kinship system, like that of the West, made for a relatively smooth transition to the conditions of an industrial society, and must be counted as a facilitating factor in industrialization. Changes that have occurred, especially among the well-to-do, modern-minded, urban population have tended to make the Japanese family even more like that of the West, while there is some evidence too of the ways in which people have been able to make use of traditional institutions to meet their needs in modern conditions, like the survival, or even the revival, of the arranged marriage in the new form of the 'interview'.

W. J. Goode's two theses – 'fit' and 'convergence'

The foregoing summary of the development of the family in modern industrial societies, including Japan, accordingly tends to support the first of the two major theses advanced by W. J. Goode in his monumental study *World Revolution and Family Patterns*, namely, that there is a 'fit' between the conjugal family and the modern industrial system. Goode uses the term 'conjugal' as a shorthand expression to signify the whole complex of characteristics which have been mentioned above – an emphasis on the nuclear family as the normal residential and catering unit, bringing up children and managing its own affairs in relative financial independence; monogamy, relatively free choice of marriage partner, egalitarianism in relations between spouses, some provision for divorce as a safeguard against marital breakdown; bilateral descent, an absence of clan or lineage structures and of joint family systems involving the right of other kin to share and interfere in the nuclear family household. His second thesis is that, accordingly, as other societies undergo industrialization, their family patterns may be expected to 'converge' upon the conjugal type.

Goode investigates these hypotheses by means of a comprehensive review of the available evidence from most of the major continents and culture areas of the world – 'the West', Arabic Islam, Africa south of the Sahara, India, China, and Japan. The coverage is not quite world-wide; in particular, Goode notes with regret the paucity of studies on eastern Europe and on Latin America, while the Islamic world outside the Arab states is also omitted. Further, in some cases it is possible to deal with the material from a single large state, as with India (Pakistan being excluded), China, and Japan. In others, however, an area consists of a number of states, as in the case of

Europe, Arabic Islam, and Africa. Goode has amassed a wide variety of evidence from these areas, including laws (together with the reports of government commissions on family law and related topics), official statistics in so far as they exist (and Goode is properly sceptical of much of this material), social surveys of every kind, public opinion polls, and the field reports of social anthropologists. The evidence is classified under a set of fairly standardized broad headings, though these are adapted as the circumstances of particular countries require. They include practices relating to the choice of mate, plural marriage (polygyny or polyandry), marriages with relatives, and age at marriage, the birth-rate and fertility, and related factors such as infanticide, abortion, and the use of contraceptives; the extended family, household, clan, and kin network beyond the nuclear family; divorce, and the remarriage of widows and divorced persons; the position of women in the wider society, women's work and women's rights, equality of the sexes; and relations internal to the family, especially those between spouses. Sometimes it proves difficult to separate matter under two or more of these headings; thus, for instance, the betrothal or marriage of children comes obviously under 'age at marriage', but it also affects choice of mate, and it almost inevitably has a bearing on the position of parents and others in the wider kin network whose authority over children is especially manifested in their ability to choose marriage partners for them before they can exercise an independent choice.

From this wide and thorough survey of the literature, Goode's conclusion is that, where changes in the family are taking place at all, there is indeed a convergence. Thus in many countries in recent decades laws have been enforced prohibiting such traditional practices as the betrothal and marriage of infants, and bringing the ages at which marriage can legally be contracted into line with those regarded as appropriate in western countries. There has been a general tendency for the choice of marriage partner to become more that of the individuals concerned, and for arranged marriages to decline in importance. Very large 'extended family' households have been shown to exist more as ideal than reality in most civilizations, and modern changes have tended towards the nuclear family households as the norm. Relations with wider kin persist and are important, even in the West, but the power and indeed the inclination of kinsfolk to interfere in the running of, or share the benefits of, the nuclear family household have been reduced. Where divorce was easy and divorce rates high, it has become more difficult and rates have fallen; where it was hard or shameful, it has tended to lose its stigma and become somewhat more frequently resorted to.

However, such changes are by no means uniform and by no means rapid. Thus in India, though infant marriage has been abolished, there is no general acceptance of the idea that young adults have the right to meet each other, engage in courtship, and decide for themselves whom to marry and when.

On the contrary, arranged marriages are still normal and girls are strictly chaperoned. Caste endogamy is still the general practice, most people support the joint family at least in principle, and though divorce has been legalized it remains hard and (apparently) shameful for Hindus. *Sati* is now a thing of the past and most people favour the remarriage of widows, but it is still far from the case that women mingle freely with men in most walks of life. Similarly, the evidence from Africa suggests that little or no change has taken place in such institutions as polygyny, clan and lineage structures, traditional courtship, or divorce practices.

The qualifications 'where changes are taking place at all' is an important one, therefore, and in a good many areas of family life we have to report no change. Perhaps the strongest point to be made in favour of Goode's thesis, however, is that there appear to be no contrary changes. Either there is no change in family patterns, or there is a change in the direction of a convergence on the conjugal family; but nowhere is there a case where change has taken place in the opposite direction. Nowhere, for example, has there been a tendency for parents to exercise *more* control over their children's marriages, for the wider kin network to be *strengthened*, for *more* men to take plural wives, or for hard and shameful divorce to get even harder and more shameful.[19]

In general, it would seem likely that the family is the most conservative of institutions, and there are indeed good reasons for believing this to be the case. The personal relations which arise in a family setting are lifelong relations; in particular, the relations between parents and their children tend to set up in infancy patterns of thought and feeling, as well as overt behaviour, which persist till the death of the parents and even after it, in so far as their memory is venerated and as people imagine how their parents would react to new situations and problems. In the same way, the most obvious model which people have of the relations between spouses is afforded by their observations of their own parents' behaviour. While they may find this not altogether attractive, and resolve to modify it in their own marital relations, nevertheless it affords a set of reference-points which may be modified but are unlikely to be abandoned altogether. Similarly, the first and most obvious lesson people get in relations between parents and children is derived from the way they themselves were brought up. Again, they may resolve to act differently themselves when they become parents; but again, the set of reference-points provided by their own upbringing is likely to persist at least while they are bringing up their own children. Such considerations alone seem likely to make the pace of change in family relations a slow one compared with the rapid changes that take place in the technological, economic, and political spheres in the modern world. For the same reason, it has often been suggested that an important function of the family in modern society is to provide the individual with a haven of refuge where he can

143

rely on warmly diffuse relations, in contrast to the specific, instrumental relations of work; a small-scale group, in contrast to the large-scale world or organizations outside; a world dominated by affection rather than calculation, and above all a world where all these things can be relied on to persist for long periods in contrast to the bewilderingly rapid changes of the world outside.[20] We could accordingly almost suggest that it is *part of the function* of the family in the modern world to provide a set of personal relations whose stability over long periods can be counted upon. Thus the findings of L. W. Doob suggest that people changing from old to new ways retain traditional attitudes to the family; I refer to this work in more detail in chapter 10.[21] Further evidence on the same point is afforded by a perceptive study of immigrants from Islamic countries to Israel by the late Yonina Talmon-Garbier, who stated that 'the initial reaction to social change is neither attenuation and decline nor mere persistence but an upsurge of kinship solidarity and heightened commitment'; and she found that 'the stability and security of kin bonds generate flexibility and receptiveness to change while instability and insecurity generate defensiveness and rigidity'.[22]

For all these reasons, then, we should expect change in the patterns of family behaviour to be relatively slow.

As has been suggested, there are strong reasons to agree with Goode that the particular forms of the family that prevailed in the West, and also in Japan, were such as to facilitate industrialization in those countries.

If this is the case, then it follows that change in the family may be expected to be more radical in those societies with other kinship systems. While there may well be a 'convergence', that is, the kinship systems of these societies may come to resemble those of the industrial nations, nevertheless the discontinuities are likely to be sharper than they were in 'Euramerica' or Japan. Further, for a time at least, the transitional forms of the family may differ substantially from those of the industrial nations, in relation to the widely different traditions which form their starting-points for change.

SUGGESTION FOR FURTHER READING

W. J. Goode, *World Revolution and Family Patterns*, Glencoe, Ill.: Free Press, 1963; paperback edition with a new preface, 1970

7 Economic development and development economics

Since the second world war there has been a great upsurge of interest on the part of economists in the problems to which this book is addressed. As the veteran economist J. E. Meade put it, the economic problems of industrial nations − balance-of-payments deficits, inflation, and the like − have become puzzles for the 'tough-minded' rather than presenting a basic appeal to the 'tender-hearted'.

There is, however, one economic problem which today presents the same sort of challenge as that presented to my generation by the mass unemployment of the 1930s − namely, the hideously great, and alas, ever widening disparity between the standards of living in the rich, developed countries and the poor, underdeveloped countries of the world ... For this reason it is the study of problems of economic development in under-developed countries which − quite rightly in my opinion − nowadays exercises the greatest attraction for the 'tender-hearted' to become economists.[1]

Economists who are attracted to this branch of their science tend accordingly to take it for granted that 'the poverty of nations' is an evil to be combated and overcome − a value-judgment with which few will quarrel. The problem is how. The task of the development economist is to provide the knowledge and understanding upon which effective action can be based to make people in the poor countries better off. That knowledge and understanding fall logically into two stages − first, the analysis of the causes of economic backwardness, and secondly an understanding of the conditions in which economic growth occurs. The first question is: Why are they so poor? When we have answered that, it is possible to go on to answer the second: What are the conditions in which economic initiatives are likely to be successful in inducing economic growth of the sort that will deliver them from their poverty?

So development economics is a 'how-to' subject − an applied science like engineering rather than a pure science like physics; an 'art' (in the wider old-fashioned sense of the word) like medicine rather than a science like physiology. Like medicine, though, it has a scientific component; just as scientific medicine from the seventeenth century onwards has been far more effective in combating suffering and death than its earlier counterpart, so it is hoped will the trained mind of the economist have something better to offer than the untrained hunches of political leaders. Many development economists are economic advisers to governments or have spent some time in that capacity, and they are especially concerned as expatriate experts in drawing up development plans for the governments of poor countries. In consequence, some tend to get into government-centred, public-policy-oriented ways of thinking in which the question 'What is to be done?' tends to be construed as 'What should the government do?' Books on development planning, indeed, have greatly enriched the literature and tend to enhance the 'how-to', prescriptive nature of the subject.

Development economists agree that economic development is not to be measured simply in terms of G.N.P. A country's G.N.P. per head may increase, for instance, simply with a rise in the price of its export staple, though no change has taken place in the conditions of its production, and nothing is happening elsewhere in the economy. Conversely, there may be technological innovation and capital accumulation without much to show for it yet in increased incomes, especially in the early stages – or the gains may be eaten up in population increase. Accordingly they write rather of 'the transformation of a tradition- or authority-bound society into a modern, innovating, experimenting, progressing one'.[2] And perhaps it is not altogether fanciful to see an analogy with psychiatry. Like madness, economic back-wardness is an unmistakable and shocking phenomenon, yet it eludes precise definition. And there is an even closer similarity when they locate the trouble at least partly *in the mind*: 'The (vicious) circle to which our analysis has led us may perhaps lay claim to a privileged place in the hierarchy of these circles inasmuch as it alone places the difficulties of development back where all difficulties of human action begin and belong: in the mind.'[3]

The 1951 United Nations (Arthur Lewis) report

Interest on the part of economists in these problems was both signalled and stimulated by a report to the United Nations in 1951 by a group of experts headed by Professor W. A. Lewis (now Sir Arthur Lewis), 'Measures for the Economic Development of Under-developed Countries'.[4] True to the pre-occupations of economists of their generation, they devoted a good deal of attention to unemployment and underemployment, and their recommendations were 'regarded as a counterpart to ... measures required to achieve full employment in economically more developed countries'. 'Under-developed', the term used in the title, was interpreted as referring to countries whose per capita real incomes were low compared with the United States, Canada, Australia, and western Europe; 'an adequate synonym would be "poor countries"'. Measures to be taken included those by governments of developing nations and by international action. 'Economic progress will not occur unless the atmosphere is favourable to it. The people must desire

146

progress, and their social, economic, legal and political institutions must be favourable to it.' Property institutions, for example, must be such as to create incentives, and legal institutions must protect the rights of tenants to the benefit derived from their improvement of the land. The public sector must perform all the tasks which in developed countries had come to be thought of as its traditional sphere, and must indeed perform them particularly well in underdeveloped countries, providing a sound infra-structure of roads and other communications, education, public health, and other public and social services. In addition, public action might be necessary in such fields as market research, geological surveys and prospecting for minerals, the establishment of new industries, and the creation of financial institutions to mobilize savings and channel them into 'desirable private enterprise' notably in the form of capital for the small private farmer and artisan. The importance of education was heavily stressed, and shown to be wider in scope than the mere training of technicians. In general, because the market might mis-allocate resources, governments must be alert to intervene in fields beyond that traditionally allotted to the public sector. Some guarded but favourable remarks were made about the desirability of fertility control.

Measures to be taken by international action included, as a first priority, arrangements for stable terms of trade, favourable to developing countries. There was a good deal of criticism of the 'unfair' policies of some industrial countries in subsidizing the home production of commodities which could be produced more cheaply in underdeveloped countries. For example, sub-sidized beet sugar production in Europe deprived tropical countries of part of their market for an important export – a point often made in later criticisms of the economic policies of European countries. Some industrial nations were further accused of encouraging, and even subsidizing, exports of primary commodities produced in competition with underdeveloped countries. Secondly, the report called for the transfer of capital from rich to poor countries on a scale 'far beyond what is currently envisaged', thereby taking the lead in calling for what we now call Aid.

W. W. Rostow and the stages of economic growth[5]

The contribution of Walt Whitman Rostow was based on his earlier work on the development of the British economy in the nineteenth century, which led him to identify five stages or categories within which, he says, all societies 'in their economic dimensions' lie: 'the traditional society, the preconditions for take-off, the take-off, the drive to maturity, and the age of high mass-consumption'. The preconditions include a shift out of agriculture and an enlargement of the scale of economic relations; in recent history this has occurred 'not endogenously but from some external intrusion by more advanced societies ... [which] shocked the traditional society and began

147

or hastened its undoing'. Family limitation is at least foreshadowed, and there is a shift from ascribed status to individual ability, a disposition to invest, and a spread of rational scientific and technological ideas.

The take-off is marked by a big rise in net investment, from 5 to over 10 per cent of net national income. Rostow identifies this as occurring in Britain between 1783 and 1802, the United States 1843–60, Japan 1878–1900, and India and China since 1950. But at this stage modern technology is applied only in a few 'leading sectors' – cotton in England, the railway in the United States – and the requisite personal qualities of enterprise in these sectors comes in many cases from a minority who form a leading elite in economic growth. Weber's 'Protestant ethic' is clearly relevant here, and Rostow acknowledges his insight, but remarks that 'John Calvin should not be made to bear quite this weight'. Other enterprising minorities besides the Calvinists have included the Samurai, Parsees, Jews, Russian civil servants, and one might add Chinese and Indian minorities overseas. I return to this point in chapter 11.

In the drive to maturity, some 10 to 20 per cent of the national income is steadily invested, and modern technology extends from the leading sector throughout the economy. Finally, a mature economy can use its resources in three ways – the pursuit of external power; the 'welfare state', redistribution, social security, and leisure; and 'high mass consumption'. This is the age above all of the private motor-car or automobile.

Rostow's book *The Stages of Economic Growth* is sub-titled 'A Non-communist Manifesto', and includes a point-by-point comparison between his own analysis and that of Marx in which he indicates the points on which he dissents from the latter and refers to communism as 'a disease of the transition'. It is not surprising, therefore, that Rostow should have been rejected by Marxist critics for his rejection of Marxism.[6]

Non-Marxist economists, however, have also been critical. Much of this criticism is summed up by Hagen; the stages of growth are not really as clear-cut as Rostow makes them out to be, and the supposed upward surge in the rate of investment turns out to have taken place in only a few countries. England, the Soviet Union, and Japan did, it is true, experience such surges, but elsewhere capital formation occurred more steadily and the division into periods is 'entirely artificial'. Hagen acknowledges, though, that Rostow contributes 'rich and perceptive suggestions of the changes that must occur if a country that was traditional is to become technically progressive'.[7] More fundamentally, Myrdal has attacked Rostow for teleology, that is for imputing to abstractions like 'history', 'society', or a 'nation' human attributes which they cannot possibly possess, especially a capacity for purposive action. This is revealed in phrases like 'the *drive* to maturity' and sentences like '[By 1851] Britain had wholeheartedly transformed itself into an industrial nation.' This leads, Myrdal says, into 'an inherent tendency to play down the importance of policies, or rather to organize them into the predetermined sequence of events'. In other words, Rostow's theories do not distinguish between changes that are *going to happen anyway*, and those that can be *made to happen* by suitable actions, especially on the part of governments.[8]

Balanced versus unbalanced growth

A perennial issue in development economics is concerned with the relative merits of 'balanced growth' on the one hand and a concentration on a 'leading sector' on the other. As long ago as 1943, in an article on development in eastern Europe, Professor Rosenstein-Rodan imagined what would happen if, say, 20,000 underemployed peasants left the land and were all put to work in one large factory making shoes. Their wages would be spent partly on food, and so agricultural production would be stimulated; but only a small proportion would be spent on shoes, and the shoe factory would quickly go bankrupt. If, however, a million underemployed peasants went to work in a thousand factories producing between them the whole range of goods on which workers and peasants spend their earnings, all would prosper. Rosenstein-Rodan accordingly advocated 'the planned creation of a complementary system', or industrialization in 'one big push'.[9] Another advocate of balanced growth was Ragnar Nurkse. Although as he said, 'Kuwait and perhaps Iraq have nothing to worry about', for most of the poorer countries reliance on expansion through world trade in their primary exports has not solved their problems; and he urged rather a balanced pattern of mutually supporting investments in a range of industries in order to create 'a forward momentum of growth'.[10]

Such ideas have been criticized by other development economists as neglecting the possibilities of international trade. Thus if the 20,000 peasants in Rosenstein-Rodan's example had some special advantage, such as cheap good leather or traditional skills and style, then they might sell their shoes in other countries and import their other manufactured wants.[11] Indeed, it is really quite easy to think up a whole set of uneconomic, unprofitable industrial enterprises linked in supply-and-demand relations and say that one has planned a 'complementary system'.[12] Thus an uneconomic hydro-electric scheme may be made to look more economic if an uneconomic cement industry is linked with it. The power from the first turbines is used to manufacture cement for the next dam, while uneconomic factories producing textiles, beer, soap, and so forth can be linked with the scheme as consumers of electric power, and protected by tariffs on an 'infant industries' argument, so concealing the uneconomic nature of the whole.

Thirdly, unbalanced growth — or at any rate an unbalanced economy — is what most poor countries have got, for as has been seen in chapter 4 the 'modern' sector tends to be devoted to primary production for export, with at

149

most some of the initial processing. In a dual economy of this nature, 'investment for exports and for marginal import substitutes, where external economies are presumably negligible, occupies a very large part of total investment. For this entire sector, the "big push" loses its specific justification from external economies.'[13]

This argument is two-edged, however, for it was precisely to get poor countries out of the rut of their dependence on primary export industries, with their weak 'spread effects' (as Myrdal calls them), that Nurkse advocated balanced growth in the first place.

A leading critic of the theory of balanced growth, and an advocate of the opposite policy of 'unbalanced development', is Professor Albert O. Hirschman.[14] The trouble with balanced growth is, he says, that 'its application requires huge amounts of precisely those abilities which we have identified as in very limited supply in underdeveloped countries', namely persons with forward-looking enterprise and managerial skills. Rosenstein-Rodan's thousand factories would need at least a thousand managers; underdeveloped countries just do not have managerial resources in such abundance, and if they had they would not be underdeveloped in the first place. Hirschman agrees with other development economists that 'The grudge against what has become known as the "enclave" type of development is due to [the] ability of primary products from mines, wells, and plantations to slip out of a country without leaving much of a trace in the rest of the economy.' He distinguishes, however, between export enclaves and those devoted to import industries. These are usually located near the ports and in the early stages may consist merely of the assembly of imported components, mixing, packaging, etc.; but he states there are many examples of industrialization working backward from the 'final touches' stage to the local production of intermediate and finally that of basic raw materials.

One of the most characteristic failings of poor countries is a failure to maintain scarce and valuable capital, as represented by 'eroding soils, stalled trucks, leaking roofs, prematurely run-down machines, unsafe bridges, clogged-up irrigation ditches'. For the development economist it is tempting to try to devise schemes that do not require maintenance, or minimize it. In the past such schemes took the form of pyramids, great walls, Roman roads, and the like; but in an age of machinery with moving parts it is hard to find such projects. Moreover, and more fundamentally, says Hirschman, they do nothing for the learning process. Another solution, he suggests, is to go to the opposite extreme, and recommend investment in projects with a 'compulsion to maintain', that is, in which failure to maintain incurs really heavy penalties. For example, in the sphere of transport a failure to maintain aircraft is likely to end in disaster, spectacular crashes in which lives are lost. Failure to maintain roads, however, only leads to inconvenience and annoyance which are spread over many people. In between, failure to

150

maintain railways is more dangerous and more likely to lead to crashes with loss of life than roads, but less so than in the case of aircraft. And so we find, he says, that poor countries run their air lines well, their railways are mediocre, and their roads are usually in a parlous state of disrepair.

Generalizing this solution, perhaps there is something to be said after all for the 'show-piece' type of development like a hydro-electric station, much criticized though such projects have been by other development economists. Such a project will at least be well planned and well maintained because its failure would be public, spectacular, visible, and reflect badly on the prestige of the country and its regime. The many small projects (like loans to progressive farmers for small-scale investment) may all go wrong, but they go wrong unnoticed.

This leads to a further argument for capital-intensive methods. Given that migrant workers, new to industry and to town life, may be inexperienced and inefficient, it may make for greater efficiency and help them to learn if they are employed in machine-paced, process-centred plants and methods, which will generally be capital-intensive ones. The contrast may then become that between efficiency on the production side of the enterprise and inefficiency on the office, administrative side, where low performance may be tolerated and nepotism survive. The efficiency of capital-intensive production may show up that contrast in a way that leads to the improvement of 'the office', and the enhanced efficiency of the administration of industrial enterprises may in turn lead to a situation in which inefficiency and corruption in public administration may no longer be tolerated.

It is along lines such as these that Hirschman advocates unbalanced growth. He agrees with Myrdal (with whose views I deal below) that this will inevitably lead to imbalance between different sections of the community. For example, an industrial region ('the North') may be the scene of growth in contrast to a relatively backward area ('the South'); or an innovative minority ('the Jews') may be enriched before other groups. Hirschman agrees with Myrdal that there are liable to be 'polarization' effects accordingly, as well as 'trickle-down' or 'spread' effects, and where he differs from Myrdal is in his more optimistic assessment that on the whole the 'spread' effects are stronger. The main point he brings out, however, is that economic development is bound to be a matter of tensions, pressures, and disequilibrium.

Nevertheless, for a number of reasons, we do not think it feasible or even desirable to suppress these tensions. In the first place, under-developed countries already operate under the *grand tension* that stems from the universal desire for economic improvement oddly combined with many resistances to change. Much is to be said for breaking down this grand tension, a highly explosive mixture of hopes and fears, into a series of smaller and more manageable tensions.

Governments have a dual task — that of inducing growth, with all the imbalance that it sets in train; and that of restoring balance. Foreign aid should

151

'embolden a country to set out on the path of unbalanced growth'. And economic advisers should be less concerned with establishing priorities than with 'discovering under what pressure people are already operating and toward what forward steps they are already being impelled'.

'Underdevelopment' and the international economy: Celso Furtado

An assumption underlying much work in development economics is that each country's economy is to be regarded as an entity in itself. It may or may not go through a series of stages of development — that is problematic. But it is assumed that the economies of the present-day industrial countries began the process of development earlier than the poor countries, so that there is a time-lag. The poor countries are still poor, just as the now-rich countries were once poor, a century or two ago. Underdevelopment is roughly synonymous with backwardness; and the problem is whether, and if so in what conditions, the poor countries will 'catch up'. As has been seen, it is in the work of Rostow that assumptions of this sort are most explicitly made, but they appear to underlie that of development economists like those I have reviewed above; and they are explicitly disputed by others, to whom I now turn.

As I suggested in chapter 1, a reason for taking the country as the unit of analysis is that it is the unit for which statistics are collected and analysed. More important still perhaps in the present context, it is the area within which a government controls such things as the currency and tariffs, and thereby influences economic life; and it is for the governments of countries that many development economists work as economic advisers. Enough has been said, however, to indicate a proper caution; and the adventitious and even artificial nature of the present-day countries of the world and their boundaries is a theme to which I return below in chapters 9 and 12.

Some development economists are accordingly open to criticism for the narrowness with which they focus on the individual country and its economy. This may be regarded as a case of illegitimate isolation, and it has been made a central point in Marxist critiques of development economics.[15] It is not only Marxists, however, who insist that the poverty of the poor countries has to be seen in relation to a world economy centred in the rich countries; the same point is made among others by Dudley Seers and by Myrdal, with whose work I deal below. As I emphasized in chapter 4, the situation of the present-day poor countries is different from that of the industrial countries at earlier periods in their development in one fundamental respect; they live in the same world as the rich industrial countries, with consequences which include technological dependence and the 'big firm, small country' syndrome.

An economist who has taken this aspect of the matter fully into consideration is Celso Furtado, one of a school of Latin American economists who have been striving in recent years to adapt the framework of traditional economic analysis — classical, Marxist, and Keynesian — to present-day realities in poor countries.[16] For Furtado, 'backwardness' is quite different from 'underdevelopment'. Mere backwardness implies only a basically agricultural economy. Underdevelopment, however, implies the existence of a dualistic economy or structural dualism. Historically this occurred as a result of the expansion of the European industrial economy into already inhabited regions, with the creation of 'hybrid structures, part tending to behave as a capitalist system, part perpetuating the features of the previously existing system'. The insertion of a capitalist wedge might take the form of productive activities intended for export, or a mine controlled by a capitalistic enterprise. Such an economy is characterized by two forms of remuneration for work, two technologies at extremely different levels, and two concepts of the organization of production. Stable equilibrium models are inappropriate, and something more like Myrdal's scheme of cumulative causation is more effective in explaining this case.

The main impulse to growth in such an economy comes from exogenous factors through the activities of the exporting sector. Incomes generated by foreign enterprises in the capitalistic 'wedge' are partly distributed locally in the form of wages and taxes. The rest is remitted to the metropolitan country, and it is this part which 'establishes the dynamic characteristics of the capitalist system'. The really important decisions are about what to do with the profits — whether to remit them out of the poor country, or reinvest them locally, and if so how; and it is these decisions that are made by outsiders.

The resulting lack of capital for local reinvestment under local control, the technological gap, and the abundance of labour which characterize such an economy led Furtado to write of underdevelopment as 'a state of factor unbalance reflecting a lack of adjustment between the availability of factors and the technology of their use, so that it is impossible to achieve full utilization of both capital and labour simultaneously'.

It is not denied that something which can be called development does occur in such circumstances; underdevelopment is not incompatible with development. Indeed, in a country like Brazil there are not two main sectors but three: 'a subsistence structure, a structure oriented mainly towards export, and an industrial nucleus connected with the domestic market and sufficiently diversified to produce a part of the capital goods it needs for its own growth'. The problems of such an economy are many, and they include the small number of people affected by development, the slow decline of the subsistence sector, and chronic balance-of-payments difficulties. Underdevelopment, then, is a specific phenomenon. It is not a necessary

153

stage in the formation of modern capitalistic economies, it cannot be explained by analogy with the past experience of developed economies, and it calls accordingly for an effort to understand it in its own right.

Gunnar Myrdal

Dr Gunnar Myrdal came to the study of 'the poverty of nations' after he had carried out a massive study of race relations in the United States, and then as head of the Economic Commission for Europe had become involved with the problems of regional disparities. From 1957 to 1961, while Fru Alva Myrdal was Swedish ambassador in India, he embarked on a massive study of the economic problems of India and other South Asian countries, which he completed in 1968.[17]

Myrdal set out his general approach in a series of lectures in Cairo in 1955. Regional imbalances can occur on a small scale with, for instance, a mill fire in one of Britain's northern textile towns. Workers lose their jobs, shops lose money, some who are free to do so move away, and the whole place takes on a shabby, run-down appearance. On a bigger scale, whole regions can be depressed or retarded (Tyneside, West Cumberland) while others are booming (Birmingham, West London). Retarded regions have a narrower base for local taxation — in British terminology they 'lose rateable value' — because many firms and shops have closed down, while house prices and rateable values fall. So local authorities must either put up local tax-rates, which will impose further burdens on remaining firms and deter others from coming, or let the standard of public services deteriorate, so that roads in disrepair and undermanned schools deter people from coming or from staying. Meanwhile the regions where economic activity is booming attract migrants, and since migration is always selective — it is always the young adults who move, especially men — the booming areas gain the strongest and most enterprising workers, while the depressed areas are left with a disproportionate burden of dependency. Capital movements, like those of people, have a cumulative effect. In the centres of expansion, increased demand spurs investment, which further increases incomes and stimulates further investment. Trade too operates with a similar bias. The widening of the market favours industries in centres of expansion, especially if they are working under conditions of increasing returns, which Myrdal says is usually the case. The handicrafts and old industries in retarded regions are thwarted accordingly.

There are accordingly strong elements of a vicious circle about this kind of regional imbalance, to which Myrdal gives the name of 'backwash effects'. As we know, it takes very strong and determined action by central governments to redress regional imbalances. Really big inducements have to be paid out of central government funds in the way of tax concessions, employment bonuses, and the like to persuade firms to set up new businesses in depressed areas. The central governments of democratic industrial countries, however, are often prepared to go to such lengths, because even unemployed workers and depressed peasants have the vote; universal suffrage tends to lead to policies favouring poorer regions and poorer classes.

Against 'backwash effects', there are also 'spread effects'; and like other development economists Myrdal sets out the gains which accrue round a centre of expansion from increased outlets for agricultural products, while in regions further away producing raw materials even consumer-goods industries will be given a spur. But, as already noted, Myrdal differs from Hirschman mainly in giving far more weight to the backwash or polarization effects. Moreover, the spread effects are greater in countries which are on the whole richer, because transport and communications are better, people are better educated, and there is a 'more dynamic communion of ideas and values'. Even in Europe regional inequalities are greater in countries like Italy, Turkey, and Spain than they are in Britain or Switzerland, and these inequalities are increasing in the poorer countries while they are diminishing in the richer.

Many of these 'backwash effects' are compounded when instead of regions within a country under a single central government, we are dealing with inequalities between countries. International trade has, in fact, had strong backwash effects, undercutting traditional handicrafts like the weaving and metal-working industries of Asian countries. In the past, capital movements from Europe went to some extent into the export enclaves of countries like India, and also into their public utilities such as railways, but the really big movements of capital were those which were devoted to setting up areas of European settlement in empty or nearly empty areas in the temperate zones. International migration is very limited in scale compared with internal migration within countries, being hampered by nationality laws, immigration restrictions, and in some cases, colour bars.

In general, then, Myrdal held that international boundaries weakened spread effects. Differences in law, administration, *mores*, language, and values 'make national boundaries much more effective barriers to the spread of expansionary momentum'.

Colonial rule had brought many benefits to poor countries, including roads, ports, and railways, political security, law and order, a civil service, sanitation and education, and contacts with the outer world. On the other hand, it had also brought restrictions in many places on the growth of indigenous industry, over and above the purely economic effects of undercutting of handicraft industries by cheaper machine-made products. 'Enforced bilateralism', sometimes politely called 'close economic and cultural ties', between metropolitan countries and their colonies had restricted the scope of the markets open to the latter. Racial and cultural differences between European and native peoples had been associated with practices of segregation which had hampered the transfer of cultures, especially including technical skills and a spirit of enterprise. The end of colonial rule had left some states with a genuine sense of unity and common purpose, such as India, but in other cases artificial states with little spirit of unity.

It was with that general framework of ideas that Myrdal approached his grand study of 'the poverty of nations' in South Asia. I have drawn extensively on the findings of that study in writing the present book, and it would be unnecessary as well as tedious to recapitulate them here. For present purposes it is appropriate to concentrate on the revised and extended general framework of ideas which Myrdal sets out in appendix 2 of *Asian Drama*, in which he criticizes other economists' analyses of the mechanisms of development and underdevelopment, and states his own approach as revised in the course of his study.

We conceive of the situation in each South Asian country – as in any other country – as a *social system*. The system consists of a great number of *conditions* that are causally interrelated, in that a change in one will cause changes in the others. We classify the conditions in six broad categories:

1 output and incomes;
2 conditions of production;
3 levels of living;
4 attitudes toward life and work;
5 institutions;
6 policies.

For Myrdal, in the South Asian countries the conditions in all his six categories 'can be categorically called *undesirable* because a one-way change in them is deemed desirable for engendering and sustaining development'. Data on output and incomes are useful as an index of the 'level of under-development', but not as a definition of underdevelopment. 'The movement of the whole system upwards is what all of us in fact mean by development.'

Many previous writers had analysed the existing condition of poor countries in terms of 'vicious circles', rather as I have briefly done in chapter 4. Poor people do not eat enough, cannot work hard, and so are poor. The process can be reversed and turned into a 'virtuous circle' – a poor man is given more to eat, his health improves, he is physically stronger, he can work harder and get more to eat. While Myrdal does not dissent from this analysis, be recognizes its somewhat tautological nature (poor countries are poor because they are poor) and regards it as far too limited in scope. He writes of

the astonishing stability of most social systems in history. Balance, far from being the fortuitous result of an unusual and obviously unstable combination of forces, seems to be the rule, not the rare exception. The great bulk of historical, anthropological, and sociological evidence and thought suggests that social stability and equilibrium is the norm and that all societies, and under-developed societies in particular, possess institutions of a strongly stabilizing character. In view of those findings the real mystery is how they can escape from equilibrium and develop. The Western experience of scientific, technological, and economic advance may well be unique: a series of extraordinary circumstances.

The main resistance to change in the social system, he says, 'stems from attitudes and institutions (categories 4 and 5). They are part of an inherited culture and are not easily or rapidly moved in either direction.'

Myrdal, then, is unusual among development economists in the importance which he attaches to the general setting of social and political institutions within which economic activity takes place. That said, it must be admitted that he is less successful in tracing out in specific detail the consequences, for example, of the Hindu joint family and inheritance system, religion, and caste for Indian economic life; and he is drawn into political naïvety, especially when he urges 'the effective abolition of caste'. So while he is perhaps too sociological to please the economists, he is not sufficiently so to please the sociologists. If I have singled out his work for specially full consideration, it is partly because we are all in his debt for the empirical findings he has amassed on the South Asian countries; and partly precisely because of his institutional bias. If he can be criticized along the lines I have suggested, despite his greater awareness of the importance of institutional factors, then how much more so may lesser and less sensitive economists?

'The limitations of the special case': Seers and Streeten

Despite a growing interest in the economic problems of poor countries, some development economists have regretted that their branch of economics has not made greater headway within the science generally. They have appeared accordingly in the role of critics of the ideas and doctrines inherited from the past which, they say, are ill adapted to the realities and needs of economic life in the greater part of the world today.

A vigorous critical attack on traditional economics from this point of view is that by Dudley Seers.[18] Just as the previous generation of economists failed to cope realistically with economic fluctuations until after the depression of the 1930s had brought political catastrophe in Europe, he says, so 'economics now seems very slow to adapt itself to the requirements of the main task of the day — the elimination of acute poverty in Africa, Asia, and Latin America'. The main reason for this in Seers' view is that the economics we have inherited is essentially the analytical study of the developed industrial economy. Both in time and space, however, that is an extremely rare and special case — in time there have been such economies for little more than a century, in space they cover only a small part of the earth's surface and include a minority of its inhabitants.

157

Thus textbooks and lecture courses of conventional economics, with titles like 'Economic principles', 'Banking', or 'Public finance', turn out on inspection to be analytical and somewhat theoretical descriptions of those aspects of the economy of the United States, Britain, or other advanced industrial countries. Yet these textbooks are used in the universities of non-industrial countries, too, often being translated into languages like Spanish for the purpose, and despite the manifest inappropriateness of much of their empirical content quite apart from their theoretical perspective. The case is little better with books written for use in the Soviet Union and recommended, again in Spanish translation, in the universities of a country like Cuba. Some Marxist analysis is highly relevant, for example, 'the "industrial reserve army" of the unemployed is after all to be seen in the streets' in many a Latin American country, while the attitudes of the landowning classes confirm Marx' analysis, and foreign-owned plantations exemplify imperialism. But there is no attempt to adapt the analysis or content to underdeveloped countries as they are today, says Seers, nor is there any scholarly analysis of their growth processes.

Seers spells out in detail the characteristic features of the special case — the developed industrial economy — and shows how special they are. He particularly emphasizes that 'non-industrial economies cannot be understood unless studied in the context of the world economy'. It is conceded that people should know something about developed industrial societies; many economists will spend their whole working lives in them, while economists in non-industrial societies need to know about their characteristics if they are to understand their impact. All this is well and good, says Seers, provided it is recognized that the developed industrial society *is* a highly special case and considered as such. What he strongly argues for is the study of comparative economics, perhaps with the slogan 'Economics is the study of economies'.

Another economist who has drawn attention to some of the limitations and biases shown by economists trained in western industrial societies is Paul Streeten, who sums up these limitations under four heads:

(1) 'Adapted *ceteris paribus* or automatic *mutatis mutandis*'. This refers to a tendency to assume that either things not immediately undergoing change will stay put, or that they will change in a direction harmonizing with the induced change. 'Thus for instance it is assumed that people either want to work, whether equipment is available or not (*ceteris paribus*), or that they will be automatically *induced* to want to work as a result of the provision of equipment' (*mutatis mutandis*).

(2) 'One-factor analysis'. Under this head Streeten draws attention to what can only be termed the changes in fashion among economists, who stress first one particular factor and then another in their efforts to diagnose the root causes of underdevelopment and recommend measures to remedy it. 'If the

158

Physiocrats stressed Land as the source of all wealth and the classical economists Labour, Capital has recently played the strategic role ... Education is now the craze ... [or] "investment in human beings" ... "Research and development" are already popular, and perhaps we shall soon study the returns from appropriate child training, which produces experimental innovating personalities, or from expenditure on child prevention.' (Both of the last-named have in fact occurred, and are mentioned in chapters 2 and 10 of this book.)

(3) 'Misplaced aggregation'. This refers to a tendency to lump together for analytical and statistical purposes things that are really very diverse, while

(4) 'Illegitimate isolation' refers to the complementary tendency to separate things that are really interrelated. For example, 'savings' are usually thought of as distinct from 'consumption' and also from 'investment'. In poor countries, however, some savings may take place only in relation to specific investments — that is, people save for a particular purpose, whereas in industrial societies the process can more realistically be thought of in two stages in which people first save and then decide how they will invest their savings. Moreover, as has been suggested, some expenditure like improved diet or health services which in industrial societies would be called consumption may be regarded as investment in poor countries since it may have the direct effect of raising output.[19]

'Indigenous economics': Polly Hill

Another critic of conventionally trained economists in their approach to poor countries is Dr Polly Hill Humphreys, who carried out an important pioneer study of migrant cocoa farmers in southern Ghana and went on to a series of studies of 'grass roots' economic development in West Africa by methods which combined economic analysis with the field techniques of the social anthropologist.[20] In a plea for indigenous economics, as she names this approach to 'the basic fabric of economic life', she points out that during the colonial period economists were concerned with the points of contact between West African and European economies — external trade, the acts of exportation and importation as such — rather than with the production of crops or the way in which internal distribution was carried on. There was a neglect of such important matters as the study of indigenous systems of land tenure and the way in which native producers raised capital and managed labour, and a number of myths grew up about West African economic behaviour, a kind of 'economic folklore', which became accepted by sheer reiteration in books and official publications. Thus it was wrongly believed that 'it was the expatriate trader who taught the West Africans ... the elementary facts of economic life'; it was further assumed that the basic fabric of economic life was either so simple as to be devoid of interest to

159

economists, or so complex (because of local land tenure, kinship and inheritance, communal work systems, etc.) as to be beyond his sphere of interest and even of his comprehension. 'Not until social and political systems have been "modernized" will economic processes become intelligible. By hastening the collapse of "tribalism", economists hope to move rapidly towards the day when they will understand events.'

The neglect of indigenous economics during the colonial period has not been rectified since independence; on the contrary, according to Dr Humphreys, it has taken hold of the attitudes of modern West African governments, who deplore the backwardness of the peasants and are apt to initiate large-scale mechanization programmes without adequate consideration of the consequences. Further, the whole ideology of underdevelopment specialists is opposed to indigenous studies. Theoreticians, econometricians, and planners share a philosophy based on the past success of their science in solving economic problems, particularly mass unemployment in western countries. They are reluctant to incorporate into their models ideas drawn from anthropological research, to look at the humdrum problems involved in the collection of the statistical data which they so finely manipulate, and to reserve judgment in cases where their knowledge is inadequate.

Nevertheless,

although it is true that the indigenous economist stands in some way opposed to the 'development economist', he is as much concerned with processes of change and modernization which he tends to regard from a non-governmental standpoint . . . While his subject is similar, in a general way, to conventional (or Western) economics, the factors which require emphasis in any situation may be unexpected, so that those who guess on the basis of Western experience are apt to go wrong even on fundamentals; he insists that the economic behaviour of individual West Africans is basically 'rational' and responsive, but that the structure of this rationality requires studying in the field.

Though Dr Humphreys' essays are devoted to descriptive analysis rather than recommendations, it is fair to point to the type of policy which her approach would appear to imply. As she says, 'we must study the farmer, not patronize him: we must assume that he knows his business better than we do, unless there is evidence to the contrary (. . . this is not to say that the farmer will be unappreciative of skilled technical advice and help)'. This seems to imply looking for and encouraging growing points in the indigenous economy, which is rather like Hirschman's injunction to 'discover under what pressures people are operating and toward what forward steps they are already being impelled'. It suggests that the economic adviser to the government of a poor country should search out groups like Mrs Humphreys' migrant cocoa farmers, seine fishermen, and cattle-owners, who are clearly innovating, investing, and developing new ways of improving their standard of living; finding out if there are gratuitous obstacles to their efforts to help themselves and if without injustice to other groups suitable action by a public authority can remove those obstacles. If, for instance, seine fishermen are found to have a problem with the custody of large sums of cash, which invite theft, then a suitable measure would be to encourage a bank to set up a branch on the beach. Or if arrangements for the marketing of cattle are inadequate on the Accra plains, again the action which central or local government can take is obvious.

The need for wider perspectives

Dr Humphreys' criticisms have a wider significance if they are taken in the context of a somewhat uneasy relation between development economists on the one hand and sociologists, social anthropologists, and political scientists on the other.

Development economics is an applied science or 'art' which, as stated at the beginning of this chapter, aspires to be of practical application in raising the living standards of the people of the poor countries. It is inevitably based on a built-in value judgment. No one, of course, disagrees with that value judgment; on the contrary, the desirability of raising living standards in the poor countries commands the assent and fires the zeal of men of goodwill everywhere, including sociologists and social anthropologists. But to put it bluntly, sociologists and social anthropologists have an innate objection to the treatment of major social institutions as merely obstacles to development. From a sociological point of view, a culture is to be regarded as made up of a number of key institutional areas or complexes, always including the family and kinship, magic and religion, social differentiation, social control, and the economy. Not only are social institutions objects of study in themselves — as legitimate, concrete isolates of culture, in Malinowski's phrase[21] — but they are integral to a way of life, and they embody values which the people concerned regard as ends in themselves. It is perfectly true — it is indeed usually the case — that the study of the basic institutions of a society may reveal that the non-rational beliefs and ideas involved are serving as verbal cloaks to conceal the vested interests of privileged groups or individuals, and that there is generally inconsistency between stated norms and actual practice, a good deal of rationalization, myth-making, and ideology involved. As has been well said, to the sociologist 'nothing is sacred, least of all the sacred itself'; and this is partly what gives sociology a bad name, for it is the uneasy sense that the most unquestioned of beliefs and values are to be questioned whenever a sociologist gets to work that leads ordinary sensible men to think of the subject as subversive, or potentially subversive, of all that they hold dear.[22]

For a sociologist, then, it is not only the system of indigenous social

161

institutions which an economist might regard as 'obstacles to development' which would be the proper objects of study; it would also be the government and its economic adviser. In other words, the government of a country, its economic adviser, and the development ideology itself, are all component parts of the total situation; and they and the interactions between them are all objects of analysis for the sociologist. It may, indeed, be almost literally a matter of collision between two sacred cows. If development economists call in question the literal sacred cows of Hinduism, so is the sociologist entitled to call in question the sacred cow of economic development − *even though he wholeheartedly agrees that it is sacred,* or at least a very highly desirable end.

So it is the development economist's tendency to take it for granted that economic development is the overriding priority among the aims of government policies in poor countries − or that if it is not then it ought to be − that leads to political naïvety. As Leys points out in a brilliant essay,[23] economic development is not in fact 'pursued as a sole or even a prime objective by people in poor countries to the extent the writers on development have often assumed'. Even for ordinary men and women, 'economic goals are not necessarily "paramount"'. People have other aims and ambitions, like building temples or pursuing clan disputes. They may be justifiably sceptical of the actual measures proposed to them for improving their incomes; and these may involve accepting non-economic costs like 'humiliating dependency on a host of (generally) young "change agents"'. Doubts and ambivalences like these among ordinary people will in nearly every case be mirrored through the political system, and even though that system may not be very obviously 'democratic' it will almost always be responsive in some degree to local pressures and factions.

A political leadership dedicated above all to economic growth, willing and able to pursue this goal at the expense of all others and able to rely on the party, the bureaucracy and the army to contain the resentment and reaction that will be entailed, is to say the least highly exceptional.

Of course, political leaders normally (though not invariably) want a rapid rate of economic growth. But it is only one among many objectives which they *want* to pursue. The word 'want' is used deliberately, rather than 'must'. Exasperated economists in planning ministries not infrequently come to view the situation as follows: 'their' minister (the Minister of Planning) genuinely *wants* to do what is needed to secure an improved rate of growth. But he is *obliged*, by reason of the need to stay in power, to compromise with all sorts of conflicting political interests − to agree to wage settlements which destroy the income assumptions of the plan; to build more than the planned number of schools; to locate industries, or roads, in economically far from ideal places and so on ... The planners are apt to conclude that, in spite of the politicians' presumed *desire* for planned growth, they fundamentally lack the moral fibre to do what is necessary to achieve it; the problem is pictured as one of the 'will to develop' ...

Of course, politicians do vary in determination, honesty, singleness of mind, and so on. But, speaking generally, political leaders do not *want* one particular goal beyond all others. Like the ordinary people whose affairs they try to manage, they have a multiplicity of goals they want to achieve and most of the time they are pursuing them all more or less simultaneously. It is only if one presupposes that economic goals (or any other kind) are the only *really* legitimate ones that one is driven to such feeble interpretations as that politicians, of all people – in this toughest of political contexts! – are systematically lacking in will.

SUGGESTIONS FOR FURTHER READING

Dudley Seers and Leonard Joy (eds.), *Development in a Divided World*, Harmondsworth: Penguin, 1971

W. Arthur Lewis, *Development Planning*, London: Allen and Unwin, 1966

Gerald M. Meier, *Leading Issues in Economic Development*, second edition, Oxford: Oxford University Press, 1970

Paul Streeten, *The Frontiers of Development Studies*, London: Macmillan, 1972

8   But is it possible?

Economic development versus environmental
conservation — a controversy considered

The purpose of this chapter is to consider the conflict at the present time
between the economic-development ideology on the one hand and another
cause to which public attention is being urgently directed in the industrial
countries, namely the desirability of measures to curb population growth
and conserve environmental balance and non-renewable resources. There is
in fact a head-on collision between the views of some development economists, who foresee economic growth without end or limit, and the environmentalists who regard the most affluent industrial countries as already
overdeveloped and call explicitly for a reduction in the level of economic
activity there.

On one side of this controversy Hagen is quite explicit: 'there is no technical
or economic reason why growth should not continue indefinitely'. In the
United States, the G.N.P. per head at the time of the civil war was about
$250 at 1967 prices. In 1966 it was $3,760. A further multiplication by a
factor of fifteen during the next two centuries would bring it to $56,000.

There is no technical or economic reason why the figure should not reach that level
before the end of the 22nd century, or why income levels elsewhere in the world
should not reach similar multiples of their present levels. Rising production depletes
natural resources, but when it does new ones are invented — aluminium, plastics,
generation of energy from nuclear fission. A man would be rash today who would
predict confidently that income will reach the level indicated in 200 or 250 years.
Too many non-technical factors may interfere. For example, the holocaust of nuclear
world war may interfere. Or too many individuals, alienated by social tensions, may
'drop out' from prosecuting technical progress. But it is worthwhile to make the
point forcefully that the process being studied in this volume is potentially an indefinitely continuing one.[1]

On the other side, Paul and Anne Ehrlich are equally dogmatic:

In general, underdeveloped countries (UDCs) differ from developed countries (DCs)
in a number of ways. UDCs are not industrialized. They tend to have inefficient,
usually subsistence agricultural systems, extremely low gross national products and
per capita incomes, high illiteracy rates, and incredibly high rates of population
growth. For reasons that are made clear in this book, most of these countries will
never, under any conceivable circumstances, be 'developed' in the sense in which
the United States is today. They could quite accurately be called the 'never-to-be-
developed countries'.

164

In the Ehrlichs' judgment, the earth is overpopulated already. 'The limits of human capability to produce food by conventional means have very nearly been reached.' In some places, indeed, a reduction in the area under cultivation and the de-stocking of flocks and herds are highly advisable measures if overgrazing, loss of soil fertility, and erosion are to be averted, and they quote as an example a study of Turkish agriculture by Georg Borgstrom. 'World agriculture today is an ecological disaster area.' Turning to resources other than food, the annual production of minerals like iron, copper, and lead would have to be increased six- to eight-fold if the world's population used them at the same rate as Americans. However, this understates the case, for to bring the present world population up to American standards of equipment — railways, motor-cars (automobiles), electric wiring, structural steel, etc. — would require the extraction of far larger amounts of minerals at much faster rates, ranging from 75 times as much for iron to 250 times as much for tin. 'Our environment cannot stand "world industrialization"', they exclaim. Even if the extraction and smelting of minerals on such a scale were imaginable, the amounts of energy consumed would be likely to endanger the heat balance of the earth, with possibly disastrous effects on climate. Moreover, the partial industrialization of the earth has already caused pollution of the air and water which is intolerable, and may have started irreversible modifications in vital cycles.

As will appear below, the Ehrlichs' pessimistic views and forecasts are not unanimously endorsed by other competent scientists working in relevant fields. Some of them, indeed, are strongly controverted. At the same time, statements by citizens of affluent industrial societies to the effect that the people of poor countries can never hope to enjoy a similar affluence are likely to be unpalatable to the latter. To say 'We have it but you cannot have it too' could even be interpreted as the ideology of the privileged, determined to retain their relative privilege. Such considerations are clearly far from the Ehrlichs' minds, yet it can scarcely be denied that their words could bear such a malicious misinterpretation. The Ehrlichs show some awareness of this aspect of their message, but see no escape from it:

The 'have-nots' of the world are in an unprecedented position today: they are aware of what the 'haves' enjoy ... our fine homes, our highly varied diet ... our automobiles, airplanes, tractors, refrigerators, and other appliances. Naturally they want to share our affluence. They have what Adlai Stevenson called 'rising expectations'. But, a few simple calculations show that they also have plummeting prospects.[2]

Ehrlich and Harriman have elsewhere compared the earth with a spaceship in trouble — 'its life-support systems malfunctioning, running out of vital supplies, and half its overcrowded passengers hungry'. The trouble is accentuated by the division between 'first-class passengers' and the rest, with the former squabbling over most of the available supplies and the latter living and dying mostly in misery. Clearly a more equitable distribution is called

165

for, yet 'the greatest good of the greatest number' is impracticable because it calls for a double maximization. 'What must be done is to determine how much "good" should be available for each person', and then limit the population to the optimum for which the basic needs of food, shelter, and health can be made available without impairing the 'basic life-support systems' of the planet. In this 'conversion process', Ehrlich and Harriman do not hesitate to write of the industrial nations as 'over-developed' and call explicitly for their 'de-development'. The underdeveloped countries should at the same time be 'semi-developed', that is, their standard of living should be improved, but not to the extent of raising their G.N.P. per head to modern American levels.[3]

The directions in which we must move are clear; the conversion process is, in outline, simple.

1. Population control must be achieved in both over-developed countries (ODCs) and under-developed countries (UDCs)
2. The ODCs must be de-developed
3. The UDCs must be semi-developed
4. The procedures must be set up for monitoring and regulating the world system in a continuous effort to maintain an optimum population— resource—environment situation.

It should be added that not all natural scientists take as uncompromising a view as Ehrlich. The views of the more extreme environmentalists or conservationists, indeed, have been sharply criticized by John Maddox as exaggerated and alarmist, lacking in historical perspective and innocent of economic understanding. Moreover, they risk alienating poor countries 'not yet rich enough to aspire to the kind of freedom from pollution on which the more prosperous nations have set their sights'; and this was illustrated by the difficulty of finding a common platform for the international conference on the human environment which was held in Stockholm in June 1972.[4]

Equally, not all economists share Hagen's view of the possibility of indefinite growth. Thus Lord Balogh has pointed out that criticism, or at least doubts, about growth are not new, and not all economists have been single-minded in its pursuit. J. K. Galbraith's *The Affluent Society* is an important contrary instance. However, a total abandonment of a commitment to growth would leave unanswered vital questions about inequality. 'Why nil growth?' asks Balogh. 'What is to be done with the poor, and with what?'[5]

Hagen on the one hand and Ehrlich on the other take extreme positions, then, in a controversy in which others are seeking middle ground. Nevertheless, current discussions do seriously raise the question whether it is realistic to think of the attainment by the people of the present-day poor countries of a standard of living resembling that of the rich industrial nations. Some mention of this controversy can hardly be avoided in a book of this nature, and though ill-equipped to attempt such a task, and reluctant to draw definite conclusions, I have tried in what follows at least to give some outline indication of the nature of the issues which are involved.

It is common ground in this debate that, at the very least, population growth makes the raising of standards of living more difficult, and checking human fertility is an important condition for such improvement. Controversies surround four interrelated issues, which may be summarily called those of pollution, food, non-renewable resources, and energy.

Pollution

People in the industrial nations have vastly increased their output both of agricultural and industrial products over the last two hundred years, but only, it is suggested, by the use of methods which have already caused unacceptable levels of pollution of the air and water. Were these methods to be extended and become general in the poor countries too, the self-righting mechanisms of the natural world and its various cycles might be seriously or even irreversibly impaired. For example, the extensive burning of fossil fuels in the typical processes of the industrial economy — heat engines, metal-smelting, etc. — have given rise to anxiety both on account of the carbon dioxide which is released into the atmosphere and the heat which is generated. The burning of fossil fuels certainly increases the heat energy in the earth's atmosphere, over and above the amount currently received and absorbed from the sun, and this suggested that there might be a change in the heat balance with possibly long-term effects upon climate. Changes in average temperatures since the start of the industrial revolution, however, have been small and erratic, and do not suggest any serious interference with the earth's energy balance. Moreover, the amounts of energy released by the combustion of fossil fuels are minute compared with those received from the sun — something of the order of 1 to 20,000. However, local effects may be more serious, and there are anxieties about such questions as the heating of rivers from the discharge of cooling-water from factories and power stations. As to carbon dioxide, the fear is that this also might lead to a world-wide rise in temperature since this gas has a strong tendency to absorb radiation at the wavelengths at which it is mostly emitted from the earth. More carbon dioxide in the atmosphere would accordingly mean that more of this radiation was trapped, and give rise to what has been called a 'greenhouse effect'. However, though it is stated that the carbon dioxide level in the atmosphere has definitely increased, as has been stated there is no clear evidence of any particular trend in temperature. Some authorities have speculated that the 'greenhouse effect' may be being offset by the increased screening of the earth by dust and smoke, partly from industry, partly from the increased extent of agricultural burning in the tropics, and partly also from volcanic eruption:

167

In any event, the higher levels of carbon dioxide may not persist for long. For one thing, the oceans, which contain sixty times as much carbon dioxide as the atmosphere does, will begin to absorb the excess as the mixing of the intermediate and deeper levels of water proceeds. For another, the increased atmospheric content of carbon dioxide will stimulate a more rapid growth of plants — a phenomenon that has been utilized in greenhouses.[6]

Such considerations emphasize the extent to which the human use of combustion in industrial and other processes depends on the activities of green plants to restore the oxygen—carbon dioxide balance. Oxygen, in fact, only occurs in the atmosphere at all because living organisms keep putting it there; it is a highly reactive element and unless continually renewed would soon combine with other elements and be lost to the atmosphere. The dependence of an industrial society on the organic oxygen cycle is highlighted by a calculation which suggests that in the land area of the forty-eight coterminous states of America, the amount of oxygen produced by photosynthesis in plant life amounts to only 60 per cent of the amount used in the combustion of fossil fuels. The balance is made up by a net 'import' of oxygen by atmospheric circulation from outside the boundaries of the U.S.A., mostly it is thought from the marine diatoms in the Pacific (and it is now estimated that about 70 per cent of the earth's annual supply of oxygen comes from the oceans). While the availability of oxygen for industrial combustion may not be an immediate limitation to the industrial development of other countries — indeed, the world seems more likely to run out of fossil fuels before it runs out of atmospheric oxygen to burn them — it does point to the dependence on a cycle which could be impaired by the pollution of the oceans. If what has happened to Lake Erie and some other bodies of enclosed water were to happen to the Pacific Ocean — if, for example, DDT pollution were to increase, or if large quantities of defoliants were to be released into the oceans — then, it is suggested, we would start running out of oxygen.[7]

It should be added, however, that some other authorities — like Professor Bunting, whom I quote below — have dismissed such fears as exaggerated. The scale of human industrial activity and its pollution of the atmosphere remain puny compared with natural hazards. Indeed, the Ehrlichs themselves emphasize this when they refer to the effects of major volcanic eruptions like those of Sumbawa in 1815 or Krakatoa in 1883. Where the climatic effects of human industry are so small as to be hardly detectable with available measurements, the pollution of the atmosphere by vast quantities of ash in those volcanic eruptions had climatic effects which were dramatically obvious all over the world. In 1816 there was said to be 'no summer at all' in the northern United States, while in Britain the lowest summer temperatures ever recorded were in that year and in others following similar eruptions.[8]

A class of substances about which there is a direct clash of opinion is that of the nitrogenous fertilizers. In some industrial countries, where farmers have used these substances on a large scale, they have drained into lakes and rivers and there stimulated plant growth, notably that of certain algae. This unwonted and excessive growth has been followed by the rapid decay of unusually large quantities of plant material, which had depleted the oxygen dissolved in the water, so that fish have died. Lake Erie has come to be regarded as a leading example of the pollution of a natural mass of fresh water by this and other means; its bed is reported now to be covered by a thick layer of material rich in phosphorus and nitrogen compounds.[9] For reasons of this kind, the ecologists have expressed serious reservations about the use of nitrogenous fertilizers on a large scale, at just the time when the hopes for agricultural improvement in poor countries have come to depend in part on plans to increase their production and use in those countries. The F.A.O. have reported with satisfaction the prospects for enormously increased production of fertilizers in Africa,[10] and Lipton concludes 'there is no doubt that enormous expansion of fertiliser use would pay many of the farmers of the Third World'.[11]

Perhaps the most acute controversy, however, surrounds the use of chlorinated hydrocarbons like DDT as insecticides. Following the publication of Rachel Carson's *Silent Spring* in 1962, these substances came under suspicion on the ground that — unlike some other insecticides such as pyrethrum — they were relatively stable and persistent. Once used on a large scale, then, they tended to be accumulated in higher and higher concentrations in the bodies of animals which fed successively on crops which had been treated with DDT, on predatory animals which fed on those animals, and so on, until they reached toxic proportions in some of the higher predators like the birds of prey. They could also be accumulated in a similar manner in the human body, with unknown but possibly serious effects. Many scientists and other influential people accordingly called for legislation to control and reduce the use of these substances.

In 1971, however, the F.A.O. found it necessary to counter this trend. While acknowledging that chlorinated hydrocarbons had been misused, wildlife had been harmed, and high levels of residues had been found in humans, nevertheless the F.A.O. and the World Health Organization stood by a policy decision of 1969 approving the continued use of DDT while urging that it should be kept to an absolute minimum. DDT was essential to malaria control, and a decision experimentally to cease using it in Ceylon (Sri Lanka) had resulted in a return of the disease to epidemic levels.[12] Support for these views of F.A.O. and W.H.O. came shortly afterwards from two distinguished scientists. Thomas Jukes,[13] professor of medical physics at Berkeley, stated that no effective substitute had been found for DDT in the fight against malaria, and suggested that this side of the controversy had not been publicized because most ecologists are healthy, well-to-do whites. Discounting fears about the possible toxic effects of DDT, he stated that 'in the light of

169

the health record of the people most heavily exposed to it, there is no reason to suppose that the millions of people protected against vector-borne diseases are at any risk from their small exposure to DDT'. This was a small risk to put in the balance against the 960 million people who were subject to endemic malaria and are now free of it, and the further 288 million who live in areas where it is being vigorously attacked. And in November 1971, in a lecture at the F.A.O. annual conference, Dr Norman Borlaug was even more outspoken. Dr Borlaug was awarded the Nobel Peace prize in 1970 for his work on Mexican wheat and counts accordingly as one of the authors of the 'green revolution'. He thought that the continued success of that revolution depends on whether farmers would be allowed to go on using agricultural chemicals. 'If agriculture is denied their use because of unwise legislation that is now being promoted by a powerful group of hysterical lobbyists who are provoking fear by predicting doom for the world through chemical poisoning, then the world will be doomed not by chemical poisoning but from starvation.' A legislative ban on the use of DDT and similar substances in the U.S.A. might be followed by a demand for a world-wide ban that would increase crop losses and put up food prices. 'This must not be permitted until an even more effective and safer insecticide is available, for no chemical has done as much as DDT to improve the health, economic and social benefits of the people of the developing nations.'[14]

There is the further point that, precisely because the dangers of pollution have been so intensively publicized in recent years, it is highly likely that appropriate remedial action will be taken. Indeed, the first successes of anti-pollution laws in industrial countries are already to be seen. In this movement the 1956 Clean Air Act in Britain may well come to be regarded as a pioneer, and though it was neither particularly stringent nor sophisticated it has resulted in air pollution by smoke being reduced by something like three-quarters in the worst-affected areas. In Britain too, considerable progress has been made in reducing the pollution of rivers, and in recent years fish have returned to the London reaches of the Thames for the first time in a century. A combination of public laws with the adoption of appropriate techniques by industrial enterprises in this and other countries seems more likely than not to be a continuing trend, and pollution of the environment may well cease accordingly to be regarded as an inevitable concomitant of industrial development and scientific agriculture.

Food

In the early 1950s, there were grave fears that world population was outstripping food supply, and the world was approaching a Malthusian crisis. By the early 1970s the spectre had receded. It is true that in some areas,

especially Africa, population is growing faster than food supply, but according to leading authorities the production and consumption of food per head
in the poor countries as a whole has increased over the last twenty years.
Thus Professor Bunting has stated that if we take the average supply of food
per head in 1952—6 as 100, the index for the developing world as a whole
in 1970 was 104. For the Far East (including India but excluding Japan) it
was 107, though in Africa it was 94. But there was certainly no sign of the
impending disasters which had been scheduled by some prophets of doom for
around 1975. Bunting also thought that fears for the 'death of the oceans' had
been greatly exaggerated, and urban and industrial effluents were far more
important in this context than agricultural chemicals and DDT; nevertheless,
greater care and precision with the latter was called for, and there were
promising results from ultra-low-volume spraying.[15]

Another moderately optimistic view is that of Lord Todd:

Since around 1950 worldwide agricultural productivity has risen by about 3%
annually and the average population increase has been just under 2%. If worldwide
per capita food consumption had remained constant at the 1955 level then by 1975,
and in spite of the population increase, it is calculated that there would have been
a world surplus of 40 million tons of wheat and 75 million tons of rice. But because
of rising *per capita* food consumption and the control of agricultural production
practised in the more highly developed producing countries (the US, Australia, etc.)
this will not occur... It has been calculated that if all land now being cultivated
were managed as it is in Holland it could support 60 billion people (that is, 6×10^{10})
on a typical Dutch diet; if managed as in Japan it could support 90 billion people
on a typical Japanese diet.

It is not denied that there are limits, yet technological improvements are still
occurring, and more land could still be brought into cultivation. And there
are the further potential developments of 'unorthodox' food production from
algae, yeasts, and the like; not as matters of science fiction, either, for 'there
are already two plants going into operation in Europe to produce good protein by growing yeast on petroleum as a carbon source'. The question, Lord
Todd suggests, is not so much whether we can produce the food, but rather
'Do we really want to have such huge numbers of people?'[16]

The dramatic change in the world food situation over the last twenty years
has been associated with a number of developments which have been collectively called the 'green revolution'. This has included the breeding of
improved strains of the basic food crops, especially wheat and rice. In
Mexico, the government agricultural research department under Dr Borlaug,
financed by the Rockefeller Foundation, successfully bred new wheat strains
which raised the country's food production at an average of 7 per cent
annually while the population increased at 3 per cent and turned Mexico
from a wheat-importing to a wheat-exporting country. In India a similar

171

partnership between government research and American foundation money — Ford and Rockefeller — has also had a spectacular success with improved wheat strains, increasing production from 67 million tons in 1966 to 104 million in 1970. Meanwhile in the Philippines the International Rice Research Institute developed a whole series of improved rice strains including the famous one named IR8 and a further improved successor IR24, which again shifted the balance and turned the Philippines into a rice-exporting country. These improved strains have been associated with the use of fertilizers and irrigation, and the control of pests and diseases, a side of the 'green revolution' which I have already touched on above.

Food has accordingly become abundant and cheap at a time when earlier estimates suggested it would become scarce and dear. However, the 'green revolution' has not been without its attendant economic disturbances. Countries which had come to rely on grain exporting, like Burma and Thailand, face economic dislocations as countries like the Philippines become first self-supporting in rice and then try to export in an already glutted market.[17] Furthermore, there have been effects upon the distribution of incomes within the rice-growing countries. According to a report by the Swedish economist Erich Jacoby, the new technology which has made possible multiple yields or additional crops 'depends on assured water supply and the use of expensive modern farm equipment. The rural masses do not have either.' The increased productivity of land is available mainly on larger holdings and to well-to-do farmers able to apply capital-intensive methods, while it also makes land-owners better off as a result of higher land values and rents. For example, in central Luzon in the Philippines, the new strains of rice make possible well over 100 per cent increase in yield for only 50 per cent extra labour. In other words, the labour input per ton of rice is one-third lower than before. Rising productivity of labour has made for rising unemployment in this case, since there is no great increase in the demand for rice on the home market, while as for exports, as has been noted already, every country is producing more rice and the market is glutted. The new technology puts a premium on effective management, exact calculation, market-oriented production, a reliable labour force, and modern machinery. Traditional forms of tenancy, share-cropping, and seasonal work no longer fulfil these requirements, with the result that a lot of people lose their livelihoods. Unemployment and low incomes further depress food prices and lead to further efforts by the big farmers to cut costs, and the general result is the enhancement (or as Jacoby calls it the 'deterioration') of inequality and social stratification in rural areas.[18] It was these effects which led a political scientist from a 'green revolution' country to comment on the irony of the award to Dr Borlaug of the Nobel *Peace* prize (rather than one of the science prizes) when the result of his discoveries had been to create class conflict and a potentially revolutionary situation in those countries.

172

'Non-renewable resources'

Apart from fossil fuels, which I deal with below, the phrase 'non-renewable resources' in the context of current discussions refers to substances like metals of which only a finite stock exists in the earth, as against renewable resources like those derived from agriculture. The suggestion made by Ehrlich and others is that the minority of the planet's 'first-class passengers' are already making excessive inroads into these resources. Were the consumption patterns of modern America to become general throughout the world's population, then it would be impossible to satisfy their demand for iron, copper, and so on.

This view, however, seems to overlook two important considerations. First, although there is only a finite quantity of the substances in question, they are not lost by being mined and put into human use; they may be discarded, but can if necessary be recovered and reused. All the iron that there ever was in the earth is there still; some of it may have been transformed into motor-cars and other artefacts, which have been worn out and deposited on the scrap heap, but it is still there and can be used again if wanted. If wanted badly enough, that is. It is really a matter of comparing from time to time the cost of getting fresh supplies of a metal by mining it from previously un-touched deposits in the earth's surface with the cost of recovering it from the municipal refuse tip or the car-breakers' yard. And there is, after all, such a thing as a scrap-metal industry whose business is concerned precisely with this question.

What, indeed, do we mean exactly when we say that we shall one day 'run out of' a particular resource? The process is likely to be gradual rather than abrupt; as the more easily accessible deposits of a mineral are worked out, then the attention of mining enterprises is drawn to the less accessible ones, the ones with lower concentrations or more troublesome impurities, the ones involving higher transport costs or other inconveniences. This would entail a gradual tendency for the price to rise, and presumably at some point in this process the scrap-metal industry finds that it can market recovered supplies at a price which competes with newly mined. In so far as we do 'run out of' non-renewable resources, therefore, we may expect that recycling through the recovery and salvage of scrap will become more important. In other words, we shall know when we have 'run out of' minerals by the extent to which municipal refuse tips are being quarried and used as low-grade ores.

The second point is that this does not seem to be happening yet to any very substantial extent. Though the recovery especially of non-ferrous metals from scrap does make some contribution to supplies, freshly mined supplies still compete effectively enough to inhibit any really large-scale reductions of the mountains of rusting tin cans and old cars which still disfigure the landscape of industrial countries. Likewise, the price of copper shows no

173

steady or sustained tendency to rise; indeed, it would be good news for Zambia and some other poor countries if it did, but on the contrary, as has been seen in chapter 4, the problem for copper-producers in recent decades has been how to avoid being undercut by aluminium.

Energy

All the energy which is available to us for human use is derived ultimately, after the lapse of a longer or shorter time, from the sun. Some solar energy is used by humans instantaneously, as when we lie on a beach and gratefully absorb its warmth. Solar energy which powers atmospheric depressions, and of which man may use a tiny proportion to drive sailing ships or windmills, is used within a few hours or days. Energy from atmospheric circulation may also be used after a slightly longer time when rain falls on high ground and runs back through water mills or hydro-electric power stations. Here the time-lapse depends on the capacity of the lake or dam in which the potential energy is stored. This may range from a few days in the case of a simple water mill powered by a river or stream to a few years in the case of a large modern dam, or even as much as a century when the largest lakes are used. For example, the arrangements for controlling Lake Victoria envisage 'century storage', averaging out the controlled outflow of the lake with the vagaries of the rainfall over that kind of period. Much of the energy which we use ourselves in our own muscles is derived from the sun after a time-lapse of the order of a year, assuming the growth of annual crops like the food grains; some over a small number of years, as we eat meat or fish that has been growing and feeding on plants for periods of that order. The same is true, of course, of the energy of domestic animals like the horse which are put to human use. When people burn firewood for warmth, cook-ing, or other purposes, they are using solar energy after a period represented by the age of the tree when it was pruned or felled, a period normally of less than a century.

In pre-industrial technologies, the time-lapse between the arrival of solar energy at the earth and its use by man is (or was) characteristically rather short. Most work was done by human and animal muscles, and the pre-dominant fuel was wood. Thus the energy cycle involved the possibility of regeneration or recycling over a comparatively short period. Given wise husbandry and a population not so dense as to press upon resources, land used for growing food and fodder crops, or for pasture, could be used again another year. Likewise the forest cropped for firewood could regenerate within years or decades; indeed, a balance could be struck between the annual growth of a given area of forest and the off-take of timber for fire-wood, building, furniture, and other uses. Not of course that a balanced cycle of this kind has been universal or even particularly characteristic of pre-

174

industrial economies. On the contrary, we know only too well that 'primitive' technologies too have ruined forests and caused soil erosion, and that the impairment of vital cycles is not something for which industrial technologies alone are responsible. The history of Britain, for instance, is the history of continuous deforestation from the Bronze Age to the present day, though it is fair to add that the inroads made into the indigenous forest in these islands by the comparatively sparse populations of pre-industrial man were far outdone by the havoc wrought by a few decades of charcoal-burning for iron-smelting in the early industrial period.[19]

With the rise of industrial technology, a new dimension has been added in the use of solar energy after very much longer time-lapses, to be measured in millions of years. That extra dimension is, of course, the use of fossil fuels. As has been seen in chapter 2, it was the use of these sources of energy that gave the decisive impetus to the industrial revolution in history. Moreover, it has been made clear in chapter 4 that the most striking difference between the real resources available to the people of the rich and poor countries respectively lies in the vastly larger quantities of energy available to the former.

Yet the fossil fuels are a non-renewable resource, or indeed one should rather say *the* non-renewable resource. The solar energy that is used when we burn coal and oil is derived from that which fell on the earth millions of years ago. In the case of metals I argued that they were not lost, and could be recovered. In the case of coal and oil the same is true in a sense — the carbon dioxide which results from their combustion will be absorbed by plants, a proportion of which may conceivably rot down into peat beds which will form the coal seams of the future. But this can occur only after a lapse of millions of years, and certainly not within the kind of time-span that is of any relevance to human life over the next few decades or centuries, with which we are concerned. As Cipolla has put it:

One can summarize the story of our happy generations in the following way. For millions of years wealth was stored and cumulated. Then, someone in the family discovered the hoard — and started to dissipate it. We are now living through this fabulous dissipation. Humanity is today consuming more coal in a single year than was generated in a hundred centuries or so during the process of carbonization.[20]

It should be added that nobody knows the extent of the deposits of fossil fuels available to man, and that astonishing discoveries continue to be made. As recently as fifteen years ago, for example, nobody thought there might be oil and gas under the North Sea; today, it is certain that Britain and Norway will be producing much of their own requirements of both within a few years, and with prospecting now moving to the western coasts of Britain there is the distinct possibility that by the end of the century this will be one of the major oil-producing areas of the world.[21] Coal meanwhile is declining as

175

an energy source in industrial countries. In the United States, for example, in 1910 coal provided three-quarters of all the energy used, while by 1970 its share had dropped to less than a quarter.[22] In Britain similarly coal output dropped from around 200 million tons a year in the 1950s to around 130 million tons in the early 1970s, and its share in total energy has dropped to less than half.[23] Yet this is not because either country is 'running out of' coal; on the contrary, it is purely a matter of costs, in which coal-mining as a labour-intensive industry in an affluent society is at a disadvantage compared with the capital-intensive production of oil and natural gas. At the same time current estimates indicate that no more than 1 or 2 per cent of the minable coal in the earth has yet been extracted, though deeper inroads have been made into oil and gas. The coal is still there if we need to go back to using it, though it will be at a higher cost than in the past.

Nevertheless, no one questions that the resources of fossil fuels are finite. Accordingly if a greatly increased use of energy by man is to be possible over a long term as the people of the poorer countries improve their standard of living and use more energy then a timely development will be the search for alternative sources of energy. The current possibilities seem to be two-fold. One is the greatly increased use of nuclear power; the other is to increase the proportion of solar energy currently falling on the earth which is put to human use, and the efficiency with which it is used.

Nuclear energy is the source with the longest time-lapse of all. Although no exception to the statement that all energy is ultimately derived from the sun, yet it is also a very special case. A nuclear reaction represents the conversion of matter into energy, and the matter in question is derived from the sun only in the same sense as the whole earth is derived from the sun. From one point of view, therefore, nuclear energy depends on fossil fuels too. The first such 'fuel' to be used was, and is, uranium-235, a rare isotope of a metal which is itself rare, uranium-238 or 'normal' uranium. Uranium-235 was used at first because it is the only naturally occurring element which without exposure to extreme conditions is capable of 'fissioning', or splitting, with the release of energy. The concentration of uranium-235 into workable quantities represents a major initial investment of energy, which has of course to be derived from 'conventional' fossil fuel sources, first in mining uranium and smelting it, and then in separating out the uranium-235, which occurs in a concentration of less than 1 per cent in natural uranium. Moreover, the small known extent of uranium ores in the earth's surface makes it possible to be sure that 'if nuclear energy depended entirely on uranium-235, the nuclear-fuel epoch would be brief'.[24] Prolonging it will depend on the building of 'breeder reactors', which besides making use of the energy released by the fission process, also transform commoner elements into fissile ones — uranium-238 into plutonium-239, or thorium-232 into uranium-233. This opens up the possibility of using materials which are present in far greater abundance than the original uranium ores. Even so common a material as granite, for example, contains uranium and thorium in workable quantities, and it is estimated that a ton of granite contains as much energy as fifteen tons of coal, besides other minerals required for the purpose of modern industrial technology.[25]

A further possibility, beyond the fission reactions which are already in use, lies in fusion reactions. Fission reactions are those which involve a large atom splitting into smaller ones; fusion reactions, contrariwise, involve small atoms fusing to make bigger ones, again with the emission of energy. A fusion reaction which is in principle very simple involves the fusion of two atoms of deuterium or 'heavy hydrogen', while another which may, it is thought, be more workable in practice is the fusion of deuterium with tritium. Deuterium occurs as an isotope of ordinary hydrogen in that commonest of all materials water, and its separation is believed likely to involve relatively small amounts of energy compared with the quantities that would be released in a fusion reaction. If tritium should be used, however, like uranium-235 this is a rare isotope of a rare element, lithium. Fusion reactions, though simple in principle, are hard to achieve in practice since they involve the production on earth of conditions approaching those in the sun — extremely high temperatures — and the containment of these conditions in a limited volume by means of extremely intense magnetic fields. Just as fission reactions involved a heavy initial investment of energy in the 'fuel', so fusion reactions will involve enormous currents in huge electro-magnets and so forth. Though they may release energy in abundance, they can only be started where electrical energy is already available in abundance. In other words, the costs will certainly be high.

Indeed, while the development of atomic transformation represents a scientific and engineering triumph over the last thirty years, from the economic point of view its impact has been a good deal short of revolutionary. It is extremely difficult to be precise about questions of cost, because the reasons for which the governments of some major industrial countries have initiated nuclear energy programmes have had a good deal to do with military requirements and have only been partly concerned with the economic production of energy for peaceful industrial uses. Besides making plutonium and other materials for nuclear bombs, atomic energy authorities have also been involved in designing reactors for purposes like submarine motors whose performance is judged on non-economic criteria. Military deliveries may not be costed at all, and if they are then the figures are obviously kept secret, so it is practically impossible for those outside government to have any real idea of the true costs of atomic energy. However, the very fact that during the last thirty years nuclear energy has not replaced the fossil fuels to a greater extent presumably reflects its high cost. In 1972 Lord Robens wrote that 'what we have proved with our nuclear power programme is that we can generate very expensive electricity';[26] but that was before the four-fold rise in the price of oil late in 1973, which along with big increases in miners' wages in Britain no doubt altered the relative costs. The latest estimates at the time of writing, indeed, have suggested that in terms of the running costs of fuel alone the advantage is now with nuclear energy, and it is only the extremely high capital costs that still tell against it.

For both economic and technical reasons nuclear energy is a matter of large-scale indivisibilities. Economically, it comes at the end of a long cumulation or 'build-up', with the investment of enormous amounts of conventionally generated electricity into extracting the first workable quantities of nuclear 'fuel', and then the building of breeder reactors, a process which is still as yet scarcely under way in the most advanced industrial countries. And technically, because of the massive safety precautions that are involved. The hazards in the development of nuclear energy are indeed terrifying. In particular, breeder reactors produce large quantities of plutonium, an element which occurs in nature only in minute traces for the very good reason that it is unstable and disintegrates with the emission of energy in the form of radiation. So 'fiendishly toxic' is this metal that the escape of as little as a milligram would amount to a serious hazard to life and health; yet current plans in the big industrial countries envisage the existence of plutonium by the thousands of tons by the year 2000.[27] Meanwhile the problems of the disposal of radioactive wastes are also daunting. Clearly such hazards can be contained only at enormous cost. Perhaps the true role of this form of energy has yet to be played; it may be, as it were, waiting in the wings, to step on stage only when the safety problems have been mastered, and when the pricing-up of the fossil fuels makes it at last an economic proposition despite the high capital costs. For these reasons, it is possible to doubt whether nuclear energy will make much contribution to the energy needs of the present-day poor countries. Only the very largest of the poor countries, like India and China, are in fact able to muster resources to make the exceedingly heavy initial investment which nuclear energy demands, whether viewed in terms of money or of energy.

One further point about nuclear energy concerns the final use to which humans put the energy which they use. At present the two most-favoured types of energy output are represented by electricity and the small internal combustion engine, most of all the motor-car or automobile, and these stand at opposite extremes of scale and divisibility. Electrical energy is generated in large power stations with great economies of scale, and distributed through grid networks which equal or exceed in scale that of a modern nation-state. At the other extreme, the small internal combustion engine represents a source of power which is portable, mobile, self-contained, and above all completely under the user's control. It is clear that a power source of this type has its great attractions, and that wherever possible people are

178

likely to try to equip themselves accordingly, as indeed we have seen in the adaptation of the internal combustion engine to uses like farm and garden cultivation, fishing, forestry, and small-scale manufacturing as well as the obvious one of personal and family transport in the ubiquitous motor-car or automobile.

While nuclear power seems likely to have a role in electricity generation, then, it is unlikely on present indications to be able to meet the evident demand for the second sort of power source. For this, it may be suggested, a liquid fuel like petrol (gasoline) will be wanted for any foreseeable future. A source that suggests itself here is alcohol. Although internal combustion engines hitherto have not run as well on alcohol as on petrol, nevertheless as a fuel it has certain advantages. It lacks the mineral impurities like sulphur which cause pollution when fossil petroleum fuels are burnt; and above all it can be produced from vegetable sources, representing the short-lapse or current use of solar energy to which presumably we shall one day have to return.

This brings us to the other broad range of possibilities, namely those involving the greater and more efficient use of solar power either directly or after short lapses of time – a policy which for the thrifty-minded has the appealing implication of depending more on current income and less on squandering a capital inheritance.

Some 173,000 million megawatts (10^{12} watts) of energy a year reach the earth from the sun. Of this total, 52,000 million megawatts are directly reflected, leaving about 120,000 million megawatts to enter the energy systems of the earth. Most of this stirs up the atmosphere and is dissipated in depressions and storms; some goes into photosynthesis and so enters the life cycle. By contrast, the human use of energy is tiny – only some 6.6 million megawatts a year at present, or about one-twenty-thousandth as much as the solar energy absorbed by the earth. Most of this, as has been seen, is generated by burning fossil fuels and so is additional to the solar energy currently received. It has been estimated that if a human population three times its present size were to use energy at the current average rate of the U.S.A., then this would amount to some 110 million megawatts a year, still under one-thousandth of the energy absorbed from the sun.[28] It is in the more effective use of this energy that the greatest possibilities would appear to lie.

Some of the required technology is already to hand. One obvious possibility is the greater use of hydro-electric power, and it is estimated that only 8.5 per cent of the potential water power available is used at present. Moreover, the three regions with the greatest potential – Africa, South America, and south-east Asia – are among the poor regions at the present time. Another possible way of replacing fossil fuel sources is to use more solar heat for space heating in temperate climates where it is necessary. Experiments have been reported which seem to suggest that buildings like houses and schools can be designed to trap the sun and keep the warmth in with modern insulating materials, while the heat from electric lights and human bodies also contributes to warming a dwelling which needs topping up only on the coldest and least sunny days. The direct use of solar power in photo-cells, used successfully for special purposes including space craft, is probably likely to remain inordinately costly, but large solar reflectors might possibly concentrate heat sufficiently to drive a steam engine or some more sophis-ticated variant.[29] A possibly less ambitious, thought less efficient, use of solar power would be in growing suitable crops in tropical areas for fermenting and distilling industrial alcohol, which might replace petroleum products in internal combustion engines. Some use of solar heat might be made here for raising the temperature of the pulped ferment to near the boiling-point of alcohol, and some use might be made at night or in cloudy weather of burning plant wastes.

A final point to be made here is that since the poor countries are mostly those in the tropics and subtropics — between roughly latitude 30° N. and 20° S. — they should be well placed for any future developments involving the more direct use of solar energy, which may well be a further reason for sug-gesting that this is the most likely direction in which to look for the kind of technological development which will play a part in a raising of the income levels of the poor countries.

SUGGESTIONS FOR FURTHER READING

Paul R. Ehrlich and Anne Ehrlich, *Population, Resources, Environment*, San Francisco: W. H. Freeman, 1970

John Maddox, *The Doomsday Syndrome*, London: Macmillan, 1972

Scientific American, issues of September 1970 for 'The Biosphere' and September 1971 for 'Energy and Power', the latter since reprinted in book form

9 Cultural diversity, language, education, and the mass media

Cultural diversity

In the neolithic world of limited communications, human communities in relative isolation developed widely different cultures. Culture in this context implies a whole way of life — a complex whole including language, material culture or technology, social institutions, and ideas embodying religious, aesthetic, and moral values. A culture is a combination of these elements in a form recognizably different from that of other cultures, even though there might be some elements in common with them — for example, neighbouring societies might get their living in similar ways, but speak different languages and have different forms of political organization. This view of culture leads to some difficulties of definition in practice; it may be a moot point whether to class two tongues as different languages or dialects of the same language, and it is hard to put a precise boundary on a map around a culture or the society whose culture it represents. For this reason, it is impossible to be precise about how many different cultures there are on earth — or were, before the forces which in our time have made for the breaking down of isolation. Nevertheless, difficulties of definition should not lead us to minimize the great extent and depth of cultural diversity, to which the whole science of social anthropology bears witness. As for numbers, it would be erring on the conservative side to say that the number of recognizably different human cultures runs into many thousands.

Cultural diversity, though a common characteristic of poor countries, is not equally well marked in all. In some areas, exposed for many centuries to the rule of overlordship of a dominant people, the culture of that people has more or less heavily overlaid the local indigenous folk-cultures. One major area of the world where this happened is the Arab—Muslim region; another is Latin America. In Asia, broadly speaking, cultural diversity is more marked, though even here certain unifying factors have some influence, especially religion — Islam in Pakistan and Indonesia, Buddhism in Burma and the adjoining lands. India is a special and particularly interesting case in which recognition of cultural diversity and tolerance for different ways of life and of worship were traditional features of the Hindu attitude to life, and non-Hindu communities found an accepted place within the framework of Brahministical Hindu society through the caste system. It is in Africa that cultural diversity is most marked, and this presumably reflects the short time that has elapsed since, under colonial rule, political ascendancy over wide areas was established and barriers to communication were removed.

As an illustration of cultural diversity we may consider the modern African state and former British protectorate of Uganda, a comparatively small country some four hundred miles across, whose population has increased from an estimated four million in 1900 to some eight million today.[1] This population includes some twenty-five to thirty groups, each with a distinctive language and a culture which is in at least some respects different from its neighbours. To consider languages first, the indigenous languages spoken in Uganda are classed into four main groups — Bantu, Western Nilotic, East Nilotic (which used to be called Nilo-Hamitic), and Sudanic. This classification implies a radical difference in basic grammar and vocabulary. Within the major groups the individual languages have a general resemblance to one another, but the degree of mutual comprehension differs. Between any Bantu language and any Nilotic language, however, a far wider gap occurs. Neither the grammar nor the vocabulary of one bears the slightest resemblance to the other, and even the use of tone is different. It is as big a difference as that between any European language and, say, Turkish.

Political organizations and the traditional ideas associated with them were equally diverse. In the south the pattern was of highly centralized kingdoms or chiefdoms — Buganda, Bunyoro, Toro, Ankole — with strongly authoritarian and inegalitarian attitudes about political relations and indeed human relations generally. Elsewhere, however, centralized political authority was weak or absent, and political relations were carried on at the level of feuds between lineages. In contrast to neighbouring Kenya, few of the peoples of Uganda practised circumcision or initiated young men into age-sets, and age-organization was generally weak or absent. There were, however, some exceptions to this, including the Gisu who did circumcise and initiate their young men.

Over considerable areas of what is now Uganda, indeed, there were cultural similarities with political fragmentation. In the southern Bantu-speaking areas, for example, as has been stated the languages are not very different, and there are similarities in institutions like the kinship system extending to common clans. Politically, however, the area was highly fragmented, with a kaleidoscopic pattern of small kingdoms or chiefdoms expanding, conquering their neighbours, reducing them to tributary status, establishing small empires which then fell apart after a generation to two.

In these circumstances, the effect of European intervention and the setting up of a colonial system of administration had had the effect of both simplifying the pattern and fixing it in a more definite form. In this case the British established a foothold first in Buganda, and extended their rule from that base. (The very name 'Uganda', indeed, is the Swahili version of the name of that kingdom.) As elsewhere in Africa, the boundaries of the British sphere of influence were settled by statesmen in the chancelleries of Europe drawing lines on a map — lines which parted like from like as often as they united unlikes. There is hardly a point at which the boundaries of the British protectorate which later became the state of Uganda do not divide people who had a common language and culture, and in some cases a traditional political unity.

There is a sense accordingly in which the former British protectorate and present-day state of Uganda is a highly artificial and arbitrary creation. Its unity is that of a rather short period of subjection to a common system of administration, with the establishment of a common official language – the completely alien English — and the concomitant establishment of common systems of taxation, justice, education, traffic regulations, and the like. It lacks a common indigenous language, a common culture, and most important, a common traditional sentiment of affection and loyalty — that is the continuing inheritance of groups like the former kingdoms, of smaller princedoms like Buhwezhu, or of acephalous communities like the Gisu or Konzo.

In all this, Uganda is by no means untypical, nor even a particularly extreme case among modern African states. In neighbouring Tanzania, for example, there are not twenty-five to thirty different traditional cultural groups as in Uganda, but well over a hundred. Nor has disunity at the political level in Uganda erupted into civil war as it did in Nigeria — or not quite, though relations were very tense over a long period between the kingdom of Buganda and the central government, both under colonial rule and after independence.

The word 'tribe': a current controversy

Not long ago it was usual for a social anthropologist to use the term 'tribe' when referring to the human group or community, with its distinctive culture, which he was studying. The word is indeed embodied in the titles of their books, for example Audrey Richards' *Land, Labour, and Diet in Northern Rhodesia* is sub-titled *An Economic Study of the Bemba Tribe*, and its opening sentence reads, 'The Bemba are the largest and most highly-organized tribe in North-Eastern Rhodesia.'[2] Needless to say there were no pejorative or patronising implications, and the word was used in a quite neutral descriptive sense. To be sure, social anthropologists were aware that the term was somewhat loose and inexact, and in particular that there was an ambiguity between the cultural and political usages of the word. As La Fontaine has put it: 'There are thus two types of meaning for "tribe": one which refers to cultural homogeneity, usually symbolized by a single language, and another which

183

denotes a group organized as a political unit.' One distinguished social anthropologist who consistently used the term in the more restricted sense was
Evans-Pritchard, who stated unequivocally that 'within a tribe there is law',
and in his classic studies of the Nuer used 'congeries of tribes' to refer to the
wider cultural unity of which the politically fragmented tribes were segments. On the whole, however, most other social anthropologists have preferred a definition such as that of Gulliver: 'In brief, then, the term "tribe"
can be taken to apply to any group of people which is distinguished, by its
members and by others, on the basis of cultural—regional criteria.'[3]

Colonial administrations also used the word 'tribe' and it was among the
information which people were asked to give about themselves on occasions
such as seeking employment or entering an educational institution. For purposes of this kind it has a commonsense justification; if a person's tribe was
known then one also knew such essential things as his mother tongue and
his home area. From the point of view of social science, among the most
important occasions when the inhabitants of countries like Uganda were
asked to state what tribe they belonged to was at the time of a census. Demographic data collected in this way were, of course, useful as a background to
more detailed studies by social anthropologists — indeed, at the most elementary level, one of the first things the reader wants to know about the people
whom a social anthropologist is writing about is how many of them there
are.[4] Internal migration patterns could hardly be studied without reference
to tribe, while in some cases there proved to be fertility differences and other
significant demographic differences between tribes which, at the very least,
called for investigation. A knowledge of the number of people who belonged
to each tribe, and consequently who spoke each of the vernacular languages,
was presumably indispensable for educational planning, while by comparing
the tribal composition of students at an educational institution (as I did in
the case of Makerere College) with the populations of the tribes from which
they came, it was possible to lay bare the patterns of regional and ethnic
inequalities in the incidence of higher education.[5]

In the colonial situation, a person's tribe came to constitute an important
aspect of his ascribed status, and this led to intertribal rivalries and conflicts in
modern society. In many cases some tribes dominated certain employments;
this arose partly as a result of stereotyping on the part of the employers who
believed, for example, that some tribes were physically strong, others quick-
witted, etc.; and partly as a result of attempts to reduce the competition of
the labour market by creating partial monopolies on the part of the workers
themselves.

Factional rivalries in modern situations such as employment, education,
and housing accordingly tended to be accompanied by a heightening of tribal
consciousness at a time when tribal identity was being transferred into new,
non-traditional situations. Thus Parkin has traced the rivalries between

the immigrant Luo and the local Ganda in the politics of a Kampala housing estate,[6] while Grillo has shown how the Luo and the Luyia—Samia factions grappled for control of the Railway African Union in Uganda.[7]

Finally, after independence tribal rivalries have broken out in a good many
new states over the most important prize of all — the control of the state with
all its power and resources.

It is not hard to understand accordingly why modern governments
in poor countries, especially in Africa, should have come to regard factionalism and particularism of this kind as a negative force to be opposed, a
danger to be checked. Tribalism has indeed got a very bad name as a
result of events like the Nigerian civil war, the Katanga separatism that
wrecked the Congo, the Buganda separatism that might well have
wrecked Uganda, and similar movements. It is not in the least surprising,
therefore, that modern African governments and political leaders try to play
down tribal differences in their efforts to engender national unity, however
artificial and arbitrary the nations to which the new sentiments of loyalty
are to be attached. Thus the government of Tanzania departed from the
practice of its colonial predecessors and in 1967 omitted any question on
tribe from the census that was taken in that year.[8] For the reasons which
have been suggested above, from the point of view of social science this step
is to be regretted as a failure to collect useful information likely to be of value,
among other things, in planning the development of the countries in question. Some African political leaders have attacked the very concept of tribe as
if it were an invention of the colonial powers — a view which, as Audrey
Richards has said, involves turning a blind eye to the immense diversity of
African cultures.[9] Though an intelligible assertion, this seems clearly to be
a disingenuous one. It is hard indeed to imagine how colonial officials could
have had the time or energy, even supposing they had the inclination, to
invent such things as the differences between Bantu and Nilo-Hamitic languages, or the different political systems of the interlacustrine Bantu and the
Nilotic peoples of Uganda.

In deference to the feelings of modern African political leaders and
intellectuals on this issue, many social scientists in recent years have tried to
avoid using the word 'tribe', even though this merely entails using another
word or phrase such as 'ethnic group', 'cultural group', 'people', or, in the
context of language, 'mother-tongue group'. Some have gone further; thus
Vincent writes, 'Surely the "tribe" may best be viewed as a colonial administrative unit given legitimacy, and, indeed, in some cases, reality, by colonial
recognition?'[10] while in a similar vein Apthorpe states, 'Yet certainly in
Anglophone Africa, what happened was rather that the colonial regimes
administratively *created* tribes as we think of them today.'[11] Such a view
pays scant regard to the pre-existing cultural diversity and seems a clear case
of what Myrdal has called 'diplomacy by terminology'. Merely to suppress a

185

word does nothing to alter the massive facts of cultural diversity and political fragmentation which characterize many new states in the Third World.

Language

Most people who live in industrial nations are accustomed to a situation in which practically everybody in the same country speaks the same language, which is also the official language of the state for the purposes of government and administration. Some industrial states are 'linguistic states' in the sense that their language is peculiar to them, and not widely spoken elsewhere — Japan and Sweden are examples. In others, the national language is also widely spoken and officially recognized in other countries also — French, for example, in Belgium, Switzerland, and Canada; German in Austria and Switzerland; and of course English in the former British dominions like New Zealand and Australia.

In many of the poor countries, however, the diversity of languages is much more marked, and the local indigenous languages have only a limited currency and do not serve as languages of wider communication. The immediate implication is that many people in poor countries are forced to be linguists in a way which most people in rich countries are not. In order to cope with situations like employment, the public education system, dealings with official authorities, and even ordinary everyday communication in shop and street, they have to learn at least one other language besides their mother tongue, and in many cases more.[12]

On the whole it is men who are under the greater necessity to learn other languages. Men enter employment, migrate to towns, seek work on plantations or mines, and generally engage in a wider social milieu. At present in poor countries most women stay at home, where their social relations are confined to the household and neighbourhood, milieux where the vernacular prevails. Local languages accordingly continue to be mother tongues, learned by children of both sexes. Moreover, among men different situations may call for the learning of different languages. Manual workers may need to know an oral lingua franca or pidgin for purposes of work or trade, where those who aspire to managerial or bureaucratic status may need to know a different literary language. Further, since some people need to know the formal, literary language, and it is not always possible to know in advance which people they will be, such elite languages may have to be taught in schools to many who will have little or no use for them in later life.

At first sight, an extreme case of cultural and linguistic diversity might appear to be that of Tanzania, with its recognized vernaculars numbering well over a hundred. However, certain features of the situation in Tanzania render it less complex and (from the point of view of official policy) less intractable than might appear. With only a few exceptions, nearly all the

186

indigenous languages are Bantu. For the last hundred years or more, Swahili has become widely spoken and understood throughout the area. This is basically a Bantu language in grammar and structure, though its vocabulary includes a large number of words borrowed from Arabic, from Portuguese (as a result of Portuguese activities at the coast of Africa in past centuries), and from English. Its Bantu structure ensures that it is readily learned by the majority of people in Tanzania, while its enriched vocabulary gives it sufficient resources to be able to accommodate many of the needs of modern life. (For example, it has in a fully developed system of number what many Bantu languages lack.) It has been committed to writing, mainly in Roman script in the last hundred years or so though there is also a somewhat limited older literature in Arabic script, in which the language can also be written. It is in fact widely spoken in Tanzania, indeed almost universally so by men, though probably to a lesser extent by women. Its adoption as a national language was accordingly natural, though it carries a rather serious disadvantage in that Swahili is not really a language of wider communication. Though spoken quite widely in some neighbouring African countries, especially Kenya, and to a more limited extent in Uganda and Zaire, it does not give access to a wide world of science, technology, literature, trade, or diplomacy. There is, accordingly, a continuing need for the teaching and use of English, the legacy of the colonial period. Since it is impossible to know in advance in a society as devoted to equality and as opposed to elitism and privilege as Tanzania who are going to be the future diplomats, scientists, and so forth, the teaching of English retains an important place in the secondary school curriculum. Educated young Tanzanians accordingly have to learn three languages – the vernacular mother tongue, Swahili, and English – unless they live at the coast or in Zanzibar, where Swahili is the mother tongue.

In neighbouring Uganda, under colonial rule no lingua franca gained so strong a foothold. Considerable numbers of men in fact know Swahili, especially those in trade and employment. Its use was, however, deprecated and opposed by the Ganda people, who under British overrule occupied a privileged position of hegemony, and who disliked Swahili because of its associations with colonial rule. It was a houseboys' language, they said, spoken by white bwanas when addressing their servants in Kenya. They had a point, too, that it was not the mother tongue of any indigenous group in the protectorate. It did, however, become the language of the army, since under colonial government Uganda units formed part of a regiment – the King's African Rifles – which drew units also from Kenya, Tanganyika, and Nyasaland (as they were then named) and in which Swahili was the obvious lingua franca. At the same time, fears of Ganda hegemony on the part of the other tribes of the protectorate led to resistance to any suggestion that Luganda (the Ganda language) should become the general lingua franca there, and after independence, accordingly, the only choice for an official

187

language was the completely alien English. One advantage of this situation was nevertheless that in the education system it was possible to go straight from the vernacular to English, without the intervening step of Swahili. Ganda disdain for Swahili later caught up with them in an unpleasant and unexpected way. As related by Mazrui, after the downfall of the Kabaka of Buganda and the suppression of the Ganda kingdom, 'a linguistic test [began] to be used as a way of determining the degree of humiliation to which a captured person was to be subjected'; soldiers tended to beat up any black man who could not answer them fluently in Swahili, and whom they thought likely accordingly to be a subject of the departed Kabaka — including on one occasion a Jamaican colleague of Mazrui.[13]

The decision to adopt a local language as the official language of a new state, therefore, while it may be a natural choice and one which can focus national consciousness, can also have politically divisive effects if the language is that of a group whose dominance is feared and resented, and it may also lead to a partial abandonment of a language of wider communication. These are points of more general application, as will appear below.

At present only a small handful of African states are based on a single language and culture — Somalia, Lesotho, Swaziland, and Malagasy (Madagascar). Even in these states there is a problem of the relation between the national language and the language, or languages, required for wider communication. Thus, in Somalia, though 95 per cent of the people speak Somali, there are no less than three languages of wider communication — English and Italian, the legacies of colonial rule respectively in the north and the south, and Arabic.[14] Similarly, in Lesotho many men learn Afrikaans as well as English in the course of their visits to work in the Republic of South Africa. These states are not typical, and the great majority of African states are as multi-cultural and multi-lingual as Uganda, Ethiopia, or Nigeria.

Traditional African cultures did not for the most part include any indigenous system of writing, a generalization to which cases like Swahili in Arabic script afford only partial exceptions. For the most part, African languages were committed to writing only within the last century or so, usually by Christian missionaries, and in the Roman script. One consequence of this has been that though many Africans have to learn more than one tongue, they do not have to learn more than one script. Roman is not a particularly easy script to learn, and many children have difficulty with it. It associates shapes with sounds in a completely arbitrary manner, the associated conventions of spelling are equally arbitrary, and there is difficulty in proceeding from phonemes to words and concepts, and thence to sentences. These difficulties are reflected in the controversies which rage in the teaching profession in western countries over initial teaching alphabets, methods of teaching, and the like. Nevertheless though the task is hard it is comparatively limited; the alphabet does, after all, consist of only twenty-six letters, and

188

once mastered this script affords the key, not only to the speaker's own language, but also to other languages, especially including European languages of world currency like French, English, and Spanish.

At the opposite extreme to this position is that in China, where there are several spoken languages but only one ideographic script. The term 'ideographic' implies that the written symbols for 'man', 'woman', 'house', etc., consist of stylized pictures; indeed, the non-lingual signs which are now appearing outside public lavatories in Britain represent a decision to adopt, in effect, an ideographic system for these basic needs. An ideographic script has two very great advantages. It is very easy to learn in the early stages; literally child's play, indeed, and it is reported that dyslexia is much rarer in Japan than in western countries. The other advantage is that literate people can communicate in writing without the slightest difficulty even though they may not be able to understand one another's spoken language. Chinese street signs and newspapers can be understood throughout China without translation, and the same is ever more importantly true of books. The common ideographic script is, accordingly, regarded as an indispensable aspect of national unity. On the other hand, it has also serious disadvantages. The simplicity and obviousness of the ideographs for commonplace objects and concepts are replaced by extreme complexity and difficulty in devising ideographs for more advanced concepts, especially abstractions. Indeed, at the high levels of thought and communication the written language becomes a matter of allusion and convention that demands an enormous expenditure of time and effort to learn. Thus, in contrast to the 26 phonetic symbols of Roman script, ordinary literate Chinese may know about 3,000 ideographic symbols, though newspapers use from 6,000 to 7,000, and the most highly educated people may know as many as 30,000 to 50,000. In traditional China this meant that the education of the elite was almost wholly literary, in the narrowest possible sense of the word; it consisted very largely of learning how to write and read the thousands of more complex ideographs symbolizing advanced concepts. In the modern world this multiplicity of symbols has further and very practical disadvantages when it comes to techniques like printing and typing. The present Chinese government has accordingly the long-term aim of introducing the Roman script, but it is recognized that this will be a very slow process. Ultimately the aim is for all Chinese to know Mandarin, the dominant spoken language of China, whether as the mother tongue or as a second language. When that is achieved, then Mandarin written in Roman script, with all its conveniences, will be available as the written language. Meanwhile, a start has been made with the issue of street signs in which the Chinese characters are accompanied by the Mandarin— Roman equivalent.

India, like China, is a country with a rich and complex heritage of literary culture. In India, however, as well as a number of spoken languages there

189

are also a number of traditional scripts — each of the major languages has its own script, and there are also scripts of ritual significance, such as the Gurmukh script in which Punjabi is written for the purposes of the Sikh religion. Each of these scripts, and the language and culture associated with it, is not unnaturally regarded as a priceless heritage and jealously defended, so that the early history of independent India was marked by violent political controversies over language and the rearrangement of the provincial administration of that large country into linguistic states. There is moreover the further complication of English, which under British rule was the official language and accordingly the language of opportunity for the intellectual and bureaucratic elite. Many families, indeed, at the highest levels of society adopted English, and it has been remarked that in the controversies that accompanied the development of secondary and higher education in the nineteenth century it was ironically enough the Indian intellectuals who were the 'Anglicists', favouring the wholehearted adoption of the English language and its associated culture, while the British officials tended to be 'Orientalists' and included men with a deeply genuine respect for Indian traditional culture who exerted themselves to rescue Sanskrit from oblivion.

The government of independent India accordingly faced a set of dilemmas over language. On the one hand, from an outward-looking point of view the existence of a substantial class of highly educated and articulate people fluent in English could be seen as a considerable national asset, favouring the communication of scientific and cultural ideas with the outer world as well as facilitating diplomatic and business contacts. On the other hand, such an elite was correspondingly cut off from the great majority of their fellow-countrymen. There was no conceivable possibility of English being spoken by the majority of the population, and accordingly its use as the official language served further to emphasize the distance between government and people, a distinction that had no relation to the reality of political life after the departure of the British, and was resented by many outside the intellectual elite. The decision in 1963 to adopt Hindi in the Devanagri script as the official language of the union, though it brought government nearer the people in that sense, was also a highly controversial one since people in non-Hindi-speaking areas felt they were being disadvantaged. So when in 1965 the new law was brought into force, riots broke out in Madras and elsewhere, and the government was forced to retreat to the position that English would continue to be recognized as long as non-Hindi-speaking people wanted it.

I have suggested above that many people in poor countries are 'forced to be linguists'. Very generally throughout the non-industrial world, indeed, there is pressure of circumstances on men (less so on women) to be bilingual, learning a second language of wider communication as well as the vernacular mother tongue. In India, however, people have to be not bilingual but trilingual, and (to coin a term) they have to be tri-scriptal as well; for they have to learn first the language of the state, with its traditional script, then Hindi in Devanagri script, and then English in Roman script. This has led to complaints that the curriculum of the child has become 'congested on the linguistic side before anything else is learned'. More time spent on language teaching means, of course, less time available for substantive subjects like mathematics, science, and history: and there are said also to be indirect effects in the emphasis on memory work and rote learning, which spread to the way in which other subjects are taught as well as the smaller amount of time available for them. Schools, indeed, then to retain an old-fashioned literary and academic character, and it is on this basis that Myrdal exclaims that 'people are not merely being insufficiently educated; they are being mis-educated on a huge scale'.[15]

The situation in some other South Asian countries resembles that in India. In Sri Lanka, for instance, there are three languages — Sinhalese and Tamil, each with its own script, and English with Roman script. In Pakistan the language spoken by the biggest number of people is Punjabi, with a script different from that used for the official language Urdu. Both regional and national languages have to be taught in Burma and Thailand. Another example of linguistic complexity is the Philippines, where there are several Malayo-Polynesian vernacular languages of which the one spoken by the biggest number is Cebuano. Another, however, was chosen as the national language since it was the vernacular language of the region of Manila, had greater prestige, and was spoken more widely as a second language; this was Tagalog, renamed Pilipino as a sop to national pride. Spanish has been of great importance in the islands for many centuries, and continues to be taught and used in schools; while English has also been taught in the primary schools since the beginning of the American administration, and is widely recognized to be the best language for wider communication with the outside world. At least, however, all these languages, including the vernaculars, are written in Roman script.[16]

'Bi-scriptalism' is called for in Arabic countries in so far as Roman is needed in conjunction with English or French as languages of wider communication. However, the Arabic language and script constitute important means of communication and unity not only within states in the Arab—Muslim area, but also between them; and this unit is heightened by association with the religion of Islam, and many institutions derived from it such as the laws of marriage and inheritance. But perhaps the area of the Third World in which the problems of cultural and linguistic diversity are least intractable is Latin America, with its common heritage of the Spanish language (or in Brazil the Portuguese) together again with associated cultural features including literature, religion, and law.

191

Sociology of the Third World

Education

Some indication of the educational state of the people of poor countries may be gained from United Nations statistics on illiteracy, school attendance, and the size of the educated elite, though unfortunately the figures are both incomplete and out of date, referring mostly to dates around 1960. Illiteracy rates are seen to be substantial everywhere in the Third World, though they seem to be associated more with regional differences and special historical circumstances than with precise levels of G.N.P. The region where illiteracy

TABLE 9.1 *Educational indicators in selected countries: illiteracy*

Country, date	Ages to which data refer[a]	% illiterate	
		Male	Female
U.S.S.R., 1959	9–49	0.7	2.2
Poland, 1960	14+	3.0	6.2
Bulgaria, 1956		7.3	21.9
Yugoslavia, 1961	10+	9.9	28.8
Spain, 1960		8.4	17.7
Portugal, 1960		30.6	44.6
Mexico, 1960		29.8	39.3
Jamaica, 1960		21.4	15.2
Venezuela, 1961		30.2	38.3
Peru, 1961	17+	25.6	52.4
Chile, 1960		14.6	17.7
Jordan, 1961		49.9	84.8
Syria, 1960	10+	46.5	83.2
Iraq, 1957	5+	73.1	92.4
Iran, 1956		80.2	94.5
Pakistan, 1961		71.1	92.6
India, 1961	All ages	65.6	87.1
Thailand, 1960		20.7	43.9
Malaysia, 1957–60[b]		39.4	75.9
Philippines, 1960		25.8	30.5
Indonesia, 1961		42.8	70.4
Senegal, 1960–1	14+	89.6	98.9
Sudan, 1956		92.6	98.4

[a]Age 15 and over unless otherwise stated.
[b]Excluding Singapore.
Source: *United Nations Demographic Yearbook*, 1963 and 1964.

192

was least extensive around 1960 was that of Central and South America, where though there were differences between countries substantially more than half the people were reported as literate and in most countries half or more of the women. Such rates were not very different from those in the poorer countries of Europe.

Illiteracy was more widespread in the Arab–Muslim world, Pakistan, and India, though the proportion illiterate was rather lower in some other South Asian countries such as the Philippines, where an extensive system of public education was one of the legacies of a period of American administration. The really high rates of illiteracy were those for African countries, in some of which, as will be seen from table 9.1, 90 per cent of the men and virtually all the women were unable to read or write.

Efforts to spread the basic skill of literacy are seen mainly in the school attendance figures shown in table 9.2. Although some countries have had mass literacy campaigns aimed at adults, and have devoted some attention to adult education, generally speaking such measures take low priority in the allocation of scarce resources compared with the education of children, which teachers and officials in Ministries of Education tend to see as their main, or even virtually their only proper task. As will be seen, in most of the

TABLE 9.2   *Educational indicators in selected countries: school attendance rates*

Country, date	Age group	% attending school	
		Boys	Girls
U.S.A., 1960	5–14	89.9	90.0
Portugal, 1960	5–14	58.0	55.3
Yugoslavia, 1961	7–14	85.0	79.3
Mexico, 1960	6–14	57.4	55.3
Jamaica, 1960	5–14	82.5	84.6
Venezuela, 1961	5–14	62.7	61.8
Peru, 1961	5–14	43.4	36.5
Chile, 1960	5–14	64.6	63.3
Pakistan, 1961	5–14	23.3	11.2
Malaysia (east), 1960	5–14	50.8	35.1
Philippines, 1960	6–14	48.5	49.7
Indonesia, 1961	5–14	45.1	39.9
Ghana, 1960	6–14	49.5	29.9
Senegal, 1960–1	6–13	24.7	15.8

Source: *United Nations Demographic Yearbook*, 1963 and 1964.

193

poor countries listed in the table substantial proportions of children were going to school in 1960—1. More of the boys than of the girls were attending school, and there was a tendency for the countries with low proportions of children attending school to be concentrating more of their resources on boys than on girls. Universal schooling for girls too tends to come as a second stage in educational development; thus, the education of females in poor countries tends to be thought of as a problem in itself, and the attitudes of many parents and other influential people in poor countries is often reminiscent of Victorian attitudes in Britain — 'why educate girls when they are only going to get married?' The basic skills of literacy and the other benefits of education tend, accordingly, to be a male privilege in many poor countries. The other point indicated by table 9.2 is that as long ago as 1960—1 many countries with high illiteracy rates were changing that situation rapidly by educating their children. In some countries, indeed, there had already been a striking fall in the illiteracy rate by 1960; for example, in Ceylon (Sri Lanka) from 65.8 per cent in 1921 to 32.3 per cent in 1953, and in Mexico from 61.5 per cent in 1930 to 34.6 per cent in 1960. Since then there has been further rapid development of the public education system in most poor countries, and the proportions attending school are now much higher, so that eventually those countries will have a largely literate population. Meanwhile, however, the educated people tend to be young men, and there are few men and scarcely any women in those countries who are both educated and experienced. There is, indeed, in many poor countries a situation of potential conflict and misunderstanding between the educated young men and their uneducated elders, as well as a gap between those young men and their wives.

Tables 9.1 and 9.2 relate respectively to the basic skills of literacy and to school attendance as the means of acquiring that and related skills. Four years at school is generally regarded as the minimum to establish secure and lasting literacy, and generally speaking it has been the first priority among the educational aims of the governments of poor countries to make four years' primary schooling available to as many children as possible, the ideal being universal primary education. This raises as a second question the balance between primary, secondary, and higher education in poor countries, and the question of what happens to children who complete the basic primary schooling and who wish (or whose parents wish them) to go on. Generally speaking, secondary education has been regarded as a second priority in countries with limited resources unable to do everything at once, so that the pyramid of school enrolments is typically a very broad, flat one — large numbers of children enter school, but a much smaller number go on to secondary schools and the numbers going forward to higher education are minute. This is made clear by the figures in table 9.3.

As a vivid illustration of these general trends we may take the progress through the educational system of Uganda of boys and girls born there in 1950, according to the estimates made by Peter Williams. Of every 100 boys and girls born in 1950 who survived to be counted at the 1959 census, about 36 boys and 18 girls entered the first class in grant-aided primary schools in 1957. Twenty-four boys and 7 or 8 girls reached the sixth and last primary class in 1962, but only 9 boys and 3 girls entered junior secondary school in 1963 and were still in the second class there in 1964. Five children entered the senior secondary school, or otherwise entered a ninth year of education

TABLE 9.3   *Educational indicators in selected countries: school enrolments by stage of education*

Country, date	Stage of education	Number of pupils enrolled	
		Boys	Girls
England and Wales, 1966	Primary	2,444,775	2,313,259
	Secondary	1,699,000	1,603,797
	Higher	195,737	114,969
Poland, 1967	1st level	2,946,324	2,759,946
	2nd level	904,845	859,742
	3rd level	174,740	114,048
Mexico, 1967	1st level	4,062,533	3,709,724
	2nd level	691,101	430,644
	3rd level	127,531	26,758
Pakistan, 1966	1st level	5,357,610	1,940,711
	2nd level	2,226,137	525,362
	3rd level	245,191	46,763
Malaysia, 1967 (excluding Singapore)	1st level	820,262	715,830
	2nd level	319,813	209,627
	3rd level	10,238	5,741
Senegal, 1965	1st level	139,365	79,430
	2nd level	25,434	9,210
	3rd level	2,265	490
Swaziland, 1968	1st level	31,816	30,266
	2nd level	3,654	2,916
	3rd level	62	7

Source: *United Nations Statistical Yearbook*, 1969.

in 1965; and at current trends it was expected that only 2 or 3 would reach Secondary Six, complete 14 years' schooling, and be potential university entrants in 1970.[17]

In many such countries, indeed, a critical bottleneck occurs in the secondary or senior secondary schools, in which the claims of all the government departments — health, agriculture, animal industry, and so forth — for trainable junior field staff for development schemes competes acutely with the demands for commercial and clerical employment, and with the needs of the education system itself for the 'feed-back' through the colleges of education of teachers for its own expansion. This situation, indeed, has led some people concerned in education in poor countries to question the wisdom of too absolute a priority being given to the aim of universal primary education, and there are those who advocate a more balanced growth of primary and secondary schools. It is at the secondary level accordingly that aid from the outside world and the services of expatriates may in some cases make a really strategic contribution. Further, there is an inexorable gradualness about the expansion of an education system which results from the extremely long 'gestation period' of any changes that are introduced in it. Thus, even if it were possible to double the intake of secondary schools overnight, it would be four to six years (depending on the precise division of the schools system, and the definition of 'secondary') before any increase could take place in the numbers of young people leaving secondary schools, which as has been suggested is often the critical bottleneck. Assuming a further three years' course in colleges of education, it would be seven to nine years before an increased flow of teachers would be available for the further expansion of the primary and secondary school system. In many industrial countries, the build-up to a system of universal education took place over long periods, many decades and even up to a century or more in some cases. By contrast, similar development has been telescoped in some poor countries into thirty years or so. In Kenya, for example, there was virtually no education for Africans in the 1920s; by the 1950s, practically all the boys and about half the girls were attending school at least for a time.

Table 9.4 is an attempt to extract from United Nations statistics indications of a third important variable — the size of what might be termed the educated elite, though that term is clearly in elastic and a relative one. Here the absolute numbers rather than percentages are given, for though the population of the country obviously affects its needs for highly educated men and women, some of the needs are indivisible — every state, for example, has a prime minister and a cabinet, ministries to be staffed with senior civil servants, embassies to the United Nations and at least a few major foreign states, and the like, and it is a vitally important question to ask what are a country's resources of highly educated people for those tasks, besides others like the needs of the education system, the health service, and so forth which are more or less proportionate to population. The point that is brought out very strongly by the figures in table 9.4 is how very small and precious are those resources in some of the poor countries. Some exceptions must be made to this generalization, notably India where there is, if anything, a surplus of highly qualified men, and graduate unemployment, or employment in work far below graduate

TABLE 9.4   *Educational indicators in selected countries: the size of the educated elite*

Country, date	Population (approximate) (millions)	Number of persons having some higher education		Criterion: number of years of education[a]
		Men	Women	
U.S.A., 1960	181	10,381,321	9,042,255	10 and over
U.S.S.R., 1959	210	2,753,018	2,762,356	10 and over
Spain, 1960	30	218,170	32,671	'Higher level'[b]
Portugal, 1960	9	54,099	17,420	12 and over
Poland, 1960	30	375,860	196,560	11 and over
Yugoslavia, 1961	18.6	148,458	48,214	'Higher level'[b]
Mexico, 1960	35	180,967	64,438	12 and over
Jamaica, 1960	1.6	2,406	890	'Higher level'[b]
Peru, 1961	10.4	81,800	37,500	'Higher level'[b]
Chile, 1960	8	54,526	27,441	11 and over
Jordan, 1961	1.7	5,717	1,302	11 and over
Syria, 1960	4.6	10,044	1,331	Graduates
Iraq, 1957	6.3	17,411	3,227	'Higher level'[b]
Iran, 1956	19	29,643	2,828	12 and over
Pakistan, 1961	95	73,838	8,231	University degree below Master's
		28,387	3,083	Master's or Doctor's degree
Thailand, 1960	26	62,945	32,192	11 and over
		8,552	1,836	Graduates
Malaysia, 1957[c]	7.3	44,261	9,667	12 and over
Philippines, 1960	27	494,125	433,141	10 and over
Indonesia, 1961	96	41,679	14,158	Completed university or academy
Ghana, 1960	6.7	18,450	5,860	'Higher level'[b]
Uganda, 1959	6.5	33,000	6,000	10 and over

[a] Including in some cases an incomplete final year.
[b] Not otherwise stated.
[c] Excluding Singapore.
Source: *United Nations Demographic Yearbook*, 1963 and 1964.

potential, is said to be a common phenomenon. In most poor countries, however, the small numbers of highly educated men and the minute numbers of highly educated women mean that they are in short supply in relation to the tasks of building up a modern state with modern public administration and public services, notably including the needs of education itself.

The role which educated elites play in the life of poor countries is indeed crucial. These are the people who have effectively undergone a double acculturation, first into the local vernacular folk-culture and then into the metropolitan or cosmopolitan culture of the world of science and scholarship, administration and international affairs. The roles which they occupy in the social structure are pivotal accordingly. For example, in my own study of the educated elite in East Africa I found most former students of Makerere, the local university college, were working in the public service as teachers, medical practitioners, in the government agricultural and veterinary services, and other similar occupations. In the great majority of cases, it could be said that their work consisted of mediating between the two cultures. At the same time, while their professional and intellectual equipment was that of the wider world culture, their own roots and their personal and family life were largely that of the changing African society. While they were drawn mostly from families with above-average education and exposure to western cultural influence – particularly through attachment to Christian missions – virtually all had at least some near kin who were living a traditional style of life as subsistence peasants and who had little or no schooling. Almost all had at least one illiterate relative, a grandparent or a parent's sibling (uncle or aunt) if not a parent. Moreover, because of the preponderance of boys over girls in secondary and higher education, many of these educated men had been unable to find equally educated wives. (Indeed, fear of being forced into an arranged marriage with an illiterate girl was a common theme in under-graduate literary and dramatic compositions.) The style of life at home was accordingly in most cases largely traditional African rather than modern western, and this was accentuated by the fact that the households of many educated men included poor relatives as well as unrelated domestic servants whose ways and skills were related to the rural tribal economy and society rather than that of the modern urban milieu.[18]

In many poor countries (South America being an exception) the recent withdrawal of colonial officials and the grant of political independence created vacancies in roles at the very top of the social and political structures of those countries, from the head of state and cabinet ministers to the senior posts in the civil service, the 'para-statal bodies' like broadcasting and electricity generating boards, the universities, schools, the police and the law, and other public institutions. At the same time, many large international business corporations like the great oil companies took steps to recruit local managers and remove as many white faces from top offices as possible, the

Roman Catholic and Anglican churches ordained local bishops, and so on. For a short time, the rise of the local educated elites in some countries was spectacular. Men in their late twenties and early thirties became cabinet ministers and heads of government departments, scholars of modest attainments became professors and vice-chancellors, sergeant-majors became generals almost overnight. Once the top posts were filled, of course, a more normal pace of promotion prevailed, and this resulted in acute frustration among men who arrived near the top only a year or two too late, to find their path to the top blocked perhaps for decades by a man very little their superior either in age or attainments, a frustration that is thought to have had something to do with some of the political upheavals and military coups, for example that led by three lieutenants in Ghana in 1967.[19]

Men who had taken over the positions of power and responsibility formerly held by white colonial officials, businessmen, and so on were naturally inclined to expect similar rewards. They moved into the same houses, drove or were driven in similar cars, led a similar kind of life in terms of their daily routine, and had the same kind of needs accordingly. Moreover, the style of life of the rich and powerful is one related to world rather than local standards. A head of state and senior officials must be able to entertain men and women of similar rank from other countries, and failure to do so would be felt to be humiliating, not least by the people of the country concerned. A senior treasury official must be able to withstand bank hospitality when he travels in his country's service to London, Zurich, or New York or attends conferences in Addis Ababa, Delhi, or Santiago.

Such circumstances clearly have a good deal to do with the wide disparities which characterize the economy and society of poor countries, as emphasized in chapter 4. The conclusion that poor countries had merely exchanged a rich, privileged, powerful black elite for a white one was readily drawn, and bitter attacks on the new 'national bourgeoisie' are to be found in the writings of left-wing writers like Frantz Fanon.[20] In Merton's phrase such groups have more often been the object of vilification than of sociological study,[21] though there are some studies especially of African elites.[22]

Another important aspect of the educated elite is its sheer size in absolute numbers rather than as a proportion of the population, for this is of significance as indicating the possible viability of the national language for the purposes of a national culture (using the term here, exceptionally, in its narrow evaluative sense of 'higher culture'). What is the size of the market or public for 'quality' newspapers, an avant-garde theatre, serious novels, new poems, or learned scientific journals? Where a big country like America, France, or Japan can be largely self-contained in such matters and develop a higher culture in the national language, at the other end of the scale there would clearly be little scope for a *Journal of Physics* in the Somali language, or even a Somali equivalent of a semi-popular journal like *New Society*. So physicists and social scientists in Somalia will clearly have to rely on a foreign language like English for communication in their professional discipline, and the same goes for university and secondary school students. Such considerations reinforce the point made above about the paramount need to introduce a language of wider communication early in the school system, and switch over to using it as the medium of instruction at some stage, usually in secondary schools after about the sixth year of education. The need is even stronger in the case of multi-cultural and multi-lingual states like most of those of modern Africa, where even the achievements of modern writers such as Achebe, Soyinka, and Ngugi have been in the English language for lack of a sufficiently numerous educated public in any one vernacular.

This situation reinforces the foreignness of education, which is one of its pervading features in most poor countries. In some areas, indeed, the very institution of a school – a place where children assemble, to be taught by specially qualified adults – is a cultural innovation (reverting at this point to the non-evaluative anthropological usage of the term culture). No society lacks institutionalized means socializing the young and transferring traditional knowledge and values, but in many pre-industrial societies the ways in which this was done did not correspond to our preconceived notion of the school. In many African traditional cultures, young people learned by doing and by helping their parents and others older than themselves In some cases institutions like tribute labour had educational functions – young men and women called to work at the chief's court saw and heard what went on there. In some African societies there were highly institutionalized and formal initiation ceremonies marking the transition from juvenile to adult status, *rites de passage* which included tests of fortitude and some formal instruction in the duties of young men and young women, and these were, in some cases, carried out in seclusion, extended over a period, and were called 'schools' accordingly.[23] Although one or two attempts were made to reconcile the new style of education with traditional initiation rites, in general the two were in conflict. Thus in Lesotho the reluctance of the mission schools to accept initiated boys, or allow them to resume their studies, has resulted in a sharp division between those men who have enjoyed the benefits of modern education and hold the positions of overt power and prestige in the modern system accordingly, but who are held in contempt as mere boys by the men who have undergone the rigours of the initiation lodge and further proved their manhood in the mines of South Africa.[24]

Lesotho is an extreme case, but it was quite common in Africa for the setting up of schools by the first Christian missionaries to be met with indifference or hostility among the local people, who had to be persuaded to send their children to school – adult converts were told it was their duty, while both missionaries and government officials put pressure on chiefs to show an example by sending at least one of their sons.[25] In some places an initial hostility was rather rapidly succeeded by a rush of enthusiastic acceptance, when the advantages in terms of employment in government service, commerce, and other modern opportunities came to be recognized, and colonial administrations who not long before had been with difficulty pioneering modern education were now criticized for not doing more and doing it faster. However, though there is certainly a clamour for education in modern Africa, not everybody is clamouring. The acceptance of modern education has not equally affected all tribes or all areas, and though people in the areas most affected by the rise of modern industry, commerce, and administration – like the Kikuyu – are sharply aware of the gains from education (or perhaps more important the losses which follow from not being educated), in the remoter areas there may still be a good deal of reservation about the value of this experience in the life of a boy, and still more in that of a girl. Some tribes have become wholeheartedly education-minded where others have not, in ways that are not always easy to explain, whether in terms of the indigenous social structure or the history of missionary penetration and government activity.[26]

The school was not quite so complete a cultural innovation in areas outside Africa, and in the traditional civilizations like those of the Arab–Muslim world and of India there were institutions resembling schools in the modern sense. It might be thought accordingly that the break between old and new forms of education would be less sharp, and the possibility of building the new on the old foundations would be greater in those areas; but broadly speaking that has not proved to be the case. Thus in Muslim countries the *kuttab* or Koran school has generally proved resistant to modernization, though Egypt is a partial exception,[27] and the *madrasah* or higher college too has proved very conservative despite attempts in some countries to introduce into the curriculum modern subjects such as mathematics and the history and geography of the Arab world. In Tunisia, for example, 'it proved impossible to graft a curriculum suited to the modern age on to the traditional framework of Zitouna', the indigenous university, which despite attempts at reform continued to train its students mainly for religious positions or posts in the Islamic courts. The initiative passed accordingly to a newly founded secondary school, Sadiqi College, with a western-style pedagogical system 'nationalized' to the extent of stressing training in Arabic and Islamic studies; and Sadiqi rather than Zitouna set the pattern for the development of Tunisian education.[28]

In India similarly the traditional systems of lower schools (*pathsala*) and higher colleges (*tols, vidyalayas, chatuspathis*) were at a low ebb when British education on British lines made a fresh start in the nineteenth century. The result has been mentioned above; the educated intellectual and administrative class thought in English and spoke it at home, and hardly knew how to read and write any Indian language. Though they were accordingly thoroughly westernized, with flexible minds open to scientific ways of thought and modern political ideas, they were also cut off from the great mass of the people; and the indigenous languages, literatures, and philosophies remained stagnant and sterilized, deprived of the vitalizing influences of the best minds. Uneasiness about this situation led in the latter part of the nineteenth century to the formation of modernizing Indian movements of thought, religion, and education under the influence of figures such as Rabindranath Tagore, Aurobindo, Vivekananda, and Raja Ram Mohan Roy, and the foundation of new experimental schools and colleges intended to balance Indian and western cultures. At the time of independence, accordingly, Kabir could write of three systems of education in India:

The products of the three systems of education live in the same country, feel the same type of needs, and must meet the same challenge of the modern age. The existence of parallel and at times incompatible beliefs and ideas among the different communities had had an adverse effect ... A man lives simultaneously in many ages. We have examples of Indian scientists who are in touch with the latest movements of scientific thought and are at the same time immersed emotionally in customs which defy all reason.[29]

It is clear from these examples that one of the major tasks in the development of education in poor, non-western countries is seen as that of harmonizing two cultures — or at least of trying to reduce the dissonance between them. The question of language, and the relative position of the vernacular and the language of wider communication, is seen accordingly in a larger perspective. On the one hand, there is the local traditional culture expressed in a vernacular language. As the mother-tongue culture this is likely to have a strong emotional hold over the minds of the great majority of people; where a language of wider communication may serve to do just that, to communicate, it is in the vernacular that people are likely to be persuaded at the level of emotion and commitment.[30] Moreover, the vernacular serves as the repository of a folk-wisdom ranging from earthy matters like soil and crops through shrewd observations of human nature and social relations to the expression of literary themes in a culture that may be by no means negligible in its content and value. And since it is viewed as a precious cultural inheritance, it will be emotionally defended, so that educationists are likely to be under pressure to respect and maintain it. On the other hand, without sacrificing the vernacular heritage, the educators in poor countries have also to introduce and widely spread the modern culture of science and mathematics, political ideas and administrative methods, associated with a world language giving access to wider communication and with its own rich heritage of literature; and English (for example) is not just a tool subject, it is also the language of Shakespeare.

Among the critical shortages in educational development in poor countries is often that of textbooks and other educational materials related to the local environment. There are many 'horror stories' about the importation of unsuitable material and inappropriate methods into the schools of the Third World — of African pupils being taught about the coalfields of England or the dissolution of the monasteries, of Algerian Muslim children taught to refer to 'nos ancêtres les Galles', of the 300-acre demonstration farms attached to agricultural colleges in countries where the average peasant holding is less than 10 acres, and of the teaching of science by means of the bunsen burner in countries with no indigenous source of gas. Many such stories are told about the colonial period, and are cited as examples of 'cultural imperialism', the foisting of an alien culture on a subject people. But not all the 'horrors' came at once to an end with political independence, and there were reasons for them more substantial than the cultural arrogance of white missionaries and colonial officials. It is in fact a large task to write the appropriate textbooks; in many cases the basic research has not been done, and even where it has, there is still a laborious process of secondary research and the amassing of suitable material before a book can be written and published and local teachers familiarized with its use. To write such books, indeed, and to carry out the necessary background research is one highly important function of the staffs of the universities in poor countries.

Moreover, there are limits to the process of 'indigenizing' or 'localizing' the content of education in poor countries. It would of course be absurd if, for example, students in East Africa were to learn about the coalfields of England without first studying the rift valleys of East Africa. It is not so obviously absurd that they should be taught about the coalfields of England at all. It is a matter of balance, emphasis, and order of presentation. To continue with the same example, regional geography is generally accepted as a proper subject in the school curriculum at the appropriate stage of education, and if pupils in the rich industrial countries of North America and Europe study the geography of Asia, Africa, and South America there seems no reason why the study of Europe and North America should be omitted from the geography syllabuses of poor countries. Education in any country presumably includes among its aims, first that of helping pupils to a greater knowledge and deeper understanding of their own immediate environment and experience, and then enlarging their mental horizons by putting that immediate environment into a wider setting of other countries and continents and other historical periods. In the enthusiasm to purge the curriculum of alien content there can be the corresponding danger of going to the other extreme and adopting a narrowly parochial or even chauvinistic perspective.

According to Jolly, low-income countries as a group are spending about the same proportion of their resources on education as the richer countries. That proportion is rising; over the last decade, public expenditure on education in many poor countries has risen from 2—4 per cent to 4—6 per cent.[31] Such facts indicate the high priority that is being given to education in poor countries, since with fewer resources and a smaller surplus available after meeting basic needs there is presumably less room for manoeuvre. On the other hand, that they are spending similar proportions of their much smaller average income indicates the limitation of the resources available. Thus Sir Arthur Lewis has estimated that to give each child eight years' education costs (or would cost) 0.8 per cent of national income in the United States, 1.7 per cent in Jamaica, 2.8 per cent in Ghana, and 4 per cent in Nigeria.[32]

As was suggested in chapter 4, the principal factor in such differences is that teachers are relatively more highly paid — by comparison, that is, with average incomes — in poor countries. Another contributory factor is the tendency for more secondary education to be carried on in boarding schools than is usual in rich countries. Though economists have attacked so expensive a form of provision, and urged a rapid switch to day secondary schooling, this may not always be very practicable. A secondary school in a poor country may draw its pupils from a catchment area extending for scores or even hundreds of miles, far beyond daily travelling distance. If they have to find their own accommodation they may do so in conditions which are conducive neither to their health nor their education; thus a common arrangement in Kampala was for children to be boarded with kinsfolk who shamelessly exploited their services in return for squalid accommodation and a poor diet. Schools which had originally set out with the firm intention of remaining day schools found that in the end they had to accept responsibility for the conditions in which their pupils lived, established hostels, and became in effect boarding schools accordingly.

Moreover, not only have the poor countries fewer resources to devote to education, they also have more to do with them, since they are (as we have seen) engaged not merely in maintaining a level of educational provision but in raising it, and raising it rather rapidly; and this entails disproportionately high expenditure in establishing new schools and colleges of education and training teachers for a rapidly expanding school system. And the claims of education on resources are yet further compounded by high birth-rates, high proportions of dependent children, and high rates of population growth.

Whether educational expenditure is properly to be regarded as consumption or investment is a moot point among development economists. Many are sympathetic towards education, and have maintained that it ought to be regarded as investment; indeed, the phrase 'investment in man' has become almost a cliché in the context of such discussions. In terms of hard economics such an approach may not be entirely justified. Thus, despite a general impression that educational expenditure has a high rate of return, even though it may be over a rather long term, a study in India found 'the rate of return on real investment in India to be substantially higher than the rate of return

204

on investment in education.'[33] It may be suggested that such considerations seem a little academic. The governments of poor countries are in most cases clearly committed to allocate a high proportion of their resources to develop education; they are under strong pressures to do so, since there is a clamour for education (even though it may not be an entirely unanimous clamour) among the people of those countries; and there are few people in any country who would seriously maintain that such expenditure is wrong or ill advised, though they might have suggestions to make about the priorities that should be applied and the quality of scope of education which are appropriate. Whether such expenditure is labelled 'investment in human resources' and justified in terms of the increase in average incomes that is hoped for as a result, or whether it is regarded as directly enhancing the lives of human beings and justified directly on those grounds alone, seems to be a question of rather secondary importance. The point has been well put by Sir Arthur Lewis:[34]

Education does not have to be productive in order to justify itself; it is valuable for its own sake, and, when compared with other consumption expenditures, giving young people more education is just as valuable as giving them gramophones. In the end, each Government must set its own pace, having regard to how much store its people set by having greater opportunities for education, and how much increase in taxation they are willing to face for the purpose.

The mass media of communication

The predominant form of communication in non-industrial and non-literate societies is by word of mouth. In the affluent industrial societies, oral communication tends to be regarded as slow, inaccurate, and unreliable – a second-best means of getting information, to be described in such pejorative terms as 'mere rumour'. It is well to remember that in poor countries whose systems of mass impersonal communication through print, radio, and the like are as yet rudimentary, 'rumour' may still play a more important part in disseminating information – however garbled – and in setting the public mood. It is against this background that we may consider the uneven distribution in the world of the means by which information is disseminated.

Parallel with the income gap there is an information gap. The figures given in chapter 4 show that the mass media of communication are among the goods and services which are unequally distributed among the countries and people of the world. Information costs, and poor countries have little of it in the same way as and for the same reason that they lack other goods and services. Furthermore, as Schramm has clearly shown, most of the news that circulates in the world is news about rich countries distributed to the people of rich countries. Most of the world's news, indeed, is gathered and distributed through five major international news agency networks which are centred in rich countries, including Tass, the Soviet news agency. Apart from local news, the media in poor countries are filled with news from rich countries, hardly at all with news from other poor countries. For example, in three representative newspapers in Pakistan in 1961 there was as much news about the Soviet Union as there was about India (13 per cent), more about France and the United Kingdom (16 per cent and 17 per cent respectively), and more than twice as much about the United States (33 per cent of all foreign news); while there was little or nothing about countries such as Egypt or Brazil. Similarly in the Argentine press only 6 per cent of the foreign news was about neighbouring Brazil, compared with 11 per cent about the United Kingdom, 12 per cent about the Soviet Union, 15 per cent about France, and 43 per cent about the United States.[35]

It might seem at first sight as if the press is particularly well adapted to the conditions of poor countries. Its capital cost is fairly low and there is a direct revenue from sales, as newspapers can be distributed through local retail networks along with other goods. The press is well suited to serve small local communities each with its own language, as in many parts of Africa and Asia; equally, a newspaper can be run in conjunction with other activities by groups like trade unions, political parties, and churches. Un-like radio and television, a newspaper does not have to be allocated a frequency; there are no compelling technical necessities, therefore, for a system of government licensing, and if governments interfere it is for ideo-logical rather than technical reasons. This is indeed the basis for the tradi-tional independence of the press and the ideology of competition and private enterprise which characterize it, except of course under authoritarian regimes.

There are, however, a number of limitations. Although the reader is not involved in any capital outlay, as with a radio receiver, the recurrent cost may not be particularly low; thus according to Schramm a workman in California with what he earns in an hour could buy fifty copies of a 40-page newspaper, while in Indonesia an hour's labour would buy seven copies of a 4-page paper.[36] To some extent, though, this can be offset if one copy is passed from hand to hand or read aloud in small groups. An even more serious limitation is that it demands literacy, and this in itself has probably been the chief reason for the relative lack of a local press in the vernacular, for which this medium would otherwise appear to be well suited. As already noted in the case of the market for books in Africa, most people who can read and write can also understand a lingua franca or language of wider communication, and such an elite, even though their educational attain-ments may be relatively modest, tend accordingly to turn to a national news-paper in a language such as English rather than to the weekly vernacular newssheet. This appears to be one reason why the local press has fared no better in poor countries than in rich, despite the diversity of languages which

206

would appear to favour it. In poor countries too the national dailies get the lion's share of the advertising of both private firms and government agencies. Though the cost of advertising in a local paper is usually low in terms of actual outlay, it is usually high in relation to the number of people who see each advertisement. It may be worth paying ten times as much for a column-inch in a national daily if it is seen by fifty times as many people. Large organizations aiming at a national public distribute their advertising accordingly, and advertising in the local press appeals mainly to small firms with limited resources selling only in a local market. Furthermore, the national daily in a poor country is often amply financed and equipped with foreign capital, and may employ some foreign staff on the production and management side, while the locally owned and managed vernacular papers lack these advantages. And finally, there are countries where the government has found the relative freedom of the privately owned local press politically embarrassing, whereas the foreign-owned national daily is more likely to be anxious to retain its foothold in the country and tries to avoid giving offence. The local press may accordingly be subjected to harassments ranging from the withdrawal of government advertising to the destruction of its premises and the intimidation of its staff by the youth wing of the government party. By such means the press may be muzzled in fact, even though there is formal legal freedom of expression and no official censorship.

The film is generally regarded as a medium of entertainment rather than of information, though it is hard to separate the two, and allowance must be made for the 'demonstration effect' which occurs when cinema audiences are familiarized with a material way of life other than their own, for instance, by seeing films with a contemporary American setting, and exposed to value-assumptions, usually implied rather than expressed, about social behaviour and political and religious beliefs. Great importance has indeed been attached to films as a vehicle for propaganda, notably in the Soviet Union in the 1920s and 1930s; however, such considerations do not seem to be of great importance today in relation to the poor countries. Films are on the whole rather costly to make, and a film industry is viable only in relation to a large market. The showing of films also involves capital costs in the projection equipment, and in most cases a building with seating; and it is easier if there is an electricity mains supply, though use can be made of portable equipment mounted on a van for small audiences. On the other hand, as in the case of the press, the consumer is not involved in any capital outlay, and paying the price of admission is a recurrent cost which may not be a very large one.

Generally speaking, the film industry has been in decline in the industrial nations over the last twenty years or so, as cinema-going as a social activity has been largely displaced by television-viewing at home. This has affected the amount of film material which is available for export to poor countries,

207

and possibly imposed some further limitation on the medium in those countries. There is, however, one notable exception to these generalizations. Alone among the poor countries, India has a large and vigorous film industry, and is indeed the only poor country which vies with countries like the United States, Britain, the Soviet Union, France, and Japan in this field. The main factor in this situation seems to be the great extent of the market for Indian films. Though language differences are something of a limitation here, it is one that can be partly overcome by subtitling. The climate makes elaborate heated buildings unnecessary, and permits some open-air showing at very low cost to audiences sitting on wooden benches. For these reasons, cinema-going probably continues to be a social habit in India when it has ceased to be so in rich industrial countries.

In contrast to press and film, the broadcasting media of radio and television lack a direct revenue from sales. Partly for this and other economic reasons, and partly also from their duty under international agreements to allocate 'channels' or frequencies and license transmitting stations accordingly, governments have to be involved in broadcasting to a greater extent than in the other media. To be sure, the institutions which have been evolved to deal with these necessities are not the same in all countries, and indeed the poor countries today have three widely different 'models' for possible ways to organize and finance broadcasting – the virtually completely private-enterprise model of the United States, with no licence fee and financed entirely from advertising; the virtually completely central control of all broadcasting by the state and the party, as in the Soviet Union; and the public corporation, set up by the government and financed from statutory licence revenue collected by the state, with a ban on advertising and some degree of independence from direct political control, as with the British Broadcasting Corporation.[37]

Radio is in many ways well adapted to the circumstances of a poor country. Though the capital cost of a transmitter is rather higher than that of a printing press or a film studio, it is not beyond the means of most such countries; indeed, the 'pirate radio' transmitter ships that in recent years broadcast off the coasts of Britain and other European countries indicate the kind of scale on which the initial capital is needed. A medium-wave transmitter, which is from many points of view the most convenient and economical, can be heard adequately by day and night over a distance of about fifty miles, with another fifty over which reception by day is adequate but there is fading at night. This accords well enough with the size of linguistic areas like the larger tribes of Africa, though there are places where the situation is more fragmented. From the point of view of the listener, a capital outlay is required of a few pounds for a radio receiver. This is a considerable sum in relation to low income levels, but not so large as to be beyond the means of all. Even if every household cannot afford a receiver, at least some of the better-off inhabitants can. In local communities in poor countries there is very commonly a radio in the local shop, while travellers by taxi are usually regaled by the output of a car radio with volume turned well up. Radio receivers are not tied to mains electricity, though without it there is the further recurrent cost of batteries. Radios have joined clothes, bicycles, and corrugated roofing materials among the so-called 'target goods' which migrant workers in many poor countries save for and try to take home with them. Above all, radio breaks through the literacy barrier more decisively than any other medium of communication.

Television is far more expensive than radio at every stage. The capital costs of the transmitting equipment, the recurrent overhead costs of studios, the production costs of each programme, and the cost to the consumer of buying or hiring a receiving set, are all anything up to ten times greater for television than they are for radio. Moreover, television reception depends to a much greater extent on mains electricity, and in poor countries is limited accordingly to towns. Finally, television is greedy for the services of highly skilled and highly specialized technicians, both at the production end and in the maintenance of receivers. Some countries have gone to considerable lengths to equip schools with television, only to find that many schools miss most of the educational broadcasts because the set is out of action.

The high costs of producing television programmes, and the scarcity of staff who are capable of making them, involve many poor countries — or those of them which have television networks at all — in filling out much of their broadcasting time with imported material. It has even been surmised that the reluctance of the South African authorities to set up a television service in the past has had something to do with this factor — whereas it would have been easy to satisfy the English-speaking audience with imported American and British programmes, all Afrikaans programmes would have had to be produced locally, and this situation would have been likely to create a built-in imbalance between the interests of the two major white groups. Although South Africa is something of a special case in this as in other ways, it may be possible to see here an instance of a wider problem of relevance to other multi-cultural and multi-lingual states — the equitable or politically acceptable division of television time between different languages, including local vernaculars, the official language, and a foreign language such as English. Where the effort is made to be fair to a number of language groups, the result may be that an evening's viewing is cut up into short programmes, one in each language, and none of very great interest or merit from the point of view of the majority. Though such difficulties arise also in the case of radio, the relatively low cost of setting up separate transmitters for each major language group and the greater ease with which sound material of at least local interest can be produced, put on tape, and reproduced make it easier to overcome them without undue cost.

It is often suggested, indeed, that prestige considerations rather than a careful consideration of costs and benefits have led some poor countries' government to decide to set up television services when it would be better to stick to radio.

Some authorities attach particular importance to the development of the mass media as a factor facilitating and precipitating change in poor countries, and not merely the consequence of greater resources. Daniel Lerner is a leading exponent of this view. In comparing a number of countries around the early 1950s he found strong correlations between urbanization, industrialization (measured as the proportion of adult males engaged in occupations other than agriculture), literacy, and media exposure, the last-named being a statistical amalgam of newspaper circulations and the numbers of radios and cinema seats. The correlation with urbanization was strong although it was not linear; a critical minimum of urbanization for literacy and the media appeared to occur when around 10 per cent of the population lived in towns of over 50,000, while above 25 per cent urbanization there was little correlation with literacy. Surveys carried out among people living in a number of Middle Eastern countries confirmed the view that media exposure was correlated with other indices of modernization among individuals as well as between nations. Thus in Turkey people could be classed as 'moderns' if they regularly read newspapers and listened to the radio, 'traditionals' if they seldom did either, and 'transitionals' if they were occasionally exposed to both; in most cases such people said they would like to read or listen oftener than they could. 'Moderns' were found to have higher incomes than 'transitionals' and 'traditionals', more of them lived in towns, more of them had high-status occupations, and they were more educated. On all these tests 'traditionals' scored low, while 'transitionals' were in between. 'Moderns' were further found to know more about world news, the United Nations, and foreign peoples. They were much more able to imagine themselves in other societies or social roles, for example, being President of Turkey, or living in the United States — a capacity to which Lerner attached great importance and terms 'empathy'. And 'moderns' were less inclined to be unhappy about the state of the world and about the latest news that they had heard, and less frustrated by feeling unable to help to solve their country's problems.

Such correlations do not strictly speaking enable us to establish causation. Thus Lerner's 'moderns' may have been less prone to feel unhappy about the state of the world because they tended to be better-off people with high-status jobs living in towns, rather than because they frequently read newspapers or listened to the radio. Similarly, they may have been able to afford newspapers and radio because they were well paid, or their media exposure and their highly paid occupation alike may have resulted from their having the good fortune to be highly educated. Presumably there are rather intricate interconnections of cause and effect involved, and it would probably be very hard to single out one factor as the prime mover. There are moreover certain objections to too sharp a contrast being drawn between 'traditional' and 'modern', whether those terms are applied to persons or to cultural influences, and I return to this theme in a later chapter. What Lerner's studies do incontestably show is that there is a strong tendency for the factors he has investigated — occupation, education, income, residence, and media exposure — to cluster together.[38]

A smaller but very suggestive study from this point of view is that by Deutschmann in a mountain village in Colombia. For the purpose of this particular analysis, Deutschmann omitted all the literate and educated people from his sample, and divided the illiterate people into two groups with respectively high and low media exposure. Wide and striking differences then appeared between the attitudes of the two groups on such questions as whether they would resort to a hospital for a childbirth, or call in the local midwife, and whether they had high or low scores on a test of political knowledge. Media exposure was further shown to make a considerable difference to the adoption of new farm practices, a theme of much research to which I allude in the next chapter.[39]

In many such studies there is a tendency to interpret processes of change in terms of the 'two-step flow' of information and opinion which was found to occur among Americans in studies of the media in political behaviour in the 1940s. According to this view, local groups include 'opinion leaders' who are more heavily exposed to the media than their fellows — more assiduous newspaper readers, radio listeners, and the like. Since such people are more likely than others to have heard the latest news, they are more often in the position of telling others what is happening than being told by them, and this gives them prestige in the group. This in turn leads to their being asked, not only about facts, but also about their opinions and evaluations of the facts, and gives them the opportunity to exert a certain amount of influence.[40] Although opinion leaders and the two-step flow may not be universal features of all human groups — and research in Britain has specifically looked for them and found them to be absent[41] — there is a tendency among American writers to assume that they are. Such ideas clearly underlie much of the work of Lerner, and there is a general association between the 'opinion leaders' of earlier studies and Lerner's 'moderns'. These are the innovators, the leaders, the change agents, with horizons wider than those of the local community and its traditional ways.

It is for reasons of this kind that authorities like Lerner and Schramm suggest that the mass media have a specially important part to play in the development of poor countries. In Lerner's work it is taken for granted that development is desirable, and it is viewed as the process through which the poor countries become more like the rich industrial ones, especially the United States. This is not only because the United States is the most highly

developed in purely economic terms; value is also put on electoral democracy
with a system that allows of more than one political party, and among the
characteristics of countries that are counted in Lerner's comparisons one
important variable is 'political participation'.

When the underdeveloped lands of the world are tested by our model of modernity,
the enormous hurdles in the path to modernization stand out more clearly. What the
West accomplished gradually over three past centuries is not so easy for the East
to achieve rapidly in the present century . . .

We come, then, to political participation. Democratic governance comes late,
historically, and typically appears as a crowning institution of the participant society.
That the voting coefficient is so high indicates that these 54 countries have achieved
stable growth at a high level of modernity. In these countries the urban literate tends
to be also a newspaper reader, a cash customer and a voter.

Lerner here makes explicit his concept of modernity as a cluster of traits
which include economic development (the 'cash customer'), urbanism, literacy, exposure to the media, and political participation. The discovery that
these variables are strongly positively correlated is for him not merely a
finding of interest for social science; these traits are also good and desirable
from the point of view of his own system of value judgments. So the significance which he attaches to the media is related to their power to set in
motion the 'common psychological mechanism' which underlies the process
of modernization, namely that of 'empathy' or 'psychic mobility' — the
capacity to imagine things otherwise than they are, and to project oneself in
imagination into other social roles and other states of society. It was empathy
that distinguished the grocer from the chief in the Turkish village whose
transformation is sensitively and perceptively described in the opening
chapter of Lerner's book; and it was the American films the grocer had seen
in Ankara that gave him his image of a wider world, including a well-stocked
supermarket.[42]

In a somewhat similar fashion, Schramm lists the part which the media
can play in processes of change which he clearly regards as desirable. They
can widen horizons, raise aspirations, create a climate for development, and
focus attention on issues which the government of a poor country regards
as important for development like new health or farming practices. Though
relatively ineffective in changing strongly held attitudes or valued practices,
the media can enforce social norms, affect attitudes lightly held, slightly
canalize stronger attitudes, and help to form tastes. And they can help in
bringing about understanding participation in the decision-making process.[43]

Not everybody presumably shares this favourable view of the mass media.
A somewhat casual impression, indeed, suggests that many people, especially

intellectuals, in industrial societies take a rather low view of the media to which they are exposed, and it is paradoxical accordingly that some of them place so high a value on it as a means to the development of poor countries. Both the press and television are frequently indicted for 'trivializing', for inaccuracy, for lack of balance, and for irresponsibility both in the selection of news, the manner in which they present it, and the intrusions which their agents (reporters, cameramen) make into private lives and public ceremonials.

Concerns of this nature have been reflected in the social sciences in anxious analyses like that of Kornhauser, with its model of 'mass society' in which the political leadership operates a one-way communication directly with the unorganized, atomized, amorphous masses of the people through the media without the two-way process of interchange involving strongly organized intermediate groups such as political parties, trade unions, churches, and other interest- and pressure-groups that characterize truly democratic societies.[44] In a somewhat similar vein, C. Wright Mills included manipulation of the media among other aspects of the general control of American life by a 'power elite'. Such manipulation manifested itself in 'banalization' and 'stereotyping', in 'a sort of psychological illiteracy that is facilitated by the media', which distract the listener or viewer and obscure rather than facilitate his chance to understand himself and his world.[45]

Such gloomy analyses have been controverted by other American social scientists like Daniel Bell and David Riesman. Bell denies that there is any tendency for the United States to be an 'atomized' society of lonely, isolated individuals, and remarks that on the contrary Americans are 'a nation of joiners'. As for the allegation that the mass media debase popular taste, Americans spend more on classical music than on baseball, while sales of books have doubled in a decade. Riesman believes that, so far from the media distracting people's attention from serious problems, in fact they give more attention to politics and problems of public policy than their audiences actually want.[46] But to pursue these controversies would take us beyond the scope of a book on the poor countries. The point is that a judicious sociological scepticism may be appropriate about the evaluation that is placed upon the development of the mass media in poor countries. If there are grounds for anxiety about their quality and their effects on the political and social life of industrial countries, how much more so about the situation in poor countries where the standards of accuracy and impartiality in the reporting and selection of news are on the whole even lower, where the lack of alternative channels of information make people even more dependent on one version of the news, and where governments are at least equally likely to lean on the media to present matters in a light not unfavourable to themselves.

SUGGESTIONS FOR FURTHER READING

Dankwart A. Rustow, *A World of Nations*, Washington, D.C.: Brookings Institution, 1967

J. A. Fishman, C. A. Ferguson, and J. Das Gupta (eds.), *Language Problems of Developing Nations*, New York: Wiley and Sons, 1968

W. H. Whiteley (ed.), *Language Use and Social Change*, Oxford: Oxford University Press for International African Institute, 1971

P. H. Gulliver (ed.), *Tradition and Transition in East Africa*, London: Routledge and Kegan Paul, 1969

Wilbur Schramm, *Mass Media and National Development*, Stanford: Stanford University Press and U.N.E.S.C.O., 1964

10 Some psychological aspects of change

Change in society involves people in changing their ways. From this general statement it follows that related to the kinds of change which are considered in this book there are a number of questions or problems for investigation in social psychology. For example, what sort of people initiate change, what sort of people respond favourably to change, and contrariwise what sort of people resist change? In terms, that is, of the differences between individual personalities, can we make any statements about the characteristics, the aptitudes, the attitudes, and the beliefs of people who respectively embrace change and resist it? In what sort of social situations, with what degree of exposure to what kinds of information and persuasion, do people learn effectively or ineffectively to adapt themselves to new situations and turn them to their own advantage, or contrariwise fail to learn?

Leonard W. Doob and 'becoming more civilized'[1]

A pioneer study in this general field was that of Professor L. W. Doob of Yale University, whose previous work had included research on public opinion and propaganda. It is a study, to quote Doob's own words, of 'two principal questions ... concerning people in less civilized societies: 1. Why do they become more civilized in certain respects? 2. What happens to them as they become more civilized? ... What changes occur in their way of thinking, in their systems of self-guiding rewards, in their beliefs, and in their personalities?'

In this study the traditional—modern dichotomy was taken for granted, and there was an attempt to specify 'the attributes of less civilized people' in terms such as the smallness of scale of social relations, security and restriction, faith and absolutism, unity of behaviour, and simplicity. Doob's methods consisted first of a comprehensive reading of the literature on societies undergoing change in the contemporary world, most of it the work of anthropologists. To the insights and hypotheses raised by the literature he added a series of interviews which he carried out himself during the 1950s in four societies of Africa and the West Indies (Luo, Ganda, Zulu, and Jamaica) comparing in each case the responses of the old with the young and the more highly educated with the less educated and illiterate. He drew also on

215

psychological studies comparing Indians and whites in America, and material from the Middle East study directed by Daniel Lerner to which reference was made in the previous chapter; and he adopted much the same distinctions as those which Lerner made between 'traditional', 'transitional', and 'modern' people.

Among Doob's twenty-seven hypotheses, some were quite specific and lent themselves to confirmation or denial from the data. Thus consistent differences were found in his interviews to support the hypothesis that people 'changing centrally from old to new ways' have longer time-horizons. Similarly, people changing in other respects were found to retain traditional attitudes towards family forms and practices — a finding which is in accord with the analysis in chapter 6 of this book. And though the evidence was not quite conclusive, it seemed likely that people changing their ways were apt to join new groups demonstrating the new ways, and to put more value on traits like initiative, independence, and self-confidence.

'People who are confronted with alternative beliefs and values' were found to be 'likely to retain traditional ones which appear to serve a continuing need and to reject those which do not, but always to retain some of the traditional views'. Even among the most educated groups there was scarcely a case in which at least one member of the sample did not assent to a traditional belief or value, even though their general traditionalism was significantly weaker than the less educated. Similar results were obtained in comparing young and old. Elaborating the initial hypothesis, Doob suggests that traditional beliefs and values may be adhered to because they are taught at an early age. The 'continuing need' may include a need to harmonize the views respectively of younger and more-educated with those of older and less-educated members of the same family group, or at least to reduce the dissonance between them, as I suggested in the last chapter. Doob links this with the well-known phenomena of syncretism in religious and magical beliefs and practices — the tendency for traditional magic to continue to coexist side by side with newly introduced Christianity, for example. Further, he suggests that 'people changing centrally are liable to remain in a state of conflict concerning the advantages and disadvantages of both old and new beliefs and values'. And misunderstandings are likely to arise between the three categories of people — the unchanged, those who are changing, and those who have changed their ways. But there was little evidence either way for the hypothesis that after people 'change centrally' they are less likely to be dogmatic about their own beliefs and values.

In the later chapters of his book, Doob becomes more concerned to advance and explore hypotheses than to test them. One theory which he puts forward concerns what might be called the 'piecemealness' of change. Where there is 'heavily reinforced behaviour that remains satisfying', it 'is likely to change only after some of its components have been changed' — in other words it is more likely to change piecemeal than all at once. Similarly, where a new form of behaviour is difficult to learn, it is likely to be learned piecemeal rather than wholly adopted on one occasion. There is something in common here with Rogers' analysis of the characteristics of innovations which make them more or less readily adopted, with which I deal below. Doob suggests that 'the proficiency with which people change from old to new ways is likely to be increased when they seek a central goal that transcends the specific form of behaviour being changed'. The central goal may be simply that of 'becoming more civilized', or it may be more complex. The Ganda are cited as a case in point of an African people whose overriding aim in the twentieth century appears to have been that of making a successful adjustment to the modern world without ceasing to be distinctively Ganda or renouncing their cultural inheritance and sense of identity. Western ways were adopted quickly and thoroughly when they appeared to be instrumental to that end — money, education, modern technology, and even Christianity. The distinction between ends which are central and those which are incidental or instrumental, or in Doob's word 'segmental', leads him to advance the corollary hypothesis that 'people who retain strong central values are motivated to learn segmental forms of behaviour that do not appear to be at variance with those values'. Presumably the whole history of Japan since the Meiji Restoration affords an even more striking case in point. Another corollary puts in general terms the experience of colonial rebellions: 'People who have changed centrally from old to new ways and who then perceive that they are being prevented from achieving some central goal are likely to learn to seek aggressively a different central goal.' Some of the hypotheses near the end of the list, indeed, appear to be so wide and vague as to be matters for general assent rather than specific verification — what, for example, are we to make of 'All societies eventually become civilized in a distinctive manner or perish'?

So although Doob begins with Lerner's opposition of 'traditional' to 'modern', his analysis of central goals and peripheral adaptations among the Ganda casts some doubt on the usefulness of this opposition. In other ways, too, his work transcends its limitations, and though its breadth and near-comprehensiveness render much of it inconclusive, it remains a source of stimulating and suggestive ideas in its field.

Everett M. Rogers and the diffusion of innovation[2]

Rogers is an agricultural scientist whose initial interest in agricultural innovations in the United States broadened into a study of the spread of farm practices in the world as a whole, and to the study of innovations in general. He amassed much data on innovation in the fields of medicine and education, and some also on family limitation, public health, and industry, to put along-

217

side that in his original field of interest in agriculture, and his bibliography lists some six hundred references to studies in this general field.

Rogers defines an innovation as an idea perceived as new by the individual. Diffusion is the process through which a new idea spreads from a source — its original invention by a creative individual — to its adoption by users. Adoption implies a decision to continue full use of the idea as distinct from a decision merely to try it. A typical time-sequence of events is involved in the behaviour of the user or potential user; first he becomes aware of the idea, then he decides to try it, and then continues in full use, the three stages being named 'awareness', 'trial', and 'adoption' accordingly. The adoption period is the time which elapses between the user's first hearing of the idea and his decision to continue full use. 'Innovativeness' is the term Rogers uses for the proneness or propensity of an individual to adopt innovations. People differ in their innovativeness, and can variously be classified as innovators, early adopters, early and late majority, or laggards, according to the length of time it takes them compared with others to adopt a new practice.

Rogers concluded from a number of studies that some cultures are more favourable to innovation in a quite general way than others. For example, his own researches in Wisconsin had led him to the conclusion that farmers of Danish descent there were far more innovative than those of Polish descent, even though all were immigrants into the common cultural environment of a single American state. Rogers' discussion of this in terms of a distinction between 'traditional' and 'modern' norms is in general accord with the views of authorities like Lerner which were summarized in the last chapter.

The adoption process, which involves both learning and decision-making, is elaborated into five stages — (1) awareness, (2) interest, (3) evaluation, (4) trial, and (5) adoption. Rogers carried out a cross-analysis of these five stages with his analysis of individuals' innovativeness, and this showed that early adopters not only start on the process ahead of others, but also go through each of the five stages more quickly.

The characteristics of the innovation matter, however. The innovations which are easily and quickly adopted tend to be those whose relative advantage over previously established methods is immediately obvious and a source of clear gain to the adopter. Readily adopted innovations are also those which are compatible with existing values and past experience, and are simple (from the point of view of the user, that is; a television set is a highly complex product, but all the user has to do is switch it on and off). Readily adopted innovations, other things being equal, are those which are divisible. A user is more likely to give a new method a trial if he can do so on a small scale, as for example when a farmer tries out something on a small portion of his land, without committing all his resources to it. Innovations are less likely to be adopted if they involve going over completely to the new method

218

without the possibility of a small-scale trial. Finally, new ideas are more readily adopted if they are communicable. A new breed of farm crop, for example, may advertise itself by its visibly better yields.

From the point of view of development and change in poor countries, some of Rogers' most important findings are in his detailed analysis of adopter categories and individual differences in innovativeness. Early adopters were found to be younger than others, to have higher social status, and to be wealthier — whether as a result of having adopted innovations in the past, or as a factor that enabled them to innovate in the present because their resources were sufficient to fall back on if an experimental innovation failed. Early adopters were found also to have distinctive personality characteristics, including less rigidity and greater rationality. In the light of the discussion of the media of communication in the last chapter, it is of particular interest that Rogers concluded that early adopters made more use than others of impersonal sources of information like the public press and the technical journals appropriate to their occupations, such as farming weeklies or medical journals. Late adopters by contrast tended to rely more on personal sources like the word of mouth of neighbours or professional colleagues. Further, early adopters relied more on 'cosmopolite' sources — national or international journals, for example — compared with the 'localite' sources of late adopters. Early adopters were more commonly in direct touch with the sources of new ideas themselves; for example, farmers might be in direct correspondence with agricultural scientists. They had a wider range of sources of information and wider horizons generally. They tended to travel more — some American farmers, for example, had literally travelled the world in search of new ideas of possible applicability to their own farms. And in terms of the 'two-step flow' of information, they were more likely to be opinion leaders.

In relation to such characteristics, innovators sometimes saw themselves and were seen by others as deviants from the local social system. At home and in the company of their neighbours they might be regarded as eccentric; but 'they identify [themselves] with other reference groups outside their community who consensually validate their behaviour'. It is a case, Rogers says, of being 'in step with a different drummer'.

Finally, Rogers draws attention to the importance of change agents, that is persons who are professionally concerned with the adoption of innovations — whether by recommending those they consider desirable, or trying to prevent those they regard as harmful or inappropriate. Examples of such professions are public health officials, teachers, and agricultural extension officials. Many change agents work in the service of central or local governments, or other public bodies such as universities; some in the private sector, for example, salesmen of agricultural machinery. Many of the East African elite whom I mentioned in the last chapter could be called change agents in this sense of the term.

219

William Ogionwo and Nigerian progressive farmers[3]

Following Rogers' work, a study was carried out by William Ogionwo, a Nigerian social psychologist, to inquire more deeply into the circumstances and characteristics associated with the adoption of innovations. Ogionwo's sample consisted of a thousand cash-crop farmers in Nigeria, together with a further two hundred who did not grow a cash crop. Most of the cash-crop farmers in the sample were drawn from lists kept by the government agricultural service as having received a government subsidy in respect of some recommended farm practice. Such farmers were officially termed 'progressive' and Ogionwo's sample probably over-represented them in comparison with the peasant population of Nigeria generally; however, the aim was not to investigate a representative sample but rather to compare farmers of different degrees of 'progressiveness' or innovativeness, and for this purpose it was important to ensure that the sample included an adequate number of the more 'progressive'. Ogionwo's main purpose was to correlate farmers' innovativeness with their economic position, with some of their social characteristics such as age, level of education, and information contact, and some of their attitudes such as traditionalism, family sentiment, rationality, and change-proneness. Innovativeness in this case was measured by the proportion of government-recommended farm practices which the farmer had in fact adopted. Which farm practices were recommended by the government agricultural service depended on the region, but according to each region's particular circumstances of climate, cash crop, and similar factors it was possible to draw up a list of about twelve to fifteen practices which the government recommended, and it was then easy to ascertain which of them the farmer had adopted. In many cases, indeed, independent verification was available, since as already mentioned most of the sample had found their way into official lists as having received a government subsidy for carrying out one or other of the locally recommended practices. Some of the data which were then correlated with innovativenss were comparatively simple, such as age; other qualities, especially the more psychological attributes such as rationality and change-proneness, were probed by means of a number of questions.

The most important of Ogionwo's findings are summarized in table 10.1. The factors most strongly correlated with innovativeness proved to be gross farm income, level of living, change-proneness, and rationality. In Nigeria as elsewhere it is clearly the case that the more innovative farmers are better off, and this may operate both as cause and as effect — farmers with greater resources are more likely to take the risk involved in going over to a new practice. The finding about change-proneness is reassuring rather than surprising, and it indicates that people who say they are ready to try new ideas prove to be so in action as well as in words. Rationality in Ogionwo's schedule involved 'the use of deliberation, planning, and the best available sources of information and advice as a means of achieving ends', and this

220

TABLE 10.1. *The correlates of innovativeness among Nigerian farmers*

Variable	Partial correlation coefficient	% of total variation explained	Group total	Conclusion
Economic				
1 Gross farm income	0.425	18.06		Strongly related to innovativeness
2 Acres of crop land	0.046	0.21		Not related to innovativeness
3 Size of plant	0.025	0.06		Not related to innovativeness
			18.33	
Social				
4 Age	−0.158	2.50		Inversely related to innovativeness (younger farmers more innovative but not very strongly so)
5 Education	0.171	2.92		Related, but not very strongly so
6 Level of living	0.325	10.56		Quite strongly related to innovativeness
7 Social participation	0.116	1.35		Positively but weakly related
8 Information contact	0.189	3.57		Related to innovativeness
9 Mobility	0.054	0.29		Not related to innovativeness
			21.19	
Personal				
10 Resignation	−0.013	0.02		Not related to innovativeness
11 Traditionalism	−0.029	0.08		Not related to innovativeness
12 Deviancy	0.119	1.42		Positively but weakly related
13 Familism	0.021	0.04		Not related to innovativeness
14 Change-proneness	0.415	17.22		Strongly related to innovativeness
15 Rationality	0.214	4.58		Related to innovativeness
			23.35[a]	

[a]Failure to agree with items results from rounding.
Source: W. W. Ogionwo, 'The adoption of technological innovations in Nigeria'.

quality too was shown to be correlated with innovativeness, albeit less strongly so. Young farmers were somewhat more likely to adopt new ways. Information contact, education and social participation were also positively correlated with innovativeness, but these correlations were somewhat weaker. Innovative farmers were found to be deviant rather than conformist, and somewhat more likely to reply affirmatively to test statements like 'I never worry about being different from others'; but here again the correlation was not very strong. Mobility was found not to be correlated with innovativeness, despite the initial hypothesis that people who had moved around and seen more of the world might be more inclined to adopt new practices.

Neither resignation, traditionalism, nor familism proved to be significantly correlated with innovativeness. These findings are of some importance as they run counter to the ideas of Lerner, Doob, and other American social scientists, who tend to assume that tradition and modernity are diametrically opposed and that attachment to the family and resignation to fate or to the will of God are likewise to be regarded as obstacles to modernity and development. Ogionwo considers these questions in some detail. People can adopt new methods because they are seen as more effective means to achieving traditional ends. Thus a farmer may be motivated to adopt government-recommended practices in the belief that they will increase his income in order to enable him better to discharge his family responsibilities. Or he may adopt because people whom he respects as traditional authorities are recommending or urging him to do so. In Buganda, for example, cotton-growing was introduced in the early years of the twentieth century by the combined efforts of the colonial government's agricultural department, the Anglican mission, and the chiefs. There were even cases of people being coerced by the traditional authorities into growing their first crop of cotton, though it did not take long to appreciate the advantages of so remunerative a cash crop.

Tradition and modernity can ... be mutually reinforcing rather than in conflict. Theories of economic growth often view such systems as the extended family and caste structure as impediments to economic growth. But it is now pointed out that such relations are complex and can vary from one context to another. The extended family as an unalloyed impediment to economic growth has been exaggerated through failing to balance its role in the division of labour, the supply of skill and training and in the accumulation of capital (one dimension) against its tendencies towards status demand and the oft-cited 'plague of family parasitism' (a second dimension). Efforts on the part of whole compounds (extended families) to become mobile, to attempt improvements as well as their ritual positions are by no means new to Nigerian life ...

The all too common practice of pitting tradition and modernity against each other as paired opposites tends to overlook the mixtures and blends which reality displays. Above all, it becomes an ideology of anti-traditionalism, denying the

222

necessary and usable ways in which the past serves as support, especially in the sphere of values and political legitimation, to the present and the future. We need a perspective towards change which does not deny the specific and contextual character of events. You can have a modernizing tradition. For example, both the Ganda and the British take enormous pride in claiming to be consistently in advance of their neighbours — the Ganda in adopting Christianity and so becoming 'civilized', and the British in developing railways and jet propulsion. There is also the case of Buganda as, in Apter's apt phrase, a 'modernizing autocracy' — the autocracy part being, of course, completely traditional.

Information was collected in some detail about the use and effectiveness of different media of information, and this too is of interest in relation to the general ideas of Lerner, Schramm, and others. Almost all farmers heard the radio — 88 per cent — and many of those who did not own radios themselves listened to farming programmes in neighbours' houses. The printed word naturally reached a smaller proportion of farmers, about 38 per cent of whom had never been to school at all; less than a half of the sample read news-papers, and about a third received 'printed extension' material directed specifically at farmers. Following Katz and Lazarsfeld, Ogionwo distin-guished between 'exposure' and 'effectiveness', the latter being defined in terms of importance in helping farmers to decide whether to adopt a re-commended practice. By this test the most effective influences involved personal contact and the spoken word; the peer group of neighbours, kins-men, and friends was the most important influence, followed by 'oral exten-sion', that is word of mouth of an extension officer. However, this test of effectiveness is not really decisive. In so far as a 'two-step flow' is in operation, it may be that change agents and opinion leaders get their information from the media, printed or unprinted, and pass it on to others orally. 'Learning of a practice from relatives and other farmers is somewhat analogous to lifting oneself by one's own boot-straps, for ego's peers are not likely to be much better informed than ego. The farmer who learns from his peers is learning second- or third-hand information which may have lost its accuracy.' Ogionwo summarizes his findings thus:

Personal media tended to be more important than *formal* mass media both in terms of 'total exposure' and 'effective exposure'. But this tendency was not evident when we examined type of information source and the degree of effectiveness. In view of the limited coverage of the printed media, 'unprinted mass media' emerged as the main source of influence apart from 'oral extension'. And it was radio that accounted for the importance of 'unprinted mass media'. It can thus be suggested that the best medium of spreading agricultural information is the radio, provided there is a close personal follow-up by extension officers to assure farmers that 'yes, it is right for you'. The printed word reaches only the literate minority, who are not notably more innovative than the non-literate majority, though hard technical information in print is important for the extension officers.

Clearly, the networks of information and influence involved in decisions like these are complex. It is, however, a mistake to think only in terms of the flow of information to an individual who then decides whether or not to act on it. Group interaction is of great importance:

In our investigation, we started with the traditional assumption that individuals have to make up their minds about whether or not to adopt a recommended farm practice, and that once their minds are made up they would go ahead and use it ... But the experience of our investigation suggests that in certain societies (and certainly in the society concerned) the individual is not a free agent ... He is very often subject to all sorts of pressure to adopt or not to adopt; family, friends, community norms, may all bombard him. It is of interest, therefore, to discover whether the adoption of farm practices in Nigeria requires individual or collective decision.

Ogionwo concludes with a plea for a recognition of the importance of a two-way flow of information. Not only is there a question of the effectiveness or otherwise with which the government's recommendations are communicated 'down' to farmers; there is also the question of the flow of information 'upwards' from the farmers to the government.

The matter of bringing up the 'feed-back' of farmers' opinions to the government needs more extensive study since it forms the very basis for the success or failure of the development programme. The farmers, on whom the ultimate success of the agricultural schemes depend, must be confident of the possibility of improvement and their own ability to foster that improvement ... Agricultural development involves the risk of change; people must believe that it is likely to pay dividends and that, if it does not, they are at least assured against the loss of what they now have — even if that is the barest subsistence ... Since even the best-informed planners cannot anticipate every eventuality, the development administration must, at the same time, remain sensitive to village-level reactions and be prepared to adapt the minutiae of its plans to the local conditions.

In order that this dialogue may take place, there must be an effective and continuous means of taking government information down to the villages and bringing the 'feed-back' of rural opinion up to the government. And to the extent that good communication presupposes both the machinery of communication and the desire to communicate, a degree of mutual confidence between the two sectors is an essential third estate of the communication process.

David C. McClelland and achievement motivation[4]

McClelland is an American psychologist who first established that a need for achievement, or *n* Ach, exists as a source of motivation to a different extent in different individuals, and also in different cultures. His colleague Winterbottom was then able to show that the development of *n* Ach takes place fairly early in childhood, and depends on parents' expecting of their children a 'self-reliant mastery' at an appropriate age, namely about eight years. 'Self-

224

reliant mastery' includes such things as knowing their way about the neighbourhood, being active and energetic, trying hard to do things for themselves, and doing well in competition with other children. If all this is called for too soon, then children react with discouragement and a reduced self-confidence; if too late, then their *n* Ach remains low. Among contemporary nations, Japanese parents on the average 'hit it right on the nose' by expecting these qualities of their children at the right age, while Brazilians demanded them too young and Germans left it too late.

McClelland points out that these findings are consistent with, and give a further depth of understanding to, the classic theory of Max Weber linking the Protestant ethic and the spirit of capitalism, since a 'self-reliant mastery' is what we may confidently suppose Puritan parents expected of their children.

A number of historical studies demonstrated that an upsurge of achievement themes in popular literature, children's stories, and other cultural manifestations was associated, after a time-lag, with an upsurge of economic activity. Such a relation was shown, for example, between *n* Ach derived from English popular literature between 1500 and 1800, and coal shipments to London, with a time-lag of thirty to fifty years. Similarly, *n* Ach in medieval Spain was related to the tonnage of shipping cleared for the New World. In both cases 'the initial high level of *n* Achievement is followed some time later by a period of economic growth which subsides fairly abruptly after the level of *n* Achievement has decisively dropped'.

Turning to contemporary societies, McClelland found a close correlation between *n* Ach on the one hand, and G.N.P., electric power, or both combined on the other. Comparing the 1925 with the 1950 level of this measure for a large number of countries he showed that *n* Ach is 'positively correlated with subsequent economic growth, and very significantly so for the electrical output measure or for both measures combined'.

The implications for development in the poor countries are obvious. Achievement motivation has been shown without exception to be related to economic development both in the contemporary world and historically, though there is usually a time-lag between the period at which children are being brought up in conditions which arouse high *n* Ach and the country's subsequent actual achievements when they are grown up and reach positions in which they influence its development. In the long term the number of people with high *n* Ach and the *n* Ach level of the people generally could presumably be raised by suitable changes in the generally accepted methods of bringing up children. In at least one sphere this is largely under the direct control of governments, namely in the schools, and there seems no reason why a government which takes McClelland's findings seriously should not act directly on, for example, the content of children's first school reading books.

In the immediate future, the economists' 'short term', however, the poor

225

countries will presumably have to make do with whatever resources of achievement motivation their adult populations already possess. McClelland has spelled out the immediate recommendations that follow from his findings.

First, 'the leadership of a country should promote an achievement mystique by every means at its disposal'. A leader who in McClelland's view has notably done so is President Nyerere of Tanzania, whose writings contain frequent references to the ideal of self-reliance: 'Between MONEY and PEOPLE it is obvious that the people and their HARD WORK are the foundation, and money is one of the fruits of that hard work. This is the meaning of self-reliance' (The Arusha Declaration). McClelland comments:

In these and other passages President Nyerere clearly shows an understanding of what the psychologist is saying: it hasn't been money as such that has produced development — ever; rather it has been a particular motive — the need to achieve — that has been critical; he calls it *hard work* which has a common sense relationship to the need to achieve — though it is not precisely the same since many peasants all over the world work very hard without producing rapid economic growth.

Secondly, McClelland advocates motivational training for businessmen, and cites the success of ten-day training seminars which were developed in India for this purpose. More than half the business leaders so trained showed marked increases in business activity. In the two years after attending the seminar they invested twice as much and created twice as many jobs as a comparable group who had not undergone the course. The institutions in which achievement motivation is encouraged among businessmen should be able also to offer material aid in the form of loans and credit. Businessmen attending the seminars would then be planning with reality in mind, while at the same time those conducting the seminars are in a good position to study seminar participants and their plans during training and follow up their progress afterwards. And these institutions should be part of the whole structure of economic planning in the country, so that the seminars could be a means of implementing the general development plans.

Thirdly, higher education for women as well as for men should be insisted on.

The recommendation may seem paradoxical since by and large it is the men who will be responsible for development of the economy. Yet ... no modern industrialized nation has so far developed which has not stressed getting women into the higher levels of the working force ... Achievement cannot be stressed for one-half the population only — namely, the male half. It appears not to be possible to maintain an achievement ideology in a population which is so to speak 'half slave and half free'. Furthermore, women as wives and mothers play enormously important roles in encouraging achievement in the male half of the population.[5]

At the same time it is necessary to make a number of criticisms of McClelland's work. Achievement motivation is not a simple concept but has

226

many aspects, the relations between which are not clear. First, it obviously involves a disposition to *set oneself tasks* rather than have tasks set from out-side — an inner drive, that is, rather than a response to externally perceived stimuli or situations. It is not clear how closely this is related to a second component, namely the satisfaction gained from *performing a task well* whether it is self-imposed or externally induced. This again is analytically separable, and should be distinguished from, a satisfaction gained from *performing a task better than others*, excelling in a competitive situation, or 'winning'. Excelling over others is further to be distinguished from *gaining others' recognition* of one's own superior (or even intrinsically good) performance of a task, and gaining general social approval from significant others — notably, of course, one's mother in early childhood at least. Recognition must again be dis-tinguished from *symbolic reward*. Thus to elaborate a favourite American folk saying, and one that is not far from the trend of McClelland's thought, 'if you make a better mousetrap (people may hate you for it but) they will beat a path to your door'. And this again is to be distinguished from a desire to *assert one-self over others* in such a way that those others *accept one's leadership*; and here the rubric in Winterbottom's test may be recalled which asked mothers, 'At what age would you expect a son of yours to have learned to be able to lead other children and assert himself in children's groups?' And on the last point one may remark that cultures differ widely in their evaluation of such be-haviour in children. While presumably it would be praised by American parents, in the sub-culture of English intellectuals it would be more likely to evoke the response, 'Never, I should hope'.

It is indeed difficult to escape the impression that the ideas of McClelland and his colleagues are not entirely free from ethnocentrism, painstaking though they have been to work on a basis of verifiable scientific method. This is further shown in McClelland's handling of the concept of other-regarding or other-directed behaviour, which is first diluted from altruism to 'paying attention to the opinion of others as a way of guiding one's own behaviour' and hence degraded into mere market morality. The inner drive of a selfless doctor, like the legendary Albert Schweitzer, toiling for the health of his underprivileged fellow men; the devotion of an administrator exercising his abilities for what he conceives to be the public good; and the determination of a businessman to achieve the success for his firm which high profits will symbolize — how the concept of the achievement motive applies to each of these three, the way it is compounded with other drives and motivations, in what kind of social situations and in the light of what kind of values — questions of this sort are left unclear. Yet it is obvious that all three and indeed many more varieties of achievement motivation will be required to manage the affairs of the poor countries and effect any appreciable amelior-ation of the lot of their people.

11   Religion and economic development: cause and effect

Sociological studies of religious behaviour in relation to economic development fall into two main categories. In one, religious doctrines and practices are regarded as causative factors in economic development, especially the part played by religious minority groups in initiating business activity. In the second, religious phenomena are seen as effects of economic development, and especially as reactions to the disturbance of social relations associated with drastic social changes, whether those changes are associated with industrialization or with other causes.

Religion and economic innovation

The main work to be considered under this heading is the monumental study of Max Weber linking the Protestant ethic with the spirit of capitalism.[1] Weber's work has acquired the status of a classic of sociology, and is so well known as to require only the briefest summary here.

The grand question which dominated Weber's thought was why the industrial revolution and the capitalist social order that accompanied it should have emerged in north-western Europe at the time they did, and not elsewhere or another historical period. Indeed, a detached and unbiased observer, supposing such a person could have existed and undertaken the necessary travel, surveying human civilizations about the year 1600 would undoubtedly have pointed to China as the most highly developed. He might have hesitated whether to put India or the Islamic world in second place, and it is unlikely that he would have put Europe higher than fourth. Yet by 1800 the domination of Europe was unchallenged, and European society was entering a period of spectacularly rapid economic development. Clearly this unprecedented shift in the balance of world civilization owed much to technological factors, and these have been detailed in chapters 2 and 3 — first a rather narrow superiority in guns and sails, and then the rise of industry associated with Savery's steam engine in 1698.

However, though Weber acknowledges the importance of the application of science at the outset of his work, he does not otherwise integrate it into his explanatory scheme, and concentrates rather on the nature of capitalist enterprise. It is a quite elementary mistake — one which he says should be

228

dispelled 'in the kindergarten of cultural history' — to identify capitalism with the pursuit of gain. Rational book-keeping, formally free labour, the separation of business from the household and of corporate business property from personal property (e.g. limited liability), and the concept of citizenship — all these were distinctive institutional attributes of western European society. But the mere possession of these attributes, even in combination, was not enough. The whole structure had as it were to be brought to life, and what inspired it and gave it direction Weber calls the spirit of capitalism.

The advent of this spirit antedated the rise of the capitalist order itself, and the critical historical period for Weber's analysis is the seventeenth century, with the rise of the Calvinist sects and the Puritans in America as well as Europe. At that time the originally harsh Calvinist doctrine of pre-destination was rendered compatible with the concept of a man's calling, the work to which he has been called by divine command, which it is his individual responsibility to perform, and for which he is alone accountable. Weber shows how the new doctrines embodied the old monastic ideal of asceticism, yet rejected monasticism itself as a wasteful form of idleness. Those called of God should be in the world and not of it. Yet to expend the fruits of their labours in pleasure or display was also sinful. The combination of this-worldly asceticism with the concept of the calling to work was clearly a powerful one for leading men to accumulate and invest where others might have been content to accumulate and enjoy the display of their wealth. More directly relevant to our own theme is the way in which, as Weber shows, the asceticism of the original Puritans was later vulgarized and secularized into the injunctions of Benjamin Franklin, which Weber quotes at length and with great effect as illustrating in its purest form the spirit of capitalism. The concept of the divine calling has turned, as Weber puts it, into 'the ideal of the honest man of recognized credit, and above all the idea of the duty of the individual toward the increase of his capital, which is assumed as an end in itself'.[2]

In support of his thesis of the uniqueness of European Puritanism, Weber considers the religions of ancient Judaism and of the East, which he knew from his assiduously comprehensive study of the literature then available in European languages. In China, despite the high state of the arts and crafts and the great urban tradition, the currency was frequently mismanaged, the legal and customary institutions favouring business organization were lack-ing, and there was no adequate system of book-keeping such as would spur Chinese businessmen to allow adequately for the depreciation and replace-ment of their physical capital. Moreover, though rationality was certainly strongly present in Chinese thought, both orthodox Confucianism and Taoism and the heterodoxies such as Buddhism tolerated a development of magic. 'Like the educated Hellene, the educated Confucian adhered to magical conceptions with a mixture of scepticism while occasionally submitting to demonology ... The preservation of this magic garden was one of the tendencies innate to Confucian ethics.'[3]

Turning to India, Weber analyses both the character of Hindu thought and society, especially the caste system, and also the movements of protest against orthodox Brahministical Hinduism, especially Buddhism. The effects of the caste system on economic life he regards as essentially negative. It was not so much that particular beliefs or ritual prescriptions in themselves placed insuperable obstacles in the way of economic development, for example by making it difficult for men of different castes to work together in the same factory. Obstacles like that could have been circumvented if the will had been there, just as the ritual ban on usury was in fact circumvented in the early development of European capitalism. 'The core of the obstruction was rather imbedded in the 'spirit' of the whole system',[4] he writes, which makes it extremely unlikely that an economic and technical revolution such as industrial capitalism could have originated from within Indian society; while if it were introduced from outside, as under British rule, then its development would be correspondingly hampered.

As I have already suggested, although he did not altogether neglect the rise of science, Weber may not have made it sufficiently integral to his analysis. The authority of the church over men's minds, supremely symbolized in the treatment of Galileo, was broken by the Protestant reformation, and its collapse left in the end no defence for dogma against rational scientific inquiry. Not that the Protestant sects themselves espoused a scientific view of man and the universe; on the contrary, they were in many cases as dogmatic and obscurantist as the parent church itself, as in another age the agonized mental struggles of a man like Gosse have testified.[5] But when the sceptical rebellious scientist was struggling against Protestant dogmatism, he could in the last resort advance the unanswerable argument of freedom of conscience. The Protestant reformation of the sixteenth and seventeenth centuries can thus be seen as clearing away important obstacles to the rise of science in the seventeenth century, and hence the industrial revolution in the eighteenth.

On historical grounds, Weber's thesis has been subjected to penetrating criticism by Professor Hugh Trevor-Roper in its application to the original rise of capitalism in north-western Europe.

The idea that large-scale industrial capitalism was ideologically impossible before the Reformation is exploded by the simple fact that it existed ... Until the invention of the steam engine, its scope may have been limited, but within that scope it probably reached its highest peak in the age of the Fugger. After that there were convulsions which caused the great capitalists to migrate, with their skills and workmen, to new centres.

The convulsions in question were those of the counter-reformation. 'The novelty lay not in the entrepreneurs themselves, but the circumstances which drove them to emigrate ... not so much Protestantism and the expelled entrepreneurs as Catholicism and the expelling societies.' The alliance between church and state – particularly the Spanish state, which at that time ruled the Netherlands and parts of Italy – suddenly resolved to persecute the ideas of Erasmus and his followers. It was this hardening of the counter-reformation that drove out the merchant aristocracies – some to Protestant countries, others to less intolerant Catholic kingdoms like France – and put them into an uncomfortable and unsought-for dilemma between the Lutheran and Calvinist versions of Protestantism. They chose the latter, though neither represented the easy-going Erasmianism they would probably have preferred, and Trevor-Roper suggests that many of them were not really very good Calvinists at heart. By far the more important thing about them was that they were migrants.

Neither Holland nor Scotland nor Geneva nor the Palatinate – the four obvious Calvinist societies – produced their own entrepreneurs. The compulsory Calvinist teaching with which the natives of those communities were indoctrinated had no such effect. Almost all the great entrepreneurs were immigrants.

Secondly, the majority of these immigrants were Netherlanders: some of them, perhaps, were Calvinists only because they were Netherlanders.

So the counter-reformation resulted in a Flemish diaspora in which the Flemings became the industrial elite of Europe, with the Jews in second place.[6] Trevor-Roper accordingly identifies migrant status rather than doctrinal attachment as the critical factor in the making of an enterprising minority; the point is of wider application, and I return to it below.

Another criticism of Weber's thesis, this time in its application to India, is that of Professor Trevor Ling. The notably enterprising character of Indians abroad in countries like Burma and Malaya should alone cast doubt on it, though it is fair to Weber to say that these developments were only just about to manifest themselves at the time when Weber was recording his negative conclusion. However, at the very time in 1905–11 when Weber was collecting his material and writing his study, which was originally published in 1912, events were taking place in India itself which were to falsify it decisively.

From the point of view of Weber's verdict on India the unkindest twist of fate was that in 1911, the first really notable large scale example of all-Indian industrial capitalism, the Tata Iron & Steel Company, began production. J. N. Tata ... died in 1904, but the scheme was taken up and pursued by his son, Dorabji Tata. In 1906 rich resources of iron ore were discovered in ... Bihar, which the Maharaja was prepared to allow Tata to work, in return for royalties on the ore. The capital needed for the construction of the plant was £1¾ million. A prospectus was issued by Tata in August 1907. Nationalist fervour was at its height and the leaders of the movement were urging all Indians to join in and support the Swadeshi movement – to support Indian-owned production of every kind, and to boycott British goods. The result was

231

that 'from early morning till late at night the Tata offices in Bombay were beseiged by an eager crowd of native investors, old and young . . . at the end of three weeks the entire capital for the construction requirement was secured, every penny contributed by some 8,000 Indians'. The construction of the plant was begun in 1909. In 1911, when Weber was writing his *Hinduismus und Buddhismus*, the first iron ore was being produced by an Indian company.[7]

Some recent studies have followed Weber's in attributing economic backwardness to cultural factors including especially religious ideas, values, and practices. As an example we may take a controversy over the economic retardation of the Malays relative to the other groups in the plural society of Malaya, namely Chinese and Indians. In an article which initiated the controversy, Parkinson pointed to the resistance to change of Malays generally, which was exemplified in their refusal to follow the government's urgings to grow a second rice crop each year, use wet rice fields instead of dry upland for their rice seed-beds, and adopt other recommended improvements. Parkinson showed that these resistances were at least partly rational, but he thought religious and magical beliefs were also relevant, for example in waiting for a propitious day before transplanting; and 'the Islamic belief that all things are emanations from God . . . tends to make them fatalistic in their approach to life'.[8] Wilder disagreed with Parkinson's diagnosis of 'Islamic fatalism', saying that it presents a caricature of the Malay as 'a blind, irrational slave of history and custom'. Indeed, in one respect Islam could be said to exercise a favourable influence on economic development, namely the *haj*. Saving the money to pay the fare to Mecca gave peasants a goal to which they directed their lives and built up patterns of saving and rational forms of economic organization.[9] Parkinson, however, insisted that this was not a productive use of savings. Money being saved for the *haj* remained largely idle, and was barren and unproductive from the point of view of economic development.[10]

Another case in point is Burma. Mya Maung has analysed the blend of new and traditional thought in the Burmese way to socialism, first enunciated in 1947 and embodied in the national plan launched in 1958. The word *Pyidawtha* used for this programme carries overtones of 'a happy and prosperous state with the additional vision of a utopian blend of traditionalism and modernity'. His central theme is that socialist planning has failed to change the cultural patterns of traditional Burmese life, especially including Buddhist cultural values. Efforts to present *Pyidawtha* as a blend of old and new — ranging from the glorification of a golden past and the revival of religion to exhortations to eat unpolished rice — merely conceal their incompatibility, as do the presentation of socialist ideas in words taken from the vocabulary of Burmese Buddhist thought, especially the use of the Buddhist concept of impermanency (*anate-sa*) for the Marxist dialectical materialism. In fact, 'State action has failed to diffuse the socialist concept of the identity

232

of interest between the state and the individual', and has indeed deepened the traditional view of government as an enemy to be wooed and feared. 'Similarly, the socialist concept of collective effort and co-operative life within a classless society is contrary to traditional Buddhist cultural values such as Karma (*Kan* in Burmese) ... Distaste for business enterprise (*a-the*) is present in the traditional Burmese culture.'[11]

Ling has remarked, however, that Maung's general statement about the resistance to change of Buddhist culture represents an inadmissible simplification. Theravada Buddhism is only one strand in Burmese culture, and the differences between Buddhist and non-Buddhist elements may be important at precisely the points at which economic activity is significant.[12]

Melford Spiro makes the further point that even Theravada Buddhism is not a single strand, and there are at least three major systems — nibbanic Buddhism, whose concern is with release from the unending circle ('The Wheel') of death and rebirth, causation and frustration; kammatic Buddhism, whose concern is not so much with release from the Wheel as with improving one's position in the next incarnation; and apotropaic Buddhism, which is concerned with man's worldly welfare, the curing of illness, protection from demons, the prevention of droughts, and so on. In relation to economic activity, Spiro says,

the soteriology of nibbanic Buddhism provides no bridge of any kind to the world. Far from being a means to salvation, worldly activity in nibbanic Buddhism is its irreducible obstacle; rather than a proof, worldly activity constitutes a disproof for one's chances of being saved. But this is not true of the soteriology of kammatic Buddhism, i.e. that of most practising Buddhists. It, on the contrary, provides profound incentives to worldly (economic) behaviour, for economic success is a necessary means for soteriological action, which in turn has important consequences, social and economic alike ... It is only through economic action that one can hope to acquire the most soteriologically valuable merit, the merit acquired through giving (*dana*). To be sure, merit is also acquired through morality (*sila*); but giving is the royal road, and (short of inheriting it) the wealth required for giving must be accumulated by economic action.

Many Burmans keep merit account-books, Spiro reports, and the quest for wealth provides a powerful motivation for work. But *dana* is confined to religious giving, and is not a motive for what we should understand as 'charity' like giving money to hospitals. The most spectacular forms of *dana* consist of building pagodas and endowing monasteries, and these earn men great social prestige — expressed in the formal title of 'pagoda builder' or 'monastery builder' which is prefixed to their names for life, like the Muslim *Haji* — as well as the assurance of pleasure in a future existence. Social prestige as well as salvation is also to be gained from lavish expenditure on one's son's ritual initiation, and another meritorious form of *dana* which is sanctioned by publicity is the collective offering of new robes and other gifts

233

to monks and on monks' funerals. Spiro goes into considerable detail about the money value of religious giving of this kind, and concludes that in a typical Burmese village something like 25 to 30 per cent of the net disposable cash income is spent on *dana* and related activities. As in the case of saving for the *haj*, such facts may be interpreted from two different points of view. On the one hand, *dana* affords a motive for work, saving, and a systematic management of resources; on the other, the methodically accumulated savings are neither invested, as Weber put it, for 'forever renewed profit by means of continuous, rational, capitalistic enterprise', nor are they well expended for social welfare.

This is all too well recognised by some of the Burmese themselves, although they are too few to change the system. Thus the headman of one village said to me that 'the entire township spends about 10 per cent of its income on provisioning monks, but far less than 1 per cent on education. If we spent, say, 9 per cent on monks and 1 per cent on education, surely that would not harm Buddhism, and how much better off our children would be.'[13]

Another study directly inspired by Weber's analysis is that by Bocock of the Ismailis in Tanzania.[14] The Asian population of East Africa as a whole played a notable part in its economic development, pioneering trade and small-scale manufacturing industry and dominating the world of finance and the professions, and among this population two communities rivalled each other for leadership — the Shia Ismailia Khoja and the Patidars. The Ismailis are a Muslim group owing spiritual allegiance to the Aga Khan whom they regard as the extant Imam, while the Patidars are a Hindu community of the general character of a caste. H. S. Morris, who also studied these groups, singled out the Ismailis as the pace-making group.[15]

An important factor in the Ismailis' success was the role and personality of the redoubtable Aga Khan III, Sir Sultan Muhammad Shah, 1877—1960. Believed as he was to be the known, revealed Imam, all his words were regarded as divinely inspired, and he used his power of *ex cathedra* utterance to urge his followers to modernize their attitudes and practices. In the sphere of social welfare, for example, he opposed infant marriage and advocated modern methods of child care; he stimulated the Ismaili communities to efforts of communal self-help in health and education; and he mobilized their lavish gifts to his person to set up trust funds for investment in the enterprises of Ismaili business men. To all appearances the Ismailis in East Africa played the same kind of initiatory role in economic development as the Puritans in Europe, and did so in much the same kind of way and by the same kind of means — hard work, frugality, trustworthiness, and consistently shrewd re-investment of profits in lines of development where further profits were to be expected. To one who lived in East Africa the comparison with 'the Protestant ethic' has the air of a commonplace.

234

In a point-by-point comparison of the Ismaili faith with Calvinism, however, Bocock notes the differences as well as the similarities. Where Calvinism was positively individualist, Ismailism relies more on community self-help. On its own Bocock doubts if it could have produced the positive push towards individualism; it was only in contact with British capitalism that the Ismailis were able to adopt some rational capitalist methods, especially when urged to do so by their divincly inspired leader. There is a superficial similarity in the doctrines of predestination of both Calvinism and Islam, but the latter does not put its adherent under the same terrible strain as the former to prove that he is among the elect by his diligence in everyday work. Islam is much more relaxed, and teaches that by giving alms, morality, and prayer he can attain heaven. 'Unlike the puritanical Calvinist, the Muslim, including the Ismailis, can enjoy using and consuming his wealth in this life, within reasonable limits.' Both religions are notably congregational in their forms of organization, and the local community of Ismailis who meet daily in Jamat Khan, the Ismaili mosque, constitute also a community exercising moral control over it members and providing them — when they are in good standing — with mutual aid and credit networks. Islam generally, including Ismailism, has more room for mysticism than did Calvinism. Both encourage education, but Islam is much more tolerant of magic and does not condemn its use by the faithful in allaying anxieties over things like illness, family and personal problems, and travel.

What is the general import of studies of this kind linking religion as a causative factor with economic development? Clearly Weber's thesis is not lightly to be dismissed; as Trevor-Roper has said, it has a 'solid, if elusive, core of truth', though his reliance on so large an abstraction as 'the spirit of capitalism' makes his analysis difficult either to confirm or refute by reference to newly discovered facts. Moreover, Weber's central preoccupation was with the original emergence of industrial capitalism, a unique historical phenomenon after which nothing could ever be the same again. As I have emphasized, all subsequent economic development has taken place in a world in which capitalist industry was already in existence, and we are dealing with a process of diffusion rather than with the original emergence; and this too makes it difficult to test Weber's ideas by reference to events elsewhere in the world after the industrial revolution in Europe.

In these circumstances there is a decided tendency to weakness in the explanations that are advanced both of economic backwardness and of economic initiative in terms of the religious and general cultural values of the group concerned. This is seen most clearly in the inconsistency between explanations of backwardness in terms of the culture of a people who, when they appear outside their own country as a minority in another, abruptly become associated with innovative energy and economic initiative. Sometimes the contortions of the analysis in these cases can only be described as comic. For example, it is possible to explain the economic backwardness of China before the communist triumph of 1964 in terms of passivity, the Confucian ideal of the cultivated man of the world, lavish expenditure on funerals and weddings, non-rational magical beliefs, and the like; and all this seems very plausible when applied to China itself. Yet when Chinese emigrated to Indonesia, Malaya, Singapore, Thailand, or even to Hong Kong they suddenly became the energetic innovators whose industry and enterprise stimulated the economy of the region into new life; and it does not seem to have been the case that the religious beliefs and ritual customs of the overseas Chinese were in any important respect different from those of the homeland. In exactly the same way, the economic backwardness of India is attributed to the other-worldly mysticism of the Hindu faith, the ban on cow-slaughter, the caste system, and similar cultural factors. Yet Indians overseas have been the dynamic source of economic development, initiating industries, pioneering trade, and through kinship and credit networks maintaining financial and trading links with the world outside the countries to which they migrated — East Africa, Burma, Malaya, and elsewhere. And whatever may be said about 'Islamic fatalism' as an obstacle to development among the indigenous Malays, it clearly did not constitute the slightest obstacle to the spectacular success of immigrant Muslim groups like the Ismailis in East Africa.

Clearly we must look elsewhere for explanations of the innovating energy frequently shown by migrant minorities despite the backwardness of their home cultures. Here it is possible to do no more than suggest hypotheses.

First, there may be a process of selection of personality types. Migrants may possibly be the more enterprising people — indeed, the ones who show their enterprise by migrating.

Secondly, there may be demographic effects. Migrants tend to be young men, followed by young women. Migrant communities are characteristically short of older people and of teenage children, being made up of young parents and their young children. There are usually more men than women. This means that the ratio of economically active people in the community is higher than would be the case in a 'normal', settled group; or, looking at it the other way, the dependency ratio is lower.

Thirdly, migrants may be free from some at least of the customary constraints on enterprise and initiative that are effective in the home society and culture. For example, it may be that one factor in the prosperity of the Chinese overseas in the nineteenth century was that they had not got the mandarinate on their backs. Morris reports that among Indians in Uganda it was impossible to observe the minutiae of the caste system, however committed they were to its general principles. Rules of exogamy were strictly observed — were insisted on, indeed, with special emphasis as if to demonstrate a general adherence to the Hindu way of life; but it would have been simply unrealistic to observe prohibitions such as those which would

236

have prevented neighbouring families in a remote trading centre in Africa from accepting goods and water from each other. Morris writes accordingly of 'the secular outlook of most of the immigrants', and quotes one of his informants as saying: 'The gods are unwilling to cross the sea. Most of them, I think, stayed in India. The women brought over a few that are important to them; but for me, it will be time to pray to God when I go back to India.'[16]

Fourthly, immigrant groups are in many cases excluded from control of the traditionally legitimate resources that go with high social prestige. These include especially land and political power. The same hypothesis, indeed, may be extended also to non-immigrant minorities like the original Calvinist and Puritan sects in England and Germany. If at the same time such groups are moved to emulation of the rich and powerful (or in the jargon of sociology if they exhibit reference-group behaviour) then success in business may be the only way in which they can rise in the world. This hypothesis would appear to fit cases like the Chinese overseas especially in colonial times, and the East African Asian groups like the Ismailis both under colonial rule, when they were excluded by Europeans from land and power, and after independence when it is Africans who have seized both. Clearly a hypothesis of this kind assumes the general framework of a plural society.

Hypotheses such as these turn more on considerations of minority status and the effects of migration than on the specific features of the culture of the group in question and it may be that the qualities of method, industry, thrift, and asceticism which enable such a group to survive and prosper are developed in response to a situation rather than brought in with their cultural luggage.

Religious movements as effects of profound social disturbance

In many societies and at different periods where there has been a profound disturbance of established forms of social relations, leading to large numbers of people being deprived of access to resources upon which they had been accustomed to rely, such a disturbance has been followed by the rise of religious movements of a characteristic type. These movements have been variously called messianic, millenarian, nativistic, and prophetic. The term *messianic* implies a comparison with ancient Hebrew beliefs in a saviour who should come to deliver his people. *Millenarian* and the equivalent *chiliastic* refer strictly to the doctrine among some Christian sects that Christ will return and reign in bodily presence for a thousand years; in sociological usage the same terms have been given a slightly extended meaning to cover beliefs of the same general nature in an impending overthrow of the present order of society by supernatural means and the coming of a new order in which 'the last shall be first and the first, last'. *Nativistic* in the colonial context referred to a movement reasserting the values and practices of the

237

native culture as against white administration and Christian missions. *Prophetic* relates to the fact that such movements commonly have leaders who prophesy the new order and urge their followers to adopt the appropriate moral and ritual usages to prepare for it.

Hundreds of such movements are known, and they have occurred from ancient times to the present day. A historical survey by Norman Cohn begins with apocalyptic prophecies among the Jews of the ancient world, notably including the 'stream of militant apocalyptic' and the promise of a saviour, the Messiah, which marked the period from 63 B.C. to A.D. 72. In medieval Europe, Cohn traces the rise and fall of sects like the Joachimites in the twelfth century who protested against the wealth and worldliness of the church and expected the millennium in 1260, when an 'angelic pope' was to convert the world to voluntary poverty. Although there were generally few links between the fanatical few inspired by millenarian visions and the broad masses of the peasants whose economic interests were threatened, occasionally under the stress of events the two types of movement might come together. Examples are the part played by John Ball in the English peasants' revolt in 1381, and the Taborites during the Hussite revolt in Bohemia in 1419–21.[17]

Among the factors which Cohn suggests may favour the rise of millenarian movements, he lists catastrophe or the fear of catastrophe, famine, plague, or massacre, and he points out that several of the Crusades were preceded by famines, which presumably engendered desperation that could readily turn to fanaticism. 'The supposed defection of the authority traditionally responsible for regulating the relations between society and the powers governing the cosmos' is noted, and many of these movements bewailed the ruin of the church as the agency of salvation. And such movements flourish in 'a society which recognises that the relative power and prosperity of different sections (classes, ethnic groups, etc.) can change', yet includes 'elements which cannot organise for the purpose of defending and furthering their interests by secular means'.[18]

In recent history the most profound social disturbances have been those associated with European expansion, colonial rule, and the advent of a new order of society in relation to the growth of the modern industrial state. There is a considerable literature on the religious movements that have arisen in response to these upheavals, and most of all on anti-European millenarian movements in colonial situations. Cohn's work is of particular importance accordingly in reminding us that such movements are by no means confined to recent history or to those particular causes.

A pioneer work in this field is the summary and analysis by Peter Worsley of the cargo cults of Melanesia. An early cult of this type was the Tuka movement which arose in Fiji in the 1870s and 1880s, led by a man named Ndugumoi who organized his followers in a quasi-military fashion under 'sergeants' and 'scribes' with high officers called 'destroying angels'. It was mystically revealed to Ndugumoi that the ancestors were shortly to return to Fiji, the shops would be jammed with calico, tinned salmon, and other goods for the faithful, but unbelievers would die or become the slaves and servants of believers. The whites had deliberately deceived them. The bible was really written about the divine Twins of local legend, but the whites had substituted the names Jehovah and Jesus for the names of the Twins. The false Europeans were pretending to be surveying the reef with their instruments, but really they were scanning the horizon for the vessels in which the Twins were returning with the ancestors.

The Tuka cult was followed by a large number of similar movements all over the area of New Guinea and the islands to the east, in which its main themes were taken up repeatedly — the belief in an imminent millennium in which ships would bring ample supplies of the new goods for the benefit of the local people; the further assertion that the missionaries were conniving in the injustice by means of a deceit in which they were deliberately withholding part of the bible; the organization of the faithful to expel the whites and to prepare for the coming of the cargo. In later cargo cults, prophets succeeded in persuading people to stop cultivating and instead build harbours, and after the 1939—45 war in which aircraft and radio became familiar to the islanders these were reflected in cults which prepared by clearing the bush to make airstrips, putting up poles and making wooden radios.

Colonial governments were generally uneasy about such movements, and in some cases acted repressively against them. In some cases this unease was prompted by a paternal concern for the welfare of people who under the influence of group hysteria neglected to make ordinary provision for themselves by cultivating. At other times the cult posed a direct challenge to law and order, as for instance when in 1923 a white plantation owner in New Hebrides was killed as a sacrificial victim symbolizing other Europeans, or when the adherents of a cult formed large crowds in a state of high emotion near police or mission stations. Many of the leaders of cargo cults were imprisoned or restrained in mental hospitals.[19]

Worsley's work, though comprehensive and full of insight, was carried out from documentary sources; but the correctness of his analysis was confirmed in the course of a field study by the Australian anthropologist Peter Lawrence. Lawrence describes how he came upon a cargo cult almost by accident when, after two months in the field, he heard it said that his mother and sister were expected with a shipload of goods, and he was asked to inspect a site for an airstrip. Now that they had, as they put it, 'their own European', things were obviously going to change, the secret they had awaited for years would be theirs; he would 'open the road of the cargo' by contacting God, who would send their and his ancestors with goods to Sydney for onward transmission to him and them.[20]

Much of Lawrence's book is devoted to the rise and fall of Yali, who became the leader of a cargo cult on the Rai coast in 1946—50. Yali had been a policeman and then during the 1939—45 war a soldier with a heroically distinguished record. Shortly after the war he gained the further approval of the government for his initiative in community development in his home district, but his very popularity with his own people was in the end his undoing. Their dawning belief in his superhuman qualities led to his being cast in the role of the leader of a cargo cult, with which after prolonged misgivings he eventually identified himself.

Beliefs in the essentials of the 'cargo' doctrine seem indeed to be well-nigh ineradicable, and a recent publication assures us that they still continue.[21]

The literature on messianic cults has been summarized by Vittorio Lanternari,[22] who traces among other movements the series of prophetic cults among the North American Indians. These began in 1799 when a man named Ganioda'yo or Handsome Lake had a vision when near to death and recovered to pass on the message of the three spirits who had visited him with a new doctrine of salvation. This 'Great Message' was a combination of Christian and traditional Indian teachings; conciliatory in tone, it was commended by Thomas Jefferson as 'positive and effective'. During the nineteenth century, however, conflict between the North American Indians and the white Americans who rapidly grew in numbers and occupied more and more of their land was reflected in prophetic movements which were unambiguously anti-white. These culminated in the so-called Ghost Dances between 1870 and 1890, though it is interesting to note that at least two of these movements gained some white supporters from among the followers of the Mormon prophet Joseph Smith — another group at odds with the dominant white American society. They ended in 1890 when a cult under the leadership of the prophet Wovoka spurred a last hopeless armed uprising among the Sioux, which was defeated at the battle of Wounded Knee.

Following the defeat of the Ghost Dance, some Indians now turned to cults of a very different character. Peyote is a small cactus a part of which when eaten has a mildly hallucinatory effect, and the central rite of the peyote cults consists of the search for peace through its use. The imagery of the movement, though various, has common themes in the revival and restoration of one near to death, which may be held to symbolize the desperation of individuals whose cultural identity seemed threatened by the all-engulfing industrial civilization of white America. The tone is peaceful and conciliatory, with the playing down of intertribal conflicts, an amalgamation of Christian and Indian symbolic elements, and a general tendency towards withdrawal from rather than opposition to the white man and his civilization. Though they came under the suspicion of Protestant missionaries, the peyote cults were long defended by Commissioner John Collier of the U.S. Bureau of

Indian Affairs, who after taking scientific advice decided that the peyote was so mild in its effects, and the cults so important to the sense of identity of many Indians, that they should be allowed to continue. With the general apprehension about narcotic and hallucinatory drugs in America in recent years, however, the attack has been renewed, and peyote was ruled illegal by a court decision in California in 1964.

As a postscript to the foregoing, it is of interest that the peyote cult was 'discovered' by the English writer Aldous Huxley who lived for many years in California and knew the plant by the name of mesca or mescal. Huxley's use of mescaline to induce states of mysticism and heightened consciousness, about which he wrote in *The Doors of Perception* (1954), led directly to the use of peyote and other drugs in the movement of 'chemical mysticism' which grew up in literary circles (e.g. the 'Beatnik' poets) and the cinema industry in California in the 1950s, and hence to the advocacy of far more powerful synthetic hallucinatory drugs in the 1960s.[23] Perhaps these developments can be seen as representing yet another form of rejection of and withdrawal from modern industrial society, this time on the part not of the deprived and dispossessed but the affluent elite of such a society.

In Africa, pioneer studies of Bantu independent churches were carried out by the Swedish missionary Bengt Sundkler, who worked among the Zulu people from 1937 to 1942. Sundkler found that there were no fewer than eight hundred such sects in South Africa alone, and he broadly classifies them into the 'Ethiopian' and 'Zionist' types, using names which the sects commonly and characteristically gave themselves.*

'Ethiopian' sects were either direct or indirect offshoots of white mission churches, whose forms of organization and doctrines of biblical interpretations they followed on the whole very closely. Their essential character could be summed up in the slogan 'Africa for the Africans!' 'Ethiopia' was equated with 'Africa', and biblical references to 'Ethiopia' were cited in support of claims for the antiquity of an African church; it was also identified with the modern kingdom of Ethiopia, both interpretations of the name being inextricably intermingled. Some of these churches had links with Negro

---

* In sociological usage, a *church* is the religious organization embracing a whole community; a *denomination* one of a number of accepted forms of religious organization competing for membership and resources in a tolerant or secular state; a *sect* a group united by beliefs and practices somewhat at odds with the accepted norms of a society, and especially such a group in the initial stages of its formation. A *cult* is distinguished from a sect by its relative lack of conscious, purposeful organization; the term is applied to beliefs and practices that are not, or not yet, those of a distinct group with a definite structure and membership. Difficulty arises when the term a social scientist would apply to a particular group differs from the name by which that group is known to its own members. Many groups which are from the point of view of sociology 'sects' call themselves 'churches'; indeed, the claim to be church and not a mere sect may be integral to the ideology of the group in question. Accordingly, some scholars in this field, including Sundkler, adopt the terminology of the groups they study rather than that of social science.

sects (as they were then called) in the United States, forged in some cases by Marcus Garvey, a Jamaican who travelled all over the black world during the 1920s and 30s spreading the idea of independent black churches as a means to liberation. Their essential aims were to be both Christian and African — truly Christian in the essentials of doctrine and practice with only minor modifications to accommodate the second aim, that of being completely self-governing and independent of white control.

In contrast, the 'Zionist' group of sects were essentially syncretistic, combining some Christian ideas and practices with Bantu elements such as speaking in tongues, purification rites, and taboos. They combated African witchcraft and similar practices, but Sundkler wrote that 'the weapons with which they fight the struggle belong to an arsenal of old Zulu religion'. The name 'Zionist' constituted a kind of mythical charter linking baptizing African prophets with an apostolic succession embracing John the Baptist, the River Jordan, Mount Zion, Jerusalem, and in some cases Nazareth. It followed that their identification tended to be with ancient Israel, the Holy Land, rather than with Ethiopia (the modern state of Israel had not come into being at the time of Sundkler's field work, and no reference was intended to Zionism as a political movement among modern Jews). Some also had links with the Zion church of Zion City, Illinois, U.S.A. Sundkler emphasizes, however, that the boundary between the two types was ill defined. An individual sect might well change its doctrines and practices and move from one category into the other, while there were many borderline cases in which it was hard to tell whether 'Ethiopian' or 'Zionist' doctrines predominated.[24]

Following Sundkler's work, a number of East African religious movements were studied in depth during the 1950s by F. B. Welbourn. Among them was that founded in Uganda in 1929 by two young Anglican teachers, Reuben Spartas Mukasa and Obadaiah Basajjakitalo, as 'the African Orthodox Church — a church established for all right-thinking Africans, men who wish to be free in their own house, not always being thought of as boys'. Welbourn also studied the churches which grew up in association with the independent schools movement among the Kikuyu, which was in turn a part of the reaction to conquest and white settlement in the much harsher atmosphere of Kenya.[25] That reaction had its political aspects in the African nationalist parties and movements which arose during the period from 1920 onwards, most of them to be suppressed by the colonial administration in a conflict which eventually took the form of an armed revolt and guerilla movement to which Europeans gave the name of 'Mau Mau'. There has been a good deal of dispute about the character of this movement; the colonial administration at first regarded it as yet another 'dini' or religious movement, and it certainly had its ritual side in the form of oathing ceremonies. Later interpretations have characterized it as an African nationalist political movement and rejected explanations in religious terms.[26] The truth may well be that it

242

was both, or more exactly that it was hard to disentangle the religious, educational, political, and military aspects of a broad movement of revolt among the Kikuyu against white settlement, Christian missions, and colonial rule. There was in fact a large and numerous growth of sects in Kenya, ranging from groups which, like Sundkler's 'Ethiopians', aspired to be fully Christian though free from foreign control, through syncretistic movements which admitted a good many more elements from the traditional African cultures of the region, to cults whose predominant character was that of a chauvinistic revival of traditional or quasi-traditional beliefs and practices. I gave an outline account of some of these movements in my general description of East African society,[27] while a notable later study is that by Sangree of the situation in Tiriki, a small area of western Kenya.[28]

In West Africa, Dr Geoffrey Parrinder's comprehensive study of religion in the city of Ibadan includes full descriptions of the separatist sects, one of the most picturesque of which was the Sacred Cherubim and Seraphim Society whose practices were drawn from Muslim as well as Christian and pagan customs.[29] Another detailed study of West African religious practices is that by the psychiatrist Dr Margaret Field, for whom they form a background to the detailed case-studies of mental patients.[30] Field emphasizes the continuity between Hebraic, Christian, Muslim, and pagan West African beliefs and practices. Quite apart from the possibility of common origins, 'Christianity has been in West Africa for five centuries', as she puts it; it is not a question of a sudden contact with a complete cultural innovation. She rejects the notion that a supposed conflict between Christian and pagan ideas — 'the opposing pulls of tribal gods and the dictates of Christianity' — is responsible for neurosis or other forms of mental trouble. In particular, beliefs in spirit possession are common to all three of the main religious traditions in West Africa, and it is these which are vital to the new shrines at which 'the troubles and desires of ordinary people' find expression and solace.

Movements variously called schisms, secessions, separatist sects, and independent churches have in fact been reported from all parts of black Africa, and four more examples must suffice. In Zaïre, then the Belgian Congo, Simon Kimbangu began to see visions and was credited with the power to heal the sick about 1921, and quickly attracted a large following, to the detriment both of the Roman Catholic missions and work on the railway and the plantations. Within months he was arrested, tried, and sentenced to death, which was commuted to life imprisonment; he died in prison in 1951. Missionary hostility notwithstanding, the movement continued to grow throughout Belgian rule. It was legalized in 1959 and took the title *Eglise de Jesus-Christ sur la terre par le prophète Simon Kimbangu* (E.J.C.S.K.), and it continues to be a considerable body with a mass following in the new republic of Zaïre.[31]

243

Joseph Booth was responsible, directly or indirectly, for starting no less than seven African sects between 1892 and 1910 in the country then named Nyasaland, now Malawi, an area which before the formal declaration of a British protectorate had been ruled in effect for nearly thirty years by Scottish and Anglican missions. As a Baptist and a radical, Booth incurred the suspicion of missions and government alike in his activities as a kind of free-lance missionary, attached successively to parent bodies including Seventh-Day Adventists. He travelled between southern Africa and the United States, in touch with the Watch Tower movement known as Jehovah's Witnesses as well as with 'Ethiopian' sects in South Africa, and supporting African followers in both continents. One such was Elliot Kamwana, to whom Booth taught the Watch Tower doctrine which he returned to Nyasaland to preach, supplied from time to time by Booth with their literature. Watch Tower spread widely throughout colonial Africa, becoming almost wholly independent of the parent American sect, and acquiring a militantly anti-white tone in which the coming millennium was viewed mainly in terms of liberation from colonial rule. The name was rendered into Bantu languages as Ki-Tower or Kitawala, and as lately as the 1950s it was still causing alarm among missions and governments. Another was John Chilembwe, who was influenced by the National Baptist Convention (a black civil rights movement) in the United States, and returned to Nyasaland with a number of black Americans to found the Providence Industrial Mission. After they left in 1906, Chilembwe's mission became the centre for African militancy, and in 1915 he led an armed rising in the Shire Highlands.[32]

In 1953 a Bemba woman named Alice, whose followers called her Lenshina (Regina, Queen) received a call to start a new religious movement which two years later broke away from the Presbyterian church and attracted large numbers of followers from both Protestant and Catholic missions. Known as the Lumpa (Itinerating) church it spread northward into Tanzania and sent a mission southwards to Salisbury in Rhodesia. At its height the movement is said to have had a hundred thousand members. Trouble began when they refused to pay taxes, and in 1964 this led to the movement taking the form of an armed rebellion against the authority of the newly independent African state of Zambia. Bloody clashes ensued and several hundred people were killed before the movement was crushed. Alice was put into restriction, but the movement is said still to have some twenty thousand members, half of them in exile across the border in Zaïre.

An exhaustive compilation of the data on movements of this kind in Africa south of the Sahara has been carried out by the Reverend David Barrett, who amassed over 1,300 published accounts of movements numbering by 1966 the staggering total of over five thousand. Barrett admits disarmingly in his preface:

In 1957, a massive secession involving 16,000 members took place from the Anglican Church in western Kenya. The African bishop there had at that time serving under him some thirty African clergy, and a handful of missionary clergy from the Church Missionary Society including myself. We all imagined that the disturbance was a new and unique kind of phenomenon caused by purely local factors and personalities, and the whole affair was handled from the start on that assumption . . .

What this demonstrates is the alarming fact that decisions of the utmost importance can be made in good faith yet in virtual ignorance of strikingly similar parallels elsewhere, and hence of the underlying realities of the crisis and the dilemma that it poses.[33]

But perhaps the biggest of all these movements was the Taiping rebellion, the most important of a series of religious revolts in China from the eighteenth century onwards, whose suppression, according to Yang, ranked with border defence as one of the two great tasks of the imperial army.[34]

Taiping was led by Hung Hsiu-Chuan, son of a peasant of the Hakka tribe, who studied unsuccessfully for the state examinations and became instead a village teacher. In 1837, when he was twenty-three, he came across a Protestant missionary pamphlet from which he learned the elements of Christian belief. In the following year he saw visions which he interpreted to mean that he was the son of God, a younger brother of Jesus, and charged with a mission to establish *Taiping tien kuo*, 'heavenly kingdom of great peace'. Hung later underwent two months' instruction at a mission station, but he had little understanding of Christianity.[35]

From 1847 the followers of Taiping were in open revolt, and with their homes burned and their goods confiscated by government troops they took to a sort of primitive communism. From 1852 to 1856 they extended their hold into Hunan and down the Yangtse, capturing Nanking, the imperial southern capital, where Hung, now styled 'Heavenly King', established his residence. Despite severe internal dissensions and fighting in Nanking, the movement held the city until 1864 when it fell to the 'ever-victorious army' of Tseng Kuo-Fan, an army which included Charles George Gordon among its European and American mercenary units.

Taiping's zeal for social reform embraced common property; over and above subsistence needs, families were to hand over crops and money to a central granary and bank. It advocated land reform, with moderate taxes; the equality of women; temperance in the use of alcohol and tobacco, and the suppression of opium; and iconoclasm, which entailed the destruction of works of art embodying outworn beliefs. Foreigners were not regarded as inferior; all men were equal, and some foreign ideas were good, notably those of Christianity; but foreigners ought not to be exempted from Chinese law, and the movement expressed the resentment which many Chinese felt at what they regarded as the imperial government's surrender in this regard. After the capture of Nanking, the movement appears to have lost its moral fervour, and Franke describes its leaders as succumbing to the traditional vices of display, nepotism, and factionalism. This led to cynicism and demoralization in its army, especially when opposed by Tseng, a man of high ideal and upright character. Further, it failed to cooperate with other movements of revolt, although several peasant rebellions and one other religious revolt were going on at the same time. But it certainly shook the empire to its foundations, and both the Kuomintang and the communists may well have learned much from Taiping.

Religious movements of the general type that has been illustrated in the preceding paragraphs, selective though those illustrations inevitably are, clearly have many features in common. In nearly every case they have arisen among people who regard themselves as deprived or disadvantaged; in Lanternari's phrase, they are religions of the oppressed. They have arisen from a sense of injustice or humiliation, in which people have felt that they have been unfairly made worse off than they formerly were, or that they are now unfairly worse off than a privileged group with whom they compare their lot. Such feelings of discontent and resentment of the social order tend to take a religious form when the possibility of changing the social order by action in this world appears to be blocked. This is the case when the privileged group clearly possess a control of the situation that is unlikely to be weakened by the actions of the underprivileged, for example, through political action, through the legal system, or through rebellion or revolution — though religious movements of this kind do in some cases engender the fanaticism that leads to desperate rebellion, usually with disastrous consequences.

In the literature on recent movements of this kind the explanatory emphasis has most commonly been on situations that may in general terms be characterized as colonial, in which people of non-European descent and appearance have been dominated by Europeans or 'whites' of European descent. Thus the religious movements among the North American Indians arose in the conflict between them and white Americans; African independent churches arose in the colonial situation or in the situation in South Africa which can be characterized as internalized colonialism (see chapter 3); cargo cults in Melanesia arose under white Australian rule; and the Taiping rebellion arose in large part as a reaction to the incursions of Europeans into China in the 1840s.

Thus Sundkler attributes African independency in South Africa to the particular features of life in that country — the colour bar, residential segregation, the land question, segregation in employment and the restrictions upon African trade unions, social constraints upon informal interaction between people of different skin colour. The colour bar was extended to the life of the Christian churches — by the Netherlands Reformed churches with their 'golden rule', explicitly stated and theologically defended, of *'geen gelijkstelling* — no equality in Church or State', and by some other white churches as a matter of fact and everyday practice, though Sundkler adds that 'some Churches with firm episcopal authority have broken with this rule, both on principle and also in actual practice'.

'Net vir Blankes —For Europeans Only' is figuratively but no less virtually written on many church doors in the Union [of South Africa, now the Republic]. And this fact is one of the reasons for the emergence of Independent Bantu Churches ... As a rule, an African cannot with impunity enter a White church for an ordinary religious service. I have listened to scores of Independent church leaders who have related instances of how they have been turned away from White church services because of their black skin. The resentment over these pinpricks has added to the general aversion to the White man's Christianity.[36]

Such explanations seem to be insufficiently general. A colour bar as rigid as that in South Africa is not to be paralleled elsewhere in the world, yet separatist sects have arisen elsewhere. In the situation described by Barrett in Kenya, an Anglican church with a mostly African clergy was not immune from a separatist movement; yet clearly there was no literal or metaphorical 'For whites only' notice over church doors there. Similarly, the British protectorates of Uganda and Nyasaland were mildly administered and both the established missions and the colonial administration encouraged African advancement in education, economic life, and (though more hesitantly) in public affairs; yet the mere atmosphere of paternalism, without any objective oppression, was sufficient to engender separatist movements like the African Greek Orthodox church in Uganda, and those associated with Joseph Booth, Elliott Kamwana, and John Chilembwe in Nyasaland.

Another hypothesis found in the literature is that separatism arose in areas in which there was much Protestant missionary activity. According to this view, the Roman Catholic church abominates schism; the Protestant churches, however, themselves began as schismatic sects, and so can hardly oppose separatism on fundamental theological grounds. In so bald a form this hypothesis too is untenable; the virtual monopoly that the Roman Catholic missions enjoyed in the Congo under Belgian rule did not stop the rise of the Kimbangu-ist movement there.

At the same time, these explanations are not wholly false. It does seem to be the case that the more pronounced the white domination, and the more rigid the colour bar, the greater the tendency to form separatist independent religious movements. Thus among the five thousand or so African independent churches, some two thousand are now estimated to be in the Republic of South Africa. In terms of their membership or following, too, of a total separatist community of seven million in all Africa, Barrett estimates that three million are in South Africa.[37]

Further, it is too simple to equate religious movements of this type with colonial rule, for they do not come to an end with political indepen-

247

dence. As has been seen, the Kimbangu-ist church continues to attract a mass following in the republic of Zaïre twelve years after Belgian rule came to an end. Similarly, the Lumpa church of Alice Lenshina clashed violently with the authorities in independent Zambia. Moreover, this simple equation ignores the evidence of numerous movements that have arisen within societies like those of medieval Europe.

Another broad type of explanatory hypothesis is that which regards syncretistic, prophetic religious movements as arising from the contact (or impact, or clash) of Christianity upon an indigenous system of religious beliefs and practices. Such explanations are 'anthropological' in the sense that they consider the religious phenomena in rather strictly local terms. Thus Peter Lawrence has shown the relation between the Melanesian cargo cults and the traditional beliefs:

Material and social culture was accepted as an automatic concomitant of living. Human beings had complete rights to it because their various deities . . . had invented it and perpetuated it for them, while their ancestors, although rarely creators, helped them exploit it. In return, men ensured the continued co-operation of deities and ancestors by the performance of ritual . . . Spatially, because men, deities and spirits of the dead co-existed in the same geographical environment and had the same corporeal nature, their interaction was as pragmatic as that between human beings themselves. That these superhuman beings should handle material objects presented no conceptual problems. Important 'work' involved both a compound of secular and ritual techniques and collaboration from deities and ancestors, no distinction being made between different degrees of reality.[38]

Somewhat similarly though in more general terms Lanternari draws attention to the syncretism involved in the beliefs and practices of many prophetic movements, in terms such as 'the cultural clash between populations in very different stages of development'.

Here again it must be suggested that these explanations, though not false, are incomplete and insufficient. To view religious movements of the type in question purely in terms of a local clash of cultures is to fail to take into account the networks of influence, ideology, and social relations which we have found to operate —networks which since the early nineteenth century have been world-wide in scale. Thus the African Greek Orthodox church in Uganda was stimulated by Marcus Garvey's Universal Negro Improvement Association in America, its original connexion was with a Garveyite church in South Africa, and its later links were with the Greek Orthodox church. Or consider the networks in which Joseph Booth was involved, moving as he did between England, Australia, the United States, and southern Africa and setting up links between the American Jehovah's Witnesses and the black Kitawala movement of Elliott Kamwana, besides involving himself in 'Ethiopian' movements in South Africa and initiating half a dozen other movements in what is now Malawi. Yet another example is afforded by the links between the white Mormons of Joseph Smith in America and the prophetic movement of Smohalla among the North American Indians.

While all these explanations have some validity, therefore, none is seen as being sufficient in itself to account for so vast and complex a range of movements as that of the type which has been discussed here. Perhaps the most sensitive and comprehensive treatment of the subject is that of John Milton Yinger, who writes of sects and cults as arising among 'groups caught in conditions of severe disprivilege'. Whether such groups are racially and culturally defined following conquest by a militarily and industrially more advanced society, or dominated by a more powerful segment of their own society, their old way of life has been brought under severe pressure and can no longer be maintained.

A new style of life including a new religion, is needed; yet the religion of the conqueror, though often strongly urged by missionary activity, is not fully meaningful and adequate. It is embedded in the whole social system of the dominant group – a system only partly experienced and understood by the conquered or minority groups.

The traditional separation of individuals and tribes imposes serious problems in the new context. Formerly separate, and even antagonistic, groups now find themselves caught up in common situation. Unifying themes are needed.

Among the many ways that people find of struggling with such a situation, religious movements often have an important bridging function, however bizarre they may appear and however seriously they may carry the threats of conflict.

Yinger cites the cargo cults, the 1890 Ghost Dance, and the Jehovah's Witnesses as examples of what he calls 'attack' cults:

Such religious attacks on the dominant society are not limited to conquered peoples. If, within a society, a group lacks an independent and successful past which can serve as the focus of the millennial dream, they can affirm that they are the true defenders of a tradition shared with their oppressors, who have fallen into sinful ways; they alone are 'Jehovah's Witnesses' ... Thus the Jehovah's Witnesses also attack the rich and powerful, although there is no racial theme involved, as did the members of the Fiji Tuka cult and the Indian Ghost Dance; and they attack the society by downgrading its institutions and refusing to accord it final loyalty.

Such religious movements, as Yinger mildly puts it, are seldom regarded with favour by the dominant group: 'Through the years, many of the leaders of the Cargo cults in Melanesia have been jailed and the movements suppressed. The Ghost Dance was smashed militarily at the Battle of Wounded Knee. Hundreds of Jehovah's Witnesses have been jailed in the United States because their search for salvation involved a sharp disagreement with dominant institutions.' The 'attack' type of cult, however, is fairly short-lived. If hope for the restoration of the old culture and the independence of the sub-

249

ject group fades, then there is likely to be a transition to a more accommodative type of cult, like the peyote cult which followed the suppression of the Ghost Dance. On the other hand, the 'success' of the sect, and more especially if its members under its influence gain improved social status, Protestant-ethic-style, then what began as a militant sect becomes a denomination accepting its place as one of several alternative forms of religion, tolerated by society and accommodating itself to the existing order.

The success or failure of movements of this kind, Yinger insists, should not been seen only from the point of view of the dominant group and its values. It depends what we mean by success. If we mean, do they allow the continuation of societies like those of the North American Indians in a drastically altered environment, rescuing them from total destruction, and giving individuals a new dignity and self-respect in conditions of cultural confusion, suffering, and demoralization? — then the answer may well be Yes, they serve these functions reasonably well. If we mean by success the relatively graceful destruction of such societies and the absorption of individuals into the dominant society, the answer may be No; but to apply such a test would be to stretch functionalism severely and perhaps distort it with an ethnocentric bias.[39]

12 The political characteristics of new states in poor countries

Several themes which afford a background to the political life of poor countries have been introduced in previous chapters; these include their poverty itself, their colonial heritage, 'tribalism' or communalism and the plural society, language, the communications network, education and the educated elite. The aim of this chapter is to draw those themes together in a consideration of the distinctive characteristics of the political life of poor countries. This necessitates a definition of what we mean by politics. From this point of view, the distinctively political aspect of human behaviour is that concerned with making the major decisions about the life of a group, or determining what is sometimes called 'policy'. Politics is not the implementation of the rules which regulate the life of a group — that is administration. Politics is concerned rather with making and changing the rules, including 'changing the rules for changing the rules'. This naturally involves competition, rivalry, and manoeuvre between individuals and groups for the control of resources — men, money, and above all power. The most important power resource in most societies is the state, that unique institution which in Weber's classic definition successfully asserts a monopoly of legitimate force within a defined geographical area. Politics in the narrow sense is generally thought of accordingly as being 'about' who controls the state power and for what purposes it is used. It is of great importance, however, to consider politics in a wider perspective. In most poor countries the state is unequivocally an institution — the most important and powerful institution, indeed — of the 'modern sector' as we characterized it in chapter 4. In the 'non-modern' or 'traditional' sectors, pre-existing methods of exercising power and making decisions continue to a large extent, articulating only to a limited extent and at particular points with the politics of the state. (The study of that very process of articulation between the two systems, indeed, is a major and largely unexplored field for social science research.) In the study of the politics of poor countries, accordingly, it is specially necessary to keep in mind the politics of local communities, such as the village, province, or tribal area, even though — or rather, precisely because — such communities are explicitly deprived of, and often at odds with, the central power of the state.

The meaninglessness of 'political development'

In all societies somebody makes the large, final decisions. They may be wise or foolish decisions, well or ill informed, well or ill considered. They may represent the people's choice, or reflect the intrigues of cliques and cabals. The discussion that precedes them — and there is always such a discussion, just as there are always issues that demand decision —may be carried on in public or in private, at a high or a low intellectual level. Unfortunately there does not seem to be any clearly marked evolutionary trend in these matters. There are technologically primitive societies in which major decisions are made in a spirit of wisdom by trusted men after public debate; there are modern industrial societies in which decisions of major public policy emerge after private intrigue or 'inner-party' debate, and seem to reflect a clash of personalities and vested interests rather than a magnanimous consideration of the public good.

With administration it is a different matter. Public accounts are no longer kept by tying knots in pieces of cord, as in ancient Peru, or cutting notches in pieces of wood, as in medieval England, while messages are no longer sent by hand of a man on a horse. The administrative offices of all contemporary states use typewriters, filing cabinets, telephones, and the new technology for storing and retrieving information. But that does not make the political decisions any wiser. It is possible accordingly to speak of administrative modernization, but that is a comparatively trivial aspect of the matter.

Political modernization is sometimes taken to refer to the outward forms of political institutions, and our judgment in these matters may even (with another relapse into triviality) be affected by the buildings associated with those institutions. Thus a new state which has an institution named a National Assembly, meeting in a modern-looking assembly hall, may give an impression of political modernity which may be belied by the actual content of the business transacted by that assembly, its relative ineffectiveness, its liability to be influenced by corruption, and so forth. On the other hand, there are countries whose form of government looks antique, even anachronistic, yet which seem to manage to cope with the world of the late twentieth century and make decisions which are not lacking in political acumen and even wisdom. The African kingdoms of Ethiopia and Swaziland will perhaps illustrate the point. And, for that matter, the government of many states to which no one would seriously deny the apellation 'modern' are not lacking in their picturesque antique formalities; the state opening of the British Parliament makes the point well enough.

The terms 'political modernization' and 'political development' are given widely various meanings by different authors, and these have been well summarized by Dodd.[1] Some see political development as a movement towards an end-state regarded as self-evidently desirable and probably inevitable, though what that end-state is depends, of course, on the political convictions of the writer — it may be a communist society, American liberal two-party democracy, an Islamic state, etc. Many Americans regard 'participation' as a key variable, including both the spread of the franchise and 'a general attitude towards equality which allows equality of opportunity to participate in politics and compete for government office'. Another meaning attached to 'political development' is the capacity to initiate and sustain economic development, and a willingness and capacity to carry out reforms which remove obstacles to it — land reforms, for example. 'The expansion and centralization of governmental power, and the differentiation and specialization (and subsequent integration) of political functions and structures' is another criterion. And finally there is 'the capacity to adapt to a higher level of adaptability; to learn how to learn, how to learn, how to . . .', or what might be called the ability to cope. It is clear enough that most if not all of these criteria involve the exercise of personal judgment. Does the government of the United States or the Soviet Union really 'cope' any better than those of India or Ethiopia? There are difficulties too about 'participation'. The franchise clearly will not do, for the formal right to cast a vote is of no real meaning if voters have no effective choice of party or candidate (as in the Soviet Union) or if elections are held but once in the history of the state (as in Indonesia). By the same token, to apply the test of a two-party democratic system, or 'fundamental democratization' brings us up against the greatest of all contrary instances in the Soviet Union — which no one would deny is a modern industrial state. Political development, modernity, and modernization appear, then, to be matters of judgment rather than objective measurement.

The colonial heritage

As was pointed out in chapter 3, most poor countries are the successor states of colonial regimes, and by far the biggest single resource which was left by the colonial power to its successor was a state — the monopoly of legitimate force over a defined geographical area, with associated resources of administration, taxation, and so forth. It was for control of that unique resource that the most acute struggle was waged in the period around independence. Moreover, most poor countries lack other sources of wealth and prestige such as large business corporations, for they tend to be under foreign control. In the absence accordingly of alternative ways for an ambitious individual to attain control of large resources, the uniqueness of the state as the supremely desirable prize is thrown into even sharper prominence.

Sometimes the forms of government which have been adopted, initially at

253

least, have been modelled closely on those of the former colonial power. One obvious example is the 'Westminster model' adopted by many former British colonies, and sometimes ridiculed for slavish adherence to small details like the design of the mace or the wigs of the clerks at the table. One important reason for this was that, though its insistence did not extend to inessential detail, it was a general condition for the grant of self-government by Britain that parliamentary democracy should be a working reality. In part, however, the adoption of this model reflected an admiration for parliamentary democracy on the part of some members of the political elites of those countries; and indeed, the anti-colonial ideology might in some cases take the form of a simple demand that the political rights and freedoms enjoyed by the British people should be shared by those of their colonies. For example, the Nigerian leader Dr Nnamdi Azikiwe quoted from Locke and Burke in support of declarations such as the following:

Thanks to the growth of political consciousness in this country, our people are becoming acquainted with the practice of parliamentary democracy. This has been used as a criterion to determine the political maturity of any people under the rule of others, and we can be no exception. [1952]

The domestic policy of Nigeria will be framed on the assumption that Nigeria shall continue to be a parliamentary democracy. [1952][2]

In some other cases, however, the experience of colonial rule has led to the rejection rather than the acceptance of the practices of the colonial power. In particular, the precedents of Spain and Portugal had little appeal for the successor states of South and Central America. The practices of the United States had some prestige there, as they have in other parts of the world, but there is a good deal of ambivalence in Latin American attitudes towards 'the colossus of the north', and a disposition to reject 'Yanqui' models accordingly. ('Poor Mexico!' as General Diaz is reported to have exclaimed, 'so far from God, so near to the United States!') A tendency to look instead for distinctively Latin models has led many of these states to adopt features of the French constitution, out of a regard for France as the cultural centre of the Latin world and 'the notion that civilization radiates from Paris'.[3]

A particular legacy of Spanish and Portuguese rule in Latin America has been the position of the Roman Catholic church. These states inherited a 'national vicariate' or state patronage of the church, and most are still officially Catholic (Mexico is an exception). It would appear from Willems' account, however, that the formal supremacy of the church is belied by its actual weakness. The clergy are few in number, many rural parishes being without incumbents, while at the same time priests are employed by wealthy families as tutors for their children. Rural life is little touched by clergy who pay hasty and occasional visits, and superstitions flourish. Anti-clerical sentiments are widespread, and there is a common view that 'the Church is something for the rich and women'.[4] Such a discrepancy between formal authority on the one hand and actual power, influence, or control on the other is a common characteristic of poor countries, and constitutes a theme to which I return below.

In more general ways, the style and content of politics after independence as well as its formal institutions have been shaped by the particular experiences of colonial rule. Thus Pye has drawn out the contrasts in south-east Asia, where the British in Burma bequeathed an image of authority committed to the 'proper way of doing things' which was closer to administrative rule than that of popular politicians. The Dutch in Indonesia pursued a policy of cultural relativism, much admired in its time, but one in which the acceptance that there were two essentially respectable worlds left no room for the transitional man seeking to become westernized without severing his roots. The result has been 'a highly ambiguous image of the desirable qualities of political authority'. In French Indo-China a different ambiguity prevailed between association and assimilation. French policy permitted the emergence of a remarkably westernized elite, but it was an elite 'who had lost their claim to leadership of the traditional elements of their society [and] could only re-establish such a claim by conspicuously rejecting their affiliations with the French'. Finally, American rule in the Philippines left two distinctive legacies – a highly developed system of public education, and a tradition of rule by elected politicians looking after their supporters' particular interests rather than by competent, impartial administrators.[5] In the same way, Rustow has pointed out the effects of the short and unhappy episode of French and British colonial rule in Arab countries between the two world wars.[6]

In many African and Asian countries (the Philippines, as noted, being an exception) as important part of the colonial legacy has been an administration accustomed to think of itself as independent of and superior to the wiles and intrigues of politics. This has led since independence to what Riggs calls the 'interference complex' – mutual accusations of 'interference' by politicians and bureaucrats. The natural claims of the new political leaders to make the important decisions involve the former power-holding elite, the administration, in stepping down gracefully in favour of men whom they may despise and fear. Small wonder, says Riggs, that they protest that such matters as the making of appointments, contracts, and allocations fall within the 'administrative' sphere and ought not to be subject to 'political interference'.[7] The conflict may be particularly acute over military matters, and army officers particularly jealous of political interference in matters which affect the national security and prestige; I return to this point below.

255

Anti-colonial ideologies

To pick up another theme from chapter 3, a further effect of colonial rule in many of the new states has been in the nature of the ideology of the groups, individuals, and 'parties' which took over the government.*

It is usual to class these ideologies as 'nationalist', but the term is more often than not misleading. As Worsley has pointed out, the word 'nationalism' has at least three different meanings. In what might be called the 'classical' sense in which it was used in nineteenth-century Europe, a movement like that of Polish nationalism was based on the sentiment that a people who shared a common language, culture, and historical identity ought to be regarded as a nation and united in a single state. A nationalism of that nature was based on a common language, Polish; on a distinctive religious affiliation, Roman Catholic as against Russian Orthodoxy to the east and German Protestantism to the west; and on distinctive historical traditions, including the memories of a period when Poland had been an independent kingdom. As a political movement, Polish nationalism was aimed at the establishment of an independent Polish state and the ending of the partition of the country between the empires of Germany, Austria, and Russia. Similarly, nationalist movements in Italy and Germany were aimed at the unification of fragmented small states in an area with a common language and historical traditions, while movements like Czech, Greek, and Irish nationalism aimed at the 'liberation' of those peoples from the foreign rule of the Austrian, Ottoman, and British empires respectively. In the latter cases religion as well as language and a cultural heritage played a part in delineating the community which felt itself to be 'different', 'oppressed', and under rule that could be thought of as 'foreign'.

While nationalism in the new states of Africa and Asia is certainly based on the desire to end foreign rule, and has that much in common with many of the nineteenth-century European nationalisms, it differs in most other respects. It consists essentially of an effort to create sentiments of loyalty to the successor state of a colonial administration. As has been emphasized in chapter 9, most of these are highly arbitrary and in a sense 'artificial' creations, whose borders part like from like as often as they embrace unlike peoples under a single state system. There is not a single symbol capable of being attached to 'Uganda', for instance, which can compare with those that could be attached to 'Poland' – no equivalents for the Polish language, for the common attachment to the Roman Catholic church, for the traditions of the court of King Wladislaw. If

* As with 'church' and 'sect', there is a difficulty about terminology here. The word 'party' has been put in inverted commas as a reminder that organizations bearing that name in poor countries are not necessarily to be thought of in the same terms as the political parties of modern industrial states. See pp. 257–61 below.

there is loyalty and attachment to 'Uganda' it must be of the head and not of the heart.

Indeed, it has been convincingly argued that the true twentieth-century counterpart of the nineteenth-century European nationalism is African tribalism.[8] The groups with a common language, a common culture, and a sense of common identity are tribes, not the new states. The emotional sentiments involved in attachments to the new states are shallow indeed compared with the depth and vitality of those toward fellow-tribesmen, traditional forms of social and political organization, and (where applicable) traditional rulers like the Kabaka of Buganda. Yet tribalism is rightly regarded as dangerously destructive of 'national' unity in the new states of modern Africa. As President Nyerere has said,

There are obvious weaknesses on the African continent. We have artificial 'nations' carved out at the Berlin Conference: we are struggling to build these nations into stable units of human society . . . Whenever we try to talk in terms of larger units on the African continent, we are told that it can't be done; we are told that the units we would so create would be 'artificial'. As if they could be any more artificial than the 'national' units on which we are now building! . . .

African nationalism is meaningless, is dangerous, is anachronistic, if it is not at the same time Pan-Africanism.[9]

This well illustrates the way in which the difficulties inherent in the first two kinds of nationalism in the twentieth century may be resolved by an appeal to a third type of attachment, a 'Pan-' movement. As Worsley has succinctly put it, such movements transcend state boundaries and are built on much wider affiliations. These may be religious, as in the case of Pan-Islamism; linguistic and cultural, as with Slavophilism and Pan-Arabism; those of physical appearance, as *négritude* and Garveyism; or continental, as Pan-Africanism.[10]

Inheritance elites and 'parties' in the successor states

The overriding aim of the political 'parties' which were the immediate successors of the colonial regimes was accordingly self-government, or the end of colonial rule by white foreigners. Slogans rather than detailed policies — Free-Dom! Uhuru! — sufficed to embody the universal aim of ending foreign rule. Tiresome questions like 'Who is the self who is to govern?' were brushed aside, in the same spirit as Fanon brushed aside the inquiries of intellectuals and democrats about the objectives of the Algerian resistance to French rule. A tendency to vagueness about what was to happen after independence could be countered by attachment to a charismatic leader as a symbol of the popular aspirations. For example, Apter has related how the 'more delicate nationalism' of the elite who founded the United Gold Coast Convention in 1946 and

257

called for self-government 'in the shortest possible time' gave way to the more robust slogan of Kwame Nkrumah's Convention People's Party, 'self-government now'. Nkrumah was indeed idolized:

Great hopes for a new society centred around his person, around the symbols of 'Free-Dom!', the C.P.P. rallying cry, and around the demand for 'self-government now'. 'Forward Ever, Backward Never' was the slogan of the party. Around the slogans and the demands, around the green, white, and red of the C.P.P. banners, around the almost mythical person of Kwame Nkrumah there slowly emerged a faithful flock, shepherded by the leader into the paths of nationalism and independence.[11]

A second major theme in the ideologies of the successor states has been economic development, and in many of them there has been a preference for economic arrangements that could be called 'socialist'. It was a central point in the anti-colonial ideology that, in the terms of Lenin and other communist writers, imperialism was the highest form of capitalism; if one was condemned the other was at least suspect. Thus the Ghanaian apologist Kofi Baako wrote of 'imperialism and its twin sister capitalism', and Nkrumah proclaimed himself to be 'a Marxian socialist and an undenominational Christian. I am no communist and have never been one.' However, the term 'socialist' has not been interpreted rigidly or narrowly. Thus while several of the new states of Africa profess attachment to 'African socialism', the term is interpreted in widely different ways. There is a rejection of the materialist premises of the Marxist—Leninist tradition; thus President Senghor has written eloquently of 'spiritual values' which he thinks were lost to Soviet communism under Stalin, Nkrumah saw no contradiction between socialism and Christianity, and President Nyerere has linked African socialism with an image of traditional kinship solidarity in the evocative word *ujamaa*. And when it comes to actual policies when in power, there are wide divergences, for example between the actions of the government of Tanzania in nationalizing large private businesses and that of Kenya in refusing to do so. In Kenya, indeed, Africanization rather than nationalization has become the aim; foreign firms are under pressure to train and employ Africans at managerial levels, and Africans are encouraged to develop indigenous commercial banks, even though this must result in the growth of an indigenous business class committed to capitalism — yet these measures were advocated in a government paper entitled 'African socialism'.[12] Thus while capitalism has been generally rejected, in name if not in fact, by many of the new states of Asia and Africa, there has not been a general inclination wholeheartedly to embrace the alternative of Soviet-style economic development with a centrally planned economy. So both the major ideologies of the rich industrial states, communism and private enterprise, have been viewed with grave reservations if not rejected outright; and along with this has gone an attitude favouring disengagement from the rivalries and conflicts between the two great power blocs, and a search for a positive neutrality. From this point of view, the 'Third World' is different; the great divide is not that between capitalist and communist industrial states, between the United States and the Soviet Union and their respective allies, but between the rich industrial world as a whole and the poor countries, or as Dia called them the 'proletarian nations'.

Yet while ideologies like African socialism clearly include the aspiration that the emergence of antagonistic classes, like those of nineteenth-century Europe, can be avoided in the newly developing countries, there is neverthe-less a clear strand of elitism in them. If there is socialism, it tends to be socialism planned by an elite. As Paul Sigmund has pointed out, many nationalist leaders see strong government as the only way to achieve modern-ization and development, and they coin phrases like Sukarno's 'guided democracy', Ayub Khan's 'basic democracy', and Sékou Touré's 'democratic dictatorship' to express the clear leadership which the government or ruling party must give the people.[13] Thus in Ghana, as Apter expressed it, there was a tendency to assert that 'the C.P.P. formed the nucleus of a new society. This required the party to "generalise" itself into society'; and he quotes Nkrumah's speech on the subject of academic freedom versus the ideological education of youth:

The Convention People's Party is a powerful force, more powerful indeed than anything that has yet appeared in the history of Ghana. It is a uniting force that guides and pilots the nation, and is the nerve centre of the positive operations in the struggle for African irridentism. Its supremacy cannot be challenged. The Convention People's Party is Ghana, and Ghana is the Convention People's Party.[14]

Such a tendency to assert and declare that the 'party' that had led the country into independence represented in some almost mythical way the 'true will of the people' was a deeply underlying factor in the tendency towards one-party systems in many of the new states.

Despite their pretensions to be the authentic national movements, how-ever, it is clear from a number of accounts that the 'parties' which rule many of the new states are in fact weak — another example of the discrepancy between formal authority and actual power. For example, it is stated of the founders of the Senegalese national 'party' that they drew into the party's organization the leaders of a wide variety of special-interest groups, often picturesquely named, like the Union pour la Défense des Intérêts du Quartier de Guet-n-Dar et des Pêcheurs, founded because 'they had no market for their salted fish, no stable prices; because they felt forgotten, their streets were ugly and unlit, their water supply was short'.[15] Similarly, the Parti Démocratique de Côte d'Ivoire according to Staniland began as an alliance of voluntary as-sociations — a planters' cooperative in which Houphouet himself became prominent, ethnic associations, the teachers' union, and intellectuals' societies. Clearly neither organizational coherence nor ideological precision is to be expected of such diverse groups. Further, the actual working of the party diverged substantially from its official structure, with committees at the district level as often nominated as elected; and only four annual congresses were held in twenty years, giving little opportunity to unseat party officials. Staniland draws the important conclusion that 'However much P.D.C.I. leaders emphasise the grass-roots context of the militant period, historically the evidence would support an opposed hypothesis, one of deliberate involvement of people at the district level by leaders of a party at the territorial level in a conflict which originated at a still higher level.'[16]

Another instance of the weakness of the national 'party' is afforded by Gertzel's account of the Kenya African National Union. During the last few years of colonial rule, rival leaders whose power was based on strong local support at the district level preferred not to have a strong national party organization which might enable one leader to gain control. This remained the position for some years after independence in 1963, when it is clear that K.A.N.U. existed in little more than name: 'No meeting of the National Executive or the Governing Council was called between 1963 and 1966 . . . KANU headquarters in Nairobi remained empty except for the occasional minor official. The telephone was disconnected because the account was not paid. Party finances were said to be in disarray. At district level branches were equally lacking in formal organization, and membership dues were not collected.'[17]

The origins of many of the national 'parties' as confederations of petty interest groups, and their dependence for whatever organizational strength they possess upon such groups, has in some cases led to an insistence that such groups should throw in their lot wholly with the 'party' and divest themselves of other links. For example, in Ghana first the T.U.C. had to break its links with the International Confederation of Free Trade Unions, then the independent farmers' cooperative movement was eliminated in favour of a new movement, and thirdly the Boy Scout movement was eclipsed by the Young Pioneers, though not abolished. When the Bishop of Accra, an Anglican missionary, objected to the form of indoctrination that was taking place in the Young Pioneers, he was forced to leave the country.[18] Such actions clearly manifest once more the discrepancy between formal authority and actual control — a sense of the actual weakness of the national 'party' despite its pretensions as the one national movement. A further example of the same syndrome is the nervous suspicion shown in many new states towards the national university, and it is significant that the context of Nkrumah's statement, quoted below, was that of academic freedom versus ideological education:

There are some persons, both staff and students, who mistakenly believe that the words 'academic freedom' carry with them a spirit of hostility to our Party and the Government, the same Party of the workers and the farmers and the same Government whose money founded the University and maintains it, and who provides them with their education in the hope that they will one day repay their countrymen by giving loyal and devoted service to the Government of the people. The Convention People's Party cannot allow this confusion of academic freedom with disloyalty and anti-Government ideas. In future we shall attach the greatest importance to the ideological education of the Youth.[19]

As Staniland has pointed out in relation to Africa, there are two fundamentally different lines of interpretation of politics in the late colonial and immediately post-colonial period. One holds that independence came as a direct result of the pressures of mass movements, the leaders of which succeeded in dislodging colonial powers and who were concerned in integrating sectional interests into 'the nation'. These leaders were concerned after independence with raising everybody's living standards; they were democratic and egalitarian, and represented the forces of modernization against opposed traditionalism, represented by the chiefs. The second, and perhaps truer, interpretation is that colonial development created an indigenous elite who had to some extent assimilated the values and practices of the colonial power. After the second world war this group gained a measure of political participation in the affairs of the colony or *territoire*.

In attempting to enlarge this participation, it found itself in conflict with colonial interests and resorted to a tactical politicization of arenas below the national level ... Only the vaguest formulation of *general* goals was possible or desirable (rigid definition would have made it harder to get so much support) ... Decolonization consisted of a bargain between a seriously weakened colonial autocracy and the local 'inheritance elite'.[20]

The first line of interpretation represents, to put it bluntly, the myth now put out by the 'inheritance elite'. The national 'parties' which represented in Staniland's terms the 'tactical politicization' of petty interest groups by the 'inheritance elite', are accordingly quite different in nature from the political parties characteristic of industrial countries, even parties as diverse as (say) the Democratic Party of the U.S.A., the Conservative Party of Great Britain, and the Communist Party of the Soviet Union. As with 'church' and 'sect', we should not be misled by the name 'party' which occurs in the official titles of such movements into thinking of them in the same terms. Further, just as I have already mentioned the discrepancy between proclaimed authority and actual power which is characteristic of politics in poor countries, so the dual interpretations outlined by Staniland illustrate a second and related tendency to state as if it were fact what is really no more than a hope, an aspiration, or

261

even a desperate wish — a tendency which, adopting a term of Riggs, we may call 'double-talk'.[21]

Communal breakaway movements

In many of the new states of Asia and Africa there has been a strong and persistent tendency for the integrity of the new state to be threatened by tribes, regions, or communities otherwise delineated to break away and assert a separate independence. Sometimes these separatist movements have resulted in spectacular conflicts and erupted into bitter and bloody wars.

Economic and ethnic factors have combined in many such cases to engender a sense that some region or people was not getting a fair share of the resources of a new state. As a background to such conflicts it should be remembered, as was pointed out in chapter 4, that economic development tends to be uneven, and some regions go ahead faster than others. In some cases it has been the leading region that has become impatient with a situation in which it has been contributing to the central revenues of a larger state from which other and more backward regions have been getting most of the benefit, and has come to feel accordingly that it would be better off going it alone (e.g. Buganda, Katanga). In other cases it has been the poorer regions that have experienced 'backwash' and attributed it to exploitation by the leading region (e.g. Bangladesh), or have resisted the secession of that region when it appeared to be trying to make off with the loot (as the Nigerian federation resisted the secession of 'Biafra').

Such instances serve to highlight a general tendency in poor countries to what is, somewhat temperately and formally, described as the weakness of local government. Fears that local regional or tribal patriotisms are liable to result in the break-up of the state altogether are often, as has been seen, well grounded. The governments of new states are inclined to maintain as much central control as they possibly can, and leave as little initiative as possible to local bodies, precisely because they know they cannot trust the latter to act as loyal local representatives in the exercise of devolved powers. This is one of the reasons why, as Riggs has pointed out, new states in poor countries are particularly liable to overcentralization. Riggs quotes many reports by advisers from World Bank missions and similar bodies to the governments of poor countries pointing out this defect and recommending decentralization; but the results have been disappointing, and the source of such malfunctions lies deeper than the level at which a purely administrative reform can be effective.

From this perspective, extreme centralization of authority can be seen as a desperate attempt to bring the bureaucracy and society under control. Indeed, when effective control weapons are so notably lacking, the cheapest and most obvious remaining weapon is the power of formal authority. Unfortunately, this nominal power turns out to be without potency, resulting, often enough, in a final resort to violence and coercion. Thus 'overcentralization' is a vain hope, a groundless aspiration and pretence, masking the actual dispersion and localization of control which is the hidden reality. The mark of prismatic power distribution is 'equivocality', not 'centralization'.[22]

Accordingly, what in formal terms is called 'overcentralization' and 'the weakness of local government' in new states can be regarded from another point of view as just the opposite – the *strength* of local political processes, beyond the power of the centre to control, and the corresponding *weakness* of the centre. Once more we find a discrepancy between formal authority and actual power or control.

Coercion

Riggs' 'final resort to violence and coercion' is indeed often exemplified in the ferocious brutality with which the army and police of a poor state behave when they go into action against a communal breakaway movement. The actions of such states often display in a dramatic form this aspect of 'equivocality' in the sharp contrast between the laxity with which the law is normally enforced and the bloody ferocity which the agencies of the state are capable of showing on some particular occasions. Besides the suppression of breakaway movements, those occasions include urban riots, strikes, student protests, and peasants' revolts. At the level of violence to individuals, too, it is consistent with this general analysis that many of the new states have retained or revived the death penalty and the use of judicial corporal punishment. Thus Milner and his co-authors have shown that in many African countries the treatment of offenders by these methods was falling into disuse in the late colonial period, in line with the movements of penal reform that were taking place in the metropolitan countries of Europe. Since 1960, however, while a country like Britain has abolished both the death penalty and judicial corporal punishment altogether, a country like Tanzania has moved in quite the opposite direction, introducing mandatory corporal punishment for certain offences despite the publicly expressed misgivings of the Commissioner of Prisons. In the same way many of the new states of black Africa have resorted to public executions. Such developments appear to be motivated at least in part by a desire to do something drastic in a situation that is felt to be getting out of hand and to respond to popular clamour for such action to show that the state's authority cannot be lightly flouted. In the case of the state which makes the greatest use of the death penalty of all, South Africa, there is a further factor; the generally authoritarian cast of mind which is associated with beliefs in racial supremacy also tends to favour the drastically punitive treatment of offenders.[23]

Political middlemen and the articulation between local and national politics

One consequence of the uncertain control of the state over local political processes is the importance of 'middlemen', to whom some social anthropologists have given attention in the societies they have studied. A pioneer in this field was Max Gluckman, who in his studies of Zulu society in the 1930s gave prominence to the occupants of what he called 'inter-hierarchical positions or roles' of this kind, the hierarchies in question being respectively those of Zulu society and those of the white South African government. One class of such roles was that of the government-recognized chiefs and village headman, and Gluckman quotes the saying that the chief was the only member of the administration who never went to Britain on leave. Another class of inter-hierarchical roles were those occupied by white men like the District Officer, the Native Commissioner, and the agricultural and other technical officers. Just as the black chiefs became to some extent imbued with the ideas of the administration, so the white administrative officers in many cases came to have much sympathy with those of the Zulu, and Gluckman hints at a tendency for the official policies of Pretoria to be somewhat modified when it came to their actual execution in Zululand.[24]

Summing up a number of such studies (including F. G. Bailey's of 'parapolitical systems' in an Orissa village, and Friedrich's unforgettable portrait of a *cacique* or local boss in a Mexican rural community), Swartz has pointed out that the middleman's authority or influence is exerted in a situation in which there is a gap or incongruity between political cultures. For example, a national scheme of elections and representative officials may be at odds with a local traditional system of authoritative chiefs or informal control through the consensus of older men. Further, scattered communities may have diverse interests, communications are generally poor, and the spheres of influence or power exerted by formal authorities overlap and conflict with one another. Political middlemen themselves may not fully understand the situations in which they act, but they manage somehow to be sensitive to the cues afforded by other people's actions in the different systems, and to work out *ad hoc* practical techniques for resolving conflicts and getting what they want.[25]

On the whole, however, there is rather a dearth of studies of middlemen and the more general subject of the articulation between local community politics and that of the larger state system. More research is needed in this important area, calling for a combination of the approaches of social anthropology and political science.

The 'soft state'

Another way of expressing the discrepancy between authority and control, and the relative autonomy of indigenous political processes at the local level, is by Myrdal's term the 'soft state'. By this he means that 'policies decided on are often not enforced, if they are enacted at all', and that 'the authorities, even when framing policies are reluctant to place obligations on people'. In particular there is a reluctance or inability to apply effective measures against corruption. Such reluctance and inability have little or nothing to do with particular political systems in the different South Asian countries; they are 'strikingly similar in their inability to institute fundamental reforms and enforce social discipline. Whether democratic or authoritarian, they are all in this sense "soft states".' Mydral gives yet another illustration of the tendency for such a situation to give rise to 'double-talk': officials in the economic planning ministries express 'two opposing views, simultaneously held' — on the one hand the need for radical social and economic change, on the other that they must proceed with caution, upsetting the traditional social order as little as possible. 'And when they do legislate radical institutional reforms — for instance on taxation or in regard to property rights in the villages — they permit the laws to contain loopholes of all sorts and even let them remain unenforced.'[26]

In such circumstances, laws may be put on the statute book because they will look well there, possibly from the point of view of 'world opinion', even though they may bear little or no relation to the actual practices of life in the country. Or a law may be enacted as a declaration of intent, a statement of principle, a pointer to the direction in which it is one day hoped to move, like the formal proscription of caste in the constitution of India, even though everybody knows that there is not the slightest possibility of seriously implementing such a principle.

Corruption

Consideration of the 'soft state' leads naturally to the subject of corruption. This has been mentioned in chapter 4, but it is a subject with both economic and political aspects — it is, indeed, precisely concerned with the interrelation of economic and political behaviour, which are in any case hard to separate — and it cannot be omitted from a consideration of politics in poor countries.

If a 'soft state' is one in which formal rules (laws, officially stated administrative rules and practices, etc.) are applied capriciously and in a lax manner rather than rigorously and consistently, then it is one in which private advantage can be gained and private bargains struck concerning the enforcement or non-enforcement of the rules, as when a businessman bribes a tax official to accept a low return of his income or assets, paying of course less than the tax saved by the transaction. Besides money, another inducement is kinship sentiment, and another is the favour of superiors. Thus a superior may ask a subordinate to do something illegal for him. If the subordinate refuses he forfeits his superior's favour; if he complies, he is for ever afterwards under the threat of blackmail.

In a society in which law and order are administered in a lax and capricious manner, the individual cannot rely on the police and the law for his protection, whether the reliability of his contracts, the security of his possessions, or even the safety of his person. The patronage of a powerful person may seem to be a better guarantee of security in any or all of these senses. Where such a relation is formally and explicitly the basis of social and political relations, of course, we have a feudal system. In medieval Europe the relation between a lord and his vassal was symbolized in the act of homage, a kind of ceremonial contract in which the vassal placed himself and his possessions totally at the disposal of the lord in exchange for the lord's protection. Better the predictable, customary extortions and humiliations of the lord than the unpredictable ones of robbers and outlaws in an age in which extortion and violence were terrible, everyday commonplaces.[27] At the other extreme, the totally illegal activities of protection rackets in some industrial societies constitute a sort of clandestine feudalism in which rival gangs, like feudal lords, have an interest in protecting their client-victims against the competitive extortions of other gangs. In societies which are in an intermediate state, relations of a quasi-feudal type may prevail at a level which is also intermediate between their formal and legal recognition as in medieval Europe and their outright illegality as in (say) modern America.

One factor making for corruption in many poor countries at the present time is their character as plural societies, in which the decisive role of economic enterprise is played by alien minority groups like the Chinese in many countries of south-east Asia, the Asians in East Africa, or the Indians in Malaya and Burma. Riggs has well analysed the situation of the 'pariah entrepreneur', contrasting it with that of the truly 'private capitalist' in a fully developed industrial society. Like the private capitalist, the pariah has to consider the ordinary economic costs and risks; unlike him, he has to consider also the costs and risks involved in security and access. So he is much more concerned with politics, though he cannot afford to be directly involved. Even the capital which he nominally 'owns' he cannot effectively use without the consent of the elite — for which he has to pay. Whatever his formal rights to his property, its actual control is in fact shared, 'in a highly nebulous and imprecise way, with an assortment of powerful individuals who may intervene at any time in arbitrary and quite unpredictable ways'. The payment of the requisite tribute, says Riggs, is 'defined as shameful, involving resort to "corrupt" practices as a requisite to survival'.[28]

Scott, too, in his comparative study of corruption has noted that minority groups of this kind seldom act openly as lobbies or interest groups when measures affecting them are being formulated at the legislative stage. Businessmen, for example, know perfectly well that the tax they will actually have to pay will bear little or no relation to their liability under the tax law. It is altogether more sensible for each firm quietly to 'buy' what it needs in the way of enforcement or non-enforcement, than to campaign for a different law that would be just as formalistic as the existing one — and risk attracting un-favourable attention to boot. Occasionally, says Scott, politicians may pass laws restricting the private sector 'so as to maintain the proper ideological stance', while at the same time conniving, for a consideration, in the evasion of the law by private firms.

However, it should not be thought that corruption is confined to those sectors of the life of poor countries in which enterprising minority groups play a major role. As has already been noted, the prevalence of kinship over more impersonal sources of obligation makes for nepotism among the indigenous populations of these countries, while the lack of impact of rural community interests upon the central political system may put peasants in a position resembling in some way that of pariahs — it may be cheaper and less trouble to bribe the government inspector than to cope with the formal demands of the law, or comply with a maze of intricate regulations, which an illiterate peasant cannot read, and which may even be written in a foreign language.[29]

Unlike pariah minorities, however, peasants and the urban poor possess an alternative set of sanctions based on their sheer numbers. As Nehru said, 'Nobody, not even the greatest autocrat or tyrant, can force vast numbers of people to do this or that.' Such a statement may not be universally true — for example, forcing vast numbers of people to do this or that was precisely what Stalin achieved in the decisive period of Soviet industrialization, and to a rather lesser extent what Hitler achieved during the supremacy of the Nazi party in Europe. But such examples reinforce rather than weaken the truth of Nehru's dictum as applied to the poor countries. In the case of Hitler it was only the possession of a thoroughly modern and highly efficient military organization based on a modern industrial economy that made even a tem-porary rule of sheer power possible. In the Soviet case, as has been cogently shown by Nove, the Russian economy though devastated by the war had pre-viously reached a high level of industrial development, and there was a tradition of a highly centralized bureaucracy with adequate resources of educated manpower.[30] Stalin's writ, in short, ran throughout the Soviet Union in a way that is simply not true of even the most strong-willed ruler of a poor country today; and this of course is the whole basis of the 'soft state'. The sheer numbers of peasant populations and the urban poor in such countries often afford them some power to carry on doing more or less as they like, to overawe tax inspectors, agricultural department and health officials, and even sometimes the police, and when really roused to assert themselves through urban riots and peasant revolts. And then, as stated above, the police and army may retaliate with extreme brutality. Coercion is an alternative to corruption in a 'soft state' in which the administration of the law lacks pre-dictability, and impartiality; and this reinforces very strongly the need which people feel for a quasi-feudal relation with a powerful person who can protect them, which has been seen is one of the strongest roots of corrup-tion.

However, although there are many factors predisposing poor countries to corruption, it should not be thought of as an inevitable result either of their poverty or of other factors in their general situation. As has been noted in chapter 4, communist political regimes in particular have been conspicuously successful in preventing it. Scott cites Vietnam as an almost perfect 'experimental case', with a single historical and cultural tradition but two vastly different political systems. Under the Lao Dong (Communist) party, he says, North Vietnam has managed to minimize corruption, while even before massive foreign intervention it was widespread in South Vietnam. Presumably, this results in large part from the tight discipline and ideological rigour of a communist party, its capacity for self-scrutiny, and its energy in pervading and scrutinizing in turn all important aspects of the life of society. Perhaps it is again a fair comment to suggest that the alternative to corruption is coercion, since the scrutiny of the party over activities in other institutions in a communist state is backed by strongly coercive sanctions. In part also it must be the effect of virtually abolishing the private sector, and with it both the need and the resources for entrepreneurs, pariah or otherwise, to secure their position through tributary relations with people in power.

But some non-communist regimes too have had their successes in minimizing corruption. Scott contrasts in this respect Tunisia and Singapore on the one hand with Indonesia and Ghana on the other. In all four countries there were nationalist movements whose triumph opened the way for administrative changes. In Tunisia and Singapore, vigorous parties succeeded in changing popular attitudes toward the civil service and insisting on proper standards of performance. In Ghana and Indonesia, the dominant party was 'more a personal following than an institution', and rent by rivalries among the leaders and their cliques. Once the revolutionary fervour subsided, corruption 'flourished with renewed vigour in an unrestrained or feudalized bureaucracy'.[31]

Liability to military rule

Poor countries have proved to be particularly vulnerable to the take-over of the state power by the army (including in that term, where applicable, the navy and air force). Hardly a week goes by without our hearing of yet another army *coup* in some state of Asia, Africa, or Latin America. The movement of army vehicles into the capital or its outskirts; the seizure of the radio station; the arrest, flight, or murder of the former Prime Minister, President or other leading politicians; the general's dawn broadcast commanding the populace to remain calm — all this has become a matter of dreary routine. Then the amplified statement of the reasons why, in the judgment of senior army officers, the *coup* was necessary. The selfish intrigues of small-minded politicians, intolerable against the background of the country's needs, its

268

economic crisis, its humiliation in the eyes of the world. Political inter-ference in the administration of the country and particularly of the armed forces. Corruption (always corruption). The appointment of a military cabinet together with a few civilian leaders worthy of the public's trust. The an-nouncement of a regime of sensible administration at the hands of ex-perienced administrators capable of putting country before party and before self. The pledge to restore normal democratic political processes as soon as conditions allow — a constituent assembly dangled as a future possibility — but meanwhile the disbandment of the now totally discredited former ruling party, control of the press, control of political meetings, a curfew, the tem-porary suspension of the legislature. We have heard it many times.

The definitive study of the military in politics is that of Professor S. E. Finer,[32] and though it was published as long ago as 1962 the main lines of his analysis have been confirmed on a number of occasions since. 'The armed forces have three massive political advantages over civilian organiz-ations: a marked superiority in organization, a highly emotionalized symbolic status, and a monopoly of arms. They form a prestigious corporation or Order, enjoying overwhelming superiority in the means of applying force. The wonder, therefore, is not why this rebels against its civilian masters, but why it ever obeys them.'

In simple, small-scale, undifferentiated societies of the sort studied by social anthropologists the question of army rule does not arise. Men may bear arms in self-defence, in defence of flocks and herds against predators (whether human or non-human), and in defence of their communities, their women and children. There may even be a rudimentary form of military organization with publicly designated 'captains' or war leaders to direct operations in emergency or in raids. But the army as a separate, quasi-autonomous institution does not exist in such a society any more than banks, trade unions, or political parties exist as such.

At the other end of the scale of functional differentiation, Finer has well shown the extreme difficulty that one highly specialized and quasi-autono-mous institution (the army) encounters when it tries to take over or master other highly specialized, quasi-autonomous institutions (the banks, etc.) in a complex industrial society. The military men simply do not have the knowledge. Those who do can 'blind them with science' and use their superior expertise if they are so minded in endless tactics of delay, sub-version, passive non-cooperation, and the like. The military men can in turn no doubt acquire the necessary knowledge to avoid being continually out-witted, but only at the cost of 'civilianizing' themselves — by becoming so immersed in the life of these other complex organizations that they end up identifying themselves with the institutional outlook of the latter, submitting in the end to the 'logic of organizations' as if they were civilians.

It is in societies at the middle levels of functional differentiation of in-

269

stitutions (or in Finer's terms of 'political culture') that there is the greatest liability to military rule. Here the society is not so complex as to be beyond the capacity of the army to administer effectively, while at the same time people's loyalties are not so strongly attached to civilian institutions at the level of the national state. Associations like industrial enterprises, trade unions, churches, the press, and political parties are weak, while the state itself may be an innovation of the 'modern sector' commanding little or no emotional loyalty. It is not difficult to see how in such circumstances an army take-over may be seen by many of the people as a liberation from the corrupt rule of crooked politicians. The army may not have much of a claim to legitimacy, but if the legitimacy of civilian political institutions is at an even lower ebb there may be little or no popular resistance.

In many poor countries, the army is by far the most highly organized institution in the whole life of the nation. It is in the very nature of an army that it has a tightly disciplined chain of command in which disobedience and failure to perform one's duty are instantly checked and severely punished. In a purely technical sense, too, the army's signals branch with its network of radio and telephone links may be the most efficient system of communications in a poor country, surpassing the public postal and tele-communications organization both in its efficiency and its capacity to reach outposts far from the main centres. But purely technical superiority is not enough; the army's sense of martial purpose, its corporate spirit of loyalty also contribute to its potential. That loyalty may be given to a cause, as with Cromwell's Ironsides or Trotsky's Red Army; but much more commonly it is given to a nation, and 'the inculcation of an extreme nationalism, often of the most rabid or vulgar sort' is well-nigh universal in the training of armies.

The contributions of later writers have filled out the detail of Finer's analysis but not seriously called it in question. Janowitz has called attention to the tendency in poor countries for the army to consist mainly of ground forces and especially of the infantry, the type of forces most useful for involvement in domestic politics. Such armies are, he says, 'in essence a form of super-police'.[33] On the other hand, armies generally dislike being involved in day-by-day police work. Such an involvement is seen as likely to weaken the army's capacity to intervene successfully and with shock tactics in a moment of crisis; moreover, the army may try to avoid the stigma of having 'pushed people around' in too frequent contact with the general public. As Finer pointed out, too, for an army 'the barracks becomes the world'. Many armies are not very good at intelligence work in a civilian political setting, and for keeping their finger on the pulse of everyday affairs and generally being sensitive to the public mood they generally need to cooperate closely with the police force. Some of the most successful *coups*, indeed, have been those in which there has been the closest cooperation between army and police; an example is the collaboration of Brigadier Kotoka and Major Afrifa with the

270

Police Commissioner J. W. K. Harlley in planning Nkrumah's overthrow in Ghana in 1966.[34]

Janowitz has analysed the special characteristics of military ideology which are important in poor countries. These include the 'puritanical' element in the military outlook and its condemnation of corruption and decadence. While military men are not alone in condemning corruption, it may well be that they do so with particular vehemence and sincerity. To a man to whom the possibility of having to give his life for his country is an ever-present consideration, the thought of politicians and bureaucrats enriching themselves at their country's expense is no doubt especially obscene. The ideology of service and dedication, together with the habits of military discipline, lead military men also to insist strongly on regularity and application in the habits of civilians over whom they assume command. Thus Gutteridge reports,

Like other military administrations, the regional governments in Nigeria displayed what some would regard as puritanical tendencies, reminiscent of 'the rule of the Major-Generals' in England. The governor of the Mid-West region, Lt.-Col. David Ejoor, for instance, made an issue of the unpunctuality of civil servants by closing the doors of ministries at the opening hour of 8.0 a.m. and shaming the latecomers, of whatever rank, by making them queue outside and haranguing them in public. The overt intention to secure efficiency and to probe corruption was not unpopular with the masses and conformed to the image of the simple, dedicated military officer whose patriotism was unquestioned.[35]

Further, Janowitz points out that though many military men are conservative in their general views, they do not necessarily reject public enterprise as a viable way of organizing economic life. Their 'service before self' mentality may lead them to think that the public good is a worthier motive than private gain; indeed, even in the United States Janowitz found senior army officers to be rather contemptuous of the 'materialist' values of civilian America.[36] In some poor countries the officer corps include substantial numbers of socialists; Janowitz cites the adherence of the group of officers who seized power in Syria in 1962 to a 'constructive and just socialism', while 'the Indonesian air force, as a young and highly technologically oriented military formation, is strongly leftist'.

Finally, perhaps the most pervasive theme is the 'anti-politics' outlook of the military, a hostility to politicians and political parties. 'It is', says Janowitz, 'the politics of wanting to be above politics.'[37] So the military align themselves with the civilian administrators in the kind of mutual accusations which Riggs has called the 'interference complex', referred to above.

For example, it was a particularly sore point with the soldiers in Ghana that Nkrumah tried repeatedly and consistently to 'politicize' the army, both in the sense of involving the Ghanaian army in political struggles in Africa, and in the sense of infiltrating it with political spies. Thus Gutteridge

271

relates that, during the Congo troubles of 1960, the President's special relation with Patrice Lumumba and the activities of the two Ghanaian political representatives in Léopoldville led first to confusion of the lines of command with the U.N. contingent, and then to outright alarm that spread throughout the army. Earlier attempts to install political agents or commissars in army units had involved the fear that the normal military hierarchy would be disrupted and that a mess corporal, for example, might report on a commanding officer.

Such fears were now intensified by other factors: the formation of the President's Own Guard Regiment with help from communist countries at a time when the regular army's equipment was becoming run down and its interests neglected, tentative steps to militarize the Workers' Brigade which seemed to pose another threat to the army's professional existence, and fears that Nkrumah would order the army to take independent action against Rhodesia without proper equipment or adequate preparation. By 1963–4 there was a 'now or never' feeling about the situation, a fear that 'the only institution capable of resisting Nkrumah by force would before long lose its effectiveness because both of this kind of penetration and of the assembly of forces capable of countering it'.[38]

Many a military regime has had deep misgivings about the fateful step of displacing the civilian constitution, has done so only when it seemed there was really no choice, and has accordingly taken power with the sincerest possible intentions of relinquishing it again as soon as possible. But when is 'possible'? Regimes established with popular support, or at least compliance, have held onto power long after that support has ebbed away. Promises to hold constituent assemblies have been honoured, only for the assemblies to break up in inconclusive bickering between rival politicians. But there are three general factors which impede the handing over of power by a military regime.

First, anyone exercising power makes enemies. After a few months or years in power, the colonels may come to fear the revenge of those they have offended if the latter were allowed to succeed them. And there is no way to ensure that will not happen, short of holding onto power themselves.

Secondly, military *coups* are like bad habits. The first time the fateful deed is done it is to the accompaniment of inner conflicts, doubts, and misgivings. The second time it seems easier. A discontented group among the officer corps in a country which already has a military regime may see no reason why its own rule should be any less legitimate or acceptable than that of the group in power. If they could do it, so can we. Ghana is again a case in point; just over a year after Kotoka and Afrifa so easily marched on Accra a counter-*coup* came near to toppling their regime, and did cause the death of General Kotoka. According to Gutteridge, a promotion block was probably a potent cause of dissatisfaction. The National Liberation Council seemed inclined to

272

check unnecessary expenditure on defence, and some young officers drew the conclusion that their career prospects would be static. Their leader further accused the N.L.C. of 'feathering their nests' like the former politicians,[39] and his was not the first complaint or the last that a military regime which had taken power with the best of intentions to clean up corruption had itself succumbed to it. On this Scott's judgment is relevant; despite the personal incorruptibility of some army rulers like Ne Win, Nasser, and Ayub Khan, corruption at lower levels during their administration once more became rife.[40] Military regimes offer no long-term prospects for incorruptible government.

Thirdly, even in those cases in which the army has genuinely relinquished power to a civilian regime, it has only been to see the rise of a group unacceptable to them on one ground or another. Or even if the civilian government consists of men originally trusted by the army, the military men may come to regard them as having mishandled the affairs of state and deposed them. Once again, Ghana affords a case in point; Dr Busia, after holding office under the army regime, and then winning the elections with which it bowed itself out, was later ousted by another army *coup* executed, like that against President Nkrumah, during his temporary absence in a period of economic crisis. It seems as though the exercise of such power is habit-forming; 'we put them there, we can take them down again' may come to epitomize the army's view. If this occurs, then the army's withdrawal from politics may be only partial. They may disengage themselves from day-by-day decisions, and cast themselves instead in the role of umpire, arbiter, and guardians in some ultimate sense of 'the best interests of the country'. Turkey is no doubt a case in point, while it may well be that it was in that spirit that the army in Chile overthrew the government of Dr Allende in the *coup* and bloodbath of September 1973.

13 The world of aid

The transfer of resources from rich countries to poor takes place in a variety of ways, differing according to the donor country or agency, the uses to which the resources are to be put, and the terms of the transfer. Not all such transfers can be classed as aid, and there are problems of definition and still more of measurement. Aid has to be seen as part of the larger picture of world economic relations along with trade and migration movements as well as capital transfers. It is, however, a major activity in the modern world and one to which sizable resources are devoted. It has accordingly become something of a world of its own, with its own specialist practitioners, technical terms, and issues and controversies. This 'world of aid' is inspired by a conventional wisdom which favours the transfer of resources from rich countries to poor, and I have taken the Pearson report as representative of that conviction, assailed though it is by radical critics both from the 'right' and from the 'left'.

The facts of aid

Organization

Since the second world war the governments of all the rich industrial countries have become involved in aiding the development of poor countries. Some have done so in continuity with a colonial past, such as France and Britain. American involvement sprang in part from the quick success of the 'Marshall plan' in restoring the war-shattered economies of Europe, a success which it was hoped might be followed with the poor countries, and in part from gifts of food for famine relief which left the U.S. government in control of 'counterpart funds' in the recipient countries, as explained below. For a mixture of motives other countries have joined in, including the distinctive contribution of the Soviet Union and eastern European countries.

By 1960, then, the governments of all the industrial countries had come to regard aid as a natural and proper activity. At the United Nations, the 1960s were designated the 'Development Decade', and under the terms of resolution 1522 of the General Assembly, which was passed in December 1960, the economically advanced nations undertook to try to provide one per cent of their national incomes as aid to the developing countries.* The term 'National income' was not precisely defined in this resolution, and an expert committee later recommended that it should be interpreted to mean G.N.P. — an interpretation which was generous to the recipient countries.[1] At about the same time, too, the Organization for Economic Cooperation and Development (O.E.C.D.) set up a Development Assistance Committee (D.A.C.) of the representatives of sixteen aid-donor countries.†

Other international agencies involved in aid include some which were set up at the end of the second world war as part of the post-war settlement but outside the United Nations — the International Monetary Fund (I.M.F.) and the International Bank for Reconstruction and Development (commonly known as the World Bank), and later the International Development Association (I.D.A.), a subsidiary of the World Bank concentrating on concessional finance to poor countries. The World Bank functions as a bank in the ordinary sense of the word in capitalist countries, raising loans in the private sector especially on Wall Street as well as from member governments. It lends mainly to governments for investment in public-sector development like railways and electricity generation, and also to a limited extent in the private sector including agriculture. One of its most important activities in the field of development has been its practice of sending missions of experts to conduct a thorough review of the economies and development needs of poor countries. The reports of these visiting missions have been influential, both in the advice they offer to the governments of poor countries, and in the guidance they give to those of donor countries.

The increasing commitment to aid and the proliferation of agencies concerned with aid have led the governments of some donor countries to set up special agencies or ministries, like the American Agency for International Development (A.I.D.), the British Overseas Development Ministry (O.D.M.), and the Ministry for Economic Co-operation (B.M.Z.) in West Germany.

The A.I.D. in the United States is an autonomous agency within the State Department, responsible under various statutes for the direction and coordination of all aid activities, and jointly responsible with the Department of Agriculture for administering gifts of American food under Public Law 480 of 1954. In countries receiving a large amount of American aid, the A.I.D. maintains sizable missions which may be housed separately from the U.S. Embassy and not only administer American aid but also take an active interest in general economic development and keep in close touch with the

---

* I use that term in this chapter since it is the one conventionally used in the context of this kind of discussion.
† They consisted of the twenty rich countries listed in chapter 4, table 4.1, excluding Iceland, Finland, Luxemburg, New Zealand, and Israel, and with the addition of Portugal.

government of the recipient country, especially senior officials in the departments concerned with development.

In Britain, where as has been stated aid activities arose in continuity with the colonial past, especially with the Colonial Development and Welfare scheme, changes became necessary as many of the countries which had received 'aid' under that scheme ceased to be colonies and so became *prima facie* ineligible for assistance from that source. By the early 1960s the administration of development had become divided between a number of government departments. Under the act of 1961, the Department of Technical Co-Operation was set up in an effort to bring about greater coordination, and in October 1964 aid administration was further strengthened by the creation of the Overseas Development Ministry. This was one of the first actions of the Labour Party on assuming office, and may have reflected a personal interest by the new Prime Minister, Mr Harold Wilson, who had some years previously published a book on the general question of world development.[2] Initially, the Minister was given cabinet rank, and the expectation was that aid to poor countries should thus be given its due weight among the competing claims of different government departments and activities for a share of public resources; later, however, cabinet status was abandoned.[3]

Mention must also be made of the private voluntary organizations concerned in aid. In Britain, for example, the Save the Children Fund was established as long ago as 1919, and the Oxford Committee for Famine Relief (OXFAM) in 1942. Some of these voluntary agencies began in response to an emergency situation, like OXFAM which during the 1940s appealed for blankets and worn clothing to send to the victims of war and natural disasters; but many have taken to heart the oft-quoted saying that 'if you give a man fish you feed him for a day, if you teach him to fish you feed him for life', and become involved in projects for rural improvement and other forms of development effective in the longer term. OXFAM, for instance, reported that only about one-eighth of its aid in 1970 was devoted to relief, seven-eights to development, and the numerous projects it supported included a water development scheme in Brazil, artificial insemination of cattle in Tanzania, grain storage in India, and the rehabilitation of lepers in India.[4]

Some of the voluntary agencies are church-based, like Christian Aid and the Catholic Fund for Overseas Development; others like OXFAM are non-denominational; yet others, like the Freedom from Hunger Campaign, are international, operating through national committees. In Britain the six major voluntary agencies sent some £7.5 million in aid to poor countries in 1968–9, while an estimate for the American voluntary agencies was $491 million in 1968. While these sums are far from negligible, they make up, of course, only a small fraction of the donor countries' total aid expenditure. 'In 1967, for example, the reductions in British government aid more than offset all the funds collected by the private organizations in that year at great cost in time and effort.' The significance of the voluntary agencies lies accordingly in part in their educational and publicity activities in the donor countries. In Britain these activities are coordinated by a Voluntary Committee on Overseas Aid and Development (V.C.O.A.D.) and furthered through groups with names like Action for World Development (A.W.D.). As an example of such activities, the churches' Action for World Development organized a national campaign in December 1969 and collected over a million signatures in support of an increased British effort in aid, trade policies, and related matters.[5]

Quantity

According to recent estimates by United Nations bodies, the net transfer of resources from developed to developing countries rose from about $9,000 million in 1961 to about $14,000 million in 1969.

But though the transfer of resources grew in money terms during the 1960s, it did not grow as a proportion of the G.N.P.s of the major industrial countries, which were increasing both as a result of industrial growth and of inflation during that period. Taking the sixteen capitalist countries of the D.A.C. group, who between them provide most of the world's aid, they were nearer to the United Nations' one-per-cent target in 1961 than they were in 1969. In 1961 they contributed together 0.77 per cent of their aggregate G.N.P.; in 1969, 0.70 per cent. The United States, which in absolute terms is by far the biggest donor country, contributed 0.72 per cent of its G.N.P. at the beginning of the development decade, 0.59 per cent at the end. Proportionately to their resources, the biggest contributors throughout were France, where the proportion fell from 1.81 per cent to 1.13 per cent; Portugal, where it fell from 1.56 per cent to 1.28 per cent; and Switzerland, 1.61 per cent to 0.82 per cent. The high figure for France is largely accounted for by the special needs for reconstruction in Algeria after the civil war, while that for Portugal reflects the heavy involvement of resources, including military resources, by a comparatively poor European country in maintaining an African empire; to that extent they are accordingly special cases. In the United Kingdom the proportion fell from 0.90 per cent in 1961 to 0.78 per cent in 1969.

Other trends during the development decade included the increasing importance of private-sector capital transfers, and correspondingly the decreasing importance of official aid. (Whether private investment in poor countries merits the term aid at all is a controversial question which I discuss below.) Within the category of official aid, loans increased more than grants; there was something like a three-fold increase in lending, in fact. Technical assistance and most food aid were on a grant basis, but apart from them the amounts transferred as grants for purposes such as general budget support declined sharply. At the same time, as the decade progressed the repayment

277

of earlier loans, with interest where appropriate, became more important. The poorer nations have between them, it is estimated, international debts amounting to over $50 billion, and almost all of them are in difficulties over interest and repayments.[6]

Estimates of the transfer of resources from what the U.N. delicately call the 'centrally planned economies' differ widely. According to D.A.C. estimates, they fluctuated between $300 and $400 million a year during the 1960s and made up only about one-thirtieth or one-fortieth of all transfers to developing countries. The United Nations put the value much higher, rising from about $800 million in 1962 to $1,400–$1,500 million in 1968. At such a level they would have contributed about one-tenth of all transfers to developing countries. They were made up about equally of two forms of aid – commitments to specific projects, like the Aswan high dam in Egypt, and trade surpluses in which the donor countries in effect give unrequited exports to the recipient countries. The nature of these transactions and the difficulty of evaluating them in money terms reflect the different principles upon which the economies of communist countries are managed, and their tendency to think in 'real' terms first and attribute money values later. Attempts to relate the aid activities of communist countries to their G.N.P. are vitiated accordingly by the fact that neither numerator nor denominator can be expressed very meaningfully in money terms at all. Such estimates as have been made, however, suggest that aid transfers amount to around 0.2 per cent of the G.N.P. of the Soviet Union, up to 0.4 or 0.5 per cent in some countries such as Hungary, Bulgaria, and Czechoslovakia, and below 0.1 per cent in Poland.[7]

Even though such figures fall short of the United Nations' one-per-cent target, they represent a considerable flow of resources to the poor countries. Nevertheless, the poor countries do not depend wholly or even mainly upon aid for their development. On the contrary, the Pearson commission stated that: 'Despite a common impression that poor countries are too poor to save anything, they have in fact mobilised the bulk of their investment capital. *In the 1960s, domestic savings financed 85 per cent of total investment.*'[8] The proportion of course differed widely in different countries, and some were more dependent than the average upon foreign aid while others were virtually independent of it. Such a high figure, viewed as an argument for or against aid, cuts both ways. On the one hand it dispels any suggestion that the poor countries are doing nothing – making no efforts or sacrifices –for their own development but just accepting it in an easy cheap way from the rich donor countries. On the other hand, however, it could be argued that it would take them very little more effort and sacrifice to raise all their own development capital, and cease to be dependent upon the rich countries altogether. And a third argument would be that if the rich countries were substantially to increase their aid contribution so that it provided much more than 15 per cent of the poor countries' investment, the economic development of the latter would be accelerated and the inequality between nations reduced more rapidly than would otherwise be the case.

The arguments for aid – and against

As has already been suggested, it is for a mixture of motives that the governments of rich industrial countries have adopted the practice of regularly parting with appreciable resources and handing them over to poor countries. In this respect, aid is in no different case from many other human activities; mixed motives, indeed, are probably commoner than pure motives for human behaviour generally, and it seems unnecessary to engage in sterile debates as to whether the motives of donor governments are 'selfish' or 'unselfish'. They may in fact be both; selfish and unselfish motives may reinforce rather than contradict one another, and point in the same direction to the same kind of action.

The moral case is clear, simple, and frequently expressed. The late Lester Pearson put it simply and eloquently: 'there is a moral obligation . . . for the strong to help the weak, for those who have to share with those who have not'.[9] Others have said that 'there is something absurd about a technology which can put a man on the moon, but seems likely to fail to feed adequately many millions of men left behind on earth'.[10] Aid has been viewed as the logical extension to the world as a whole of the values embodied in the 'welfare state' within rich countries.[11] For to quote Pearson again, it is questionable if the moral foundations of those societies could remain firm and steady if, having worked to eliminate poverty and backwardness at home, they ignored them abroad and washed their hands of the plight of others.[12]

At the other extreme from such lofty moral sentiments come motives of economic and political self-interest. Aid may be viewed as export promotion, and when it is both 'tied' (as I explain below) and financed by loan it can indeed amount to little more than the grant of export credit on favourable terms. Further, the indirect effects of aid with a well-labelled import content, like a 'loss leader', may be to create a favourable image of the donor country and its industrial enterprises and so create an atmosphere in which further and more purely commercial sales may be made. Aid may thus be seen as an aspect of the competition among industrial countries for the export markets of poor countries. But as the Overseas Development Institute (O.D.I.) point out, 'if all donors compete in this way, any advantages are likely to be only temporary and the competition self-cancelling in the long run. Clearly the donors cannot benefit as a group.'

Similarly, though aid is sometimes seen in terms of retaining export markets and raw material sources for capitalist countries against commercial competition from communist countries, this argument too has little weight.

279

The poor countries in fact do very little trade with the communist world, and that share could be expanded a good deal without significantly impinging on the interests of the capitalist countries. As for access to raw materials, it seems likely, as pointed out in chapter 4, that in most cases the industrial countries could more easily find substitutes for the raw materials produced by poor countries than the poor countries could find other markets for their primary products.

A somewhat wider argument is that the economic development of the poor countries will increase their purchasing power, a proportion of which will be spent in almost every industrial country. Each donor country accordingly has an interest in furthering the general economic development of poor countries. There are limits to this argument, however; for as the O.D.I. have pointed out, in so far as the industrial countries are concerned solely with their own prosperity they will compare the returns to aid with those to internal investment in research, education, etc., and with investment in other rich countries whose propensity to import may be far greater than that of the poor countries.[13]

Arguments of political self-interest seem even weaker than those of economic self-interest. If there were ever any ideas on the part of donor governments that their aid would serve to bring about friendly, compliant relations or direct political advantages in recipient countries, then those governments must have been sadly disillusioned. Recipients of American aid have denounced American imperialism, while recipients of Soviet aid have continued to keep native communists locked up. It even seems on occasions as though the government of a country which receives aid feels thereby under a greater need to demonstrate its independence, to show that the donor government must not think that it has the recipient government in its pocket.

In between the motives of disinterested moral purpose and those of direct political and economic self-interest, there is a class of arguments for aid as tending to further the long-term general interests of all countries, including all donor countries, by promoting a better world — one less riven by acute conflicts, less shameful, a source of less anxiety than its present state. To quote Pearson again, 'There is also the appeal of enlightened and constructive self-interest . . . Who can now ask where his country will be in a few decades without asking where the world will be? If we wish that world to be secure and prosperous, we must show a common concern for the common problems of all peoples.'[14]

Such, then, is the conventional wisdom, the basic assumption that is made in the world of aid that its purpose is to promote the economic development and general welfare of the people of the poor countries.[15] Practitioners in this world readily admit that things do not always work out that way, and that aid in practice may fall short of the ideal. In other words, there may be a gap between the intentions of donor governments and the actual effect of aid in raising the standard of living in recipient countries. Such a gap is thought of in terms of failure or ineffectiveness, and it is again conceded that there may well be much to learn about how to make aid more effective. Aid practitioners see their task as learning from experience how to do better next time with the resources their governments make available, though they tend also to be forced to the conclusion that it is virtually impossible to increase the effectiveness of aid without increasing its volume.

Clearly it is hard for such a world to accommodate radical critics who dispute the assumption on which its whole existence is based, and maintain that aid may be actually harmful to poor countries — not just as a matter of failure or ineffectiveness, but systematically so. From widely different points of view that argument has, however, been advanced by P. T. Bauer and Teresa Hayter.

For Bauer, the basic argument for aid fails because he sees nothing wrong in inequality, either between persons or countries; 'a differentiated social structure may be both a reflection and an instrument of economic development'. The analogy with redistributive taxation within a country fails alike accordingly. Moreover, since aid benefits those in poor countries who are already better off — town-dwellers, politicians, civil servants, academics, and some businessmen — and is paid for out of taxes paid in part by the poor, it is 'a process by which poor people in rich countries help rich people in poor countries'. It is not indispensable for development; the rich countries themselves were all underdeveloped (as he puts it) two centuries ago, and moreover 'many underdeveloped countries have advanced very rapidly over the last half century or so without foreign aid'. Some aid projects have absorbed domestic inputs greater than the net output, and the recipient country would have been better off without them. Reliance on food aid has reinforced the tendency of governments to invest in prestige industrial projects and neglect agriculture. And aid in general is a 'dole', tending to erode or sap attitudes and beliefs conducive to self-reliance, thrift, effort, and enterprise.[16]

Hayter herself worked for some years in the world of aid, but her studies in Latin America led her to conclude that the conventional wisdom of aid constitutes 'a complicated edifice of deception' and that aid itself

can be explained only in terms of an attempt to preserve the capitalist system in the Third World. Aid is not a particularly effective instrument for achieving this; hence its current decline. But, in so far as it is effective, its contribution to the well-being of the people of the Third World is negative, since it is not in their interest that exploitation should continue.

But though she writes from an ideological position diametrically opposed to that of Bauer, there are distinct similarities in her criticisms of the effects of aid.

It may ... help to sustain, within Third World countries, a class which is dependent on the continued existence of aid ... It can be used directly as a bribe to secure the adoption of measures favourable to the providers of aid and unfavourable to its

281

recipients; it can be used, deliberately or otherwise, for projects which impoverish the mass of the population; and it usually adds to the burden of debt carried by the countries receiving it, and hence to their dependence. In one sense, aid is merely a form of subsidy for international companies paid for by the tax-payers of the imperialist countries ...

In the long term it is clearly necessary that underdeveloped countries should reduce their dependence on the industrialized countries. In this sense it could be said that the loss of 'aid' was an advantage.[17]

Terms, definitions, and issues in aid

Aid itself is not easy to define. The total net flow of resources from rich countries to poor is by no means all aid, and following D.A.C. practice the Pearson commission distinguish between

1. *Official development assistance*, consisting of funds made available by governments on concessional terms primarily to promote economic development and the welfare of developing countries. It is this category which we and the DAC describe as 'aid'.
2. *Other official flows*, comprising official export credits, some of which may have a concessional element, and net purchases by governments of bonds, loans, and participation of multilateral agencies.
3. *Private flows*, including direct investment, portfolio investments, and private export credits with maturities of longer than one year.[18]

According to this definition, then, aid is that part of the total flow of resources from rich to poor countries which is made available (a) by governments, (b) on concessional terms, and (c) primarily to promote economic development and welfare. Thus military expenditure, for example, represents one form of official flow of resources from a rich to a poor country which the government of the rich country might be inclined to class as 'aid', but which on the D.A.C.—Pearson definition should not be so counted since it is not intended 'primarily to promote economic development and welfare'. This definition, then, raises issues with which I deal below.

Official versus private

In excluding private investment from the definition of aid, neither the Pearson commission nor other like-minded authorities intended to imply that it is harmful or undesirable. On the contrary, it is a source of capital, and some part at least of the income which it generates stays in the 'host country' in the form of wages and salaries, purchases of local materials, and taxes. And it may have 'spread effects' in introducing new technology, training local people, and inducing the growth of local industries supplying the foreign-owned firm or consuming its products. At the same time there are dangers and drawbacks. It can be 'politically sensitive', giving rise to fears of 'neo-colonialism'. Protective tariffs imposed by the host government on

282

the 'infant industries' argument may merely increase the profits which a foreign company remits abroad, a tendency calling for appropriate fiscal measures to encourage local reinvestment. And there is an in-built tendency for foreign companies' engineers to prefer the capital-intensive methods with which they are familiar to others which might be more appropriate in a poor country. But this only means that foreign investment in some circumstances may be less beneficial that it could be ideally, not that it is actually harmful. Indeed, 'dollar for dollar, it may be more effective than official aid', because it is closely linked to management and technology, and because those who risk their own money may be expected to ensure its efficient use.

But Pearson rejected the view expressed by 'influential voices' in industrial countries, that private investment could and should replace official aid flows. In the first place, private-capital flows are 'simply not available' for many of the forms of public investment which are the prime need of developing countries — schools, roads, hospitals, irrigation schemes, etc. Secondly, 'the flow of private capital tends to be highly concentrated in countries with rich mineral resources and fairly high incomes. Many of the countries of Africa and Asia receive almost no private capital.' It is, in other words, the Venezuelas of this world rather than the Indias that tend to attract private investment. Thirdly, 'It is fundamental to our strategy that the need for aid should eventually subside.' Aid is thought of as a temporary, once-for-all operation. Though the time-scale is a long one, extending some three decades roughly to the end of the twentieth century, by that time it is envisaged that the pump should be primed and working, the 'take-off' should have been made, the poor countries should really and literally be the developing countries. 'Direct investment and access to capital markets would then increasingly meet the demand for development finance.' It is the view of aid as a special once-for-all effort on the part of the rich countries to stimulate the self-sustaining development of the poor countries that makes aid in the strict sense a matter for governmental rather than private action.[19]

In the same way and for the same reason, the D.A.C.–Pearson definition would exclude from aid those loans which are made by the governments of rich countries on commercial terms and for commercial purposes, like export credits. The Pearson commission re-emphasized the distinction when in making recommendations they endorsed the U.N.'s one-per-cent target, and added that 0.7 per cent should be the target for aid in the strict sense: 'We therefore recommend that each aid-giver increase commitments of official development assistance to the level necessary for net disbursements to reach 0.70 per cent of its gross national product by 1975 or shortly thereafter, but in no case later than 1980.'[20]

It remains to add that this recommendation has not been generally implemented by the donor countries. In 1971, official aid flows from the sixteen richest countries amounted to 0.35 per cent of their combined G.N.P., just half the Pearson figure, and less·than the private commercial investment flows from those countries. In particular, though British official aid at 0.41 per cent of G.N.P. was a little above the average, Britain remained one of the few donor states which had not adopted the 0.7 per cent target at the time of U.N.C.T.A.D. III in 1972.[21]

Grants versus loans

If, as already suggested, loans are not to be counted as aid even when made by governments if they are on commercial terms and for commercial purposes, the implication is that aid properly so called should consist either of outright grants or of loans on 'soft' or concessional terms.

Some aid takes the form of outright gifts of money from one government to another. This had occurred, for example, in the direct budgetary assistance that was given by the British treasury to the former 'High Commission' territories in southern Africa. With some such exceptions, however, most of the aid that is now given in the form of grants falls into two categories — technical assistance, and food aid mainly from the United States; I deal with these forms of aid in more detail in the next two sections. As has been noted, the tendency during the 1960s was for loans to grow in importance compared with grants.

Two main arguments are advanced for loans. First, they predispose the recipient government to a proper economy in the use of aid, giving them an incentive to ensure that projects are viable, that the money is well spent, and that the management is efficient. Secondly, many donor countries from time to time have balance-of-payments troubles, and the repayment of loans does something to offset the foreign-exchange costs of aid. Indeed, aid can come to be seen almost as a rotating fund, with the repayments of old loans coming in to finance further aid contributions, through there is always a flow of fresh funds as well.

On the other hand, however, the repayment of aid loans becomes a burden upon the recipient country's balance of payments. Many, if not most, poor countries are said now to be in difficulties over this, and in some the difficulties are acute.

If loans are to count as aid at all according to the Pearson criteria then they must be on 'soft' terms. In practice concessions may be made in three ways — a low or even zero rate of interest; a long repayment period; and a period of several years' grace before repayments (or interest, if charged) have to begin. The D.A.C. recommendation has been that most transfers should be at 3 per cent or less. According to the United Nations world economic survey for 1969–70,

The most generous interest rate policy in recent years has been pursued by Australia (whose transfers are all gifts), Denmark (which has charged a zero rate since 1966) and the United Kingdom (whose average rate has been about 1 per cent since

284

1966) ... There was a definite, if slight, hardening of the average rates on loans from Belgium, the United States and France (between 3 and 4 per cent) and Italy (between 4 and 5 per cent), and, as these are among the largest lenders, the result was an increase in the average developed market economy rate from 3.1 per cent on loan commitments made in 1964 to 3.8 per cent on those made in 1967.[22]

Among international agencies, the World Bank tends to lend on terms not very different from the private market, with maturities of from fifteen to twenty-five years and interest rates like 6.5 per cent. However, part of the point of setting up the International Development Authority as a subsidiary of the bank was to enable it to specialize in loans on the softest of terms to the poorest countries. I.D.A. loans are typically repayable over fifty years and carry a 'service charge' of 0.75 per cent.[23]

Technical assistance

Technical assistance takes two main forms. Expert advisers, professionals, technicians, teachers, and other highly qualified people are sent from rich countries to work for a while in poor countries, wholly or partly at the expense of donor governments (usually their own); and people of poor countries are trained at the expense of the governments of rich countries, usually in the latter but sometimes at home and sometimes in third countries. As an indication of the scale on which this takes place, the Pearson report quotes a D.A.C. estimate that in 1967 there were over 112,000 technical assistance personnel from the D.A.C. countries working in poor countries, just about half of them being teachers. In the same year some 80,000 students and trainees from poor countries were benefiting from D.A.C. countries' aid programmes, about three-quarters of that number having travelled to study in the donor countries. The figures would, of course, be larger if the contribution of communist and other non-D.A.C. countries were added. Pearson reported that this was one of the most rapidly growing forms of aid; it amounted in the late sixties to a fifth of all aid, and if current trends continued there might be a quarter of a million people involved by 1975.[24]

Such figures must, however, be seen in relation to the 'brain drain' or migration of highly qualified people from poor countries to rich in search of better pay and opportunities. Against the 112,000 technical assistance personnel working in poor countries in 1967 must be set the 40,000 professional men and women who migrated from those countries in that year.[25] At that rate, technical assistance to poor countries at any one time makes up for less than three years' flow along the brain drain. It would be hard indeed to estimate whether the one makes up for the other. For example, does an English engineer going to India for two or three years, knowing no Indian language and relatively unfamiliar with the country, make up for an Indian doctor working permanently in the National Health Service in Britain? It would not be easy to strike a balance, and the value of the latter's remittances

285

home would have to be taken into any full and realistic account. A further point is that the second type of technical assistance, in which students or trainees from poor countries are brought to be trained in rich, may itself result in a 'brain drain' in so far as some of them stay.

Technical assistance usually involves the recipient country in costs as well as the donor country. A common arrangement is for the recipient country to pay technical assistance personnel at the local rate, which is usually less than they would get at home, while the donor country pays travelling expenses, 'tops up' salaries, and pays or guarantees fringe benefits such as superannuation and position on incremental salary scales. The donor country, however, may have to provide accommodation and facilities such as research assistance, secretarial help, etc. In an example quoted in the Pearson report, for every $100 spent by the United States on technical assistance to Brazil, the Brazilian government paid $137.40.[26]

The services of expatriates under technical-assistance programmes often resemble, and may in some cases actually replace, those of officials in the technical branches of the former colonial services. Of course their impermanence — they normally serve on contracts for two or three years — creates a quite different situation from the old irremovable presence of the colonial power; but the new expatriates hardly have time to learn the language and familiarize themselves with local conditions before they go home. The former colonial services afforded men a life's career, in which they were at no disadvantage in immersing themselves completely in the problems of the country they were working in — or those of poor tropical countries generally — even if that meant getting out of touch with the latest developments in rich-country technology in their fields. Today's expatriate expert is much more likely to think in rich-country terms, and feel the pace of technical progress in those countries breathing down his neck; and this is yet another factor in the adoption of capital-intensive, rich-country methods which are not always the most appropriate.

There has accordingly been some discussion in donor countries of the possibility of setting up a technical-assistance service with a continuous career structure. The Pearson commission made such a recommendation, and it seems to have been seriously considered in both France and Britain, but rejected on the ground that it would be impossible to foresee the need for staff precisely enough and far enough ahead.[27]

The intellectual preparation of technical-assistance personnel accordingly presents some problems. It would be ideal if they knew at least a year beforehand where they were going and had time to learn an appropriate language and study the basic social, political, and economic characteristics of the country. Naturally the people who have most to give will tend to be those with hard, technical skills like forestry experts, nurses, or teachers of world languages like French and English. People like sociologists, anthropologists, political scientists, and economists may have a far deeper understanding of

286

the general nature of the societies in which they are working, yet (except perhaps for the economists) lack the professional skills which would enable them to make a contribution to a poor country under a technical-assistance programme. Ideally of course the expatriate technical expert should also be a social scientist, but such doubly qualified people are indeed rare. This gives rise to something of a dilemma, for the people who are likely to understand the social situation in which they are working have little to offer, while the technical experts who have what is needed may be lacking in understanding of the social situation in which they are to give and apply their knowledge. Perhaps this may be an appropriate point at which to make a plea for the inclusion in their preliminary training of some general social-science orientations about the poor countries.

Food aid, P.L. 480, and counterpart funds

Food aid is mainly an American speciality, and has been made available by the United States government since 1954 under Public Law 480 of that year. As a great agricultural country as well as a great industrial one, the United States from time to time experiences gluts of agricultural produce with calamitous falls in prices and in farmers' incomes, and the piling up of unsold stocks. When these coincide with famines in other parts of the world, then an obviously humane and sensible action is to load the food into American ships and send it to the famine-stricken area. Under P.L. 480 such food aid has generally been sold at reduced prices to the governments of recipient countries, who have in turn released it through normal, commercial distribution channels. In this way the United States government finds itself possessed of what are called 'counterpart funds' in the local currency; and after deducting local expenses, its practice has been to apply most of the money to projects in the recipient country which are regarded as beneficial to its economic development and general welfare. In this way the recipient country benefits twice over — first by way of famine relief, and again from the use of 'counterpart funds' for development. By far the biggest beneficiary of this form of aid has been India. During the 1960s, however, its importance dwindled.

According to the Pearson commission, food aid has been of great benefit in the past by averting disastrous shortages and saving foreign exchange. Over long periods, however, it could enable the recipient country to neglect agriculture, and it might also work against the interests of other poor countries by limiting their opportunities to export food.[28]

Project aid versus programme aid, and the question of leverage

A distinction is made in the world of aid between 'project' and 'programme' aid. As its name implies, project aid is given in respect of a particular project; for example, the government of rich country A lends the government of poor country B ten million dollars on 'soft' terms to build a hydro-electric station. In such a case, before the aid agreement is signed the officials of government

A have the task of assessing whether it is viable and practicable, and will really benefit country B. After it is signed, those officials exercise a general surveillance of the project's progress, giving or withholding instalments of aid according to an agreed schedule, and inspecting the work from time to time. From the donor's point of view an advantage of this form of aid is that it can more easily be 'tied' to the donor country's products, though that practice is deprecated in some quarters, as I explain more fully below. Another advantage is that within limits a project can be seen as 'outside politics'. A hydro-electric station will produce electric power whatever the nature of the political regime in country B, and a change of regime will not necessarily affect the project's viability, unless of course the new government deliberately abandons the project, expels foreign personnel working on it, or does something equally drastic. Government A can thus insulate itself to some extent against accusations of political interference in country B's affairs. According to this way of looking at things, a project can be assessed in purely technical terms (including economic costs and benefits in the term 'technical') that are independent of politics. Furthermore, government A can answer critics in its own country, who may wonder why they go on giving aid to a country whose government votes against them in the United Nations, behaves unspeakably to its racial minorities, nationalizes foreign assets, and generally conducts itself in an objectionable way. Such critics can be told that it is not the *government* of country B which country A is concerned to help, but its *people*. And lastly, it is thought undesirable that aid should be subject to the shifting vagaries of political alignments, or become part of the rewards and deprivations which one country can promise or threaten another in day-by-day diplomacy. It is far preferable that a poor country should be able to count on aid over a long period, and be able to draw up long-term plans accordingly, without an ever-present danger that donor countries will 'cut off aid'. Dependability of aid, on this view, is itself more likely to make for stability both in the external relations between states and their internal political arrangements.

However, in some quarters in the world of aid a contrary view has been growing up in favour of 'programme' aid. Instead of supporting specific projects, it is argued that donor countries should offer general support to the whole development plan of a poor country's government, and not concern itself overmuch about the details of its particular schemes. One argument in favour of this view is that it puts the two governments on something more nearly approaching equal terms. If government A trusts government B, then there is no need for its officials to check every detail of every development project, audit the books, inspect the site, and so forth, and it is acknowledged that such activities are somewhat humiliating to recipient country B and its government.

Another argument in favour of 'programme' aid is based on the fact that aid from all sources has contributed only about 15 per cent of all investment in poor countries in recent years. The use which those countries, and their governments, make of the remaining 85 per cent is clearly much more important for their development than is the use of aid alone. In so far as donor countries wish to bring about the best and fastest possible economic development of the recipient countries, therefore, they should concern themselves with the general economic policies and procedures of the recipient governments. Matters like import-licensing arrangements, investment codes, marketing-board price policies, tax rules, the efficiency of publicly operated utilities like railways and harbours, and the treatment of 'pariah entrepreneurs' may have greater effect on economic development than particular aid projects. Aid can thus come to be viewed as a 'major catalyst', a means of inducing recipient governments to pursue economic and social policies favourable to development and to the efficient use of all the recipient country's resources, not just the 15 per cent or so provided in the form of aid.[29]

According to this view, then, it is perfectly proper to withdraw aid from a country which suddenly adopts a policy judged contrary to its economic development, such as that of expelling an enterprising racial minority, whereas such a withdrawal would be seen as wrong by the supporters of 'project' aid. 'Programme' aid should indeed be flexible, just as the policies of the recipient government can be flexible. However, promises to increase aid, or threats to withdraw it, are seen as the final resort to the blunt weapon in aid relations. The more important and subtler influences which the donor country can exert are through its aid officials' close contacts with senior officials in the government of the recipient country, who can, so to speak, be continually encouraged to tread the paths of righteousness and forsake the ways of sin. The quiet support of the donor country's officials can be given to those of the recipient country who are judged to have the right ideas, hints can be dropped that the donor country is more likely to be impressed by one policy where another would weaken its confidence in the recipient government, and so on. This process of influencing recipient governments to adopt policies which the donor government regards as favourable to development has become known as 'leverage'.

The danger with programme aid and leverage is, of course, that besides aid being sensitive to the general policies of the recipient government in so far as they affect development, it can also be sensitive to the political and economic pressures of vested interests in the donor country. However clear-sighted and disinterested the donor country's aid agency and its officials may be in their view of the recipient country's development and welfare, they may not be able to shield themselves from those pressures. Such dangers are vividly illustrated in Hayter's account of the Peruvian crisis of 1966–7.[30]

Tying

A common practice is for donor countries to 'tie' aid to their own products. For example, in the imaginary case quoted above, the government of rich

289

industrial country A when making a loan on soft terms to the government of country B for a hydro-electric scheme may specify that the turbines, generators, transformers, and other heavy equipment must be bought in country A.

The advantages to the donor country are obvious. Tying minimizes the effect of the aid agreement on the balance of payments. Indeed, the money may never leave country A at all; it may be paid into the account which the central bank of country B maintains with the central bank of country A, and paid out from that account to industrial enterprises in country A for work done on contracts under the scheme. From one point of view, indeed, the transaction amounts to a contract or set of contracts financed by government A with industrial firms in its own country. Again, motives of self-interest and generosity may be combined. While from one point of view there is an arrangement which benefits certain firms and workers within the donor country, at the same time the work that is being done and the eventual products will benefit people in the poor recipient country. They, after all, and not the people of rich country A, get the hydro-electric station. In effect, then, government A pays some of its own firms to do work which will benefit country B.

On the other hand, tying has serious disadvantages from the point of view of the recipient country. It forces the latter to buy in what may not be the best market, or buy equipment that may not be the most suitable for its particular needs. Tying of shipping and insurance charges to the donor country may add further to the direct costs, which may be increased to an extent which the Pearson commission thought might be as high as 20 per cent.[31] Moreover, tying is among the factors which lead donor countries to prefer to support projects with a high import content. Thus to continue the same imaginary example, the government of B might include among the projects it would like to initiate (1) a scheme to build a thousand small dams, mainly with hand labour with a minimum of equipment (wheelbarrows, etc.), employing the skills of modestly qualified local surveyors in design and supervision, and potentially beneficial for irrigation, fish-farming, stock-keeping, and rural water supplies for human use; and (2) a single large hydro-electric scheme, involving a massive dam and a major generating station, employing foreign experts at the design and construction stage, and geared mainly to the potential needs of large-scale industry. As an aid project, the latter would be far more likely to commend itself to a rich industrial country like A, whose firms would obviously make more out of supplying generating equipment than wheelbarrows. Scheme (1) would moreover be less attractive to donor governments because of the high proportion of local costs. Financing local costs from outside is regarded in general as inflationary (since it generates income flows in the recipient country which correspond neither to current production nor to current saving), and for this and other reasons donor

290

countries are most averse to the practice. As the Pearson commission say, 'This policy is sometimes useful in inducing the latter [the recipient country] to maximise efforts to raise local capital, but in many countries it encourages an uneconomic bias towards capital-intensive projects with a large foreign exchange component.'[32] In other words, the combination of tying with the avoidance of responsibility for local costs is a major factor in the tendency towards an inappropriately capital-intensive technology.

It should be added, however, that we are again dealing with factors which may make aid less beneficial than it could otherwise have been, and not with considerations which tend to suggest that it is actually harmful. Suppose country B were in the position that, without aid, it could afford only one of the two schemes outlined above, and had to choose between them. Aid from country A might enable it to escape the dilemma and have both. Tying might in that case somewhat reduce the value of A's aid, but it could hardly be said to make country B worse off.

Tying was deprecated by the Pearson commission, who pointed out that it had 'spread in a contagious fashion' during the 1960s. (Each time a donor country resorts to tying, it reduces the possibility of other donor countries' benefiting from its aid, and predisposes them to tie their aid too — hence the suggestion of a 'contagion'.) According to the United Nations, indeed, all but one-eighth of all official bilateral lending was tied to purchases in the lending country during the years 1966—8. The Pearson commission urged that donor countries should move towards an agreement to untie their aid, and meanwhile should not intensify procedures. At the same time, they should 'remove regulations which limit or prevent contributions to the local costs of projects, and make a greater effort to encourage local procurement wherever economically justified.'[33]

A final point about tying — using the term in its most general sense — concerns the petty restrictions which some donor governments place on the use of their aid, restrictions which at the very least make heavy demands on scarce administrative manpower in the recipient countries. An O.D.I. report on aid to Uganda vividly illustrates what can be involved especially with the United States government. Detailed planning of the project and negotiations leading to an offer of U.S. aid are only a beginning, for Washington must be notified in voluminous detail of the invitations to tender, the form of the tender, the form of contract, the final plans, and bills of quantities. At the disbursement stage a host of detailed requirements have to be observed concerning records, progress reports, inspection, limitations on the use of funds. No goods for the scheme — whether financed from U.S. aid or not — may be bought from communist countries. A certain proportion of the imported goods must be carried in ships registered under the U.S. flag, and no goods financed with U.S. aid may be carried in ships which are 'ineligible' through having called at ports in Cuba. To comply with these requirements, quarterly shipping records of goods imported for the project are required, though Uganda has no port and goods landed at Mombasa may have been trans-shipped in other ports and formed part of a cargo for other destinations. And so on. And it is clear that, despite the truly enormous amount of clerical work involved in making these returns, the great bulk of them are never scrutinized; 'they are simply there to enable, in theory, checks to be made should queries arise'.[34]

Bilateral versus multilateral

Most aid is bilateral, that is it is given under an agreement between a donor country and a recipient country. 'Multilateral' aid is that which is given by donor countries as a group, pooling resources and working through an international agency. The preceding discussion has been expressed mainly in bilateral terms, though mention has been made of the more important agencies for multilateral aid – the World Bank group, and the United Nations and its specialized agencies. According to the Pearson report, almost nine-tenths of all official development assistance in 1967 was bilateral. They thought that more aid should be multilateral, and recommended a target of 20 per cent by 1975.

The arguments for increased multilateral aid are, first, that in theory at least, it should be more impartial, especially if it is administered by an international body on which poor recipient countries are themselves represented. From this point of view the ideal authority, or group of authorities, is that of the United Nations and its agencies such as U.N.E.S.C.O., F.A.O., and W.H.O., responsible as they are to an organization which includes communist as well as capitalist countries, rich as well as poor. Some regional organization like the Inter-American Development Bank (I.A.D.B. or I.D.B.) also fulfil this requirement at least to the extent of including both donor and recipient countries. In fact, however, a larger share of multilateral aid is handled through the World Bank group, which is an association of rich capitalist countries and not entirely immune from criticism on the ground of laissez-faire orthodoxy.

Secondly, international bodies can be invaluable agencies for coordinating aid. A World Bank report on a poor country's economy, for example, can be relied upon to be thorough and factual. Individual donor countries need hardly duplicate such a study, though they may wish to evaluate it differently and draw different conclusions for aid policy.

Thirdly, international agencies may be able to fill the gaps left by bilateral agreements. One of the reasons for these – indeed, a reason why most aid is in fact bilateral – is the natural affinity between some donor countries and some recipients, often their former colonies. These are in part based on language and culture. Language is clearly of great importance in technical assistance, especially so when it is recalled that about half of all technical-

292

assistance personnel are teachers. Thus former French colonies naturally look to France — or perhaps to Canada — for this kind of help, while former British colonies turn to Britain, the United States, or other English-speaking countries. Besides language there are many other ties, such as engineering conventions — inches or centimetres, the pitch and gauge of screws, standard electrical fittings — linking some poor countries with some metropolitan ones. However, there are countries which would do rather badly if aid were confined to bilateral agreements, and it can be part of the task of international agencies to try to ensure that such gaps are filled.

Trade versus aid

This is a somewhat wider issue than aid itself, and calls in question wider aspects of the relations between rich and poor countries. It is often said that trade is more important than aid. The more difficult problems for the economic development of poor countries, in this view, lie in the adverse terms of trade between them and the rich countries, the widely fluctuating prices which they get for their primary products (which according to the Pearson report make up nearly 90 per cent of their foreign-exchange earnings),[35] and the way in which their industrial development is hampered by the tariff barriers which rich countries erect against their industrial products. According to this view, rich countries would do more to help the economic development of poor countries by changing their trade policies than by giving aid.

From the point of view to which I am alluding, aid is sometimes seen as a 'soft option'. It may be politically easier, it suggested, for a donor government to give aid, which comes out of taxes paid by all taxpayers, than to expose particular industries or sectors to competitive undercutting from the products of poor countries by lowering tariff barriers. Thus to take a particularly sensitive example, it is suggested that it may be politically easier for the British government to give aid to India than to abolish the import duties on manufactured cotton textiles, which would help the development of textile manufacturing in India but cause terrible trouble in Lancashire.

The question of the terms of trade between rich and poor countries has aroused a good deal of controversy, and the phrase 'the ever-widening gap' is used to suggest that the rich countries trade on ever more favourable terms with the poor. But an examination of the statistics gives little ground for that view. In part it may have arisen from statistics which have used 1951 as a base year — an exceptionally favourable year for the poor countries, when the United States was stockpiling strategic materials in relation to the Korean war. Even if the base year is taken as 1948 the picture looks different, with the exceptionally favourable early fifties followed by a restoration of the previous position by 1961, a slightly adverse movement in the early sixties, and a recovery later in the decade. Further, if the comparison is made over time between raw material prices and those of manufactured goods, the trend looks more unfavourable to the poor countries than if the comparison is made between the exports of developed and developing countries. For though raw materials still predominate in their exports, the poor countries' exports of manufactured goods are increasing fast – according to the Pearson report by over 12 per cent annually.[36] And according to the U.N., the export unit value of developing countries' raw materials and fuels fell during the 1960s, but that of their foodstuffs rose, and that of their manufactured goods rose sharply. If fuels are excluded, indeed, the terms of trade moved in the poor countries' favour.[37]

Turning to restrictions on trade, the Pearson commission drew attention to a general tendency for the tariff and quota systems of rich countries to discriminate in two ways, both harmful to the interests of economic development in the poor countries. First, they discriminate against manufactured goods as compared with raw materials. Typically, raw materials are imported by rich countries duty free or at a low rate of duty, semi-manufactured goods at a higher rate, and fully manufactured goods at a higher rate still.[38] Such discrimination may, moreover, operate disproportionately heavily against the development of manufacturing in poor countries, for as Bauer has pointed out,

Tariffs are expressed as a percentage of the value of the processed product. If, as is often the case, imports of raw materials enter duty free or at low rates of duty, an apparently moderate rate of duty on the processed product often represents a very high percentage of the value added in processing and thus a correspondingly high degree of protection to those activities.[39]

Secondly, rich countries tend to charge higher rates of import duty on goods from poor countries than on similar goods from other rich countries.[40]

Questions of this nature have been discussed at three United Nations Conferences on Trade and Development (U.N.C.T.A.D.), held respectively at Geneva in 1964, New Delhi in 1968, and Santiago, Chile, in 1972. At the first the General Secretary, Dr Raul Prebisch, presented a proposal for a system of 'generalised non-reciprocal preferences' by means of which rich countries should alter their systems of tariffs, quotas, and the like positively to favour the products of poor countries. 'Generalised' implied that these preferences should apply to all the products of poor countries and not just to their raw materials, thus abolishing discrimination against the development of processing industries in poor countries, while 'non-reciprocal' implied that poor countries should not have to reciprocate by lowering their tariff protection against rich countries' products.

The initial discussion of this proposal at U.N.C.T.A.D. I soon became entangled with immensely complicated questions about the relation of the Prebisch scheme to other tariff conventions and negotiations in which different countries were involved – the General Agreement on Tariffs and Trade (G.A.T.T.), the Kennedy Round of mutual tariff reductions, British Commonwealth preference, the Yaoundé convention involving France and her former colonies. The United States, which has never liked schemes like Commonwealth preference, tried to take a stand on the principle that existing preference schemes should be abolished immediately the new system came into force, while Britain joined France and the other Common Market countries in believing that the two systems could be accommodated to one another, at least for a transitional period. At U.N.C.T.A.D. II some poor countries began to have doubts, wondering if they would not lose their existing advantages under Commonwealth preference etc., and gain little or nothing in exchange; while at U.N.C.T.A.D. III the discussion shifted to other questions including a proposal to amalgamate the General Agreement on Tariffs and Trade with the International Monetary Fund. This, if adopted, would have given the poor countries a part in the making of decisions about such vital matters as exchange rates, but it was opposed by communist countries who, of course, play no part in I.M.F. Little more than lip-service continues to be paid to the idea of generalized non-reciprocal preferences.[41]

Meanwhile, the situation has been changed significantly by the rise of the European Economic Community (E.E.C., the Common Market) followed by that of the European Free Trade Area (E.F.T.A.) and the subsequent negotiations for Britain and other E.F.T.A. countries to join an enlarged Common Market. As the Pearson commission noted in 1969, since there is soon to be free trade in industrial products between the major countries of Europe, it becomes hard to imagine how they can *give preference to* manufactured goods from poor countries.[42]

The case for intermediate technology

A number of factors have already been mentioned which make for the adoption in poor countries of technological methods and capital equipment which are inappropriate to their needs and to the pattern of their resources. In particular, the world's dominant technology can now be characterized as capital-intensive, appropriate to conditions in which there is plenty of capital, the productivity of labour is high, workers are well organized in trade unions, and wages are high accordingly. In the rich countries, in fact, there has been a cumulative process for many decades in which 'labour-saving machinery' (as it used to be called) raises the productivity of labour, trade union action raises the wages of workers to something approximating to the new marginal productivity of their labour, incomes are increased, and there is an incentive accordingly for the development of yet more labour-saving machinery. This indeed has come to be thought of as the 'virtuous circle' by which the living standards of whole populations have been raised.

295

As has been seen, these capital-intensive methods have been applied in poor countries for a variety of reasons. Often they are technically the best, most efficient, and most economical in any country. Engineers trained in the great technological universities of the world find it hard to believe that the best way of doing things in one country is not necessarily so in another. Technical-assistance personnel carry these methods with them in their heads, and are reluctant to get out of touch with ideas and developments in the rich countries where they will soon be back. Aid policies contribute to the same effect by 'tying' and by not contributing to local costs.

And the social and economic effects have also been seen in earlier chapters — the dual economy with a modern sector dominated by large international firms, the tendency for development to be centred in towns, 'development without employment' in which an 'aristocracy of labour' can earn high wages while many make a bare living in a labour-intensive indigenous private sector, and many are unemployed.

One way of expressing this is in terms of the cost per work place. It has been estimated that the average equipment cost per work place in modern industry is of the order of £2,000, while in some highly capital-intensive industries like steel works it may be as high as £10,000. Clearly it is unrealistic to think of providing jobs at this kind of level in poor countries which are short of capital; what is needed is a new technology for small-scale industry with a cost per work place one or two orders of magnitude lower than this, say around £100. One effect of this approach would be to bring it within the capability of a worker in a poor country to save enough to buy his own work place. There are implications too for the distribution of income. How, it is asked, are the jobless in a poor country to fill in their time waiting for the surpluses generated by the labour aristocracy to filter down to them? 'The only effective distribution system for income in poor countries is *work*.' Moreover, 'no-one has ever acquired skills, aptitudes and self-reliance by having his labour "saved"'.

What is needed, according to Dr E. F. Schumacher, a leading exponent of this view, is an 'intermediate technology' — one which as he puts it is intermediate between the sickle and the combine harvester, and which is, or can be brought, within the reach of the poor and by which they can become self-reliant. This does not imply 'backwardness'; on the contrary, the application of scientific principles can be just as 'modern', and just as challenging, when it is devoted to devising small-scale, capital-saving methods.[43]

The Pearson commission recognized this problem, and recommended that 'aid-suppliers devote a significant share of their research and development resources and facilities to projects specifically related to problems of developing countries'.[44] Some work has in fact been done along these lines by research institutes in industrial countries. In Britain, for example, the National Institute of Agricultural Engineering has set up an Overseas

Liaison Unit and has developed a number of low-cost agricultural machines suitable for poor countries. These include a basic one-wheel-drive tractor, a thresher for small-scale rice-growers costing less than £100 and locally manufactured in south-east Asian countries, and a hand-operated rice transplanter. The Tropical Products Institute has worked on a number of projects including the fabrication of light-weight building blocks made from rice hulls and cement, small-scale equipment for palm-oil extraction, and methods for utilizing solar energy. The Japanese have also been reported to be working on a solar water heater costing as little as six dollars and suitable for domestic water heating in countries with adequate sunshine. An American A.I.D. study of simple village technology resulted in the publication of a handbook illustrating 'do-it-yourself' methods of constructing tube wells, hand pumps, and sanitary services.[45] The task of collecting information about these and similar methods, together with data on appropriate low-cost equipment, from research institutes and private firms, and making this information known in poor countries, has been assumed by Dr Schumacher's Intermediate Technology Development Group with support from the British Overseas Development Ministry, industrial firms, and private charities.

However, while the arguments for intermediate technology may appear very cogent, they seem to offer no escape from the dilemma that whereas 'capital-intensive development' may mean high wages for the few and unemployment for the many, 'labour-intensive development' is a polite way of saying low wages. For example, in a recent television programme on this problem a hand press was shown operated by about a dozen men in a small cooperative workshop producing hub-caps for automobiles. Though this was praised as an example of self-help and intermediate technology, it may be doubted how much was added to human welfare and dignity by a dozen men in a South Asian country working repetitively for several hours a day to produce what a machine in Detroit or Coventry could turn out in a few minutes.

Such are the dilemmas of a world of disparity and involvement – a world of which a Secretary-General of the United Nations has said:

I do not wish to seem over-dramatic, but I can only conclude that the members of the United Nations have perhaps ten years to subordinate their ancient quarrels and launch a global partnership to curb the arms race, to improve the human environment, to defuse the population explosion, and to apply the required momentum for world development efforts.

If a global partnership is not forged within the next decade then I very much fear that the problems I have mentioned will have reached such staggering proportions that they will be beyond our capacity to control.[46]

Notes

Chapter 1. Introduction and argument

1 Peter Worsley, *The Third World* (London, 1964), p. 1.
2 United Nations, *Measures for the Economic Development of Under-developed Countries*, E/1986 ST/ECA/10 (3 May 1951).
3 Gunnar Myrdal, *Asian Drama: An Inquiry into the Poverty of Nations* (Harmondsworth, 1968), appendix 1.
4 Ernest Gellner, *Thought and Change* (London, 1964), p. 33n.
5 A. O. Hirschman, *The Strategy of Economic Development* (New Haven, Conn., 1958), p. 11.
6 Myrdal, *Asian Drama*, appendix 2.
7 Paul Streeten, 'How poor are the poor countries?' in Dudley Seers and Leonard Joy (eds.), *Development in a Divided World* (Harmondsworth, 1971), p. 77.
8 Auguste Comte, *Positive Politics*, vol. IV, appendix, pp. 149–50, quoted by N. S. Timasheff, *Sociological Theory, Its Nature and Growth* (New York, 1955), p. 19; *Positive Philosophy*, transl. Harriet Martineau (London, 1853), esp. vol. II, ch. VI.
9 Herbert Spencer, *Principles of Sociology*, 3rd edition (London, 1904), vol. I, part II, chs. X, XI; vol. II, part V, chs. XVII, XVIII.
10 Sir Henry Sumner Maine, *Ancient Law*, 11th edition (London, 1887), p. 170.
11 Emile Durkheim, *The Division of Labour in Society*, transl. G. Simpson (Glencoe, Ill., 1947).
12 George Lichtheim, *Marxism* (New York, 1961), pp. 143–52.
13 Ferdinand Tönnies, *Community and Society* (Gemeinschaft und Gesellschaft), trans' Charles P. Loomis (East Lansing, Mich., 1957).
14 L. T. Hobhouse, *Social Development* (London, 1924).
15 Godfrey and Monica Wilson, *The Analysis of Social Change, Based on Observations in Central Africa* (Cambridge, 1945).
16 These points were made by Professor Monica Wilson in an oral communication subsequently to the publication of *The Analysis of Social Change*.
17 Talcott Parsons and Edward A. Shils, *Toward a General Theory of Action* (Cambridge, Mass., 1951), pp. 49, 76–7.
18 Talcott Parsons, *Societies: Evolutionary and Comparative Perspectives* (Englewood Cliffs, N. J., 1966), pp. 1, 21–3.
19 Fred W. Riggs, *Administration in Developing Countries: The Theory of Prismatic Society* (Boston, 1964).

Chapter 2. Technology, society, and population

1 On the neolithic revolution, the classic treatment (and probably the source of the phrase itself) is V. Gordon Childe, *Man Makes Himself* (London, 1936), ch. 2. Other references: Don R. Arthur, *Survival* (London, 1969); Zygmunt Bauman, 'Economic growth, social structure, elite formation: the case of Poland', *International Social Science Journal*, XVI (1964) p. 203; Carlo M. Cipolla, *The Economic History of World Population*, 5th edition (Harmondsworth, 1970); S. Lilley, *Men, Machines and History* (London, 1948; revised edition 1965).

2 Carlo M. Cipolla, 'Guns and sails' in *European Culture and Overseas Expansion* (Harmondsworth, 1970).
3 J. V. Grauman, 'Population growth', *International Encyclopaedia of the Social Sciences* (1968).
4 R. W. Firth, *We the Tikopia* (London, 1936), ch. XI.
5 D. V. Glass (ed.), *Introduction to Malthus* (London, 1953), pp. 30—8.
6 The authoritative source for estimates of world population from 1650 to 1930 is still A. M. Carr-Saunders, *World Population* (Oxford, 1936). Later figures from U.N. *Demographic Yearbooks.*
7 C. P. Blacker, *Eugenics, Galton and After* (London, 1952), ch. 8.
8 M. Drake, *Population and Society in Norway, 1735—1865* (Cambridge, 1969), pp. xvii—xviii.
9 Tegner, quoted in Alva Myrdal, *Nation and Family* (London, 1945), p. 17.
10 *East Africa Royal Commission 1953—55 Report*, Cmd. 9475, appendix VII.
11 Kenneth Smith, 'Some observations on modern Malthusianism', *Population studies*, VI (1952), pp. 92—105.
12 Carr-Saunders, *World Population*, pp. 61, 90, 106—9.
13 Gunnar Myrdal, *Asian Drama: An Inquiry into the Poverty of Nations* (Harmondsworth, 1968), pp. 1443—5, 1473—80.
14 Lord Blackett, *The Gap Widens* (the Rede Lecture, 1969) (Cambridge, 1970), pp. 13, 26—7.
15 Michael Lipton, 'The international diffusion of technology' in Dudley Seers and Leonard Joy (eds.), *Development in a Divided World* (Harmondsworth, 1971), p. 48.
16 Paul Streeten, 'Economic strategies' in *ibid.* p. 149.
17 *Population Bulletin*, XXIV, no. 3 (November 1968).
18 *Partners in Development: Report of the Commission on International Development* (Washington D.C., 1969), pp. 55—8, 194—9.
19 *Population Reference Bureau Selection*, no. 33 (October 1970).
20 *Partners in Development*, pp. 57, 197.
21 John Peel and Malcolm Potts, 'The sociology of population control', paper presented to British Sociological Association annual conference, York, April 1972.

Case-study 1: India

1 Kingsley Davis, *The Population of India and Pakistan* (Princeton, 1951).
2 Myrdal, *Asian Drama*, pp. 1489—91, 1518—20, and appendix 12.
3 Population Reference Bureau, *Demographic Express* (December 1973).

Case-study 2: England and Wales

1 Carr-Saunders, *World Population*, ch. 1.
2 E. A. Wrigley, 'Family limitation in pre-industrial England', *Economic History Review*, XIX (1966), pp. 82—109.
3 G. M. Trevelyan, *English Social History* (London, 1942), pp. 339—46; T. S. Ashton, *The Industrial Revolution, 1760—1830* (London, 1948), pp. 3—6; H. J. Habbakuk, 'The economic history of modern Britain', *Journal of Economic History*, XVIII (1958), pp. 486—501.
4 R. A. Lewis, *Edwin Chadwick and the Public Health Movement, 1832—1854* (London, 1952).
5 J. A. Banks, *Prosperity and Parenthood* (London, 1954).
6 Graham Wallas, *The Life of Francis Place* (London, 1898), ch. 6; St John G. Ervine, *Francis Place* (Fabian biographical tract) (London, 1912).
7 J. H. Clapham, *An Economic History of Modern Britain, 1850—1886* (Cambridge, 1932), ch. IX; W. W. Rostow, *British Economy of the Nineteenth Century* (Oxford, 1948), chs. III, IV, VII.
8 *Royal Commission on Population Report*, Cmd. 7695; E. Lewis-Faning, *Family Limitation* (Papers of the Royal Commission on Population) (London, 1949), p. 7.

Case-study 3: Japan

1 Irene B. Taeuber, *The Population of Japan* (Princeton, 1958).

Chapter 3. The colonial episode and the race question

1 Patrick Keatley, 'Imperial Ice Age', *The Guardian*, 5 April 1965.
2 Carlo M. Cipolla, 'Guns and sails' in *European Culture and Overseas Expansion* (Harmondsworth, 1970), pp. 104—5.
3 De Kiewiet, quoted in Pierre van den Berghe, *South Africa: A Study in Conflict* (Middletown, Conn., 1965), pp. 13—14.
4 Burton Benedict, *Indians in a Plural Society: A Report on Mauritius* (Colonial Research Studies, no. 34) (London, 1961), esp. chs. II and III.
5 References on this and the previous paragraph include: Gunnar Myrdal, *An American Dilemma* (New York, 1944), and also abridged edition by Arnold M. Rose, *The Negro in America* (New York, 1948); C. W. Wagley, 'The situation of the Negro in the United States', *International Social Science Bulletin* [now *Journal*], IX, no. 4 (1957), pp. 427—38; Roger Bastide, 'Race regulations in Brazil', *ibid.* pp. 495—512; Donald Pierson, *Negroes in Brazil* (Chicago, 1942), esp. pp. 30—7.
6 G. M. Trevelyan, *English Social History*, 2nd edition (London, 1946), pp. 347, 388—9, 495—6; R. Coupland, *The British Anti-slavery Movement* (London, 1933); Eric Williams, *Capitalism and Slavery* (Chapel Hill, N. C., 1943).
7 Roland Oliver, *The Missionary Factor in East Africa* (London, 1952), ch. I; W. E. R. Ward, *The Royal Navy and the Slavers* (London, 1969).
8 Gunnar Myrdal, *Asian Drama: An Inquiry into the Poverty of Nations* (Harmondsworth, 1968), ch. 5, section 1, 'The advance of colonial rule'.
9 For a graphic presentation of this process, see A. Boyd and P. van Rensberg, *An Atlas of African Affairs* (New York, 1962), pp. 24—7. See also Roland Oliver and J. D. Fage, *A Short History of Africa* (Harmondsworth, 1962), ch. 16.
10 Harry Thuku, *Autobiography* (with assistance from Kenneth King) (Nairobi, 1970).
11 Oliver, *The Missionary Factor in East Africa*, pp. 149—62; D. A. Low, 'British public opinion and the Uganda question, October—December 1892', *Uganda Journal*, 18 (1954), pp. 81—100.
12 Such attitudes are well documented in the works of Elspeth Huxley, especially *White Man's Country* (London, 1956), a biography of Lord Delamere; see also Elspeth Huxley and Margery Perham, *Race and Politics in Kenya: A Correspondence* (London, 1944); L. H. Gann and P. Duignan, *White Settlers in Tropical Africa* (Baltimore, Md., 1962).
13 A. P. Elkin, *The Australian Aborigines*, 4th edition (Garden City, N.Y., 1964), ch. XIV. See also his 'Aborigines and Europeans in Australia', *American Anthropologist*, 53 (1951), pp. 164—86.
14 Myrdal, *Asian Drama*, pp. 449—52, 832—3, 839.
15 A. I. Richards, *Land, Labour, and Diet in Northern Rhodesia* (London, 1939), pp. 256—62; R. L. Buell, 'Forced Labour', *Encyclopaedia of the Social Sciences* (1932).
16 Myrdal, *Asian Drama*, pp. 969—71
17 Oliver, *The Missionary Factor in East Africa*, pp. 247—57.
18 W. H. Hutt, *The Economics of the Colour Bar* (London, 1964), pp. 158—9; van den Berghe, *South Africa*, ch. 8 and map facing p. 118.
19 See, for instance, Boyd and van Rensberg, *An Atlas of African Affairs*, map on p. 45.
20 For each £100 invested in the company when it began in 1903, an investor received a dividend of £2.10.0 in 1907. In 1913 his capital was written down to £50 and he got no more dividends until 1918. From then till 1925 the company paid dividends at rates of 5.5—15%, but that was only 2.75—7.5% on the original capital. No more dividends were paid until 1937, by which time the original £100 investment had been written down further to £37.10.0. After 1940, and even more after 1945, the company paid substantial dividends as it became more commercial; but even so the average rate of yield over the first fifty years was only fractionally over 3%. See C. Ehrlich, *The Uganda Company Limited: The First Fifty Years* (Kampala, 1953).
21 C. Wagley and M. Harris, 'The Indians in Brazil' in *Minorities in the New World* (New York, 1958), p. 27.

22 Carl G. Rosberg jnr and John Nottingham, *The Myth of 'Mau Mau': Nationalism in Kenya* (New York, 1966), pp. 112—25; F. B. Welbourn, *East African Rebels* (London, 1961), ch. 7.

23 The situation in East Africa is described in more detail in J. E. Goldthorpe, *Outlines of East African Society* (Kampala, 1958), ch. VIII.

24 See, for instance D. A. Low and R. C. Pratt, *Buganda and British Overrule* (London, 1960), pp. 98—101.

25 A fine expression of the sensitive awareness of local cultures and gently paternalistic attitudes of at least one former colonial administrator is to be found in the works of the late Sir Arthur Grimble, especially *A Pattern of Islands* (London, 1952).

26 Goldthorpe, *Outlines of East African Society*, ch. X.

27 J. E. Goldthorpe, *An African Elite* (Oxford, 1965).

28 van den Berghe, *South Africa*, pp. 129—30.

29 Cyril Sofer and Rhona Ross, 'Some characteristics of an East African European population', *British Journal of Sociology*, II (1951), pp. 315—27.

30 The point is made explicitly in Roger Bastide, 'Dusky Venus, black Apollo', *Race*, III (1961), pp. 10—18. See also Carl N. Degler, *Neither Black nor White* (London, 1971), esp. pp. 185—95.

31 Wagley and Harris, 'The Indians in Brazil', p. 24; Pierson, *Negroes in Brazil*, pp. 321—50.

32 Charles Wagley, *Race and Class in Rural Brazil* (Paris, 1952), pp. 23—4.

33 Bastide, 'Race relations in Brazil', pp. 495—512.

34 van den Berghe, *South Africa*, pp. 14—21, 39—42, 55—9.

35 The term 'plural society' is generally credited to J. S. Furnivall in 'The political economy of the tropical Far East', *Journal of the Royal Central Asian Society*, XXIX (1942), pp. 195—210, and in *Colonial Policy and Practice* (Cambridge, 1948). It has since been extensively used and discussed, for example, by John Rex, 'The plural society in sociological theory', *British Journal of Sociology*, X (1959), pp. 114—24.

36 Myrdal, *Asian Drama*, pp. 425, 465, 453—7.

37 Sir Charles Dundas, *African Crossroads* (London, 1955), pp. 123—130; Perham and Huxley, *Race and Politics in Kenya*, pp. 98, 100, 107; Rosberg and Nottingham, *The Myth of 'Mau Mau'*, pp. 74, 207, 304.

38 Margery Perham, 'African facts and American criticisms', *Foreign Affairs*, 22, no. 3 (1944); reprinted in her *Colonial Sequence, 1930 to 1949* (London, 1967), pp. 250ff.

39 Myrdal, *Asian Drama*, pp. 144—7.

40 John Kenneth Galbraith, in an interview with Kenneth Harris, *The Observer*, 27 November 1966.

41 Ernest Gellner, *Thought and Change* (London, 1964), p. 175.

42 *Colonial Development and Welfare Acts, 1929—70: A Brief Review*, Cmnd. 4677 (1971), table 3.

43 Sofer and Ross, 'Some characteristics of an East African European population', pp. 319—21.

44 George de Vos, 'Conflict, dominance and exploitation in human systems of social segregation: some theoretical perspectives from the study of personality in culture' in A. de Reuck and Julie Knight (eds.), *Conflict in Society* (a CIBA symposium) (London, 1966), pp. 60—81.

45 G. Andrew Maguire, *Toward 'Uhuru' in Tanzania* (Cambridge, 1969), esp. pp. 156—9 223—8.

46 Jawaharlal Nehru, *Letters from a Father to His Daughter* (Allahabad, 1929); *Glimpses of World History* (Allahabad, 1934); *An Autobiography* (London, 1936); *The Discovery of India* (Calcutta, 1946).

47 Jomo Kenyatta, *Facing Mount Kenya* (London, 1938).

48 Kenneth Kaunda, 'Some personal reflections', *Africa's Freedom* (London, 1964), pp. 26—8.

49 Kwame Nkrumah, *Ghana: An Autobiography* (Edinburgh, 1957), pp. 17—20, 42—3, 49—50, 81—4; Oginga Odinga, *Not Yet Uhuru* (London, 1967), pp. 57—9, 61; Tom Mboya, *Freedom and After* (London, 1963), pp. 27—30.

50 Aimé Césaire, 'Cahier d'un retour au pays natal', transl. Peter Worsley and quoted in his *The Third World* (London, 1964), p. 124.

51 Quoted for instance in Philip Mason, *Patterns of Dominance* (Oxford, 1970), p. 290.

52 Kwame Nkrumah, *Neo-colonialism* (London, 1965).

53 Frantz Fanon, *The Wretched of the Earth* (*Les damnés de la terre*, 1961; English transl. Constance Farrington, 1965); this quotation is from pp. 80—1 of the Penguin edition (Harmondsworth, 1967). Quotations in subsequent paragraphs are from: 'Letter to the Resident Minister' (1956) in *Toward the African Revolution* (1964; English transl., Harmondsworth, 1967); 'Algeria unveiled' in *A Dying Colonialism* (Harmondsworth, 1965), the English translation of *L'an cinq de la révolution algérienne* (1959); 'The North African syndrome' (1952) and 'French intellectuals and democrats and the Algerian revolution', both in *Toward the African Revolution*.

54 Aristide R. Zolberg, 'Frantz Fanon' in Maurice Cranston (ed.), *The New Left* (London, 1970); Peter Geismar, *Fanon* (New York, 1971).

55 These are the opening words of Jean-Paul Sartre's introduction to Frantz Fanon, *The Wretched of the Earth* (1965).

Chapter 4. Economic conditions

1 C. F. Carter, *The Science of Wealth* (London, 1966), p. 177; see also the report of an expert committee to the United Nations, *Measurement of the Flow of Resources to Developing Countries* E/4327 ST/ECA/98 (1967). It was this committee which recommended the use of G.N.P. in interpreting the term 'national income' in the U.N. resolution of 1960 setting a one-per-cent target for aid.

2 Everett E. Hagen, *The Economics of Development* (Homewood, Ill., 1968), ch. 1; see also Gunnar Myrdal, *Asian Drama: An Inquiry into the Poverty of Nations* (Harmondsworth, 1968), p. 481, quoting an earlier article by Hagen and applying it particularly to India.

3 Quoted by Myrdal, *Asian Drama*, p. 549.

4 K. H. Connell, *The Population of Ireland, 1750—1845* (Oxford, 1950), pp. 151—6.

5 H. C. Trowell, J. N. P. Davies, and R. F. A. Dean, *Kwashiorkor* (London, 1954).

6 Myrdal, *Asian Drama*, appendix 2, section 21, pp. 1912ff.

7 *Ibid.* pp. 540, 551—3.

8 *Ibid.* p. 587.

9 *Partners in Development: Report of the Commission on International Development* (Washington, D.C., 1969), p. 268.

10 Tony Killick, 'Commodity agreements as international aid', *Westminster Bank Review* (February 1967), reprinted in Gerald M. Meier (ed.), *Leading Issues in Economic Development*, 2nd edition (New York, 1970), pp. 533—8.

11 *The Economist*, 7 November 1970, pp. 64—5.

12 *Ibid.* 3 October 1970, p. 65.

13 *Ibid.* 15 January 1972, p. 40; 12 February 1972, p. 39.

14 G. L. Beckford, 'The economics of agricultural resource use and development in plantation economies', *Social and Economic Studies*, 18 (Jamaica, 1969), pp. 321—47; reprinted in Henry Bernstein (ed.), *Underdevelopment and Development* (Harmondsworth, 1973), pp. 115—51.

15 C. V. Vaitsos, 'Bargaining and the distribution of returns in the purchase of technology by developing countries', *Bulletin of the Institute of Development Studies*, 3 (1970), pp. 16—23; reprinted in Bernstein, *Underdevelopment and Development*, pp. 315—22.

16 *Partners in Development*, pp. 82—6.

17 United Nations, *World Economic Survey, 1971*, E/5144 ST/ECA/159 (1972), table D.10

18 Peter Odell, 'Against an oil cartel', *New Society*, no. 437 (11 February 1971), pp. 230—2.

19 The fact of labour migration is a commonplace in many economic and sociological studies of modern Africa. See, for instance, Godfrey Wilson, *The Economics of Detribalisation in Central Africa* (Manchester, 1942); Godfrey and Monica Wilson, *The Analysis of Social Change* (Cambridge, 1945); J. Clyde Mitchell, *The Kalela Dance* (Manchester, 1956); P. G. Powesland, *Economic Policy and Labour* (Kampala, 1957); P. H. Gulliver, *Labour Migration in a Rural Economy* (Kampala, 1955); W. Elkan, *An African Labour Force* (Kampala, 1956); see also works cited below.

20 W. Elkan, *Migrants and Proletarians* (London, 1960), p. 99.

21 Erich H. Jacoby, 'Effects of the "green revolution" in South and South-East Asia', *Modern Asian Studies*, 6, no. 1 (1972), pp. 63—9.

22 W. A. Lewis, 'Economic development with unlimited supplies of labour', *Manchester School*, XXII (1954), pp. 139—91.

23 Gerald M. Meier, 'Development without employment' in *Leading Issues in Economic Development*, 2nd edition (New York, 1970), pp. 430—9; see also his comments on Lewis in *ibid.* pp. 158—62.

24 W. Arthur Lewis, *Development Planning* (London, 1966), pp. 80—1.

25 Quoted in *Unemployment, the Unnatural Disaster* (an OXFAM special report) n.d. [?1971].

26 G. Arrighi and J. S. Saul, 'Class formation and economic development in tropical Africa', *Journal of Modern African Studies*, 6 (1968), pp. 141—69; reprinted in Bernstein, *Underdevelopment and Development*, pp. 284—397.

27 Gulliver, *Labour Migration in a Rural Economy*.

28 J. van Velsen, 'Labour migration as a positive factor in the continuity of Tonga tribal society' in A. W. Southall (ed.), *Social Change in Modern Africa* (London, 1961), pp. 230—41.

29 Myrdal, *Asian Drama*, ch. 20.

30 M. J. Sharpston, 'The economics of corruption', *New Society*, 26 November 1970, pp. 944—6.

31 Goldthorpe, *An African Elite*, p. 76.

32 Chinua Achebe, *No Longer at Ease* (London, 1960), pp. 5—6.

33 S. N. Sen, *The City of Calcutta: A Socio-economic Survey, 1954—55 to 1957—58* (Calcutta, 1960). I am indebted to M. Kirk, Esq., for access to this report.

34 W. Arthur Lewis, *Some Aspects of Economic Development* (lectures at the University of Ghana) (Accra, 1969).

35 J. A. Banks, *Prosperity and Parenthood* (London, 1954), ch. V. and pp. 134—8; D. C. Marsh, *The Changing Social Structure of England and Wales, 1871—1961* (London, 1965), pp. 118, 125—7; J. Jean Hecht, *The Domestic Servant Class in Eighteenth-century England* (London, 1956).

36 Svetlana Alliluyeva, *Twenty Letters to a Friend* (London, 1967). p. 241.

37 Myrdal, *Asian Drama*, p. 575; see also Sen, *The City of Calcutta*.

38 Richard Jolly, in Dudley Seers and Leonard Joy (eds.), *Development in a Divided World* (Harmondsworth, 1971), pp. 211, 219—21.

39 Myrdal, *Asian Drama*, ch. 12 on 'Levels of living and inequality', especially pp. 539, 545, 563—5, 569—71; and appendix 8, sections 8, 9, pp. 2098—103.

Chapter 5. The rise of towns

1 Nathan Keyfitz, 'Political—economic aspects of urbanization in South and South-East Asia' in P. M. Hauser and L. F. Schnore (eds.), *The Study of Urbanization* (New York, 1965), pp. 265—309.

2 Homer Hoyt, *World Urbanization* (1962), quoted in G. Breese, *Urbanization in Newly Developing Countries* (Englewood Cliffs, N. J., 1966), p. 16.

3 Leo A. Orleans, 'China: Population in the People's Republic', *Population Bulletin*, 27, no. 6 (December 1971), pp. 25—8.

4 E. A. Kracke, 'Sung society: change within tradition', *Far Eastern Quarterly*, XIV (1955), pp. 479—88.

5 R. E. Pahl, *Patterns of Urban Life* (London, 1970), p. 19; see also Phyllis Deane and W. A. Cole, *British Economic Growth, 1688—1959* (Cambridge, 1962), pp. 7—8.

6 Kingsley Davis, 'The urbanization of the human population', *Scientific American*, no. 213 (September 1965), pp. 40—53; reprinted in Gerald M. Breese (ed.), *The City in Newly Developing Countries* (Englewood Cliffs, N. J., 1969), pp. 5—20.

7 Breese, *Urbanization in Newly Developing Countries*, p. 19.

8 Davis, 'The urbanization of the human population'.

9 Glenn T. Trewartha, 'Chinese cities: origins and functions', *Annals of the Association of American Geographers*, XLII (1952), pp. 91—3.

10 Morton White and Lucia White, *The Intellectual versus the City* (Cambridge, Mass., 1962).

11 Daniel Lerner, *The Passing of Traditional Society* (Glencoe, Ill., 1958), pp. 58ff.

12 Sir Joseph Hutchinson, 'Reflections on African development', Presidential address to the African Studies Association of the United Kingdom, 1968.

13 President Julius K. Nyerere, *Socialism and Rural Development* (Dar es Salaam, 1967), pp. 5—6, 10—11.

14 *The Arusha Declaration* (Dar es Salaam, 1967), pp. 11, 17; Julius K. Nyerere, *Education For Self-Reliance* (Dar es Salaam, 1967).

15 S. N. Sen, *The City of Calcutta: A Socio-economic Survey, 1954—55 to 1957—58* (Calcutta, 1960).

16 Nirmal Kumar Bose, 'Calcutta: A premature metropolis', *Scientific American* (September 1965).

Chapter 6. The family and kinship in a changing world

1 E. E. Evans-Pritchard, 'The Nuer of the southern Sudan', in M. Fortes and E. E. Evans-Pritchard (eds.), *African Political Systems* (London, 1940), pp. 272—96.

2 A warning against this particular error (which may in its turn go too far towards the other extreme) is to be found in Ruth Finnegan, 'The kinship ascription of primitive societies: actuality or myth?', *International Journal of Comparative Sociology*, XI (1970), pp. 171—94.

3 Anthony Sampson, *Anatomy of Britain* (London, 1962), genealogy between pp. 34 and 35.

4 W. W. Ogionwo, 'The adoption of technological innovations in Nigeria', Ph.D. thesis, University of Leeds, 1969.

5 J. van Velsen, 'Labour migration as a positive factor in the continuity of Tonga tribal society', in A. W. Southall (ed.), *Social Change in Modern Africa* (London, 1961) pp. 320—41.

6 W. J. Goode, *World Revolution and Family Patterns* (New York, 1963), p. 76.

7 Talcott Parsons and R. F. Bales, *Family, Socialization and Interaction Process* (London, 1956), p. 20.

8 R. W. Firth (ed.), *Two Studies of Kinship in London* (London, 1956), p. 42, quoted in Goode, *World Revolution and Family Patterns*, p. 72.

9 M. Young and P. Willmott, *Family and Kinship in East London* (London, 1957); *Family and Class in a London Suburb* (London, 1960).

10 Colin Bell, *Middle Class Families* (London, 1968), pp. 90—5.

11 Peter Townsend, *The Family Life of Old People* (London, 1957).

12 Peter Laslett, 'Size and structure of the household in England over three centuries', *Population Studies*, XXIII (1969), pp. 199—223.

13 Michael Anderson, *Family Structure in Nineteenth Century Lancashire* (Cambridge, 1971).

14 Elizabeth Bott, *Family and Social Network* (London, 1957).

15 In 1967 the highest divorce rates among the major industrial nations were those of the Soviet Union (2.74 per 1,000 population) and the United States (2.64). Rates between 1 and 2 per 1,000 were reported from a number of countries including Austria, Denmark, Sweden, and South Africa (white population). Countries with

rates below 1 per 1,000 included Poland (0.85), France (0.75), England and Wales (0.88), Australia (0.82), New Zealand (0.75), Israel (0.80), and Japan (0.84); while zero rates were of course reported from countries like Italy and Eire where there was no legal provision for divorce. See *United Nations Demographic Yearbook for 1968*, special topic, marriage and divorce; see also revised figures in subsequent *Yearbooks*.

16 Chie Nakane, *Kinship and Economic Organization in Rural Japan* (London, 1967).
17 Fujiko Isono, 'The family and women in Japan', *Sociological Review*, 12 (1964), pp. 39—54.
18 Ezra F. Vogel, *Japan's New Middle Class* (Berkeley and Los Angeles, 1963), ch. VIII.
19 Goode, *World Revolution and Family Patterns* (Revised ed., 1970).
20 See, for instance, E. W. Burgess and H. J. Locke, *The Family* (New York, 1945), ch. 10; C. Kirkpatrick, *The Family* (New York, 1955), p. 133; W. J. Goode, *The Family* (Englewood Cliffs, N. J., 1964), p. 109.
21 Leonard W. Doob, *Becoming More Civilized* (New Haven, Conn., 1960), pp. 112—16.
22 Yonina Talmon-Garbier, 'Social change and kinship ties' in Reuben Hill and René König (eds.), *Families in East and West* (Paris and The Hague, 1970), pp. 511—17.

Chapter 7. Economic development and development economics

1 J. E. Meade, 'On becoming an economist', *Christ's College Magazine* (Cambridge), May 1970, p. 123.
2 Paul Streeten, 'How poor are the poor countries?' in Dudley Seers and Leonard Joy (eds.), *Development in a Divided World* (Harmondsworth, 1971), p. 77.
3 A. O. Hirschman, *The Strategy of Economic Development* (New Haven, Conn., 1958), p. 11.
4 United Nations, *Measures for the Economic Development of Under-developed Countries*, E/1986 ST/ECA/10 (3 May 1951).
5 W. W. Rostow, *British Economy of the Nineteenth Century* (Oxford, 1948); 'The take-off into sustained growth', *Economic Journal*, LXVI (1956), pp. 25—48; *The Stages of Economic Growth: A Non-communist Manifesto* (Cambridge, 1960; 2nd edition 1971).
6 For example, Paul A. Baran and E. J. Hobsbawm, 'The stages of economic growth', *Kyklos*, XIV (1961), pp. 234—42.
7 Everett E. Hagen, *The Economics of Development* (Homewood, Ill., 1968), pp. 148—9.
8 Gunnar Myrdal, *Asian Drama: An Inquiry into the Poverty of Nations* (Harmondsworth, 1968), appendix 2, pp. 1852—5.
9 P. N. Rosenstein-Rodan, 'Problems of industrialization of eastern and south-eastern Europe', *Economic Journal*, 53 (1943), pp. 205—11.
10 Ragnar Nurkse, 'The conflict between "balanced growth" and international specialization', *Lectures on Economic Development* (Istanbul, 1958); reprinted in Gerald M. Meier (ed.), *Leading Issues in Economic Development*, 2nd edition (New York, 1970), pp. 362—6.
11 Jacob Viner in a paper to the International Economic Association congress, 1956; quoted in Meier (ed.), *Leading Issues in Economic Development*, p. 399.
12 A. J. Youngson, 'Development myths', *Bulletin of the Institute of Development Studies* (University of Sussex), May 1969, pp. 22—3.
13 Howard S. Ellis, in Meier (ed.), *Leading Issues in Economic Development*, pp. 399—400.
14 Hirschman, *The Strategy of Economic Development*.
15 Andrew Gunder Frank, 'The sociology of development and the under-development of sociology', *Catalyst*, summer 1967, pp. 20—73, esp. pp. 43—4.
16 Celso Furtado, *Development and Underdevelopment*, translated from the Spanish by R. W. de Aguiar and E. C. Drysdale (Berkeley and Los Angeles, 1964); *Diagnosis of the Brazilian Crisis*, transl. Suzette Macedo (Berkeley and Los Angeles, 1965).
17 Gunnar Myrdal, *An American Dilemma: The Negro Problem and Modern Democracy* (New York, 1944); *Economic Theory and the Underdeveloped Regions* (London, 1957); *Asian Drama*.

18 Dudley Seers, 'The limitations of the special case', *Bulletin of the Oxford Institute of Economics and Statistics*, 25 (May 1963), pp. 77—98.
19 Paul Streeten, 'The use and abuse of models in development planning' in Kurt Martin and John Knapp (eds.), *The Teaching of Development Economics* (London, 1966); 'Economic models and their usefulness for planning in South Asia', appendix 3 of Myrdal, *Asian Drama*.
20 Polly Hill [Humphreys], *Studies in Rural Capitalism in West Africa* (Cambridge, 1970).
21 B. Malinowski, *A Scientific Theory of Culture* (Chapel Hill, N. C., 1944), pp. 51—2.
22 J. A. Barnes, *Sociology in Cambridge* (inaugural lecture) (Cambridge, 1970).
23 Colin Leys, 'Political perspectives' in Seers and Joy (eds.), *Development in a Divided World*, pp. 106—37.

Chapter 8. But is it possible?

1 Everett E. Hagen, *The Economics of Development* (Homewood, Ill., 1968), pp. 39—40.
2 Paul and Anne Ehrlich, *Population, Resources, Environment* (San Francisco, 1970), pp. 2, 3, 53, 145—8, 166—7, 170.
3 Paul R. Ehrlich and Richard L. Harriman, *How to Be a Survivor* (New York, 1971), pp. 1, 13—15.
4 John Maddox, *The Doomsday Syndrome* (London, 1972), pp. viii, 26—7.
5 Lord Balogh reviewing H. V. Hodson, *The Diseconomics of Growth*, *New Society*, 18 May 1972, p. 370.
6 S. Fred Singer, 'Human energy production as a process in the biosphere', *Scientific American*, September 1970, pp. 184—6.
7 L. C. Cole, 'Man and the air', *Population Bulletin*, XXIV, no. 5 (December 1968), pp. 109—10.
8 Paul and Anne Ehrlich, *Population, Resources, Environment*, pp. 146—7.
9 *Ibid*. p. 187.
10 Uvedale Tristram, 'Fertilisers in Africa: self-sufficiency in five years', *World Hunger*, II, no. 9 (May 1971), p. 13.
11 Michael Lipton, 'The international diffusion of technology' in Dudley Seers and Leonard Joy (eds.), *Development in a Divided World* (Harmondsworth, 1971), pp. 53—4.
12 *The Guardian*, 21 May 1971.
13 *The Guardian*, 4 August 1971.
14 'Dr. Borlaug condemns DDT "hysteria"', *World Hunger*, III, no. 1 (January 1972), p. 11.
15 A. H. Bunting, 'Pests, population and poverty', a lecture at the University of Nottingham in December 1971, reported in *World Hunger*, III, no. 1 (January 1972), pp. 6—10.
16 Lord Todd, in a public lecture at the University of Ghana, reported in *The Guardian*, 26 January 1972.
17 Bunting, 'Pests, population and poverty', pp. 6—10.
18 Erich H. Jacoby, 'Effects of the "green revolution" in South and South-east Asia', *Modern Asian Studies*, 6, no. 1 (1972), pp. 63—9.
19 For a vivid account of this process in Scotland, see Frank Fraser Darling and J. Morton Boyd, *The Highlands and Islands* (London, 1964), ch. 4.
20 Carlo M. Cipolla, *The Economic History of World Population*, 5th edition (Harmondsworth, 1970), p. 58.
21 *The Economist*, 18 March 1972, p. 89.
22 Singer, 'Human energy production', p. 184; Earl Cook, 'The flow of energy in an industrial society', *Scientific American*, September 1971, p. 137; see also same journal, p. 39.
23 *The Economist*, 1 April 1972, pp. 58—9.
24 M. King Hubbert, 'The energy resources of the earth', *Scientific American*, September 1971, p. 67.

25 Harrison Brown, 'Human materials production', *Scientific American*, September 1970, p. 208.
26 Lord Robens, *Ten-Year Stint* (London, 1972), p. 182.
27 *The Observer*, 24 February 1974.
28 Singer, 'Human energy production', p. 190.
29 Hubbert, 'The energy resources of the earth', pp. 61—70.

Chapter 9. Cultural diversity, language, education, and the mass media

1 On the peoples, cultures, and history of Uganda see the appropriate volumes in the International African Institute's Ethnographic Survey of Africa series; also J. E. Goldthorpe, *Outlines of East African Society*, revised edition (Kampala, 1962); J. E. Goldthorpe and F. B. Wilson, *Tribal Maps of East Africa and Zanzibar* (Kampala, 1960); A. I. Richards, *The Multicultural States of East Africa* (Montreal, 1969); L. P. Mair, *Primitive Government* (Harmondsworth, 1962); P. H. Gulliver (ed.), *Tradition and Transition in East Africa* (London, 1969); W. H. Whiteley (ed.), *Language Use and Social Change* (London, 1971), esp. ch. VII.
2 A. I. Richards, *Land, Labour, and Diet in Northern Rhodesia* (London, 1939), p. 113.
3 J. S. La Fontaine, 'Tribalism among the Gisu' in Gulliver (ed.), *Tradition and Transition in East Africa*, p. 178; E. E. Evans-Pritchard, 'The Nuer of the southern Sudan' in M. Fortes and E. E. Evans-Pritchard (eds.), *African Political Systems* (London, 1940), p. 278; Gulliver, 'Introduction' in Gulliver, (ed.), *Tradition and Transition in East Africa*, p. 24.
4 Goldthorpe and Wilson, *Tribal Maps*, p. 7 and map 3.
5 J. E. Goldthorpe, *An African Elite* (Kampala, 1965), pp. 24—32.
6 David Parkin, *Neighbors and Nationals in an African City Ward* (Berkeley and Los Angeles, 1969); 'Tribe as fact and fiction in an East African city' in Gulliver (ed.), *Tradition and Transition in East Africa*.
7 R. D. Grillo, 'The tribal factor in an East African trade union' in Gulliver (ed.), *Tradition and Transition in East Africa*.
8 Gulliver, 'Introduction', pp. 16—17, 37n.
9 Richards, *The Multicultural States of East Africa*, pp. 102, 107—8.
10 Joan Vincent, 'Anthropology and political development' in Colin Leys (ed.), *Politics and Change in Developing Countries* (Cambridge, 1969), p. 59.
11 Raymond Apthorpe, 'Does tribalism really matter?', *Transition*, no. 37 (1968), p. 18.
12 Dankwart A. Rustow, *A World of Nations* (Washington, D. C., 1967), tables 1—3, pp. 284—8.
13 Ali A. Mazrui, 'The king, the king's English, and I: a personal narrative', *Transition*, no. 38 (1971), p. 66.
14 I. M. Lewis, 'Nationalism and particularism in Somalia' in Gulliver (ed.), *Tradition and Transition in East Africa*, pp. 339—61.
15 Gunnar Myrdal, *Asian Drama: An Inquiry into the Poverty of Nations* (Harmondsworth, 1968), pp. 81—9, 1639—50, 1742—3.
16 Eugene A. Nida and William A. Wonderly, 'Communication roles of language in national societies' in Whiteley (ed.), *Language Use and Social Change*, pp. 62—3.
17 Peter Williams, *Aid in Uganda — Education* (London, 1966), p. 52.
18 Goldthorpe, *An African Elite*, pp. 32—46, 73—5.
19 William Gutteridge, *The Military in African Politics* (London, 1969), pp. 114—16.
20 Frantz Fanon, 'The pitfalls of national consciousness' in *The Wretched of the Earth* (Harmondsworth, 1967).
21 Robert K. Merton and Alice M. Kitt, 'Contributions to the theory of reference group behaviour' in R. K. Merton and Paul F. Lazarsfeld, *Continuities in Social Research: Studies in the Scope and Method of 'The American Soldier'* (Glencoe, Ill., 1950), p. 92.
22 INCIDI (The International Institute of Differing Civilizations), *The Development of a Middle Class in Tropical and Sub-tropical Countries* (Brussels, 1956); *International Social Science Bulletin* [now *Journal*] VIII, no. 3 (1956); H. H. Smythe and Mabel M.

Smythe, *The New Nigerian Elite* (Stanford, 1960); Leo Kuper, *An African Bourgeoisie* (New Haven, Conn., 1965); P. C. Lloyd, *The New Elites of Tropical Africa* (London, 1966).

23 Edwin Smith, 'Indigenous education in Africa', in E. E. Evans-Pritchard *et al.* (eds.), *Essays Presented to C. G. Seligman* (London, 1934), pp. 319—34.

24 Hugh Ashton, *The Basuto*, 2nd edition (London, 1967), pp. 46—61; Austin Coates, *Basutoland* (London, 1966), pp. 75—80, 109—11.

25 P. T. W. Baxter in A. I. Richards (ed.), *East African Chiefs* (London, 1960), p. 294.

26 Goldthorpe, *An African Elite*, pp. 24—32.

27 R. D. Matthews and M. Akrawi, *Education in Arab Countries of the Near East* (Washington, D.C., 1949), pp. 24, 40, 540.

28 Ruth Sloan and Helen Kitchen (eds.), *The Educated African* (London, 1962), ch. 3, pp. 45—6.

29 Humayun Kabir, *Indian Philosophy of Education* (Bombay, 1961), p. 209.

30 E. M. K. Mulira, *The Vernacular in African Education* (London, 1951), p. 17.

31 Richard Jolly, 'Manpower and education' in Dudley Seers and Leonard Joy (eds.), *Development in a Divided World* (Harmondsworth, 1971), p. 209.

32 Quoted in Gerald M. Meier, *Leading Issues in Economic Development*, 2nd edition (New York, 1970), p. 610.

33 *Ibid.* p. 629.

34 W. Arthur Lewis, *Development Planning* (London, 1966), p. 110.

35 Wilbur Schramm, *Mass Media and National Development* (Stanford, 1964), ch. 2, esp. fig. 1 on p. 60.

36 *Ibid.* p. 101.

37 C. A. Siepmann, *Radio, Television, and Society* (New York, 1950).

38 Daniel Lerner, *The Passing of Traditional Society* (Glencoe, Ill., 1958), chs. 2—5.

39 Paul J. Deutschmann, quoted in Schramm, *Mass Media and National Development*, pp. 74—6.

40 Paul F. Lazarsfeld *et al.*, *The People's Choice*, 2nd edition (New York, 1948), esp. ch. XVI.

41 Joseph Trenaman and Denis McQuail, *Television and the Political Image* (London, 1961), pp. 193—5.

42 Lerner, *The Passing of Traditional Society*, pp. 27—8, 60, 64—5.

43 Schramm, *Mass Media and National Development*, ch. 4.

44 William A. Kornhauser, *The Politics of Mass Society* (London, 1960).

45 C. Wright Mills, *The Power Elite* (New York, 1956), ch. 13.

46 Daniel Bell, *The End of Ideology* (Glencoe, Ill., 1960), ch. 1; David Riesman, *The Lonely Crowd* (New Haven, Conn., 1953), pp. 224—7; William Kornhauser, '"Power elite" or "veto groups"?' in Richard L. Simpson and Ida H. Simpson, *Social Organization and Behavior* (New York, 1964), pp. 199—208.

Chapter 10. Some psychological aspects of change

1 Leonard W. Doob, *Becoming More Civilized: A Psychological Exploration* (New Haven, 1960).

2 Everett M. Rogers, *Diffusion of Innovations* (New York, 1962).

3 W. W. Ogionwo, 'The adoption of technological innovations in Nigeria: a study of factors associated with adoption of farm practices', Ph.D. thesis, University of Leeds, 1969.

4 David C. McClelland, *The Achieving Society* (Princeton, 1961).

5 David C. McClelland, 'A psychological path to rapid economic development', *Mawazo*, 1, no. 4 (December 1968), pp. 9—15.

Chapter 11. Religion and economic development: cause and effect

1 Parts of Weber's posthumous *Gesammelte Aufsätze zur Religions-soziologie* (1920—1) have appeared in English translations as follows: *The Protestant Ethic and the Spirit*

of Capitalism, transl. Talcott Parsons (London, 1930); *The Religion of China*, transl. Hans H. Gerth (New York, 1951); *The Religion of India*, transl. Gerth and Don Martindale (New York, 1958); *Ancient Judaism*, transl. Gerth and Martindale (New York, 1952). The following references are to the English translations cited by title only.

2 *The Protestant Ethic*, pp. 48—63.

3 *The Religion of China*, chs. I and IV, pp. 173—95, 227—9, 243.

4 *The Religion of India*, pp. 111—12.

5 Edmund Gosse, *Father and Son: A Study of Two Temperaments* (London, 1907).

6 Hugh Trevor-Roper, *Religion, the Reformation, and Social Change* (London, 1967).

7 T. O. Ling, 'Max Weber in India', inaugural lecture at the University of Leeds, 11 December 1972.

8 Brien K. Parkinson, 'Non-economic factors in the economic retardation of the rural Malays', *Modern Asian Studies*, I, no. 1 (1967), pp. 31—46.

9 William Wilder, 'Islam, other factors and Malay backwardness: comments on an argument', *Modern Asian Studies*, II, no. 2 (1968), pp. 155—64.

10 Brien K. Parkinson, 'The economic retardation of the Malays — a rejoinder', *Modern Asian Studies*, II, no. 3 (1968), pp. 267—72.

11 Mya Maung, 'Socialism and economic development of Burma', *Asian Survey*, IV, no. 12 (1964), pp. 1182—90.

12 T. O. Ling, 'Religion and economic development in Burma and Malaya', paper presented to the Development Seminar, University of Leeds, 8 December 1971.

13 Melford E. Spiro, *Buddhism and Society: A Great Tradition and Its Burmese Vicissitudes* (London, 1971), pp. 12, 453—4, 463—7.

14 Robert J. Bocock, 'The Ismailis in Tanzania', *British Journal of Sociology*, XXII (1971), pp. 365—80.

15 H. S. Morris, *The Indians in Uganda* (London, 1968); J. E. Goldthorpe, *Outlines of East African Society* (Kampala, 1958), pp. 125—6.

16 Morris, *The Indians in Uganda*, pp. 51—4.

17 Norman Cohn, *The Pursuit of the Millennium* (London, 1957).

18 Norman Cohn, 'Medieval millenarism: its bearing on the comparative study of millenarian movements' in Louis Schneider (ed.), *Religion, Culture and Society* (New York, 1964), pp. 168—78.

19 Peter Worsley, *The Trumpet Shall Sound* (London, 1957), pp. 20—2, 144.

20 Peter Lawrence, *Road Belong Cargo* (Manchester, 1964), pp. 2—3, 116—221.

21 Robert Forster, 'The cargo cults today', *New Society*, 7 January 1971, pp. 10—12.

22 Vittorio Lanternari, *The Religions of the Oppressed*, transl. Lisa Sergio (London, 1963).

23 Weston La Barre, *The Peyote Cult*, enlarged edition (Hamden, Conn., 1964), pp. 205—6, 227—37.

24 B. G. M. Sundkler, *Bantu Prophets in South Africa* (London, 1948).

25 F. B. Welbourn, *East African Rebels: A Study of Some Independent Churches* (London, 1961).

26 C. G. Rosberg and John Nottingham, *The Myth of 'Mau Mau': Nationalism in Kenya* (New York, 1966).

27 Goldthorpe, *Outlines of East African Society*. ch. VIII.

28 Walter H. Sangree, *Age, Prayer and Politics in Tiriki, Kenya* (London, 1966), esp. chs. VI and VII.

29 Geoffrey Parrinder, *Religion in an African City* (London, 1953), ch. 6.

30 M. J. Field, *Search for Security: An Ethno-psychiatric Study of Rural Ghana* (London, 1960), part I.

31 Lanternari, *The Religions of the Oppressed*, pp. 11—28; Dominique Desanti, 'The golden anniversary of Kimbanguism, an African religion', *Continent 2000*, April 1971, pp. 7—19.

32 Lanternari, *The Religions of the Oppressed*, pp. 28—31; George Shepperson, 'The politics of African church separatist movements in British Central Africa, 1892—1916', *Africa*, XXIV (1954), pp. 233—45; George Shepperson and T. Price, *Independent African: John Chilembwe and the Nyasaland Rising of 1915* (London, 1958); R. L. Wishlade, *Sectarianism in Southern Nyasaland* (London, 1965).

33 David B. Barrett, *Schism and Renewal in Africa* (Nairobi, 1968), pp. xvii, 25, 114, 139, 285.
34 C. K. Yang, *Religion in Chinese Society* (1961), pp. 218—29, reprinted in Franz Schurmann and Orville Schell, *Imperial China* (Harmondsworth, 1967), pp. 157—68.
35 Wolfgang Franke, 'The Taiping rebellion', transl. from the German and reprinted in Schurmann and Schell, *Imperial China*, pp. 170—82; Lanternari's account differs from Franke's in this and other details.
36 Sundkler, *Bantu Prophets in South Africa*, p. 37.
37 Barrett, *Schism and Renewal in Africa*, p. 71.
38 Lawrence, *Road Belong Cargo*, pp. 225—6.
39 J. M. Yinger, 'Religion and social change: functions and dysfunctions of sects and cults among the disprivileged', *Review of Religious Research*, 4, no. 2 (1963); reprinted (abridged) in Richard D. Knudten (ed.), *The Sociology of Religion: An Anthology* (New York, 1967), pp. 482—95.

Chapter 12. The political characteristics of new states in poor countries

1 C. H. Dodd, *Political Development* (London, 1972), pp. 9—15.
2 *Zik: A Selection from the Speeches of Nnamdi Azikiwe* (1961), quoted in Paul E. Sigmund, *The Ideologies of the Developing Nations* (New York, 1963), pp. 212, 215.
3 George I. Blanksten, 'The politics of Latin America' in Gabriel A. Almond and James S. Coleman (eds.), *The Politics of the Developing Areas* (Princeton, 1960), p. 521.
4 Emilio Willems, *Followers of the New Faith: Culture Change and the Rise of Protestantism in Brazil and Chile* (Nashville, Tenn., 1967), pp. 34—44.
5 Lucian W. Pye, 'The politics of South East Asia' in Almond and Coleman (eds.), *The Politics of the Developing Areas*, pp. 87—97.
6 Dankwart A. Rustow, 'The politics of the Near East' in Almond and Coleman (eds.), *The Politics of the Developing Areas*, pp. 382ff.
7 Fred W. Riggs, *Administration in Developing Countries: The Theory of Prismatic Society* (Boston, Mass., 1964), p. 236.
8 W. J. Argyle, 'European nationalism and African tribalism' in P. H. Gulliver (ed.), *Tradition and Transition in East Africa* (London, 1969), pp. 41—57; see also George Bennett, 'Tribalism in politics' in *ibid.* pp. 59—87.
9 Speech to the second Pan-African seminar, World Assembly of Youth, 1961; quoted in Sigmund, *The Ideologies of the Developing Nations*, pp. 209—11.
10 Peter Worsley, *The Third World* (London, 1964), p. 69.
11 David E. Apter, *Ghana in Transition*, revised edition (New York, 1963), pp. 167, 173—4.
12 A brief characterization of African socialism is given in J. E. Goldthorpe, *Introduction to Sociology* (Cambridge, 1968), pp. 137—9; for a full account, see William H. Friedland and Carl G. Rosberg (eds.), *African Socialism* (Stanford, 1964).
13 Sigmund, *The Ideologies of the Developing Nations*, pp. 18—24.
14 Apter, *Ghana in Transition*, p. 326.
15 Thomas Hodgkin, *African Political Parties* (Harmondsworth, 1961), p. 48.
16 Martin Staniland, 'Single-party regimes and political change' in Colin Leys (ed.), *Politics and Change in Developing Countries* (Cambridge, 1969), pp. 147, 152.
17 Cherry Gertzel, *The Politics of Independent Kenya, 1963—68* (Nairobi, 1970), p. 58.
18 Apter, *Ghana in Transition*, pp. 345—6.
19 *Ibid.* p. 326.
20 Staniland, 'Single-party regimes and political change', p. 139.
21 Riggs, *Administration in Developing Countries*, p. 201.
22 *Ibid.* pp. 254, 282, 340.
23 Alan Milner (ed.), *African Penal Systems* (New York, 1969).
24 Max Gluckman, 'Analysis of a social system in modern Zululand', *Bantu Studies*, 14 (1940), pp. 1—30, 147—74, reprinted in Rhodes-Livingstone paper no. 28 (1958); see also his 'Inter-hierarchical roles' in Marc J. Swartz (ed.), *Local-level Politics: Social and Cultural Perspectives* (London, 1968), pp. 69—93.

25 Swartz, *Local-level Politics*, pp. 199—204.
26 Gunnar Myrdal, *Asian Drama: An Inquiry into the Poverty of Nations* (Harmondsworth, 1968), pp. 66, 101, 117, 779.
27 For a brilliant analysis of medieval European feudalism, see Marc Bloch, *Feudal Society* (London, 1961).
28 Riggs, *Administration in Developing Countries*, pp. 189—90.
29 James C. Scott, *Comparative Political Corruption* (Englewood Cliffs, N. J., 1972), pp. 15, 24—5.
30 Alec Nove, 'Soviet political organization and development' in Leys (ed.), *Politics and Change in Developing Countries*, pp. 65—84.
31 Scott, *Comparative Political Corruption*, pp. 16—19.
32 S. E. Finer, *The Man on Horseback: The Role of the Military in Politics* (London, 1962).
33 Morris Janowitz, *The Military in the Political Development of New Nations* (Chicago, 1964), pp. 32, 37.
34 William Gutteridge, *The Military in African Politics* (London, 1969), pp. 107—8.
35 *Ibid.* pp. 79—80.
36 Morris Janowitz, *The Professional Soldier* (Glencoe, Ill., 1960), pp. 228—31.
37 Janowitz, *The Military in the Political Development of New Nations*, pp. 63—5.
38 Gutteridge, *The Military in African Politics*, pp. 101—6.
39 *Ibid.* pp. 114—16.
40 Scott, *Comparative Political Corruption*, p. 10.

Chapter 13. The world of aid

1 United Nations, *Measurement of the Flow of Resources to Developing Countries*, E/4327 ST/ECA/98 (1967).
2 J. Harold Wilson, *The War on World Poverty — An Appeal to the Conscience of Mankind* (London, 1953).
3 Dudley Seers and Paul Streeten, 'Overseas development policies under the Labour government', ch. 15 of Paul Streeten, *The Frontiers of Development Studies* (London, 1972), pp. 254—96.
4 *OXFAM News*, 1970, annual report edition.
5 Andrzej Krassowski (ed.), *ODI Review*, no. 4 (1970), pp. 48—50.
6 The Economist, 20 May 1972, p. 116.
7 Sources: United Nations, *World Economic Survey, 1969—70* (1971), pp. 161—74, tables 57, 61, 62, and A.35; D.A.C. (O.E.C.D.), *Development Assistance: 1969 Review*, tables II, 1, 2, quoted in Krassowski, *ODI Review*, no. 4, p. 15.
8 *Partners in Development: Report of the Commission on International Development* (Washington, D.C., 1969), p. 30; my italics.
9 Lester B. Pearson, *The Crisis of Development* (London, 1970), p. 32.
10 William Clark, preface to Sir John Cockcroft, *Technology for Developing Countries* (London, 1966).
11 O.D.I., *Effective Aid* (1967), pp. 104—5.
12 *Partners in Development*, pp. 7—10.
13 O.D.I., *Effective Aid*, pp. 101—3.
14 *Partners in Development*, p. 9; Pearson, *The Crisis of Development*, p. 35.
15 This was reported, for instance, to have been unanimously taken for granted at a conference in 1966 of senior officials of the World Bank, United Nations agencies, and the ministries of development of major donor countries with interested academics; O.D.I., *Effective Aid*, p. 9.
16 P. T. Bauer, *Dissent on Development* (London, 1971).
17 Teresa Hayter, *Aid as Imperialism* (Harmondsworth, 1971).
18 *Partners in Development*, p. 136.
19 *Ibid.* pp. 122—3.
20 *Ibid.* pp. 147—9.
21 *The Economist*, 15 July 1972, p. 41.
22 United Nations, *World Economic Survey, 1969—70*, p. 167.

23 Hayter, *Aid as Imperialism*, p. 48; *Partners in Development*, p. 211.
24 *Partners in Development*, pp. 179—85 and table 23 of appendix II.
25 *Ibid.* p. 202.
26 *Ibid.* p. 182.
27 *Ibid.* p. 185; O.D.I., *Effective Aid*, pp. 55—64.
28 *Partners in Development*, pp. 151—2, 175—6; Adrian Moyes and Teresa Hayter, *World III* (London, 1964), p. 92.
29 O.D.I., *Effective Aid*, pp. 9, 19—21.
30 Hayter, *Aid as Imperialism*, p. 148.
31 *Partners in Development*, p. 172.
32 *Ibid.* p. 177.
33 *Partners in Development*, pp. 172—7; United Nations, *World Economic Survey, 1969—70*, p. 163.
34 Ralph Clark, *Aid in Uganda* (London, 1966), pp. 61—4.
35 *Partners in Development*, p. 81.
36 *Ibid.* p. 87.
37 Sources: Moyes and Hayter, *World III*, figs. 37—9; United Nations, *World Economic Survey, 1969—70*, table 49.
38 *Partners in Development*, p. 88.
39 Bauer, *Dissent on Development*, p. 263.
40 *Partners in Development*, pp. 87—8.
41 Teresa Hayter, 'The UNCTAD Conference', *New Society*, 11 April 1968, pp. 528—9; Krassowski, *ODI Review* no. 4, pp. 54—7; *The Economist*, 20 May 1972, p. 116; Irving Louis Horowitz, *Three Worlds of Development* (New York, 1966), which includes a detailed analysis of the issues at UNCTAD I.
42 *Partners in Development*, p. 90.
43 E. F. Schumacher and G. McRobie, 'Intermediate technology and its administration implications', *Journal of Administration Overseas*, VIII, no. 2 (April 1969), pp. 89—96; G. McRobie, 'Industrial development', paper presented to the biennial conference of the African Studies Association of the United Kingdom, Aberdeen, September 1970.
44 *Partners in Development*, p. 205.
45 Cockcroft, *Technology for Developing Countries*, pp. 14—18.
46 U Thant, 9 May 1969.

INDEX

Index

participation, 212, 253
Partners in Development (the Pearson report),
  30—2, 94, 99n, 111, 274—97
party (political), 2, 130, 162, 206—8, 212,
  253, 256—61, 269—70
patent, 98
paternalism, 242, 247
Patidars, 234
pattern variables, 9—11
Pearson, Lester B., 279—80; *see also*
  Partners in Development
peasant, 36, 101, 113, 149, 155, 160, 267;
  see also agriculture, farm, subsistence
Peel, John, 33n
Peking, 120
penal reform, 263
Perham, Margery, 47n, 67n, 68n
Perry, Commodore, U.S.N., 36
Peru, 4, 192, 193, 197
petroleum, 99—100, 119, 171, 175—9, 198
peyote, 240—1, 250
Philippines, 11, 31, 172, 191, 192, 193,
  197, 255; Pilipino, 191
phosphorus, 169
photosynthesis, 168, 179
Pierson, Donald, 43n, 62n
Place, Francis, 35
plague, 19, 20, 25
plantain, 84—7, 97
plantation, 42—51, 67, 71, 96—8, 102—3,
  122, 158, 186, 239, 243
plural society, 13, 42, 64—5, 94, 237, 251,
  266
plutonium, 176—8
Poland, 86, 192, 195, 197, 256, 278; Poles
  in U.S.A., 117
polarization, 94, 151, 155
police, 58, 61, 198, 263, 266—7, 270—1
politics, -ians, -al science, 12—13, 55, 71—2,
  96, 128—31, 143, 146, 162—3, 183—4,
  190, 198, 202, 207—13, 223, 243, 246,
  251—73, 279, 281, 288—9, 293; political
  culture, 264, 270; political middlemen,
  264
pollution, 165—70, 179
polyandry, 128, 142
polygyny, 21, 22, 128, 142—3
population, 13, 15—38, 48, 78—81, 87, 101,
  113—15, 121—7, 136, 146, 164—7, 171,
  174—5, 179, 182, 184, 197, 204, 236, 297
Portugal, -uese, 39, 42, 47, 62, 81, 89, 135,
  187, 191, 192, 193, 197, 254, 277
potato, 85—7
Potts, Malcolm, 33
power (political), 4, 12, 56, 112—13, 199,
  200, 237, 251, 255, 259—68, 272—3
Powesland, P. G., 100n

Pratt, R. C., 55n
Prebisch, Raul, 294—5
press, *see* newspapers
Preston, 135—6
primary products, 83, 94—6, 98—100, 147,
  149, 155, 280, 294
prismatic, 11—13, 263
profit, 96, 103, 118, 153, 234, 283
prophet, -ic, 237—50
protein, 85—7, 92, 110
Protestant churches, 28, 53—5, 230—1, 240,
  244—5, 247, 256; P. ethic, 10, 148, 225,
  228—35, 250
psychology, 3, 70, 212—13, 215—27
Public Law 480 (U.S.A.), 275
Punjabi, 190—1
puritan, 225, 229, 235—7, 271
Pye, Lucian W., 255

race, 8—9, 18, 39—76, 94, 154—6, 263,
  288—9
radio, 78—9, 92, 110, 205, 208—11, 223,
  268, 270
railway, 25, 49, 51, 58, 84, 94, 102, 151, 155,
  165, 185, 223, 243, 275
rate of exchange, 82, 90, 295
rate of interest on aid loans, 284—5
rationality, 220—1, 234
raw materials, 83, 94—6, 98—100, 147, 149,
  155, 280, 294
reactor, nuclear, 176—9
reference group, 111
region, -al disparities, 94, 108, 112—13,
  115, 154—5, 262—3
religion, 8—9, 13, 28, 32, 52—5, 63, 65,
  112—3, 116, 128—30, 157, 161, 181,
  190—1, 202, 207, 216, 228—50, 256—7;
  see also churches, *individual sects*
Rensberg, P. van, 44n, 52n
research, 98, 130, 280, 296—7
retailing, 3, 33, 84, 94, 104, 124—7, 206
Rex, John, 64n
Rhodesia, 47, 59, 131, 244, 272
rice, 42, 85—6, 98, 101, 171—2, 232, 297
Richards, Audrey I., 50n, 182n, 183, 185
Riesman, David, 213
Riggs, Fred W., 11—14, 255, 262—3, 266,
  271
roads, 25, 49, 58, 147, 150—1, 155, 283
Robens, Lord, 177—8
Rogers, Everett M., 217—9
Roman Catholic church, 21, 28, 54—5,
  62—3, 137, 199, 230—1, 243—4, 247,
  254—6
Roman empire, 18—20, 113; Roman script,
  187—9, 191
Romania, 86

322